Upgrade or Repair Your PC

Upgrade or Repair Your PC

Aubrey Pilgrim

McGraw-Hill

New York   San Francisco   Washington, D.C.   Auckland   Bogotá
Caracas   Lisbon   London   Madrid   Mexico City   Milan
Montreal   New Delhi   San Juan   Singapore
Sydney   Tokyo   Toronto

pbk   5 6 7 8 9 10 11 12 AGM/AGM 9 0 0 9 8 7

Product or brand names used in this book may be trade names or trademarks. Where we believe that there may be proprietary claims to such trade names or trademarks, the name has been used with an initial capital or it has been capitalized in the style used by the name claimant. Regardless of the capitalization used, all such names have been used in an editorial manner without any intent to convey endorsement of or other affiliation with the name claimant. Neither the author nor the publisher intends to express any judgment as to the validity or legal status of any such proprietary claims.

Library of Congress Cataloging-in-Publication Data
Pilgrim, Aubrey.
    Upgrade or repair your PC / by Aubrey Pilgrim.
        p.   cm.
    Includes index.
    ISBN 0-07-050114-9
    1. IBM-compatible computers—Upgrading. 2. Microcomputers—
Upgrading. 3. IBM microcomputers—Repairing. I. Title.
TK7887.5.P54   1994
004.165—dc20   94-23468
                                                                   CIP

Editorial team: Brad Schepp, Acquiring Editor
                Kellie Hagan, Book Editor
                Robert E. Ostrander, Executive Editor
                Jodi L. Tyler, Indexer
Production team: Katherine G. Brown, Director
                 Susan E. Hansford, Coding
                 Toya B. Warner, Computer Artist
                 Brenda M. Plasterer, Desktop Operator
                 Linda L. King, Proofreading   0501149
Design team: Jaclyn J. Boone, Designer   EL1

Dedication

To the memory of Gary Kildall, 1942–1994. He was the inventor of CP/M in 1973, the first PC operating system, he was the founder of Digital Research Corporation, and he developed DR DOS and many other software programs. I met him only a few times at computer shows, but he seemed to be a very modest man. He impressed me as being an engineer's engineer, an innovator, and a true pioneer in the computer industry. He was one of the unsung heroes of the computer revolution; he should have been a multibillionaire.

Contents

Acknowledgments

I want to thank my editor Brad Schepp. If he hadn't made a few irritating calls now and then, I might never have finished this book. I also want to thank Ron Powers. If he hadn't got me started writing the "save a bundle" books, I might still be working a 9-to-5 factory job. Writing is a whole lot more fun. So thank you Ron, Brad, Kimberly, Carol, Lisa, Stacey, and the rest of the crew at McGraw-Hill in beautiful Blue Ridge Summit, Pa.

—Aubrey Pilgrim, in smoggy Los Angeles
(you may write to me on CompuServe at
73740,256 or Prodigy at TJJC38A)

Introduction

One of the reasons you're probably looking at this book right now is because you want to save some money. How much can you save? It depends on a lot of things, such as how well you shop and where you shop. Software upgrades are as necessary as hardware upgrades. I guarantee that you can save several hundred dollars on your software upgrades. Check out the suggestions in chapter 17.

If you had a lot of money, you wouldn't need to upgrade an older computer. You could go out and buy the very best PC and the latest software that money could buy. Or if you *really* had a lot of money, you could hire someone to go buy it for you.

Unfortunately, there aren't many people who have that kind of money. Most of us have to try to save money wherever we can. This book can help you. You can upgrade an older computer to be equivalent to the best on the market without having to spend a fortune. Computers are made up of standardized modular units and components so you can remove and replace any or all of them very easily.

So you don't have to junk your old PC and spend a lot of money on a new one. Even if you know nothing at all about computers, this book can show you how to upgrade them. It will also show you how to troubleshoot and find the cause of most computer problems. Once you know what a problem is, it's easy to repair the computer.

If you decide to upgrade your PC or if it breaks down and you take it to a shop to be fixed, it could cost from $50 to $100 an hour just for labor. Parts are extra. And just taking your computer to a repair shop can be a real chore, especially if you live in a large city.

Pilgrim's law dictates that no matter where you live, the repair shop, sale, or whatever you need will be on the other side of town. And when you get there all the parking spots near the shop will be occupied. The nearest parking spot will be about a half mile away and, after you park and lug your computer to the shop, you'll find that several people have decided to vacate the parking spots in front. The dealer will look your computer over, then give you an estimate for the cost. Of course the cost will always exceed the estimate. You'll probably have to leave your computer in the shop and you'll be given an estimate of when it will be done. Don't expect it to be done by the time given.

This book will show you how to avoid many of these problems. It will show you how to find the cause of most problems and how to find defective components. You don't have to be an engineer or skilled technician to add or replace components in a PC. There are a lot of clear instructions and photos in this book. You can do it yourself.

Types of upgrades

There are two main types of upgrades, hardware and software. The first part of this book deals primarily with hardware upgrades and the second part is about newer and better software.

Compatible components

One of the fantastic advantages of the PC is that the components are all interchangeable. Components such as a disk drive, keyboard, and modem used in an old 286 can also be used in the latest 486 or Pentium. Since they're all interchangeable, it's very easy to plug in a new board or a faster modem. You can easily upgrade an older computer in thousands of ways.

Upgrade or repair a PS/1 or PS/2

At one time, the only way you could upgrade or repair a PS/2 was to have an IBM authorized dealer do it. The parts had to be authorized genuine IBM components installed by genuine authorized IBM dealers. Of course, everything IBM costs two to three times more than other services and products.

Times have changed. IBM has changed. They will now sell you any component they manufacture. It's now possible to purchase many PS/1 and PS/2 components on the open market, and you don't need an IBM dealer to install them. In many ways, the PS/1s and PS/2s are easier to upgrade and repair than the compatible clones. And you can really save a bundle if you do it yourself. There are a lot of photos and easy instructions in this book to show you how. Anyone can do it.

You can use this book to easily upgrade or repair a genuine IBM PS/1 or any IBM PS/2 model 25, 30, 35, or 40. These models are industry standard architecture (ISA) machines (which used to be called IBM and IBM-compatible machines).

The PS/1 and PS/2 models 25 through 40 can use much of the ten billion dollars worth of hardware that's available, but they might have only one to three slots so you'll be limited in what you can install.

It's a bit more difficult to find some upgrade or replacement parts for the microchannel architecture (MCA) models 50 and up. Other than IBM, there aren't many other manufacturers of MCA products. Since there's little competition, MCA components might be a bit more expensive than ISA products and they're not as plentiful as ISA components. But there are larger hard disks, memory upgrades, tape backup, and much more available for the MCA.

Troubleshooting a PS/1 or PS/2 system is no different than any other PC system. Chapter 20 offers many suggestions for finding and solving problems. More about the PS/1 and PS/2 in chapter 5.

Upgrading your peripherals

Besides upgrading your computer, you'll find information on how to upgrade your peripherals, which are components such as your monitor, printer, keyboard, scanner, modem/fax, floppy drives, hard drives, CD-ROM, and sound card. Upgrading these items can make your computer work better and faster, and give you more versatility and utility.

If you have young children, then you should by all means upgrade your computer with a CD-ROM. There are thousands of children's educational and game programs on CD-ROMs. We learn through our five senses. Reading lets us learn by only one sense. A CD-ROM can furnish text, graphics, animation, and voice. It offers one of the better ways of learning. If you have children and aren't providing them with every possible advantage, then they're handicapped. In order to make it in this world, we need all the advantages we can get. If you don't have a good multimedia computer and you think I'm trying to make you feel guilty, then you're absolutely right.

Software upgrades

You'll find information about upgrading to the latest software in this book. You must have software to run your computer and, by using the suggestions in chapter 17, you can save several hundred dollars. This chapter alone can save you several times what the book costs. There are hundreds of thousands of software packages, so I can't list them all. But there are some short reviews and recommendations for the more essential software.

How much can you save?

Since the titles of most of my books include the phrase "and save a bundle," I'm often asked just how much you can save. Of course, the answer depends on many different things: where you shop, how well you shop, whether you buy brand names or clone products, and what type of upgrade or repairs you want. Another variable that makes it difficult to determine how much you can save is the fact that prices continue to go down.

One writer claimed that you couldn't save much at all in building your own computer. He used the comparison of buying computer components to that of buying the components to assemble a Chevrolet. Of course, if you were buying individual parts for a Chevy it would cost five to ten times more than what a new car would cost. But there's only one company that manufactures parts for a Chevy and there are hundreds of vendors that manufacture the components for computers, all competing against one another for your dollar. It's a very competitive business. I recently assembled a Pentium PC. It has a 60-MHz Pentium VL-bus motherboard, 32MB of RAM, 1.05GB and 540MB hard drives, two floppies, a 21-inch monitor, and a Viper monitor adapter. It cost me $5,600. An equivalent system bought in a store would have cost at least $7,000 or more. If a vendor assembles a system like this, he has to charge more to cover his overhead and expenses. Also, I put just the components I wanted into my Pentium and I know the quality of those components.

Here's another example of how you can save. Say you have an old 286, but you want a new 486. A new 486 computer could cost as much as $1,500 or more. If you tried to sell the old 286 computer, you might not get more than $100 or $200 for it. However, if you spent about $500 to replace the motherboard and about $200 for extra memory, you could have a new 486 that would be every bit as good as the new $1,500 machine. It would take you less than an hour to replace the motherboard, and in that one hour you could save about $800—which is pretty good for that much time.

There are other benefits that you can't put a price on. One of the biggest benefits of doing it yourself is that you'll learn a bit about your computer. Another fantastic benefit is the feeling you'll get because you did it yourself.

Do you need to upgrade?

Some people are still driving around in 10-year-old cars. They get them to where they want to go and they're usually paid for. There are other people who wouldn't be caught dead in an old car. They must have a brand-new car every year.

There are many people who are the same when it comes to computers. There are some who still use computers that are 10 years old. I have a friend who has a small business. He still uses an old XT and programs like dBASE II and WordStar 3.0. This computer and software do all he needs them to do. He's perfectly happy with his system. There are other people who must have the biggest, most powerful, and fastest computer available, even if they have to spend the family nest-egg and take out a second mortgage.

The B-B gene

I'm convinced that there's a gene, as yet undiscovered, that influences and controls those people who must have the biggest, best, and the most expensive of everything available. This includes cars, homes, fancy clothes, and even computers. When this gene is finally discovered and documented, I suggest that it be called the "biggest and best" gene, or the B-B gene. There's little doubt in my mind that this gene exists in all of us. But it exerts a far greater influence over some than others.

Many of the people who are influenced by the B-B gene are also quite willing to pay exorbitant prices for goods that they perceive to be better than others simply because of a brand name. I've never had much money, so I try to make sure that I get all the value I can for my few dollars—which is why it's difficult for me to understand why a person would pay three or four times as much for such things as a purse or shoes or jeans simply because they have a well-advertised brand name. The same goes for computers. I don't understand why some people will buy a computer just because it has an IBM or Apple logo. For the price of an IBM or Apple, you can buy two or three equivalent, compatible, no-name computers.

One of the large computer magazines recently did a comparison test in their laboratory. They found that no-name ISA compatible clones performed as well as or better than the high-cost brand-name computers.

Please don't misunderstand. I think the B-B gene is a good thing. I'm influenced by it myself when it comes to computers. Without it, there might not be as much progress and innovation. Without the B-B gene, we might all still be living in caves and using stone tools. Without that B-B gene, we probably wouldn't have all the computer goodies that are available to us.

Some reasons you need to upgrade

That B-B gene might not exert much influence on you and your old computer might still do everything you want it to do, but there are a few reasons why you should consider upgrading.

Time

One of the foremost reasons is time. The old XT lumbers along at a speed of only 4,770,000 cycles per second (4.77 MHz). It can run most of the DOS programs, but there are some it would take hours to complete. The 486DX2-66 can process data at a speed of 66,000,000 cycles per second (66 MHz). The 486DX4 is even faster and can process data up to 100 million cycles per second (100 MHz). The 66-MHz Pentium, due to its superscalar technology, can process two instructions at a time, it can process data faster than the 100-MHz 486DX4. The Pentium's processing speed is several hundred times faster than that of the old XT.

Time is important to all of us because there's so little of it. If you're wasting time while your old computer struggles to run a simple program, then you should consider upgrading.

Software

If you have an older computer, you'll need to upgrade your hardware system to run some of the newer software, some of which simply won't run on a machine such as the XT. Some won't even run on a 286. There are some excellent Windows and OS/2 programs that can make computing much easier and faster, and accomplish things that older programs can't. There are thousands of new applications being developed every day, and an old computer might cause you to miss out on a lot of goodies.

Many programs cost from $500 to $1000, but some of them are so difficult to use that you have to spend an additional $500 to $1000 for classes and instructions. Hundreds of companies make a good business holding seminars to teach people how to use these high-cost programs. There are several books written for each of the popular programs that will teach you how to use them, and all of these programs come with instruction manuals. Most of these programs also have extensive on-disk help. If the manuals and help files were any good, there would be no need for the extra books and the seminars.

Software developers are trying to remedy this situation. They're trying very hard to make software user-friendly, and easier to learn and use. But there's still a price to pay. To make them easier to use, the programs are larger and require more memory and disk space.

Of course, software developers add much more functionality and more utility to the programs, which also makes them larger. To install and run Windows NT requires about 80 megabytes (80MB) of disk space. You'll also need a minimum of 8MB of RAM, although 16MB is better. To take advantage of the extra goodies and utility in the newer software, you'll have to upgrade so you have a lot of disk space and memory.

Used computers

This book will show you how to upgrade or repair your older computer to bring it up to date with the newest technology. If you don't have an older computer to upgrade, don't let that stop you. Buy a used one and upgrade it.

The only trouble with buying a used computer is that you might have trouble finding one. I live in the Los Angeles area, but when I check the classified ads for computers I seldom see more than two or three IBMs or IBM-compatibles listed.

About 160 million computers have been sold. Evidently, everybody is holding on to the old ones, possibly upgrading them or passing them on to the kids or relatives and buying new ones. Many large companies are buying newer, bigger, better, and faster systems, but they don't get rid of the older ones. They just pass the old computers down the line to departments who were doing without computers. Of course, an older XT or 286 is better than no computer at all. Besides, many of those people probably don't need the high power and speed of a 386 or 486.

Perhaps one reason you don't see too many used computers for sale is that computers are built primarily from semiconductors. If a system is designed properly, a transistor should last for several lifetimes. Of course, the disk drives, keyboards, and other components with moving parts will eventually wear out. But most of them can be easily replaced.

Buying a used IBM

A used computer with a genuine IBM logo on it will probably cost more than two brand-new clones. This is pure snob appeal. There's no basic difference in the workings of an IBM and a clone. You can take anything out of a clone and plug it into an IBM, and vice versa.

Some might argue that IBM is an American company so it's better quality. If you look inside an IBM, you'll find almost as many ICs and components with foreign brands as you'd find in a clone. As for quality, I've had quite a lot of experience with both IBM computers and clones, and I'm convinced that the main difference between them is the IBM logo.

Beware of used mechanical items

It's perfectly okay to buy anything electronic that's working, but I would strongly advise against buying a used printer, disk drive, or anything that's mechanical. As I said earlier, semiconductors don't wear out, but the mechanical components have a finite lifetime and will eventually fail. According to Murphy's law, they fail at the most inopportune time.

Of course, if you find a mechanical component that's almost new and you get a good buy on it, then go ahead. There are several companies who buy older hard disk drives and printers, and rebuild them. They often sell them for a very reasonable price. If you can get a good warranty on such a product, it should be all right.

Buying a bare-bones unit

You might consider buying a bare-bones system and building it up yourself. A bare-bones unit usually consists of a case, motherboard, and power supply. In order to have a functioning computer, you'll need disk drives, a keyboard, a monitor, and several other goodies. But you can buy them from different sources at the best price, and you don't have to buy them all at once. You can gradually build your system as you can afford it. This way, you'll still save money and you'll have put together your own computer. If it doesn't suit you, then you have only one person to blame.

Compatibility

A few years ago, IBM compatibility was essential. (IBM-compatible computers are now called ISA, or industry standard architecture.) IBM compatibility isn't a problem today. There's about ten billion dollars worth of ISA hardware and software today, and the software will operate on any of the ISA machines. You have a vast number of products to choose from for your upgrades.

Organization of this book

One of the problems in writing a book is that you don't know how much your readers already know. If you make it too simple, it will discourage the old pros. If you make it too technical, it will be over the heads of the newcomers. I try to take the middle ground throughout this book.

Another difficulty in writing a book like this is that the industry has grown so much that it's almost impossible to cover everything. In the medical field, there are specialists who concentrate on one area of the body. The human body is so complex that no one person can know all there is to know. The computer industry is almost to that point. Already there are people who specialize in communications, networking, and desktop publishing, to name just a few areas. There are also different kinds of programming that call for specialists. I've tried to cover as much as I could, but I can't put everything that you or someone else might want in this book. If I could, there'd be no need for all those other books. I'm sure the bookstores (not to mention the authors) wouldn't like that.

I've used plain English throughout the book and tried to avoid using computer jargon unless absolutely necessary. In some cases, there's no other way, so I've included a comprehensive glossary in the back of the book. If you come across an unfamiliar term, check for a definition in the glossary.

The future

Figure I-1 shows three key rings made by Intel from failed central processor unit (CPU) chips. On the left is a 386 chip with only 275,000 transistors in it. It measures approximately .380 of an inch by .380 of an inch. In the center is a 486 CPU. There are 1.2 million transistors in this small chip and it measures .414 of an inch by .619 of an inch. (I can remember when a single transistor was bigger than this chip.) On the right is a Pentium CPU with 3.1 million transistors. (Intel hasn't been able to copyright the 386 and 486 names. Other manufacturers have applied 386, 486, and 586 designations to their clone products, so what Intel should have called the 586 is the Pentium, which they have protected by copyright. Intel's clock tripler CPUs, the 3.3 volt 486DX4s, are just called DX4s. DX4 can also be protected by copyright.) Figure I-2 shows a DX4 with 1.6 million transistors. The DX4 can operate up to 99 MHz.

Intel manufactures several versions of each of the CPUs. Figure I-3 shows four different versions of the Pentium CPU. Intel has said they'll have CPUs with over 100 million transistors by the year 2000.

I-1 Three key rings made from CPU chips: a 386 on the left with 275,000 transistors, a 486 in the center with 1.2 million transistors, and a Pentium on the right with 3.1 million transistors.

I-2
An Intel DX4 processor, with 1.6 million transistors.

I-3 Four different versions of the Pentium CPU.

The computer industry has one of the fastest changing technologies. I discuss many of the new and improved products in this book, but I can't possibly list them all. Such a book could never be complete because thousands of new products are introduced every day.

You can be sure that faster, more powerful, and more useful computers will be on the market by the time you read this, but that doesn't mean you should wait for the newest development. Remember that there will always be newer ones out tomorrow. Besides, maybe you don't really need the newest, fastest, and most powerful computer. Perhaps you can get by with one that's almost the fastest and most powerful.

There's one truth that no one can dispute: technology does not stand still. Since the discovery of the transistor just a little over 40 years ago, there have been more technological advances than in the previous 4,000 years. And it shows no signs of slowing down. These are wonderful times that we're living in.

You can do it

Some of the hottest-selling books on the market today are those written for "dummies." I belong to Mensa, but I've bought most of these books. Some of them have some very good information, but they're usually overly simplistic and leave out a lot of important information. I love books and have hundreds in my office. One of the books that's directly opposite of these "dummies" books is *Upgrading and Repairing PCs* by Scott Mueller. It's highly technical and very good for reference. It's an excellent book, but it's quite different from this one. This book is more of a hands-on book for the average person, and covers both hardware and software.

The main point made in most of those "dummies" books is that you don't have to be a genius to use, repair, or upgrade a computer. But despite all my assurances, some of you will still have doubts or fears that you can't upgrade or repair your computer. Don't worry. It doesn't require a lot of expertise. Computer assemblies require no soldering or electronic test equipment or instruments. Computers are made up of modular components that just plug in or connect together by cables. Please believe me; you can do it—and save a bundle.

1
CHAPTER

What's inside

If you aren't familiar with the components inside your computer, it will be difficult for you to upgrade or replace them. This chapter tells you how to remove the cover, how to identify the major components, and how to remove and replace them.

Tools needed

There are a few inexpensive, basic tools that you'll need. Even if you don't expect to do much computer upgrading and repairing, these tools, shown in Fig. 1-1, are good for other uses around the home.

Screwdrivers

You should have a couple of different-sized standard (plain-head) screwdrivers and Phillips-head screwdrivers. Most computer systems use Phillips-head screws.

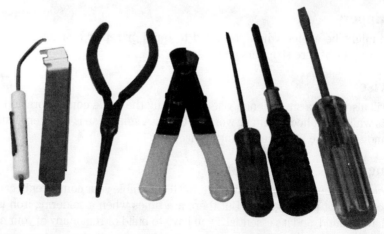

1-1 Some tools you might need.

Some have a Phillips head with a slot so you can use either a Phillips-head or standard screwdriver.

Some systems use Phillips-head screws that have a hexagonal head. You can use a ¼-inch nut driver on these screws, which makes it very easy to install and remove them.

You might find a few systems, such as Compaq, that use Torx screws. Torx screws are similar to Phillips-head screws except that they have six slots. You might be able to remove them with a Phillips-head screwdriver, but it will be much easier with a proper sized Torx screwdriver. The two sizes used most often are the T-10 and T-15.

If the screwdrivers are magnetized, it will help you to get the screws started. (Caution! Be very careful not to let a magnetized screwdriver or any magnet near your floppy disks. A magnet can erase them or partially destroy the data.)

Pliers

You'll also need a pair of standard pliers and a pair of long-nosed pliers. The long-nosed pliers are very handy for retrieving dropped screws. The flat portion of the nose is also excellent for straightening the pins on integrated circuit (IC) chips or pins on connectors.

Voltohmmeter

A voltohmmeter can be used to check for the presence or absence of voltages in your computer. A lot of problems can be traced to cables. A cable might have a break in one of the wires, especially if it's subject to a lot of use and frequent flexing. I once spent a lot of time on a bad cable. It had a broken wire that made contact until the cable was moved. A power cord such as one used by a home vacuum cleaner will often break at the plug because of the flexing. You might think you need a new vacuum cleaner unless you check the power cord. You can use a voltohmmeter to check the continuity of cables and power cords.

A voltohmmeter can also be handy around the home for checking out small appliances that might be defective. You should be able to buy a low-cost one at any electronics store.

Wire strippers

There might be a time when you need to build or repair a special cable. You should have a pair of wire strippers and cutters.

Bench vise

You will also need a small bench vise for holding the cable connectors and other small parts while you check them or work on them. A small vise is also very handy to have around the house for dozens of other uses.

Soldering iron

You probably won't need to do any soldering to assemble your computer because all the components just plug together. But there are times when a soldering iron is very handy to have around, and it's essential if you have to build or repair any of your cables.

Flashlight

A flashlight or a good bench light is essential for troubleshooting and exploring your computer. A good magnifying glass might also come in handy for reading the types and part numbers on some of the chips.

Chip pullers

Caution! Before removing any chip, make a diagram with the socket number on the motherboard and the orientation of the chip. It's very easy to forget where a chip belongs or how it should be oriented. I once removed a couple of BIOS chips. There were four sockets on the motherboard, all exactly alike. When I got ready to replace the BIOS chips, I couldn't remember which sockets they came out of. Fortunately, I had documentation for the motherboard that showed the BIOS sockets. It would have saved me a lot of time, however, if I had made a simple note before I removed the chips.

If you need to remove or replace any of the chips, such as when you're installing a new BIOS, there are standard chip pullers and extractors that you can buy. These are necessary if you expect to do a lot of removing and installing of chips.

Ordinarily, you won't be removing and changing chips very often. I have a small bent screwdriver that works very well. I also use the metal fillers used on the back panel for slots that have no boards installed. Just place the bent portion of the blank filler under one end of the IC and pry it up, then pry up the other end until it's free.

It might take a special tool to remove some of the large square chips. They usually have one corner that has been cut off, which matches the socket and assures that the chip is plugged in properly. To remove one of these chips requires a tool similar to an ice pick. It's a thin, hardened, metal probe. You use this probe to pry the chip up from the cut-off corner, although you might be able to use an ice pick or a very small screwdriver.

Most of the newer motherboards with 486 and Pentium CPUs now have a zero insertion force (ZIF) socket. This socket has split contacts for the chip's pins. A lever opens the socket contacts so the chip just falls in. When the lever is closed, the contacts are forced together so they connect with the pins.

Removing the cover

The first thing to do before removing the cover is to remove the power from the unit. Unplug the monitor, keyboard, and any other cables from the unit. But before unplugging any cable, make sure the connectors and cables are plainly marked so you can plug them back together properly. If they aren't, take some masking tape or a felt marking pen and label each cable and connector. If there's a chance that any connector might be plugged in improperly, place a mark across both connectors so the mark will line up when they're reconnected.

In the early days there were only one or two different types of cases. Most of them were similar to the IBM XT or standard AT types. The covers were held in place by five screws on the back panel, one in each corner and one at the top center. When the screws were loosened, the cover could be slipped off toward the front. There might have been several other screws on the back panel, some for the power supply and various connectors. These screws could not be removed.

Many cases today are still similar to the old XT and AT types, but there are also many new styles available. Some are the low-profile and small-footprint type, and many secure the cover differently.

Tower cases are about the same as desktop cases, except they stand on one side. There are usually six screws on the back that hold the cover in place. On most tower cases, the front bezel has a groove that accepts the front part of the cover so that no screws are needed in the front.

Case and power supply

The desktop case is still the most popular. Most desktop cases are limited to three or four bays for mounting disk drives. If you want to install two hard disks, a 1.2MB and 1.44MB floppy, you'll need one with at least four bays.

There are some low-profile cases that are similar to the IBM PS/2. They aren't even high enough to mount a vertical plug-in board. They usually have a single slot on the motherboard, and a daughterboard plugs into this slot. The daughterboard might have three to five slots for horizontally mounted plug-in boards.

The low-profile cases limit the number of plug-in slots and also the number of available drive bays. Most of them have room for only two drives: a single floppy and a hard drive. Because of these limitations, I don't recommend the low-profile systems.

Depending on your needs, you might want to buy a tower case. A tower case sits on the floor and the larger ones have space for up to eight drive bays. This would provide room for two hard drives, two floppies, a tape backup, a CD-ROM, a write once read many (WORM) drive, and one other.

Tower cases are a bit more expensive than the standard or small cases. There are three sizes of tower cases: mini, medium, and large. The smaller sizes don't have as many bays for mounting drives. Most of the tower cases, and most other cases, include a power supply with the cost. Depending on the type of case and the vendor, they'll cost from $40 up to over $100 each. Make sure that any power supply is at least 200 watts.

Static electricity warning

Caution! Once the cover is removed, before touching any of the components inside your computer make sure you discharge yourself of any static electricity. If you've ever walked across a carpeted room and got a shock when you touched a doorknob, you know what static electricity is. It's possible for a person to build up as much as 3,000 volts or more of static electricity. If you touch any of the sensitive electronic components, that static electricity could be discharged through them—which could destroy or severely damage some circuits.

Discharging yourself

When you touch a metal doorknob, you discharge built-up static electricity. A much better discharge occurs if you touch something that goes directly to the ground, such as a water pipe. Since you probably don't have a water pipe near your computer, the next best thing is to touch a bare metal part of your computer.

It's a good idea to discharge yourself by touching something that's metal and grounded before handling any electronic component or board, especially if you've walked across a carpeted room.

The power switch on your computer should be turned off. Then plug the power cable into the wall outlet. Even with the computer switch off, the third wire of the power plug, or ground wire, is still connected to the power outlet. If you traced this ground wire back to your main circuit breaker or fuse box, you would find that it's connected to a water pipe or metal rod that goes to the earth ground. The metal chassis of your computer should be connected to this earth ground by the third wire of the 110-volt power outlet.

Most boards and components have a static electricity warning label on the packaging. In most cases you have to break that warning label in order to open the package.

Motherboard

Once the cover is removed, you'll see several boards that are plugged into connectors on the large motherboard that sits on the floor of the chassis. There are usually eight slots on the motherboard for various types of plug-in boards. Here are some of the boards you might find in your computer: an adapter board for your monitor, a board for your printer, which might have connectors for a mouse or other serial devices, a board for a modem and fax, and one or more boards for your disk drive controllers.

Motherboard slots

Most motherboards have eight plug-in slots, whether the machine is a true-blue IBM XT, AT, or a clone. The motherboard slots, or connector receptacles, are for the various boards you might want to use. Plug-in boards have an edge connector with copper-etched fingers that contact the spring-loaded contacts of the motherboard slot connectors.

The XT motherboard is 9 inches wide and 12 inches long. The original AT motherboard is 12 inches wide and 13 to 14 inches long. Later, Adaptec and other companies began integrating several of the motherboard chips to reduce the size of the AT motherboard to about the same size as the XT. They called these "baby AT motherboards." Some of the early baby 286 and 386 motherboards have only seven slots. The early IBM PC had only five slots. Compare this to some high-end systems that have a motherboard with 12 slots.

The slots on these motherboards, whether the original AT size or the baby size, are placed so they line up with the openings in the back panel of the case, whether it be a large AT size, the XT size, or any of the tower cases.

The IBM PS/2 systems and the low-profile clone systems have a single slot on the motherboard for a plug-in daughterboard. This daughterboard then has from two to five slots for horizontally mounted plug-in boards. If it has five slots, there are usually three slots on one side and two on the other.

Motherboard differences

The major difference between the XT, 286, 386, 486, Pentium, and PowerPC is the motherboard. Figure 2-4 shows an XT motherboard, a 286, and an early 386. The plug-in slots are at the bottom in the photos. Notice that the 286 has six extra 36-pin slots above the standard eight 62-pin slots. Some early 386 motherboards have four extra 36-pin slots and two extra 62-pin slots. The extra 36-pin slots are for 16-bit system boards. The two extra 62-pin slots on the 386 motherboard are for proprietary 32-bit memory boards.

Having the 32-bit memory on a plug-in board had several disadvantages. It slowed the memory down a bit, used up a precious slot, was bulky, and there was little or no standardization. Later motherboard designs eliminated the extra 62-pin slots. Most motherboards now have sockets for single in-line memory modules (SIMMs). These memory sockets are tied directly to the CPU through a 32-bit bus. Figure 1-2 shows my first 486 motherboard with 4MB of SIMM memory installed.

SIMM
memory

1-2 My first 486 motherboard, with 4MB of SIMMs.

The standard 62-pin slots on all motherboards are 8-bit slots. Sixteen-bit boards were developed to use the extra 36-pin slot. Notice that all the 8-bit 62-pin slot connectors are separate from the extra 16-bit connector slots.

As you've probably deduced, an 8-bit plug-in board, even one designed for the antique XT, can also be used in any industry standard architecture (ISA) or enhanced ISA (EISA) computer. All 8-bit boards are compatible, even with the most powerful Pentium. Of course, a 16-bit board can't be plugged into an XT.

If you have one of the older PCs, your motherboard is probably mounted on nine standoffs, with nine screws or nuts on the bottom of the chassis and on top of the motherboard holding it in place. Most of the newer systems have raised channels on the floor of the chassis. The channels have wide slots that become narrow to the right (refer to Fig. 1-3). As shown in Fig. 1-4, the motherboard has white plastic standoff/retainers. These standoff/retainers are dropped into the wide portion of the slots on the raised channel. The motherboard is then pushed to the right and grooves on the plastic standoffs become engaged in the narrow portion of the channel slot.

1-3 The bottom of a desktop computer case showing the raised channels and slots for motherboard stand-offs/retainers.

1-4 The back of a motherboard, and plastic stand-offs/retainers.

A screw in the front center and one in the rear center are sufficient to hold the motherboard secure. To remove it from the case, remove the two screws and pull the motherboard toward you until the standoffs are disengaged. More about motherboards in chapter 4.

The power supply

If you have a desktop case, the power supply is located in the right rear corner of the chassis. It has a chrome-plated cover around it and a cooling fan that generates the only noise you hear, except for the disk drives, when your computer is running. The cooling fan sucks air in from the front of the computer and forces it out through the grill in the back of the power supply. All holes in the computer and blank slots in the back panel should be covered so the air is drawn only from the front grill of the computer and drawn over the components. Make sure that nothing in the front or back of the computer impedes the airflow.

The power supply usually has four screws on the back panel that holds it in place. It might also have a couple of cutouts on the bottom that interlock with the raised tabs on the floor of the chassis. To remove the power supply, remove the four screws on the back panel, then slide the power supply toward the front of the chassis to disengage the tabs. The power supply in tower systems is usually mounted in the top rear area. It's held in place with four screws through the back panel.

Transforming the voltage

The computer systems use direct current (dc). The dc voltages needed are 12 Vdc and 5 Vdc. The voltage that's provided by the wall socket is usually 110 volts alternating current (ac). The computer power supply uses rectifiers and transformers to convert the ac voltage to the proper dc voltage.

The ac voltage that comes from the wall plug alternates at 60 cycles per second, or 60 Hz. (Hz stands for Hertz. Rudolph Heinrich Hertz (1857–1894) was a German physicist who was the first to produce artificial radio waves. In order to honor Hertz, a standards committee decreed that the frequency of cycles should be called Hertz. Many old-timers still call it cycles per second.) To transform 110 volts at 60 Hz would require a large transformer, but a fairly small transformer can be used if the frequency is very high. Rectifiers are used to transform the ac to a 120-Hz chopped dc voltage. An oscillator circuit takes this 120-Hz chopped voltage and changes the frequency to over 50,000 Hz. This high-frequency voltage is input to a small transformer, which reduces the high-frequency 110 volts to 12 volts and 5 volts. Since the voltage that comes out of the transformer is ac voltage, it's again rectified and made into dc voltage.

The 110 volts in the power supply is the only voltage in your computer that might harm you, which is one reason for the cover. Another reason for the cover is to reduce any stray radiation that might emanate from the conversion process.

Early IBMs and most clones had a switch on the side of the power supply for turning on the computer. This switch turned the ac on and off. It was a bit inconvenient to reach around the back of the computer to turn it on and off, however, so many of the newer systems have a switch on the front panel. There's usually a four-wire electrical cord that goes from the power supply to the switch. When you buy a new case, this switch is often not connected to the power cord. The switch has four terminals for the power connection. Be careful when connecting the power to the switch. The power supply should come with a diagram showing how to connect the switch.

The disk drive bays

Depending on the type of case you have, you might have bays for two floppy disk drives and one or two hard drives. The bays for the floppy drives are accessible from the front. The hard drive bays might not be accessible once the cover is installed. If you're buying a new case, try to get one with at least three or more accessible bays so you have room to install two floppy drives, a CD-ROM drive, and perhaps a tape backup system.

If you have an older case that has only two accessible bays and you want to install a CD-ROM or other drive, you might consider buying a combination floppy drive that has both 5¼-inch and 3½-inch drives integrated into one system (see Fig. 1-5).

The drive bays might have slots and holes for mounting the drives. The drives have several screw holes on their sides that match up with the holes in the bays.

1-5 A combination 5¼-inch and 3½-inch drive from the CMS.

Some of the cases have slots for plastic or metal slides; the slides are attached to the drives. The drives are then inserted in the slots and pushed to the rear of the bay. A couple of screws or small flanges hold the drives in place.

Cost of components

All PCs, even the Pentium and PowerPC, use the same basic components except for the motherboard and the CPU. Since the common components are all interchangeable, you can shop around for the best buys. Look at the ads in computer magazines such as the *Computer Shopper*, *PC Magazine*, *PC World*, and *PC Computing* for an idea of what's available. These ads will also give you prices for the various components and options. You can order the components through the mail or, if you live near a large city, go to a swap meet or local store.

It's almost impossible to put a real cost on components. The prices change daily, usually downward. There are hundreds of different manufacturers and many, many options, so the prices will vary. Of course, brand names and the type of component are a factor.

There's a large variation in the cost of motherboards, depending on the brand name, whether it's a 386, 486, or Pentium. The cost also varies according to the operating frequency of the CPU; the higher the frequency, the higher the cost. At this time, a 386SX motherboard might cost as little as $60 and a 40-MHz 386DX might cost as little as $90. A 486SX might cost about $200 and a 66-MHz 486DX2 might cost $600 or more. (I paid $1,850 for my first 386DX motherboard, which operated at only 16 MHz. My first 25-MHz 486 cost me $4,450. I recently bought a 60-MHz Pentium-motherboard for $1,200.)

Table 1-1 lists some approximate prices of other common components. These prices are listed to give you an idea of what a basic system might cost at the time this was written. The prices will since have changed, probably downward.

Table 1-1. Approximate prices of common computer components

Component	Price
Power supply & case	$35–150
Monitor	$65–2000
Monitor adapter	$40–400
4MB of memory	$125–150
Multifunction board	$50–200
1.4MB floppy drive	$45–50
1.2MB floppy drive	$45–50
200MB-1GB hard drive	$200–800
Disk controller	$20–150
Keyboard	$20–150

As you can see, there's quite a large variation in the cost. The cost depends on several available options and whether the components have well-known brand names. There's also a large variation in cost from dealer to dealer. Some of the high-volume dealers charge less than the smaller ones, so it pays to shop around a bit and compare prices.

Keep in mind that these figures are only rough approximations. The market is so volatile that prices can change overnight. If you're buying through the mail you might even call to check the advertised prices before ordering. Often the advertisements have to be made up one or two months before the magazine is published, so the prices could have changed considerably.

At one time Intel was the only manufacturer of 386 and 486 chips. But Cyrix, AMD, and several other companies now have 386 and 486 CPU clones on the market. Cyrix, AMD, and NexGEN all have Pentium or 586 clones. IBM and Apple have the PowerPC to compete with the Intel Pentium. This added competition will force CPU prices down even more. And when the CPU prices go down, the motherboard prices usually go down as well.

Options

There are many common components that aren't absolutely necessary for a system. If you don't need a lot of goodies at this time, you can buy the minimum components and add to your system later. For instance, you don't need two floppy drives; you can get by fine with a single floppy drive.

Extra memory

You can get by with two megabytes of memory, but for most applications today you need at least four megabytes. Even better is 8MB or more. You can't have too much memory.

On older systems, memory chips were usually located in the left front quadrant of the motherboard. They used dual in-line pins (DIP). Almost all systems today use the single in-line memory module (SIMM). These are small boards that have miniature chips on them. The board has an edge connector that plugs into special sockets on the motherboard. The SIMM technology allows up to 128MB or more memory in a much smaller area than the 640K on the older motherboards that used the DIP chips.

A few of the older motherboards used a single in-line pin (SIP). These were miniature chips mounted on a board, which was very similar to the SIMM technology except that the boards had pins that plugged into special sockets. Very few motherboards use the SIP type of memory today.

When a computer runs a program, the program is temporarily loaded into memory and processed there. When the processing is completed, the program is then loaded back on the hard disk. There are many different types of memory, and they're discussed in chapter 6.

Floppy disk drives

You might have an old 360K floppy drive. I recommend that you buy a 5¼-inch 1.2MB and a 3½-inch 1.44MB drive. The 1.2MB drive will read and write to both the 360K and 1.2MB floppies. The 1.44MB drive will read and write to the 720K as well as the 1.44MB.

I've seen ads for 1.2MB and 1.44MB drives for as little as $75 for the pair. The combination drive has both 5¼-inch 1.2MB and 3½-inch 1.44MB drives in the standard 5¼-inch drive. It costs about $95, a bit more than separate 1.2MB and 1.44MB. The combination drive will probably be less, though, by the time you read this. There are still a few 360K and 720K drives around, but they're obsolete. Don't buy them.

You might have to buy a floppy drive controller (FDC) board for your floppy drives. Many motherboards now have the disk controller built in. If so, there will be a double row of upright pins for connecting the disk drives. If you have a hard drive, it might also have a hard/floppy drive controller (H/FDC) built in. If not, you can buy a floppy controller for about $20. If you have an IDE hard disk, you might have an FDC on the IDE interface board. See chapter 8 for more details on floppy drives.

Hard disk drives

It's possible to operate a computer without a hard disk, but it's difficult to do much productive work. If your time is worth anything at all, a hard disk can pay for itself in a very short time.

Most of the older systems used the MFM, RLL, or ESDI hard drives. They were physically large, clunky, and slow. They were also very limited in storage capacity. One of my early hard disk drives was 40MB. It was three inches high, six inches wide, and eight inches long. I paid almost $1,000 for it. Since DOS 2.0 could handle only 32MB, I had to buy special software in order to use the full 40MB. I recently bought a 1.050-gigabyte (GB) drive for $740. It's one inch high, four inches wide, and six inches long.

There are several hard disk manufacturers with hundreds of different models, sizes, and types of hard disks. The older hard drives need a controller board that plugs into one of the slots. In many cases the controller is made by some company other than the one that manufactures the hard drive.

The integrated disk electronics (IDE) drives have all the controller electronics on the drive itself, but it still needs an interface to the system. This can be built into the motherboard or you can buy a low-cost interface that plugs into one of the slots. Since controllers for the IDE drives are made and matched by the same manufacturer, they operate better. They also cost a bit less than a drive and separate controller.

The small computer system interface (SCSI, pronounced *scuzzy*) also has all of its controller functions on the disk. It needs an interface card, but a SCSI card can handle up to seven different devices.

If you have one of the older hard disks, you should consider upgrading to one of the newer, larger ones. You just can't have too much disk storage. You could keep your old hard disk and use it for a doorstop. Or you could upgrade by adding a second hard disk that matches your first one. Your controller will handle two similar drives. If you have an old MFM or RLL hard drive, however, it might be difficult to find a second drive to match it. The problem is that these drives are obsolete. No one is making them now, so even if you do find one it will probably be rather expensive. Another disadvantage is that the older drives were quite limited in their capacity; most were 30 to 40 megabytes. That isn't enough to hold one good program today. You can probably install a 200MB IDE drive for about what it would cost for a 40MB MFM.

You'd probably be better off installing an IDE and a SCSI hard drive for the second drive. One advantage of this type of system is that you can use the two drives to back up each other. It's possible that one of the drives will crash or fail, but not very likely that both will fail.

Another very inexpensive way to double your disk storage is to use a data compression system. Stac Electronics at 619-431-7474, and several other companies offer data compression software. MS-DOS now comes with data compression as a standard feature. See chapter 9 for more details on hard drives.

Monitors

There's a large variety of monitors that you can use. You can buy a monochrome monitor for about $65. I like color even if I'm just doing word processing, so I'm willing to pay a little more for color. You can buy a VGA color monitor for about $250, or you can spend up to $2,000 or more for a large screen, very-high-resolution monitor. The type of monitor you buy should match whatever you're using your computer for. If you're doing a lot of high-end graphics or computer-aided design (CAD), then you need a large screen with high resolution. If you're buying a system for the kids to play games, then a 14-inch system with .039 dot pitch would be fine.

You'll need a plug-in adapter board to drive the monitor. (Some motherboards have a built-in adapter). It might cost as little as $20 for a monochrome adapter. For standard VGA color you should be able to buy one for about $40. For very-high-resolution color it might cost up to $500. See chapter 11 for more details on monitors and adapters.

Keyboards

The keyboard is a very important part of the computer. It's the main device for communicating with the computer. There are many different types of keyboards; most of them have slight differences in the placement of the keys, the tactile feel, and special adjuncts such as trackballs, calculators, and keypads.

To run Windows and other graphical user interface (GUI) programs, it's essential to have a mouse, trackball, or other pointing device. Chapter 12 discusses keyboards and other input devices in some detail.

Modems, faxes, and communications

You can use your computer to communicate with millions of other computers, with on-line services, and with a host of other services. You can download software from bulletin boards and you can send low-cost faxes to millions of other fax sites. You'll definitely need some communications hardware and software if you want to get the most from your computer. I'll discuss communications in chapter 13.

Printers

You have a lot of options when it comes to buying your printer. There are many different manufacturers and hundreds of different types and models. There are dot-matrix, laser, ink-jet, daisywheel, and many other types of printers. Some are better for a particular application than others, so which one you choose depends on what you want to do with your computer and how much you want to spend. Chapter 14 discusses various types of printers.

Software

You need software in order to use your computer. Before you even turn it on, you need operating software such as MS-DOS, DR DOS, IBM PC DOS, or OS/2. There are billions of dollars worth of off-the-shelf software that you can use. Some of the commercial programs are a bit expensive, but there are inexpensive public-domain and shareware programs that can do just about everything the commercial programs do. See chapter 17 for more about software. Chapter 18 discusses some of the ways you can use various programs on your computer. Just a few of the thousands of things you can do with your computer are discussed.

Backups

It's very important that you keep copies or backups of all of your programs and important data. You never know when your hard disk will crash or fail. There are thousands of ways you can lose very important data. You should always have a current backup. There are many methods of backup; some use hardware and some require special software. See chapter 10 for more details.

Sources

There are many different places where you can buy all the components you need to upgrade or repair your PC. If you live near a large city, there are probably local stores that sell the parts. Local vendors and computer stores will be most happy to help you. They might charge a bit more than mail-order houses, but if anything goes wrong they'll usually be very quick to help you or make it right.

There are also frequent computer swaps in most large cities. A computer swap is just a gathering of local vendors at a fairgrounds, a stadium, or some other area. The vendors usually set up booths and tables and present their wares. You can quite often find all you need at these meets. You can go from booth to booth and compare the components and prices. The prices are usually very competitive and you might even be able to haggle a bit with the vendors.

Another good source for components is mail order. Just look at the ads in any of the computer magazines. At one time mail order was a bit risky, but it's very safe today.

If a price seems too good to be true, then the vendor has probably cut a few corners somewhere. There are some very good bargains out there, but you should be careful. Your best protection is to be fairly knowledgeable about the computer business. Computer magazines and books like the one you're holding are some of the better sources for this knowledge.

Another excellent source of knowledge and help is the local computer user groups. If you live near a large city, there will probably be several groups. Most of the people in these groups are very friendly and willing to help you with any problem.

If you're fairly new to computing, be sure to read the chapters on floppy disk drives, hard disk drives, monitors, keyboards, and the major components before you buy your parts. There are billions of dollars worth of products available, and many of them are very similar in functionality and quality. What you buy should depend primarily on what you want your computer to do—and how much you can afford to spend.

If you're knowledgeable and if you shop wisely, you can save a bundle.

2
CHAPTER

Ways to upgrade a PC

There are hundreds of ways to configure and upgrade a computer. Computers are made up of various components that just plug together. You can add hundreds of different boards, components, and peripherals to a computer. Only a very few of the ways to upgrade are discussed in this chapter.

A dream machine

If money were no object, here's what I would like in a perfect PC or dream machine:

Pentium motherboard with a 100-MHz CPU

A Pentium 100-MHz computer operates at almost twice the speed of a 60-MHz machine. It's a 3.3-volt system, so it uses less wattage and will run cooler.

PCI bus

The VESA local bus (VLB) is a useful addition to the motherboard, but it appears that the PCI system from Intel might be a bit better.

Plug-and-play BIOS in flash memory

It's sometimes very frustrating to try to install a board in a system. Most boards have to have a specific memory address and interrupt request (IRQ). There are often conflicts when two boards are set for the same IRQ or memory address. A system that's "plug and play" in both the BIOS and software makes life a bit better.

32MB of DRAM

When a program is being processed or operated on, it's loaded into dynamic random-access memory (DRAM). So for large programs you need a lot of DRAM. You can probably get by with a lot less than 32MB, but it sure is nice to know that you'll never get an "insufficient memory" error message. (It's something like having a car with a 427-horsepower engine. You might not ever need all the power, but it's nice to have it in case you do.)

512K of SRAM fast cache memory

The CPU goes back and forth to the DRAM to get portions of the program for processing. Quite often a small portion of the program is processed over and over. If the most-used portions of the program are stored in very fast static random-access memory (SRAM), the system will operate much faster. SRAM is much faster than DRAM. And, of course, it's more expensive.

540MB enhanced IDE and 1.05GB SCSI-2 hard drive

It doesn't happen too often, but it's possible for hard drives to fail. Even one failure can be disastrous. If you have both IDE and SCSI drives installed, you can quickly back up from one to the other. It's very unlikely that both of them will fail at the same time.

A JTS 540MB removable hard disk

Some people still like tape backups, but you can back up a removable hard disk much more quickly. You can also access the data randomly; data on a tape can be accessed only sequentially. If the data you need is in the middle of the tape, you have to run it to the middle. JTS systems (408-747-1315) are relatively inexpensive compared to other systems.

Combination 1.2MB/1.44MB 5.25-inch floppy drive

The 1.2MB floppy drive is almost obsolete but I still have hundreds of both 360K and 1.2MB floppy disks. There are still many companies using them for software. A combination 1.2MB 5¼-inch and 1.44MB 3½-inch drive takes up no more space than a single 1.2MB drive.

PCMCIA slots

PCMCIA stands for the Personal Computer Memory Card International Association. This association was formed to standardize the plug-in slot for memory cards for laptop and notebook computers. Besides memory, there are now dozens of different PCMCIA cards available—fax-modem cards, network cards, SCSI interface cards, and 1.8-inch hard disks on cards. Having a slot on a desktop or tower computer makes it very easy to transfer data back and forth from a laptop.

V.34 modem/fax board

The V.34 fax-modem board allows communications up to four times faster than the 14.4K fax-modem board.

Fast CD-ROM drive

CD-ROMs have become an essential part of a computer. Many software companies are now distributing their software on CD-ROMs. CorelDRAW offers a considerable discount if you ask for the software on CD-ROM rather than 3½-inch disks.

Good 16-bit sound board with DSP and speakers

It's now possible to add sound and annotations to your files, and to play audio compact discs on a CD-ROM drive. Many CD-ROMs have sound, text, graphics, and motion. If you have a CD-ROM drive, you'll definitely need a sound board.

Network interface card (NIC)

I have several other computers in my office. It's very easy to connect them together in a simple network.

21-inch multiscanning monitor

Monitors go up in cost in an almost logarithmic fashion. A 14-inch monitor might cost a little over $200. A 21-inch monitor might cost as much as $2,000. The bigger the monitor, the easier it is to see. For high-end work, you need a high-end monitor.

24-bit monitor adapter

You need a good monitor adapter to be able to display all the possible colors. A good 24-bit monitor adapter with 2MB of memory can give you true color.

Good Key Tronic keyboard

Key Tronic, at 509-928-8000, has a keyboard that can be elevated in the center and angled so there's less chance of getting carpal tunnel syndrome (CTS) or a repetitive strain injury (RSI).

Logitech wireless mouse

I often have trouble with the cord to my mouse getting tangled up. A wireless mouse would solve that problem.

Medium tower case

Most medium tower cases have eight bays, and four of them are accessible. This should take care of most needs.

Bottom-line cost

As long as I'm dreaming, I'd also like to have a Rolls Royce. But it's a whole lot easier to make your dream come true for a computer than for a Rolls Royce. A system with all of the components I listed would cost between $10,000 to $20,000 if you bought it from a computer store. A few months ago, I put together a Pentium system that has most of these components for less than $6,000. I had to settle for a 60-MHz CPU and I don't have the new Key Tronic keyboard, JTS hard disk, and Logitech wireless mouse, but I'm sure I could put together a system with all the listed components for much less than $8,000—and I'm sure you could do the same. If you have an older system, you can easily upgrade it with any of the listed components.

Ever-changing technology

Computer technology is advancing and changing faster than any other technology. It's changing so fast that by the time you get a brand-new computer home from the store it's practically obsolete. My new Pentium is only a few months old, but it's definitely out of date compared to several new products released in the last six months. If your computer is three or four years old, it belongs to the dinosaur age. But not to worry. You can upgrade your computer, no matter how old it is, to take advantage of all the latest and greatest.

There are new software and hardware products being developed every day that can't be used on some of the older systems. These new products can make life a lot easier and simpler. The answer is to upgrade your older system so you can take advantage of the new goodies.

There's a brief explanation of the components inside a computer in chapter 1. Figure 1-1 shows some of the components you need to assemble a computer. Except for the motherboard, the parts or components that make up a PC are all basically the same whether it's a PC, XT, 286, 386, 486, Pentium, or PowerPC. There are in-depth discussions of the major components in later chapters.

Simple hardware upgrade

If you're working from home or in a small office, you might have your computer, monitor, printer, and several other devices all plugged into wall outlets. Life will be a whole lot simpler if you buy a power outlet strip. These strips usually have six outlets. The better ones also have power surge protection. Whenever a large electric motor or other piece of heavy electrical equipment is turned on, it creates a very high voltage spike in nearby power lines. These surges can cause glitches and data corruption in your computer. A good surge protector shunts the spikes to the ground.

Even more convenient is a power panel that's about one inch high and about the size of a desktop computer case. I have one that I sit on top of my desktop computer. It has six outlets in the back of it, where I can plug in my computer, monitor, printer, and two auxiliary devices. I can then use the switches on the front of the panel to turn any of the devices on or off. It's very convenient.

If you live in an area where there are frequent power failures or brown-outs, maybe you should consider installing an uninterruptible power supply (UPS).

Internal upgrade

A computer is somewhat like an erector set or set of building blocks. There are a very large number of components, modules, and devices you can connect together or plug in to upgrade a computer. Here are a few major upgrades that can make your computer faster, more powerful, and more effective. They're also quite cost effective.

New plug-in boards

Over ten billion dollars worth of hardware has been developed for the industry standard architecture (ISA) machines. These machines are what used to be called IBM compatibles. The ISA standard also includes IBM machines such as the IBM PS/1 and several of the PS/2 models. The IBM PS/2 models 50 and up are microchannel architecture (MCA). These computers use plug-in boards that have a different connector than do the ISA machines. See Fig. 2-1 for a comparison of an ISA and an MCA board.

2-1
An ISA board on top and an MCA board on the bottom. Note the difference in edge connectors.

ISA machines have a large motherboard with up to eight connectors, called *expansion slots*, for plug-in boards. Plugging a board into one of these slots allows you to expand the capability of your computer. Because of the open architecture, ISA computers can be configured to perform thousands of applications. It isn't necessary to design or manufacture a computer to do a specific job. If you want to perform a task like being able to collect or measure data from a scientific process, you can use an ISA computer and plug in a special board for that task. If you need to tie several computers together in a network, there are special network interface cards (NICs) that allow you to do that. There are cards or boards that allow you to use your computer as a part-time fax machine or modem. Or you can plug in boards that allow you to use your computer to add sound and voice to your files, or use the computer as an audio system. There are hundreds of different boards that can cause a computer to perform thousands of different tasks. You can plug the boards into any one of the slots on the motherboard for a very easy upgrade.

There are also over 50,000 different programs you can use with an ISA computer. This, along with the many different plug-in boards, makes this type of computer one of the most versatile tools in history.

Upgrading your processing speed

One of the foremost reasons to upgrade is to get more speed so you can do the same job in less time. Computers operate by processing and manipulating bits of data in the form of 0s and 1s. The processing of some files might require the handling of millions of bits of data. Much of this data must be handled over and over again, so billions of iterations can be performed on a relatively small file. Older computers require several minutes to do a job that a fast 486 or Pentium can do in seconds.

You might not care how long you have to wait for a file to be processed. If so, you're a very unique person. Most people don't like to wait, even if it's only a few minutes or seconds. If they're using a computer, they hate to wait even microseconds.

In the 1950s and 60s, many high school kids would take an old jalopy and turn it into a hot rod. There were all sorts of things they could do to an old car to make it faster and more powerful. They did things like installing bigger engines, different rear-end ratios, better carburetion, improved ignition systems, and many other improvements.

There are also several ways to get more speed and acceleration from a computer. With a little tinkering you can turn your computer into a real hot rod. One way is to replace the old motherboard, roughly equivalent to replacing the engine in an old jalopy. (But it's a whole lot easier to pull out an old motherboard and install a faster one than it is to replace an engine in an old jalopy—and a lot less expensive.)

Among other important chips, the motherboard has the all-important central processing unit (CPU) and random-access memory (RAM) on it. The old XT shuffled along at 4.77 MHz. The Intel 486DX4 and Pentium can speed along at up to 100 MHz. (Motherboard replacement and instructions are discussed in more detail in chapter 4.)

Hertz and cycles per second

Frequency and Hertz means how many times per second an event happens—the speed at which an event occurs. In the old days, when I first became an electronics technician, frequency was called cycles per second, or CPS. This was a very good description of the events. But someone decided to honor Heinrich Rudolf Hertz (1857–1894), who was the first to produce radio waves. So 1 Hz is equal to 1 CPS, and 1 MHz is equal to one million cycles per second.

CPU and I/O speed

On the XT and early 286 systems, the I/O and CPU speed was about the same. But the frequency of newer CPUs has increased way beyond what some software and hardware I/O can support.

One thing that made the XT so slow is that it was an 8-bit system, operating at 4.77 MHz. This means that the CPU handled input/output (I/O) at a maximum of 8 bits at a time. The I/O is data that's input from the keyboard, a disk drive, or another input device. Once the data is processed by the CPU, it's output to the disk drives, a printer, or other output device. It takes 8 bits, or 0s and 1s, to make one byte. It takes one byte to represent a single character of the alphabet. Once the data to be processed is loaded into RAM, it's sent to the CPU over the 8-bit bus. The CPU processes portions of the data, then sends it back to RAM, or the hard disk, or wherever it needs to go.

As long as the system frequency was less than 8 MHz, the I/O frequency and CPU frequency could be the same. But in order to remain compatible with some software and hardware, the I/O speed was limited to 8 MHz. Today we have CPUs that can operate as high as 100 MHz, but on many systems the input/output speed is still limited to 8 MHz.

The XT was an 8-bit system, which means that it communicated over an 8-bit bus between the CPU, RAM, and I/O. It takes 8 bits or one byte of on/off digital voltage to make an A or B or any other character. So the XT could send or receive one character at a time over the 8-bit bus. The XT bus had 20 lines between the CPU and RAM, so it could address only 2^{20} or 1,048,576 bits of data—one megabyte.

The 286 AT was a vast improvement over the XT. The CPU operated at 6 MHz and had a 16-bit bus between the CPU, RAM, and I/O. Later the CPU speed was increased to 8 MHz, then 12 MHz. This means that the CPU processed the data at up to 12 MHz and sent it back to the RAM at the same speed. Much later some 286 CPUs were designed to run as high as 25 MHz between the CPU and RAM.

Being a 16-bit system, the 286 could handle two bytes at a time. It also added four more lines to the bus for a total of 24. So you could now address 2^{24} or 16,777,216 bits of data—16MB of memory.

The 386DX was a tremendous improvement over the 286 system. It was a 32-bit system, which means that it could transfer four bytes at a time to memory. Also, 2^{32} made it possible for the CPU to address 4,294,967,296 bytes, or 4 gigabytes (4GB) of data. Originally, the 386 operated at 16 MHz. Later, some systems were designed to operate as high as 40 MHz.

At one time several companies offered plug-in modules and plug-in boards to replace a 286 CPU with a 386 CPU, which would give you most of the advantages of the early 386. There are some companies who still sell these modules, but today this type of upgrade is no longer cost effective. The cost of motherboards has dropped so much, that it's now less expensive to replace the 286 motherboard with a 386 motherboard than to buy one of these CPU modules.

Soon after the introduction of the 386DX, Intel came out with a 386SX. The 386SX CPU sent data to RAM over a 16-bit bus, just like the 286. But the 386SX CPU processed data internally in 32-bit chunks just like the 386DX. This might seem like a step backward because it slowed the system down a bit. But once the data is loaded into the CPU, it's processed at the same speed as a 386DX. So being able to process data at 32 bits doesn't slow down the overall speed very much.

The 386SX is a low-cost alternative to the faster but more expensive 386DX, but it can run all the software that the more expensive 386DX runs. (I paid $1,825 for my first 386DX motherboard, which operated at 16 MHz. I can buy a 386DX motherboard today that operates at 40 MHz for less than $100.)

The early 486DX operated at 25 MHz. Like the 386DX, it has a 32-bit bus system between the CPU and the RAM. But it also has an improved data-handling capability and an 8K internal cache system that makes it much faster than the fastest 386. Later, the 486 CPU frequency was increased up to 33 MHz and then 50 MHz. Then the 33-MHz speed was doubled to 66 MHz.

The 486DX has a built-in math coprocessor. Intel later introduced the 486SX, which doesn't have the math coprocessor. It's a bit slower for some operations but is much less expensive. Shortly after the 486SX introduction, Intel made available their OverDrive CPUs, which are 486 CPUs that operate internally twice as fast as they do externally. For instance, an OverDrive CPU for a 25-MHz system will double the clock frequency for an internal processing speed of 50 MHz; a 33-MHz system will operate at 66 MHz internally. Since the OverDrive chips operate externally at the original speeds of 25 MHz or 33 MHz, the actual overall speed increase is about 70%.

The latest 486 is the 486DX4, which triples the 33-MHz clock speed to 99 MHz. The original Pentium operated at 60 and 66 MHz. The current versions operate at 100 MHz. It's expected that the Pentium or a later version of it will eventually operate as high as 150 MHz. We've come a long way since the early XT at 8 MHz.

In spite of all of the increases in CPU speed, the I/O speed remained at 8 MHz, the same as some of the early XTs and the 286. The I/O bus was also limited to 16 bits. This was done primarily so that the newer CPUs remained compatible with the early software and hardware. Another reason the whole systems weren't designed to operate at the higher frequencies is because higher-frequency components are much more expensive to design and build. It costs very little to double the internal frequency of the CPU; most of the CPU work is done internally anyway. The CPU might access the RAM just once, then perform several iterations on the data internally. It's very easy to remove an older CPU and replace it with a faster OverDrive chip.

On the OverDrive system, you can just remove the old CPU and drop in a 486DX2. But you can't do that with the DX4, which uses a voltage of 3.3 volts instead of the standard 5 volts. Therefore, these CPUs can be used only on a motherboard with a power supply that's specifically designed for them. Several companies are developing sockets with a built-in voltage regulator that plugs into the old socket. Just pull out the old CPU, plug in the regulating socket, then plug the CPU into the socket.

Upgrades for the PS/2

In the past, there weren't many parts and components available for upgrading PS/2 machines, except from IBM. You had to take your machine to an authorized dealer and have him install genuine IBM components. But now you can buy any component from IBM and install it yourself. Also, there are quite a lot of other sources for IBM components and parts. It's no more difficult to upgrade or repair a PS/2 than it is any other PC. The main difference in upgrading a PS/1 and PS/2 is that the components will cost much more than those for other ISA machines.

More memory

My first computer, a little Morrow CP/M machine, had a whopping 64K of memory. That was plenty for the few applications that were available, but programs were soon developed that required many times more than this. Most major software today require a minimum of 4MB. I have 32MB of DRAM installed on my Pentium computer. Even that might not be enough in the future. It's very easy and simple to install memory. For more about memory, see chapter 6.

ROM BIOS

If you really want to keep your old computer, you'll no doubt need a new ROM BIOS. The Basic Input/Output System (BIOS) is on plug-in chips on the motherboard. As the name suggests, it controls the input and output of data to the computer. In the early days, the BIOS was fairly simple because not too many applications were available. The original IBM PC didn't even support hard disk drives. BIOS chips have improved as applications have proliferated.

I have an ancient 286 machine that I put together in 1984. When 3½-inch floppy disks came out, I immediately bought a 3½-inch drive for $325. But the BIOS in my machine had been designed before the 3½-inch drive was even dreamed of so I couldn't install it. I also had problems with several new programs and applications until I bought new BIOS chips.

There are several companies who specialize in selling replacement BIOS chips. They advertise regularly in *Computer Shopper* and other computer magazines. You should be aware, though, that new BIOS chips could cost more than a complete new motherboard, which includes a new BIOS and all the other chips. Some BIOS chips cost from $40 to $60.

CMOS battery

Every time you booted up the old PC and XT, you had to input the date and time. It's helpful if the time and date is correct because every time a file is created, DOS stamps the file with the time and date. This makes it very easy to determine which of two files is the later one. Several companies made fortunes selling plug-in boards with a battery-operated clock. When the 286 was introduced, it had a clock built into the motherboard. The early systems used batteries that lasted about two or three years.

The batteries supply power for a complementary metal oxide semiconductor (CMOS) transistor circuit. Besides keeping the date and time when the power was turned off, these low-power transistors retained the system configuration. It kept a record of what types and kinds of floppies, hard drives, monitor, and keyboard were used in the system.

If your system doesn't keep accurate time, you might need to replace the battery. Early IBM 286 ATs used a battery that cost over $30. Many of the clone builders designed a system that used low-cost alkaline batteries. Most modern systems now use a tubular lithium battery that's soldered onto the motherboard. The battery is often a small blue cylinder. Several companies offer replacement batteries. Look in computer magazines like *Computer Shopper*. These batteries might also only last two or three years.

One factor in the battery life is how often you use your computer. While the computer is on, it draws power from the wall socket. When it's off, the CMOS transistors must be kept alive by the lithium battery. If your system consistently loses time, it could be that you need to replace the battery. If your battery goes completely dead, it will lose all your configuration data and you won't be able to use your computer. When this happens, some people think they need to buy a new computer. Some, in fact, have gone out and bought a new computer or a new hard drive when all they needed was a new CMOS battery.

It's fairly easy to replace your battery, but some shops will charge you $50 to $100 to do it. Besides that, you have to transport your computer. Rather than fighting the traffic and inconvenience, you can order a battery and replace it yourself. The battery should cost about $15, but some companies are charging twice that much. Tom Doyle of the Raytheon Company has put together a list of companies that supply batteries or will install them for you. Call Tom at 800-881-2562 for the dealer nearest you. The Page Computer Company at 800-886-0055, Battery Biz (818-706-0635), and Fedco Electronics at 800-542-9761 all have motherboard batteries. Call them for brochures and prices.

Most motherboards have a set of upright pins somewhere near the battery. Figure 2-2 shows a round tubular battery and a pen pointing to a set of upright pins for the connection of an external battery. Raytheon now supplies batteries that have a connector for these pins. If the pins aren't marked, you'll have to check your motherboard documentation. This is yet another reason to make sure you have documentation for all the boards and components in your system.

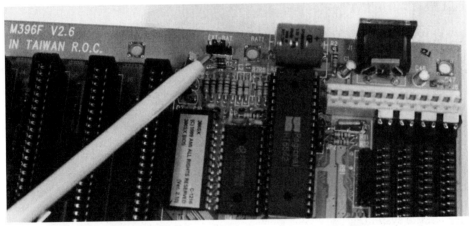

2-2 A round tubular battery. The pen is pointing to a set of upright pins for connecting an external battery.

By using the Raytheon batteries that have connectors, you won't have to do any soldering. If you're unfamiliar with how to use a soldering iron on an expensive circuit board, you could cause a lot of damage. By all means try to find a plug-in battery. Just plug in the wires from the external battery, then clip out the old battery. You must remove at least one of the terminals, otherwise the dead battery will act as a short on your new battery and will soon drain it. Clip the terminals with a pair of wire cutters, or even a knife if you have nothing else. Don't clip the leads until you've plugged in the new external battery, otherwise you'll lose all of your CMOS setup data.

Most batteries are 3.6 volts. There are a few that are 6 or 7 volts. Make sure you get the proper size and voltage for your system. Some systems use a 3.6-volt on-board battery, but they might specify a 6- or 7-volt external plug-in battery. There's usually a resistor between the pins for external batteries that drops the voltage down 3.6 volts.

Before you replace the battery, make sure you have a backup or written record of all the information in your CMOS setup. Once the battery is disconnected or if it goes completely dead, the CMOS transistors lose all their information. Some utility programs will make a backup of your CMOS setup. It isn't usually that complicated. It will have the date and time, the type of monitor and keyboard, and the type of floppies and hard drives you have. The type of hard drives is crucial. You must reinput the exact data from the original CMOS setup into the system. This data is the type of drive, which tells the system how many cylinders the disk has, how many heads, how many sectors, etc. If you don't replace the CMOS setup information exactly, you might not be able to access your hard drive. If you plug in an external battery before you clip out the old battery, you shouldn't have any problems.

Most systems will give you an opportunity to access your CMOS setup while it's going through the boot routine. Usually you have to press the Esc key, Del key, or a combination of keys. Check your documentation for which keys to press. I always forget the combination used on one of my systems, so I just hold down a key on the keyboard while it's booting up. The system beeps at me, gives me a keyboard error, and tells me to press F1 to continue or F2 for setup. Most systems will react the same way.

If you replace the battery, make sure you install it the same way. Make a diagram showing the positive and negative ends before you remove the battery. It's very easy to forget how a battery or other chip is installed. Some of the batteries on the newer motherboards come in a square chip-like device that can be plugged into a socket. I unplugged the battery on my Pentium Micronics motherboard to take a photo of it. When I got ready to plug it back in, I had forgotten how it was originally plugged in. There were no markings on the board to show how it should be installed. If I plugged it in backwards, it could ruin the CMOS chips. I was rather unhappy with myself until I remembered that I had taken some photos of the motherboard earlier. I was quite lucky because one of them showed how the device was originally plugged in. Figure 2-3 shows the newer type battery on a Pentium motherboard.

New motherboard

I recently replaced my daughter's old 286 motherboard with a 386SX. I also set up three other 386SX computers for my grandchildren. I paid $60 for each of the motherboards. These motherboards had a new BIOS and all the other chips except extra memory. The 386SX motherboards allow them to run multimedia and most other types of software. They might be a bit slower than a 486 or Pentium, but the kids don't mind.

The motherboard is the main board in your computer. It's the primary difference in all systems. Except for the motherboard, all ISA computers use the same basic components, such as disk drives, monitors, and modems.

The motherboard has the CPU, the memory, the BIOS, the bus, and several other chips and components on it. It has slots so you can plug other boards into it. If you have an old XT or 286, you can remove the motherboard and replace it with a late-model 386, 486, or Pentium. Motherboards have gone through several structural changes. Figure 2-4A shows an old XT motherboard; 2-4B shows a large standard-sized 286, 2-4C a small 386, and 2-4D a Pentium.

2-3 A new type of motherboard battery that plugs into a socket.

2-4A
An old XT motherboard.

2-4B
A standard-sized 286
motherboard.

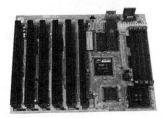

2-4C
A small 386 motherboard.

2-4D
A Pentium motherboard.

There are hundreds of vendors that sell motherboards. The competition has forced the prices down to where they're very reasonable. Replacing the motherboard is one of the better upgrades you can make. One of the newer motherboards will allow you to run any software or use any hardware that's available.

It's very easy to pull out your old motherboard and install a new one. There are detailed instructions in chapter 4.

Floppy drive upgrade

The old 360K floppy has served us well, but it's now obsolete. There are several newer drives that are inexpensive and easy to install. The 1.2MB floppy drive can read, write, and format both 360K and 1.2MB disks. They cost only a few dollars more than a 360K drive, but a 1.2MB can store over three times more data. Similarly, the 1.44MB 3½-inch drive can read, write, and format both 720K and 1.44MB disks. A 1.44MB drive costs only a few dollars more than a 720K drive, but it allows you to store twice as much data. A few vendors are still advertising and selling 360K and 720K floppy disk drives. They're obsolete; don't buy them.

A 2.88MB floppy drive is a bit more expensive, at about $75. You can buy a 1.2MB and 1.44MB drive for that amount. The 2.88MB drive might also require a special controller. Some companies are now integrating the 2.88MB controller along with the standard floppy controller and IDE interface on a single board. The 2.88MB disks are also rather expensive. You can buy a 1.44MB disk for about 35 cents, but a 2.88MB disk could cost as much as $5. I looked at the ads in a recent *Computer Shopper* magazine. I saw dozens of ads for 1.44MB and 1.2MB floppy drives and disks, one ad for a 2.88MB drive, and no ads for 2.88MB disks. I'm not sure that the 2.88MB system will ever become widespread.

The Insite Company has developed a 21MB floptical 3½-inch disk drive. If you use data compression, you can store up to 42MB on this 3½-inch floppy disk. Several other companies are now manufacturing 21MB floptical drives at a fairly reasonable cost.

The Iomega Company manufactures the Bernoulli drive. It now has a capacity of 150MB. By using data compression, which is furnished with the drive, you can store up to 300MB on the special 5¼-inch floppy disk. With just a few disks, you would never run out of disk storage. I'll discuss floppy drives in more detail in chapter 8.

Hard disk upgrade

I assume that you already have a hard disk. If you don't, then by all means you should get one. It's almost impossible to do any productive computing today without at least a 200MB hard disk. The prices have come down to less than a dollar per megabyte. I've seen 210MB drives for $189. They're very easy to install. If you have an older drive that's less than 200MB, you should probably get a second or a larger one. More about hard disks in chapter 9.

Before you do any upgrading, you should have a complete backup of your data. Some of your data might be irreplaceable. If your data is worth anything at all, it's worth backing it up. It's very easy to lose or erase files that took many hours to create. They can disappear in a fraction of a second.

You want to make sure that your hard disk is backed up at all times. You never know when it might fail, and you might accidentally erase a crucial file. There are several good backup programs available. One of them comes free with your copy of DOS (the BACKUP and RESTORE commands), but it's not very sophisticated. Commercial backup programs cost a bit of money, but their speed, versatility, and convenience make them worthwhile. Many hardware systems, such as a tape system, can be very good backup methods.

By all means have a boot disk with your AUTOEXEC.BAT, CONFIG.SYS, and the basic information from your CMOS setup. Chapter 10 discusses some of the many ways to back up your data.

Monitor

Small monochrome monitors are very inexpensive. So are the old CGA monitors. But life is too short not to have good color. New monitors have been developed with much greater resolution than the early CGAs. And the prices have come way down. A good high-resolution super VGA (SVGA) color monitor costs about the same as a monochrome one did a few years ago. There are many options and choices available.

Monochrome monitors are obsolete. Color is now very inexpensive and gives excellent resolution. I like color even if I'm doing nothing but word processing. In many applications color is essential. See chapter 11 for more about monitors.

Keyboard

If you use your computer very much, then you know the importance of the keyboard. It's the primary method of data input. If the keys are too soft or they don't suit your typing style, then you should consider upgrading. Keyboards are now very inexpensive.

PC and XT keyboards look exactly like the 286 and 386 keyboards and even have the same connector, but if you plug one into a 286 or 386, it won't work. Some later-model keyboards have a small switch underneath that allows them to work with both systems.

Adding a mouse or trackball

One of the biggest selling points of the Apple Macintosh is the fact that it's so easy to learn and use. With a mouse you just point and click. Windows 3.1 and thousands of programs make using a PC as easy as using a Macintosh. And there are thousands more programs and hardware available for the PC than for the Macintosh.

The cost of mice has come way down. As I write this, I'm using a mouse that cost all of $10. A mouse can make life in the computing lane a lot easier. Trackballs operate much the same way as a mouse but they require much less desk space. Some companies have developed keyboards with a built-in trackball.

Scanner

A scanner is essential if you plan to do any kind of desktop publishing. There are many other times when you can save a lot of time by simply scanning a printed page or drawing into your computer. There are now several different types of scanners and some very good software to go with them. Scanners are fairly inexpensive, especially the color ones, but they're very easy to install. See chapter 12 for more details on input devices.

Communications

With a modem your computer can communicate with thousands of bulletin boards, on-line services, and other computers. A modem uses a telephone line almost as easily as you do. Most bulletin boards are crammed full of public-domain and shareware programs, many of which are as good as high-cost commercial programs. Downloading just one of these programs might pay for the cost of the modem.

Very few offices or businesses could exist today without a fax machine. You can easily install a fax board in your computer and have all the benefits of this great tool. Chapter 13 discusses some of the ways to communicate using your computer.

Printers

Printers are a very important part of your computer system. If you have an old dot-matrix printer, you might be unhappy with the quality. New printers can deliver near-letter-quality type. Most of them are fast and comparatively inexpensive. Even new laser printers are coming down in price to where they're quite affordable.

There are several types of color printers, including dot-matrix printers with color ribbons, color ink-jet printers, and laser color printers. These printers are coming down in price.

Laser printers have many components in common with copy machines and scanners. Some companies, such as Canon and Okidata, have now integrated several different functions, such as a printer, copier, scanner, and fax, into a single machine.

Gutenberg started developing movable print in about 1436. We've come a long way since then. Chapter 14 discusses the many types of printers that are available.

Software

When speaking of upgrading a computer, most people think about hardware. But upgrading your software is just as important as upgrading your hardware. Without software, you can't run your computer. Software is as essential to a computer as gasoline is to an automobile. When you turn on your computer and boot it up, an operating system is loaded into memory. Memory is tied to the central processor unit (CPU).

Plug-and-play systems and Setup Advisor

Time and again I've said that it's very easy to install components and upgrade your computer. Actually, I lied just a little bit. There are some boards and components that are very difficult to install, especially if you don't have documentation for all the boards and devices already installed in your computer. Many boards and components have to have jumpers or switches set so they operate on a unique interrupt request (IRQ) and memory address. If two devices are set to use the same IRQ, there will be a conflict and it's possible that neither device will work. If you don't have the documentation that shows how the installed devices are set, you can only guess as to which IRQs are free. The Microsoft MSD command can help to some extent to identify what's inside and how it's configured. But there are times when it helps very little.

Microsoft and several other companies are working to develop a plug-and-play system. The board or device would check your computer system and determine which IRQ and memory address was free. A few such devices will be on the market by the time you read this.

The TouchStone Company, at 800-831-0450, has developed Setup Advisor, a small program that can do now what plug-and-play devices are supposed to do. Setup Advisor checks your system for any IRQ conflicts and tells you which IRQs are available. You can then play "what if" by asking what would happen if you installed something like a SoundBlaster 16 board. The program then recommends which IRQ and memory address to use. Setup Advisor has a fairly large library of components and devices that can be installed in your PC, so it knows how each one of them should be configured. If you ask "What if I installed a Novell network interface card (NIC)?" it would be able to tell you how to set it for whatever free IRQs you had.

If you ever intend to install a fax/modem board, mouse, network card, printer, or any of dozens of other devices, you should have the Setup Advisor. It could save you many hours of frustration.

How software controls the computer

The computer's memory, CPU, and many components and devices are made up of transistors that can be turned on to represent a 1 or off to represent a 0. Hardware devices and software can send electrical signals to the memory, the CPU, and devices to turn certain transistors on or off.

Software is made up of instructions that cause electrical signals to be created. If the software is typed in from a keyboard, each individual key causes a unique square wave signal voltage to be created. Each time the square wave signal goes up, it represents a one; when it goes down, it represents a zero. Software can also be read and entered from a floppy disk or hard disk. As the on and off signals are read from the disk, a square wave voltage is created and sent to the CPU and memory for processing. The operating system interprets the square wave instructions sent to the computer by the software and hardware devices.

The most popular operating software is MS-DOS, which stands for Microsoft disk-operating system. It's called a disk-operating system because in the early days there were only floppy disks. Now, the *disk* portion should be dropped from the DOS name. But it has been around for so long and is so ingrained that it'll probably always be DOS. IBM's OS/2 dropped the D some time ago.

All the ISA systems, even the 486 and Pentium, can run any of the older versions of DOS, even the old 1.0. But you'd be severely limited in what you could do with it. Depending on your applications and needs, you'll probably want to move up to the latest versions of MS-DOS, Novel DOS, OS/2, or Windows.

You don't have to be a programmer to upgrade or use your computer. There are billions of dollars worth of software that has already been developed for the IBM PC and compatibles. There's ready-made software for just about any application you can imagine. New programs and improvements are being introduced daily. This software can give you great versatility, utility, and capability.

Software to run your computer might end up costing even more than the computer. But there are ways to save hundreds of dollars and still buy first-class brand-name software. Read chapter 17 about how you can trade in an older copy or a competitor's copy of a program for an upgrade.

There are several public-domain and shareware programs that are either free or very inexpensive. Check the pages of most computer magazines for listings of shareware. Shareware is also available from most bulletin boards.

Booting up

Every time you turn on your computer, it boots up. Boot is short for bootstrap, which is taken from an old saying: "pulling yourself up by your own boot straps." When the computer is turned on, a small program in read-only memory (ROM) causes the computer to search for a boot routine on track 1 of a floppy disk in drive A. If there's a nonbootable disk in drive A, it will give you an error and ask that you correct it. If there's no disk in drive A, it will look for the routine on track 1 of drive C.

The first files loaded into memory by the boot routine are COMMAND.COM and a couple of hidden system files, IO.SYS and MSDOS.SYS. These two hidden files won't show up on a directory list. The reason these files are hidden is that they're very important and should never be changed or deleted.

After the COMMAND.COM and hidden files are loaded during bootup, the next files to be loaded are the CONFIG.SYS file and the AUTOEXEC.BAT file.

I said earlier that you didn't need to be a programmer, but there are a few simple programs you need to know how to create or change, such as CONFIG.SYS and AUTOEXEC.BAT. You'll probably have to create or at least change these two files occasionally. It's also quite helpful if you know how to create other .BAT files. I use .BAT files to access and load many of the programs I use. By typing just two or three characters, I can quickly switch to a directory and load the program. Your DOS manual contains more information about creating .BAT files.

How to benefit from your computer

You can use your computer for thousands of business applications, such as desktop publishing, telecommuting, and networking. It can also be a great educational tool. There are now thousands of educational programs for everyone from kindergarten through graduate school, and beyond. And it can also be a great recreation tool for playing games such as solitaire, chess, and hundreds of others.

Multimedia

It's now possible to turn your computer into a full orchestra. You can add sound and MIDI interfaces. You can use it to play music with a CD-ROM or sound board. You can use a computer to create music, and you can do it even if you know very little about music. You can enter one note at a time and the software can then assemble it, adding chords and other musical instruments, so it sounds like a 100-piece orchestra.

CD-ROMs

The cost of CD-ROM drives has come way down. I bought a CD-ROM drive in 1987 that cost over $1,000. I recently bought one that cost $175. I recently saw a dual-speed CD-ROM drive advertised for $129. This price also included the proprietary controller card. The more popular brand-name CD-ROM drives still cost up to $400 each at this time.

The cost of CD-ROMs has also come way down. There are now hundreds of programs that are quite reasonable. The programs include everything from games to reference material for very complex science and technological subjects. They can be an excellent educational tool.

Upgrade possibilities

There are so many other things you can do to improve and enhance the performance and capabilities of your computer that it's impossible to list them all. One reason is that new devices, hardware, and software are being developed and introduced every day. There could never be a complete, up-to-date list.

Sources

One of the better sources for information about computers and components is computer magazines. There are at least 100 of them published today. Most are filled with ads because ad revenue is what makes them possible. Several magazines are listed in chapter 19. I also discuss mail order in chapter 19. It might be one of your better alternatives for purchasing components and supplies.

Another good source is computer shows and swaps. If you live in or near a large city, there's probably one going on every weekend. I enjoy going to them even if I don't need anything. It's almost like a circus.

Of course, whenever possible you should patronize your local computer dealer. His prices might be slightly higher than those of mail-order houses or computer swaps, but he might be able to give you help and support and answer questions if you have problems.

You should also join a user group and attend meetings. You'll find people at these meetings who can help you and exchange ideas with you. Most groups also are able to acquire public-domain software and other goodies at a discount. Besides being able to download public-domain software, if you have a modem you can access bulletin boards and usually get help for many of the problems that you may have.

Troubleshooting and repairing

You have to know what's wrong with your computer in order to repair it. Chapter 20 tells you how to find most common problems and how to fix them.

In most cases you'll want to replace rather than repair. For instance, over the years several of my floppy drives have become defective. In 1983, an IBM 360K floppy disk drive cost over $400. If it became defective, it was worth it to send it out and have it repaired. You can buy a floppy drive today for less than $50. Most repair shops charge from $50 to $100 an hour for labor, plus parts. It's much easier to throw the old drive away and replace it with a new one.

I paid $325 for one of the first 1.44MB 3½-inch drives in 1988. It gave me excellent service for six years. It recently became very erratic in reading floppy disks. Evidently, the worm gear that moves the heads from track to track had become worn so it could no longer find the proper track. I pulled it out and threw it in the waste basket. I hated to part with it, but it wasn't worth the cost to have it repaired.

The same goes for most motherboards. It's possible that a circuit trace on a motherboard will break, or one of the IC chips become defective. It might take hours of time and some very sophisticated equipment to find the problem. Even then, you'd probably need to be technically skilled in order to repair or remove and resolder the component.

If you have an XT or 286 motherboard that becomes defective, throw it away. You can replace it with a 386SX motherboard for only about $60. It might not even be worthwhile to have a 386DX or 486 motherboard repaired. In most cases, it's more cost-effective to scrap the motherboard and replace it with a new one. The same goes for most of the other components in your computer. In most cases, repairing means replacing the component.

Why you should do it yourself

There are shops and several mail-order stores, that will upgrade your computer for you. Of course, these stores can't stay in business unless they make a profit, so it can be a bit expensive. It can also take a lot of time and cause a considerable amount of problems.

First you have to find someone who will do it for you at a reasonable price. Then you have to lug the computer down to the shop, usually during business hours, fight traffic, and find a place to park. Or you can package it up and send it off to a mail-order store. If you send it to a mail-order store for an upgrade, there can be a problem of communication. Just what do you want done to your computer? How much do you want to spend? When using either a local shop or a mail-order business, you must also consider the following questions: How busy is the shop? How reliable is the shop? Can you get a firm price for the total cost and a date it will be ready? How long can you wait for it?

Too old to upgrade?

A computer is never too old to be enhanced or upgraded in some manner. You can add new monitors, large-capacity hard drives, and many other peripherals to almost any of the older computers. Still, depending on what type of upgrade you want or what you want to do with your computer, you might be better off buying a new one.

If you decide that you don't want to upgrade your older computer, what do you do with it? You might decide to try to sell it. But you probably won't be able to sell the computer for what you think it's worth. The computer that you paid $2,500 for a few years ago might not be worth $500 today. Besides, you might not want to go through the bother and hassle of advertising and selling it, especially if you live in a city like Los Angeles. A recent news story reported that a gang would go to a person's house who had advertised a computer for sale, tie the person up, and then take all the computers and software it could find.

If you live near a larger city, there might be computer swap meets every so often. There will usually be a consignment table at these meets where you can sell your old hardware, but don't expect to make a lot of money off your old components.

Still another alternative is to pass your computer on to a relative or someone who's just getting started in computers. Or you can keep it and use it for word processing, a dedicated print server on a network, or voice mail. There are thousands of perfectly good DOS software packages that work very well on 286s, such as WordPerfect 6.0, WordStar 7.0, Microsoft Works, and dBASE IV. Most standard DOS programs also run very well on XTs. The programs might run a bit slower on an XT or 286 than they would on a 486, however, so you'll have to wait a few seconds or a few minutes. You might be better able to afford to waste a bit of time rather than spend money for an upgrade.

Another alternative is to donate your old computer to a school, church, or charitable organization. Depending on your tax situation, you might come out ahead by donating it and deducting it as a gift on your income tax return.

Buying a new computer

You might consider buying a completely new system, even a true-blue IBM or a Macintosh if you have a lot of money. The Macintosh, IBM, Compaq, and most other big brand-name computers cost more than an equivalent ISA clone. A low-cost ISA machine can do everything an IBM or Macintosh can do.

If you're looking at ads for a computer, read them closely. Many are a bit misleading to say the least. Many of the ads show a complete system for a very low price, then in small print say that the monitor and keyboard aren't included. I see this quite often in ads for the Macintosh. Or you might see an ad for a motherboard with a very low price, then in small print it says that it comes without the CPU.

Despite the high cost, a lot of people still buy IBM, Macintosh, and other brand-name computers. The logo and brand name means more to some people than money.

Buying a used computer

If you're lucky, you can buy a used computer and upgrade it. Look around your area and check the classified ads. Depending on how it's configured, a used XT could cost as little as $100, and a 286 about $200. Depending on what you need a computer for, this might be all you need. An XT is very good for word processing and several other applications, such as some small databases. This type of computer is also good enough for the kids to get started on. If you buy a used computer and find that you need more speed and power, you can upgrade it yourself. It's very simple to do.

If you work for a large company, chances are they're in the process of buying a more powerful system to meet additional business needs. (A basic law, based on Parkinson's law, is that a company's need for a larger computer system grows in a logarithmic fashion each year the company is in business, whether or not the business increases.) Try to find out what the manager of the computer procurement department is doing with the old computers. Some companies pass them down to people who are low on the totem pole. Many companies sell them to their employees for a good price. Talk to the manager and remind him how much goodwill such a practice can generate.

Enhancing a new computer

Even if you've just bought a brand-new computer, there are all kinds of things you can do to upgrade or enhance it. And you can do it by yourself; you don't need to send it out to have it done. If you're not too familiar with the innards of your computer, you might be afraid to tackle a project like this, but it's very easy to do. I've seen people who are absolute klutzes do it, so I know anyone can do it.

There are an endless number of applications for a computer. Because I don't know what your needs are, I'll talk about several alternatives and options in the following chapters.

New business opportunities

After you finish this book, I think you'll agree that it's very easy to upgrade a computer. Once you see how easy it is, you might even want to go into business. Worldwide, there are currently about 150 million computers in use, about half of which are older computers that could be easily upgraded. Many of these older computers are sitting in a corner not being used because they have a defective floppy disk drive or some other minor problem that could be easily fixed.

Many companies are buying new computers because they don't realize how easy and inexpensive it is to upgrade or repair their older ones. That is a terrible waste of money and resources. After you've read this book you might want to go into business upgrading and repairing older computers.

3
CHAPTER

A few minor upgrades

If you have an ISA computer, you have quite a versatile machine. There's over ten billion dollars' worth of boards and peripheral hardware you can use with your computer. With this hardware, you can upgrade or configure an ISA machine to do almost anything you can imagine.

There's also about ten billion dollars' worth of software you can use with a PC. There are still millions of XTs and 286s in use today. Many of them do everything their owners want them to, so there's no need for upgrading. But many of the software packages developed in the last few years, during the Windows era, will run only on machines such as the 386, 486, and Pentium.

You might not have to buy one of these more powerful machines in order to take advantage of the newer software and hardware. You can easily upgrade an older PC.

One of the features that makes the PC so versatile and useful are the expansion slots on the motherboard. There are hundreds of different boards you can plug into these slots to configure a PC to do almost anything you want it to do.

If you've been putting off adding or replacing a board in your computer because you were afraid you might mess something up, don't wait any longer. There's really not much that you can do to harm your computer or yourself. If you know which end of a screwdriver to use, you'll have no trouble upgrading your computer. And you can save a bundle.

Installing a new board

You might not have the money or the inclination to perform a major upgrade at this time. There are several minor upgrades that are very simple and very easy to do.

Adding a new board is one of the most common and easiest ways to upgrade. Maybe you need a modem so you can access a bulletin board system (BBS). Most BBSs are crammed full of public-domain software and other goodies. Downloading a single public-domain program might be worth more than the cost of a modem.

Just a few years ago, I bought a combination 2400-baud modem and 9600-baud fax board for a little over $900. I recently bought a 14.4-Kbps modem/fax board for $99. One reason the boards are so inexpensive now is that an entire fax/modem can be integrated on one or two VLSI chips. Some of the new modems can now transmit at a speed of 57.6 Kbps. If you plan to do a lot of telecommunications, it's well worth it to buy a new high-speed fax/modem. More about modems and faxes in chapter 13.

Maybe you need to install an adapter board for a new color monitor or a graphics monitor that you've bought, or a multi-I/O (input/output) board for COM ports for your mouse, an external modem, and printer. It's a very simple task. Here are some simple instructions to install a plug-in board:

Step 1: Remove the case cover.
First turn off the power. If you have an older desktop computer, it probably has five screws in the back that holds the cover on. There's a screw in each corner and one at the top in the center. You might find four screws in the right rear corner that holds the power supply. The air vent you see here is part of the power supply. Don't remove any screws except those that hold the case cover in place.

The inside of your computer is safe. Except for the power supply, which is completely enclosed, the highest voltage in your computer is only 12 volts. But, of course, if you're going to open your computer and add or change anything, there won't even be 12 volts in it—because the very first thing you did was to turn off the power. Right?

Caution! Once the cover is removed, make sure you touch an unpainted metal part of the chassis to discharge yourself of any static electricity. This is especially necessary if you're working in a carpeted area. You've probably walked across a room, touched a doorknob, and gotten a shock. You can build up several thousand volts of electrostatic voltage on yourself. If you touch a fragile semiconductor, you could damage it.

Another caution! Never plug in or unplug a board, cable, or any component while the power is on. The fragile transistors and semiconductors on these boards and components can be easily destroyed. It takes only a second to turn off the power.

Note: It's always a good idea to turn off the power when removing or replacing anything in your computer, but the PCMCIA system doesn't require it. You can safely "hot swap" (unplug or plug in) any PCMCIA component while the power is on.

Step 2: Make a diagram.
I mentioned this earlier, but it's worth repeating. If you're going to remove any boards, change any cables, or switch settings, make a drawing or diagram of the original setup. It's very easy to forget how a chip or cable should plugged in. Many cables and connectors can be plugged in backwards or into the wrong receptacle. I'm ashamed to admit it, but I once ruined an expensive BIOS chip because I plugged it into the wrong socket.

It takes only a minute to make a rough diagram, and it could save you money and hours of agony and frustration in trying to solve a problem that was caused because something was plugged in backwards or into the wrong receptacle.

You could also use a felt-tip marking pen or some fingernail polish and put a stripe on all the cable connectors and the board connectors before they're unplugged. Vary the location of the stripes on the connectors so when they're plugged together the stripes are lined up. You can tell immediately if it's the right connector and if it's plugged in properly.

Step 3: Set switches and jumpers.

We presently live in a "plug-and-play" era. It can be very frustrating trying to install a board that uses an IRQ and unique memory address. Eventually we're going to have "plug-and-play" systems, which will be able to automatically configure themselves to whatever IRQ or memory address is available. What a wonderful day that will be.

For now, when you buy a board or any component, always make sure that you get some kind of manual or documentation with it. Check the manual for installation instructions. It might have some switches or shorting bars you have to set to configure the board to your system, or to whatever it has to do. Your computer has certain addresses and interrupt request (IRQ) assignments. If two devices are set for the same IRQ, it will cause a conflict.

If you have several boards in your computer, they're probably already configured for certain addresses and IRQs. It would be nice to have a document or log near your computer that shows how each one is configured. That way you can look at the log and determine which IRQs and addresses are available. If you don't have such a record, perhaps you should start one with whatever board you happen to be installing.

If you have MS-DOS 6.0 or later, the MSD command can show you how your computer is configured. Just type MSD at any prompt and it will give you several diagnostic options.

Getting all the IRQs and memory addresses set properly can be very frustrating and time-consuming. The Setup Advisor from the TouchStone Company, at 1-800-531-0450, does a much better job than the MSD command. It spots existing configuration problems and helps you avoid upgrade conflicts. It can greatly simplify the installation process.

After you've set any necessary switches, look for an empty slot and plug your board in. It doesn't matter which slot. The slots are all connected to the standard bus. If you look closely at the motherboard, you can see etched lines that go across the board to the same pin on each slot connector. The contacts on one side of the 8-bit connectors are numbered A1 to A31. On the other side they're numbered B1 to B31. For example, contact B1 on every connector is ground and B9 on every connector is 12 volts. The connections on the A side are I/O and address lines.

Multilayered motherboards

In most cases, it's physically impossible to plug a board into a slot backwards. Make sure, however, that it's plugged in all the way. And be very careful when you plug the boards in. Some slot connectors are very tight, and it's often difficult to seat the board properly. If you press down too hard you could flex and damage the motherboard. The copper circuit traces on the motherboard that carry the signals to all of the various components are very complex. Some traces have to cross over other traces, so the traces that cross over others are placed on separate thin layers of plastic. The layers, as many as ten or more, are then fused together into a solid board. The traces in the various layers are connected to each other at various points and to the components where they don't interfere with other circuit traces. This several-layer design is similar to a highway system with overpasses and cloverleafs.

If you flex a motherboard too much, it's possible to break some of these traces in the various layers and ruin the motherboard. The motherboard sits on plastic stand-offs so there are areas beneath it where there's very little support.

Once you're satisfied the board is seated properly, install a screw in the back bracket to hold it in place. It helps if you have a magnetized screwdriver to hold the screws while getting them started. If you don't, you can magnetize one by rubbing it vigorously against any strong magnet. (If you have a stereo system, your large speaker has a strong magnet around the voice coil.) Be careful not to place the magnetized screwdriver, or any magnet, near any of your floppy disks because it could partially erase them.

XT DIP switches

The XT is obsolete, but there are still millions of them in existence. For many applications, they're still a very good tool. For simple word processing, they can be as good as the most powerful 486. They're also a good tool for kids or anyone just starting out in computers. One of the best things about XT computers is that you can buy them for peanuts; they're very inexpensive.

There are several things you can add to an old XT to make it better. You can add a color monitor, more memory, a new floppy drive, a hard drive, a coprocessor, modem, fax board, scanner, CD-ROM drive, or almost anything that can be added to more powerful systems.

If you're upgrading an XT or PC, you might have to reset the dual in-line pin (DIP) switches on the motherboard. The PC has two DIP switches; the XT has only one. The DIP switches need to be set for various configurations. Here are the settings for an XT at various configurations:

- 1 OFF
- 2 OFF without an 8087 coprocessor, ON with an 8087 coprocessor
- 3 OFF
- 4 ON if only 128K memory on motherboard, OFF if 256K or more on motherboard
- 5 ON for color monitor, OFF for monochrome monitor
- 6 OFF
- 7 ON if only one floppy drive, OFF for two floppy drives
- 8 ON

The motherboards of other systems will be considerably different than that of an XT. Most of them will also have DIP switches or jumpers that need to be set. You should receive some sort of documentation with your components. Be sure to check the specifications.

Installing more memory on an XT

If you have an XT, you can have up to 640K of memory. The later models have DIP sockets for this much memory in the left front quadrant of the motherboard. Some of the early models have sockets for only up to 256K. In order to add another 384K, you have to buy a memory board and plug it into one of the eight slots.

There are four banks of memory, with nine chips in each bank. The systems that come with 256K of memory use 64K chips in each bank. For 640K, they use 64K chips in two banks and 256K chips in the other two. If you need to add memory, check the type you have installed and buy the same type.

When you plug the memory chips in, make sure they're properly oriented. Pin 1 usually has a small dot or some sort of marking. All the chips should be oriented the same way. Also, make sure that all the legs are plugged in properly. It's very easy to have a leg bend underneath the chip or slip outside of the chip socket.

After you install the memory, check your documentation. You'll have to set DIP switches 3 and 4 to match the amount of memory you now have.

Installing a coprocessor

Another very easy XT upgrade is installing a coprocessor. If you do a lot of heavy number-crunching or large spreadsheet work, then you could probably benefit from a coprocessor. Some programs don't take advantage of a coprocessor. It would be a waste of money to install one if your software doesn't use it. Depending on the programs you run, a coprocessor can speed up the operation from 5 to over 100 times.

Almost all motherboards are designed with an empty socket alongside the CPU for a coprocessor. Most computers are sold without this chip. At one time the coprocessors were rather expensive, but several companies began manufacturing them and the competition forced the prices down.

Coprocessor chips all have an 87 at the end of their chip designation; for the 8088 family it's 8087, for the 286 it's 80287, and for the 386 it's 80387. The 486DX and Pentium CPUs have a coprocessor built into the chips. The 486SX doesn't have a coprocessor. If you want to add one, you'd need the 487SX.

Step 1: Remove the cover of the computer.

If you have a PC or XT, look for the 8088 CPU. It's a long, narrow chip with 40 pins. It will probably be located near the motherboard power supply connector at the back of the board, and there should be an empty socket alongside it. Figure 3-1 shows an XT motherboard on the left and a Pentium on the right. The XT coprocessor socket is at the top right corner of the board between the 8088 CPU and the white power-supply connector. You might have to disconnect the power-supply cables or remove some of the plug-in boards. Make a diagram of the boards and cables before you disconnect them.

3-1 An XT motherboard on left and a Pentium motherboard on the right. The empty 8087 socket is at the top right corner of the XT between the long 8088 CPU and the white power-supply connector.

If you're installing an 80287 or 80387 coprocessor, look for the 286 or 386 CPU, a square chip about 1½ inches square. It will probably be located near the center of the board, with an empty socket nearby. Figure 3-2 shows a small 386SX motherboard. The empty 80387 socket is at the bottom right corner of the much smaller 386SX CPU.

3-2
A small 386SX motherboard. The empty 80387 socket is at the bottom right corner near the much smaller 386SX CPU.

Step 2: Note the orientation of the chip.

There should be a small U-shaped notch at one end of the CPU that indicates pin 1. The empty slot should also have some sort of indication or outline on the board to indicate the orientation of the chip.

The 286 CPU chip is square, but the 80287 coprocessor has the same long shape and 40 pins of the 8087. The 80387 coprocessor has 128 pins and fits in the square socket near the 386 CPU. It can be plugged in only one way.

The 487 coprocessor

If you have a 486DX system, the CPU has a built-in coprocessor. The 486SX doesn't. The lack of a coprocessor and slower speed are the primary differences between the 486DX and the 486SX. You can install a 487 coprocessor on a 486SX system, however, which will give you all the benefits of a 486DX. In fact, the 487 is an actual 486DX CPU. It also costs about the same as a 486DX, which might be a bit expensive.

If you think you'll need a coprocessor later, consider buying a 486DX rather than a 486SX. More about the 486 CPUs later.

Cooling system

As long as you have the cover off, check to make sure the openings in the rear panel above any empty slots have blank covers installed. The little electrons that represent bits of data get hot as they go racing around through the semiconductors in your computer. Heat is the enemy of all semiconductors. What you hear when you turn on your computer isn't the sound of those electrons. Most of the sound you hear is the cooling fan located in the power supply.

The power-supply fan draws air from the front of the computer, pulls it over the boards and components, and forces it out through the rear opening of the power supply. To make it work efficiently, all the openings in the rear panel should have blank covers installed. There should be no obstruction in the back or front of your computer that would interfere with the flow of air through the power supply.

Some 486 and Pentium CPUs run very hot, so small fans can be installed on the CPU. Figure 3-3 shows two Pentium motherboards. The one on the right doesn't have a fan installed and the one on the left does. Incidentally, the motherboard on the left has a PCI bus (the three white sockets) and the one on the right has a VL bus. More about buses in the next chapter.

Step 3: Perform a final check.

Caution! Install only one item at a time, turn on the computer, and make sure it works. If you install two or three items and your computer doesn't work, you could have trouble determining which one is at fault.

Once you've installed your new board, coprocessor, or whatever, check it again to make sure any switches and jumpers are set, cables are installed properly, and everything is right. Then connect the keyboard and monitor, and reinstall any boards or cables that were removed. If you're satisfied everything is proper, connect the power and try the system out before you replace the cover. There have been times

3-3 Cooling fans for Pentium CPUs. The fan on the right hasn't been installed. The motherboard on the left has a PCI bus (the three white slots); the one on the right has a VL bus (the two brown slots near the center left edge).

when I installed new parts, replaced the cover, turned on the power, and it didn't work. It was usually some small thing I hadn't done or had done improperly. So I would end up having to remove the cover again. It doesn't hurt to run your computer without a cover. I have several computers and I'm constantly running tests and evaluations, and trying out new boards and products. Most of the time I don't even bother to replace the covers on them.

One reason to cover your computer is to shield and prevent it from radiating TV and radio interference. The FCC is very concerned about this, but in most cases the interference from a computer won't affect a TV set unless it's within a few feet of it.

Sources

Coprocessor chips are priced according to the speed at which they're designed to operate. The higher the frequency, the greater the cost. They cost from $50 up to $300. Look in computer magazines such as *Computer Shopper* for ads. Some coprocessor chips cost more than buying a complete motherboard.

The XT is obsolete, so there aren't many vendors who even carry the 8087. Those that do will probably charge more for the XT coprocessor than for the 287 or 387.

Coprocessor prices are coming down every day. Intel was the original developer of the chips, but there are now several companies who make them, such as AMD,

Cyrix, ULSI, Integrated Information Technology (IIT), Chips & Technology, and Weitek. Intel is usually the most expensive.

There are hundreds of other manufacturers of coprocessor chips. Here are just a few vendors who sell coprocessor chips; call them for the latest prices:

Access Computer Components	800-332-3778
Asean Computer Technologies	714-598-2828
Bulldog Computer Products	800-438-6039
California Microchip	818-884-3660
Chips For Less	214-416-0508
CompuSave	800-544-8302
Computer Discount Warehouse	800-800-2892
Dynamax Products	800-886-2882
Focus Computer Center	800-223-3411
H&J International	800-275-2447
Leo Electronics	800-421-9565
Main Street Computers	800-456-6246
Memory Plus	800-388-7587
OS Computer City	800-926-6722
Treasure Chest Computers	800-723-8282
Ulta Computers	800-755-7518
Upgrades International	800-877-6652
USA Electronics	800-332-8434
USA FLEX	800-872-3539
Worldwide Technologies	800-457-6937

BIOS upgrade

When a computer is sold, it has a BIOS that's designed to handle any software or hardware presently available. But there are thousands of new products introduced every day. So if you have an older computer, there's a lot of software and hardware you might not be able to use. You also might not be able to use a 1.44MB or 2.88MB floppy drive, or an IDE hard disk drive. You might not be able to run Windows or some of the Novell and Netware software. You could be missing out on a lot of essential utilities such as disk diagnostics, disk surface analysis, and other major component tests and diagnostics. You could also be wasting a lot of time while your BIOS tries to do its job.

BIOS chip developers constantly introduce new versions of their chips to try to keep current. Many of the new motherboards now come with a BIOS in flash memory. You can upgrade this BIOS by downloading the upgrade over a modem connection or by way of a floppy disk. The Pentium motherboard on the left of Fig. 3-3 has a flash memory chip in one of the large square chips. The Pentium motherboard on the right has a 512K EPROM chip with a white covering alongside the VLB slots.

If you have a computer that's over two years old, chances are they've developed a new BIOS that can give new life to your old computer. Replacing your ROM BIOS is rather inexpensive, and very easy to do. It's one of the better upgrades you can do for your computer to bring it up to date.

ROMs and EPROMs

ROM is an acronym for *read-only memory*. BIOS is an acronym for *basic input/output system*. The ROM BIOS is a program that has been burned onto EPROM chips. EPROM is an acronym for *erasable programmable read-only memory*, which is made up of special light-sensitive transistor circuits.

Some of the BIOS system resides in complementary metal oxide semiconductors (CMOS). These are very low-power transistor circuits that are kept alive with an on-board battery during the time the computer is off. (Note: If your computer is more than four or five years old, you might need to replace the battery. Battery replacement is discussed in chapter 2.)

The EPROM chips are made up of special transistors and are available in 64K, 128K, 256K, and 512K sizes (see Fig. 3-4). There's a clear glass window over the transistor circuits on the chip. These circuits are sensitive to ultraviolet light (UV). The transistor circuits can be electronically programmed in an EPROM programmer or burner. A program can be read from a floppy or a hard disk and fed to the burner. The individual transistors on the chip are set to either on or off to reflect the 1s and 0s of the software. So the program is copied to the chip, just as if it were being copied to another floppy or to a hard disk. Once it's programmed, the glass window of the chip is covered with opaque tape.

3-4
EPROM chips. Left to right: 64K, 128K, 256K, and 512K.

If something goes wrong and the program isn't exactly right or needs to be updated, you can erase and reprogram it. To erase the program, remove the tape from the glass window and simply expose the chip to ultraviolet light.

POST

BIOS is pretty close to BOSS, and the function of the BIOS is quite similar to that of a boss in a small factory. He gets there early, checks all the equipment to make sure it's in working order, then he opens the doors for business. This is similar to the start-up procedures that happen when you first turn your computer on. It first does a power-on self test, or POST. It checks the RAM chips for any defects. (The IBM memory check takes a considerable amount of time, and it's almost always okay. The clone makers noted this so they designed a BIOS that did a much faster check. Most of the newer BIOSs give you the option to bypass the RAM test if you want to.) The BIOS then checks the keyboard, floppy and hard disk drives, printer, and other peripherals. If it finds something wrong, it reports an error and displays a code number. (See chapter 20 for a listing of POST codes.)

Hard disk drive types

When IBM introduced the AT in 1984, the BIOS recognized only 15 types of hard drives. If your drive wasn't on the list, you were in trouble. IBM also had a diagnostic or setup diskette it used to tell the computer such things as the type of floppy drives, hard drives, and type of installed monitor. You also needed to set the time and date via the floppy drive.

The compatible BIOS developers soon came out with BIOS chips that allowed you to set up these functions from the keyboard. You didn't need the floppy disk drive. They upgraded the list from 15 to 46 different types of hard disks. A 47th type was included that let the user input any characteristics or types not included in the 46 types listed. Many of the clone ROM BIOSs also included other goodies such as letting you switch from standard speed to turbo from the keyboard. They can all now recognize a 1.44MB 3½-inch floppy. The newer releases will also recognize a 2.88MB floppy drive.

Incidentally, many hard disk controllers, monitor adapters, and several other peripheral devices have their own BIOS chips.

BIOS utilities

Many developers have added several utilities to their BIOS. Some have comprehensive diagnostics that can be used to do a low-level format on a hard disk. They can test and determine the optimum interleave factor, perform a surface analysis of the disk and mark the bad sectors, and check the performance of the hard and floppy disk drives, as well as measure their access speed, data transfer rate, and rotational speed. They can run tests on the keyboard, monitor and adapter, and serial and parallel ports.

The AMI BIOS has about the best diagnostic utilities. It's one of the few that can support COM3 and COM4. At this time, DOS supports only COM1 and COM2. If you want to use COM3 and COM4, you must use special software such as ProComm.

Boot program

When the POST is run, if everything is okay a signal is sent to drive A: to run the boot program. If there's no disk in drive A:, it then tries to find a boot program on the hard disk. This boot program initializes the peripheral equipment, runs the CONFIG.SYS and AUTOEXEC.BAT programs, and allows you to start doing business.

Interrupt control

During the day the boss, or BIOS, receives several interruptions or requests for services. These interrupts can be minor or major. Depending on the type of request, the boss might shut everything down and put everybody to work to satisfy that one request. A minor request will usually have to wait until the present task is finished.

Depending on the software and type of computer, the boss might have the facilities to accomplish several tasks at the same time, or do *multitasking*. With the proper hardware and software, the BIOS might even be able to allow several computers to access it and use its software and hardware.

The boss must be savvy enough to work with many different types of requests and orders. There are thousands of different kinds of software and hardware. The boss must be able to take the orders and route them to the proper hardware device, such as the screen, keyboard, disks, printer, and modem. Sometimes the boss will be asked to do something it doesn't have the equipment or the ability to do. Since the boss is very conscientious, he'll keep trying to accomplish the impossible task. If you leave your computer on and come back a week later, he might still be trying to satisfy the request, ignoring any requests from the keyboard to stop. Depending on the type of problem, you might have to do a "warm boot," or a Ctrl–Alt–Del key combination, to restart the computer. You might even have to turn the power off (do a "cold boot") to completely clear the computer and restart it.

The BIOS provides you with the date and time when you ask for it. It also appends the date and time to any file or program you create. As you might imagine, the BIOS is quite an important part of a computer.

Compatibility

Many chips used to make a computer, such as the CPU and RAM, are made by many different companies, such as Intel and AMD. But IBM designed and developed their own ROM BIOS for PCs using EPROM chips. Since IBM was the biggest, the industry leader, and a standard setter, a whole lot of software was written for the IBM PC and its BIOS system.

Just as it's possible to copy software from one disk to another, it's possible to copy the contents of one EPROM chip to another with the EPROM burner. It's illegal to make and distribute copies of software that's copyrighted, but that hasn't stopped a lot of people from doing it. The same is true for illegal copying of ROM chips.

In order to be compatible with IBM, several of the early clone makers copied the IBM BIOS. Naturally, IBM wasn't too happy about this and threatened to sue. Phoenix Technologies and Award Software were two of the several companies that began developing a compatible BIOS for the clone makers. Since they couldn't copy the IBM BIOS, their BIOSs could never be 100% compatible. But they did almost everything the IBM BIOS did. And in some cases, they did it better than IBM did, such as reducing the time for checking RAM.

It wasn't long before there were more compatible clones in existence than IBM PCs. It didn't take long for the software developers to take note of this fact and begin writing programs that could be run on any machine, not just IBMs. Today there are very few, if any, programs that have BIOS compatibility problems.

BIOS size

The early BIOS programs were relatively simple. PCs and XTs used a single 64K chip for the BIOS. The ATs used two 128K chips. But the ever-changing technological advances have forced changes. Most of the 286, 386, and 486 machines today use two 256K chips for a total of 512K of memory. Many of the newer computers use a single 512K chip. To print out the entire contents of a 512K BIOS ROM would require about 250 pages. A whole lot of instructions and programs can be stored in 512K of ROM.

Shadow ROM

A single 512K chip, however, slows the BIOS down considerably because the ROM is addressed in an 8-bit-wide format. If the BIOS is installed on two chips (high and low or odd and even), each can be addressed 8 bits at a time. This, then, is essentially a 16-bit system, but even 16 bits can be very slow so some of the high-end 386 and 486 systems offer an option of loading the ROM BIOS into 32-bit system RAM. This "shadow ROM" can then be addressed 32 bits at a time.

BIOS differences

I have several computers in my office. One of them has a clone 286 motherboard that was designed and built in late 1984. The vendor I bought it from tried both the Phoenix and Award BIOS in it. They both worked and I ended up with the Award BIOS. A while back I tried to install a 1.44MB floppy disk drive in it. Of course, the 1984 BIOS had never heard of such a thing. I also wanted to install a new hard drive that didn't fit any of the 15 types listed. So I decided it was time to upgrade to a new BIOS.

I went to a nearby dealer who used the Phoenix BIOS in his systems. He cautioned me that it might not work in my system, but he sold me a set. I figured that if it worked with Phoenix in the beginning it should work now, but it didn't. It wouldn't boot up at all. I went to another dealer who used the Phoenix BIOS, and he had a version that was just a bit newer. It worked perfectly.

It seemed strange that an early Phoenix BIOS would work, but a much later version wouldn't. In the early days, things were a lot simpler. There weren't nearly as many options and choices available, so there was more compatibility. Later, many manufacturers designed motherboards that were a bit different than others. They bought a BIOS license from the developers and many of them customized the firmware for their motherboards (*firmware* is software that's embedded in the ROM or other computer circuitry). A BIOS chip that has been customized for one motherboard might not work on another. Most of the upgrade BIOS vendors will give you a money-back guarantee if a replacement doesn't work.

IBM XTs and ATs

There usually isn't too much trouble in upgrading an older XT BIOS. Most of the new ones are very compatible. It's worthwhile, especially if you're installing high-density disk drives. Most of the new XT BIOSs now recognize the 1.2MB and 3½-inch drives; the old ones don't.

If you have an older true-blue IBM PC or XT, you might have some trouble getting a new IBM BIOS. You might be better off installing a clone BIOS in the IBM. It'll cost you a lot less money and time, and it'll provide more utility and capability for your computer than you had before. If you put a clone BIOS in an IBM, it won't lose any of its perceived value as long as you keep that IBM logo on the front panel.

You should be able to replace your old 286 AT BIOS with a 286 BIOS from any of the major vendors.

You might have some trouble trying to replace a PS/2 BIOS. Although the PS/2 models 25 through 40 are ISA machines, they have a BIOS that isn't compatible with the other ISA machines. If you have an older PS/2, you'll probably have to go to IBM for an upgrade. Call the IBM fax-back service at 800-426-4329 and ask for the personal systems listing. (The fax-back service is discussed further in chapter 5.)

Installing a BIOS

It's easy to remove and replace the BIOS chip or chips. You should have a copy of your CMOS setup; If you don't, make one before you remove your BIOS. If you don't have a listing of your setup, especially of your hard disk type and the number of cylinders, heads, and sectors, you might not be able to access your hardware. Once you've installed a new BIOS, you'll need to enter all the information for a complete new setup.

The companies who make BIOSs for computers use different methods of accessing the setup. They might ask you to press Ctrl–Alt–Esc, just Del, Alt–Esc, or any of several other combinations. Check your documentation. If you don't have the documentation, you can usually force the setup to appear by holding down one of the keyboard keys during bootup. The BIOS will usually detect it as a stuck key and give you the option of going to the setup or bypassing the problem. Here are the steps for a simple BIOS replacement:

Step 1: Remove the cover and locate the BIOS.

To install the new BIOS, the first thing to do is to turn off the power and remove the cover of the computer. After the cover is removed, look for the location of the BIOS chips. They could be almost anywhere. The XT BIOS chip is a single 128K chip near the center and toward the left, with a white label on it. The 286, 386, and 486 machines will have either two 256K chips or one 512K chip. You might have to remove one or more plug-in boards to get to the BIOS. Before you remove any boards or cables, make a diagram of how they're connected and installed. Be especially careful to note where the BIOS chips are located and how they're oriented. Note the small notch or other marking on the chips that indicate which end has pin 1. One of the chips will be marked either HI or ODD, or simply an H or O. The other will be marked LO, L, E, or EVEN. Most motherboards are stamped with a chip number. The integrated circuit numbers usually begin with a U. Look for the U number of each of the BIOS chips and write it down on your diagram.

Step 2: Remove the old BIOS.

After you've made your diagram, remove the chips. Use a small screwdriver to lift the chips from each end. There are metal filler covers on the back panel to cover the openings for unused slots. One of these filler covers makes a great tool for lifting out chips. Be careful that you don't get your screwdriver or lifter under the socket itself. There's space under some of the sockets. If you pry them up, it could damage the board or socket. Make sure your lifter is under the chip only; then lift one end and then the other.

Step 3: Plug in the new BIOS.

Carefully plug in the new BIOS chips. Make sure to replace the HI or ODD chip and the LO or EVEN chip in its proper socket. Caution! Make sure the chips are oriented properly so that pin 1 goes into pin 1 on the board. If you plug it in backwards, it could be destroyed. If necessary, use a flashlight to check that all the legs or pins are inserted into the sockets. If one of the pins or legs get bent, remove the chip and use a pair of long-nosed pliers to straighten it out.

Step 4: Replace the cover.

Replace any boards and cables you removed. Plug in the power cable and turn on the system. It will probably tell you that there are errors in the setup. You'll have to reenter all the setup information and set the date, time, type of drives, and type of monitor you're using. If it boots properly, then replace the cover and give yourself a pat on the back for doing a good job.

Sources

Most BIOS developers don't supply chips to end users. They usually draw up a license agreement with a motherboard manufacturer and supply them with the BIOS software on a disk. The manufacturer then uses the supplied software to burn as many BIOS chips as needed for their motherboards. The BIOS companies might also license distributors. Here are just a few mail-order vendors:

Advanced Software (800-798-2467)

They can provide a BIOS for almost any computer. They also have a low-cost diagnostic POST card and several other computer components.

DTK Computer Company (818-810-8880)

This company designs several motherboards. Unlike some of the other manufacturers, they've designed their own BIOS. If you have one of their older systems and you need to upgrade, contact your vendor or their main office.

Micro Firmware (800-767-5465)

They stock over 50 different ROM BIOS sets.

Unicore Software (800-800-2467)

They're a BIOS distributor for both Award and Quadtel.

Upgrades Etc. (800-955-3527)

They carry AMI, Phoenix, and Award. They can provide BIOS upgrades for almost any kind of computer. They also carry several other computer components.

USA Electronics (800-332-8434)

Among their many advertised components is the AMI BIOS. A spokesman at the company says the AMI will work in 95% of other computer systems.

CPU upgrades

Several companies have developed processor modules that can transform a 286 into a 386SX. The 386SX will allow you to use all the newest software, such as OS/2,

Windows NT, and other 32-bit software. At one time this was a very good upgrade option. Today, the 386SX is almost as obsolete as the XT. I wouldn't recommend this type of upgrade. Besides, if you want a 386SX, it would be much less expensive to buy a 386 motherboard and replace the 286.

Evergreen Technologies Company at 800-733-0934, has processor modules and replacement chips that can transform a 286 into a 386 or a 486 (see Fig. 3-5), and a 25-MHz 486SX into a 50-MHz 486DX2. They also have Blue Lightning CPUs from IBM that can triple the internal processing speed, and modules that can convert a 386SX or 386DX into 486 systems. The modules can double or triple whatever speed the original CPU had—from 16 MHz to 48 MHz, 20 MHz to 60 MHz, 25 MHz to 75 MHz, or 33 MHz to 99 MHz. The chips can be installed in most ISA machines, including the PS/1 and PS/2.

3-5 CPU upgrade modules from Evergreen.

Improve Technology, at 801-224-0088, also has a Make-it 486 module that can convert a 286 into a 486.

You can't just pull out a 286 or 386 CPU and replace it with a 486. So Evergreen and Improve Technology have mounted the upgrade CPU on a small board and integrated all necessary electronics on the board to do the conversion. This small module can then be plugged into a 286 or 386 socket.

Evergreen also has modules that use Intel DX4 CPUs. Since the DX4 requires 3.3 volts instead of the standard 5 volts, a voltage drop regulator is part of the socket package. The DX4 modules can be used to convert a 486SX or 25-MHz 486DX to 75-MHz 486DX, and a 33-MHz 486SX to a 100-MHz 486DX. Evergreen also has a module that can convert a 50-MHz 486DX to a 100-MHz 486DX. Evergreen has modules and CPUs that can upgrade dozens of older-model PCs.

Kingston Technology at 714-435-2600 is another company that has many different types of CPU modules and other upgrades.

Cyrix 386 to 486 CPU

The Cyrix Company at 214-994-8387 has not only cloned the 486, it has developed several CPU chips that can directly replace some of the 386SX and 386DX

CPUs. This CPU upgrade can give you most of the advantages of a 486SX or a 486DX at a very low cost.

Some of the early 16-MHz 386SX systems that were manufactured before 1991 can't be upgraded with the Cyrix replacement CPU. If you call or write the company, you can get brochures and information about available upgrade chips, and also a verification floppy disk that will check your system and determine if it can be upgraded with one of the chips. The disk is free. Call Cyrix at 800-848-2979 and request part number 90272-08. You can also write the company at the following address:

Cyrix Corporation
2703 N. Central Expressway
Richardson, TX 75080

The Cyrix replacement CPUs act much like the Intel OverDrive chips in that they double the internal speed of the processor. The speed at which a computer processes data is dependent to a large extent on the operating speed of the CPU.

The 386SX is limited to a 16-bit bus, or pathway between the CPU and the RAM. But internally the 386SX processes data in 32-bit chunks, the same as the 386DX.

Intel 486 CPUs have a built-in 8K cache. When a computer processes data, quite often the same portions of data will loop in and out of memory several times. Ordinarily, this data has to move back and forth between the CPU and RAM. If this often-used data is stored in a nearby fast cache system, it will speed up the processing to a large degree. Cyrix systems have only 1K of built-in cache. Of course, the larger the cache, the better the system is. But even 1K can vastly speed up operations compared to 386 CPUs, which have no built-in cache.

386SX to Cx486SRx2

The Cyrix Cx486SRx2 is pin-compatible with the 386DX CPU. It takes about 15 minutes to remove the case cover from your computer and install the new Cyrix CPU. This CPU can be used only with a surface-mounted 386SX that's soldered to the motherboard. The Cyrix CPU clamps onto the 386SX chip.

This Cyrix CPU doubles whatever speed the 386SX was previously running. For instance, if a 386SX was operating at 25 MHz, it will operate at 50 MHz with the new Cx486SRx2. Figure 3-6 shows a clock-doubled 386-to-486 CPU upgrade.

This chip won't give you absolute 486 performance for several reasons. One reason is that the 386SX motherboards have a 16-bit bus, both for I/O and memory. For 486 performance, you need a 32-bit memory bus. Another is that the Cx486SRx2 has only a 1K on-board cache. The 486DX2 has 8K. The 486DX motherboards have sockets for SRAM cache memory. There are no sockets to add SRAM to the 386SX motherboards. The 486 has a built-in coprocessor; Cyrix supplies a low-cost 387 coprocessor for the CPU. For software that can take advantage of it, the coprocessor can vastly increase the speed of processing, but since it's external it won't be quite as fast as a true 486DX2.

386DX to Cyrix 486DRx2

Installing a Cyrix 486DRx2 will convert a 386DX into a 486 that operates at twice the speed of the original 386. The 386 CPU is removed and the 486DRx2 plugs into the socket. It doubles the original 386 CPU operating frequency.

3-6
A clock-doubled 386-to-486 CPU
from Cyrix.

This upgrade is closer to true 486 performance since the 386DX is a 32-bit CPU. But it still has only 1K of built-in cache. Some 386 motherboards might have an SRAM cache. If a coprocessor and SRAM is used with this system it can offer performance that's close to that of a true 486DX. The 486DRx2 processor also doesn't include a coprocessor. But again, they offer a low-cost external 387. This is one of the easiest and least expensive ways I know of to upgrade to 486 power. Call the companies for brochures and current prices.

Installing CPUs and modules

This is a very easy upgrade. It takes less than 15 minutes to install a new CPU or module. Just pull off the cover, locate and remove the CPU, and plug in the new module. But before removing the old CPU, make a rough diagram of the orientation of the chips. There should be some indication of which is pin 1 on the chip or motherboard. Evergreen provides very good documentation, so you shouldn't have any problems.

If you're upgrading a 286, the original 286 chip was made in several different styles that used different types of sockets. Some of them have pins or a pin grid array (PGA), some have a plastic leaded chip carrier (PLCC) and others have a leadless chip carrier (LCC). Evergreen will send you various types of sockets used for the 286 CPU so you know which type to order. If you're upgrading anything other than a 286, just locate the CPU, remove it, and replace it with the new CPU or module.

Power precautions

If you haven't done so already, you should install a power strip. This will allow you to plug all your equipment into one source. Having five or six power cords from your computer, your monitor, printer, lamps, and other devices plugged into various outlets and extensions can be messy and potentially dangerous.

Some older or less expensive equipment might have only two-wire cords. It's possible to plug these devices in so there's a voltage potential between them, which could cause grounding problems. Check the prongs on the plug. One prong should be wider than the other. This is the ground side. The wider blade should be plugged into the wider slot in the receptacle. If at all possible, buy only components that have a three-wire power cord and plug.

You should be able to buy a power strip with six outlets for $10 to $15. Each outlet should be able to accommodate three-wire plugs. Some companies advertise very expensive power outlets with filtering. In most cases, they have a cheap capacitor and a varistor that filters some spikes from the voltage source, but there usually isn't that much need for filtering. If you do need a filter, make sure the unit has a good electronic filter that includes coils and more electronics than just a capacitor and a varistor.

I have a power distribution center, shown in Fig. 3-7. It's a metal enclosure that has switches for five different devices. I sit my monitor on it and can use it to easily turn any of the devices on or off. The power center has surge and spike protection, and a modem telephone line input connector on the back so the telephone line can be run through the power center and electrical spikes suppressed before getting to the modem.

3-7 A power distribution center, with which you can easily control five different devices. I sit my monitor on top of the center.

Uninterruptible power supply

While my part of the country (Los Angeles) has very few electrical storms, you might live in an area where there are frequent storms and power outages. If so, you might consider buying an uninterruptible power supply (UPS). This is essential if you do any crucial work on your computer. Any time the power goes off, you can lose the data you're working on. A UPS would take over and keep your computer going if the power is interrupted.

I like WordStar because you can set it to save your files to disk automatically. That way if the power is accidentally switched off or interrupted, most of your file will still be on your hard disk. (Many other word-processing programs also allow you to do this.)

The highest voltage your computer uses is 12 volts. The power supply in the computer takes the 120-volt alternating current (ac) and converts it to the direct current (dc) that the computer needs. Several UPS techniques provide uninterruptible power. Most use rechargeable batteries, and some even use automobile batteries. The cost of the various systems depends primarily on the amount of wattage needed.

The Emerson Company, at 714-380-1005, makes AccuCard, a small plug-in board with a rechargeable battery. You can plug it into any slot in your computer and, if there's a power outage, the board will immediately take over and keep the computer running long enough for you to save your data to the hard disk. There are a large number of companies that offer UPSs, and most advertise in computer magazines. Here are just a few:

Alpha Technologies	206-647-2360
American Power Conversion	401-789-5735
Best Power Technology	800-356-5794
Brooks Power Systems	215-244-0624
Clary Corporation	818-287-6111
Computer Power Products	213-323-1231
Sola Corporation	312-439-2800
Tripp Lite Corporation	312-329-1777
UPSystems	213-634-0621

Green PC

Green PCs help save energy, money, and the environment. In the past people didn't worry too much about how much energy their computer used. But there are about 150 million computers in use today, and they're using a whole lot of energy.

A lot of computers are left on 24 hours a day, seven days a week. Some people believe that leaving a computer on will make it last a bit longer. When an incandescent lamp is first turned on, a large surge of current passes through the lamp. Most lamps burn out as they're being turned on. A lamp that's never turned off will last longer than one that's frequently turned on and off. A similar thing happens in a computer. When first turned on, there's usually a high current that surges through the electronics. If it's left on, the current stabilizes. The temperature also stabilizes. Also, when the computer's first turned on the hard disk might not operate properly until it has warmed up. For these reasons, some people and some companies never turn their computers off.

Another reason a computer might be left on is if it has a modem or fax board. Many faxes and communications are sent during the night for a cheaper rate. There really isn't any scientific evidence that proves that leaving a computer on all the time will make it last longer. Besides, it will most likely be obsolete before it wears out.

The government has become concerned about the energy wasted by computers. Computers purchased by the government from now on will have to meet certain energy-saving requirements. Newer computers will also meet those requirements. If you're buying a new computer, look for the EPA Saver Star.

Even if you have an older computer, with an inexpensive upgrade you can still manage to save some energy. The NEI Company, at 800-832-4007, produces the PC Ener-G Saver, a small device that lets a printer and monitor go to sleep if there's no activity. It comes with software that lets you set whatever time you want for inactivity before the printer and monitor shut down. The monitor comes back on as soon as you start using the keyboard.

The printer will come back on line only if it receives a command to print. The computer is active only about 10 percent of the time, based on keyboard activity, so quite a lot of energy can be saved. The PC Ener-G Saver costs about $75, but it should pay for itself in energy savings within a year.

Besides directly saving wattage, when the computer and printer are off less heat is generated. If your office uses air conditioning, it can help save a bit there also. Even if the device doesn't pay for itself, it's everyone's responsibility to try to save as much energy as possible. Any amount of energy saved helps that much to conserve the environment.

Pentium

The Pentium CPU has 3.1 million transistors, over twice as many as the 486. It's much more powerful and faster than the 486. There are several Pentium motherboards available. The procedure for upgrading to a Pentium is the same as for any of the other upgrades mentioned earlier. Just remove your old motherboard and install a new Pentium. It's very easy to do.

PowerPC

Even more powerful and faster than the Pentium, the PowerPC is a joint effort by Motorola, IBM, and Apple. The CPU is a reduced instruction-set computer (RISC). It actually has fewer transistors than the Pentium, but can outperform it because of the technology used. More about the Pentium and PowerPC in chapter 7.

4
CHAPTER

Installing a new motherboard

If you have an old computer, you might tell your spouse that you need a new computer. If your spouse is in charge of the purse strings, you might be asked, "Why in the world do you need a new computer? You haven't worn out your old one yet."

The purse string holder has got you. Those little electrons racing around inside the computer don't cause any wear at all. Except for the mechanical devices, such as the disk drives, it's very difficult to wear out a computer. But the ever-changing technology causes computers to quickly become obsolete. The old XT and 286 were excellent machines for their time. But their time has past. They're as obsolete as the old Model T Ford. Like the old Model T, these old machines can still get you to your destination, but slowly and without many of the modern conveniences. If your time is worth anything at all, it's worth upgrading.

You can say to the tight-fisted spouse, "Well how about if I just replace my motherboard?" Your spouse will probably go along with that. A new motherboard is the most important and most cost-effective upgrade you can make. It's also one of the easiest upgrades. A new motherboard can give you most of the benefits of a new system at a fairly reasonable cost. Just pull out your old motherboard and install a new 386SX, 386DX, 486SX, 486DX, Pentium, or even PowerPC.

You might have spent as much as $2,500 or more for your old XT or 286. And this was in the days when each dollar was worth about three times what it is today. If you try to sell these old machines, you probably won't get more than $100 to $300 for them. But if you spend $100 to $300 for a new motherboard, the computer can be worth as much as a new $1,200 or $1,500 machine. You can definitely save money by spending a little to upgrade.

Incidentally, instead of selling your old computer, you might consider donating it to a local school or a charity and deduct the gift from your income tax. The computers might be obsolete, but they can serve very well for beginners.

If you decide to sell your old system or donate it, you can buy the components and build a new system from scratch. Or you can buy a bare-bones system and add the items and components that you want to it. It's very easy to do.

Using old components

Even if you're moving up from the oldest PC or XT, you might still be able to use some of your old components, such as the case, plug-in boards, and disk drives, in your new system. All the components in PCs are basically the same, except for the motherboard.

Of course, if you decide to install a new 486 or Pentium motherboard, you probably won't want to use your old monochrome or CGA monitor. You'll also want to move up to larger-capacity hard drives and newer floppy drives. But if you're on a tight budget, you can always use your old components until you can afford the newer goodies.

Backward compatibility

All newer systems are backward compatible, so they can run and use the older hardware and software. This backward compatibility has been a slight problem and bottleneck to developing new products. If the old systems were abandoned, new products could be made to run much faster and be less expensive. But if new incompatible products were introduced, it would be disastrous and extremely costly to millions of users.

Intel and other industry leaders determined that it's much more important to protect the consumers who've invested so heavily in earlier products. We're seeing a small crack in the solidarity, though, in IBM's decision to develop the PowerPC. At this time there's not much native software for the PowerPC, but it will be able to run some software by using emulation and recompilation. It can also use the billions of dollars worth of ISA standard hardware.

Keyboard differences

If you decide to use your old components when you upgrade, you might not be able to use your old keyboard. Although the XT and AT keyboards look exactly alike and have the same connector, the XT keyboard won't work on AT systems, which include the 286, 386, 486, Pentium, and PowerPC. These systems have a scanner frequency that's different from the original PC and XT.

Though the XT is obsolete, some of the keyboard manufacturers still provide a small switch on the back that allows them to be switched from one type to the other. Some of the newer keyboards can automatically sense what system they're plugged into and automatically switch over. If you buy a new keyboard that has a switch, make sure the switch is set to the correct position.

Many motherboard options

If you decide to install a new motherboard, you have a lot of options and choices. There are hundreds of different manufacturers. Of course, every one of them wants to differentiate their product, so they're all a bit different in some respect. Even though they're all a bit different, however, they're all still compatible and will accept all the usual hardware and software.

At one time there were only two types of motherboards: the XT and the AT 286. Now there are hundreds of different types and variations of motherboards. One reason is that Intel and several other clone companies now manufacture a large number of different CPUs. The motherboard and computer type depends on whatever CPU is installed, such as the 386SX, 386DX, 486SX, 486DX, Pentium, and the PowerPC. There are several different versions for each of these systems. Intel alone manufactures over 50 different CPUs. Many of the versions are based on the operating frequency of the CPU.

As you can see, there are a lot of different options. What you choose should depend on what you want to do with your computer and, of course, how much you want to spend.

What is the motherboard?

The motherboard is the largest and most important board in your system. It contains the central processing unit (CPU) and all the chips and electronics that makes computing possible.

The original 286 case was a bit larger than the XT's. The XT case was five inches high, 19½ inches wide, and 16½ inches deep. The 286 case was six inches high, 21½ inches wide, and 16½ inches deep. The XT motherboard was 8¾ inches wide and 12 inches long. The 286 motherboard was 12 inches wide and 13¾ inches long. By combining several chips into single very large-scale integrated (VLSI) chips, the clone builders soon developed a "baby" 286 motherboard that was the same width as the XT, except it was one inch longer. The new baby 286 could still fit in the XT case. Since that time, all new motherboards have been as small or smaller than the baby 286. The baby size is now the new standard, even for the Pentium and PowerPC.

There are a large number of different types and sizes of cases available today. Baby motherboards can be installed in any desktop or tower case. The holes and slots usually line up with no problem.

Expansion slots

The motherboard usually lies on the floor of the chassis. Most motherboards have eight slots or connectors for plug-in boards. Some motherboards, such as those used in the PS/2 and low-profile systems, might have only a single slot for a daughterboard. The daughterboard will have two to five slots.

Some motherboards will have fewer slots if they have built-in functions. The Micronics PCI motherboard shown in Fig. 4-1 has only five slots for plug-in boards, but it has three slots for peripheral component interconnect (PCI) boards. Several billion dollars' worth of boards have been developed for the PC. You can plug one or more of these boards into a slot to expand the utility and function of your computer.

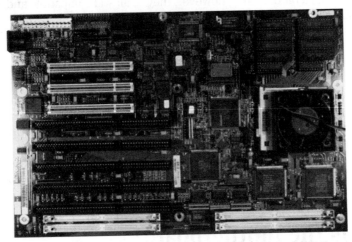

4-1 A Micronics motherboard with only five plug-in slots, but three PCI slots.

There never seems to be enough slots, and there are so many different boards you can use in them. Because of this problem, some special motherboards have up to 12 slots. Of course, you have to have a standard-sized board to accommodate this many slots, and also a special case to accommodate extra slots for rear panel connections.

Expansion bus

The slot connectors have two rows of contacts that mate with both sides of the edge connector of the plug-in boards. Each contact in each slot is connected to the same contact on all the other slots. This is called a *bus*. Since all slots have the same bus connections, a plug-in board can be inserted into any one of the slots.

Bus is more or less a generic term. It could be just etched circuits on a board, some wires, or anything that provides a signal path. There are several different types of buses: the input/output (I/O) bus, a memory bus, ISA, EISA, VESA local bus (VLB), Intel peripheral component interconnect (PCI) bus, and Personal Computer Memory Card International Association (PCMCIA) bus.

Buses are also differentiated by their width and number of lines. The XT has an 8-bit bus, the 286 has a 16-bit bus, and the 386 and 486 have a 32-bit memory bus, but their I/O bus is still 16 bits. This means that any board or peripheral that wants to communicate with these two CPUs has to do so over the 16-bit I/O bus. The EISA and high-end MCA systems have a 32-bit I/O bus system.

The VLB and the PCI bus allows certain peripherals, such as hard drives, video adapters, and network interface cards (NICs) to communicate over the special 32-

bit bus. The PCI and version 2.0 of the VLB allows the Pentium peripherals to communicate on a 64-bit bus.

Most PCs, even the 386, 486, Pentium, EISA, and MCA systems, operate at an I/O speed of 8 to 10 MHz so they're downward compatible with early software and hardware. The fact that they're compatible allows you to use the early software and hardware, but it can be a real bottleneck for some operations and applications where speed is important.

The CPU

Motherboards are named and differentiated according to the CPU chip that's installed in them. The XT has an 8088, the 286 has an 80286 CPU, the 386 an 80386 CPU, the 486 an 80486 CPU, and the Pentium has what should have been called an 80586 CPU.

Within these designations, there are several other CPU variations, such as the 386SX and 486SX. There are also differences according to the speed and frequency of the CPU. For instance, there are 16-MHz, 20-MHz, 25-MHz, 33-MHz, and 40-MHz 386s. There are even more variations of the 486 CPU, and several variations of the Pentium. Table 4-1 lists several of these CPUs and their differences.

Table 4-1. Differences in various CPU chips

	XT	**286**	**386**	**486**	**DX4**	**Pentium**	**PowerPC**
Transistors	29K	134K	275K	1.2MB	1.6MB	3.1MB	2.6MB
Frequency	4.7–10	6–25	16–40	25–66	75–100	60–100	60–150
MIPS	.75	2.66	11.4	54	75	112	150
Bits	8	16	32	32	32	64	64
Memory	640K	16MB	4GB	4GB	4GB	4GB	4GB
Coprocessor	No	No	No	Yes	Yes	Yes	Yes
Built-in cache	0	0	0	8K	16K	16K	16K

Intel first developed the 4004 processor in 1971. It had 2,300 transistors on the chip, which was an amazing development. In the early 1980s, the 8088 was developed with 29,000 transistors. Since that time, Intel has introduced newer and more powerful CPUs every three or four years.

Benefits of competition

For some time, Intel was the only source for 80x86 CPUs. Because they had no competition, the prices were always high, especially during the period after an initial release. The price of the CPU determines to a large extent the price of the motherboard. I paid $1,825 for my first 386 motherboard, which operated at only 16 MHz. Today I can buy a 386SX motherboard that operates at 40 MHz for about $60. I paid $4,450 for my first 486 motherboard, which operated at 20 MHz. Today I can buy a 486SX motherboard that operates at 33 MHz for about $200. I could even buy a 486DX2-66, which operates at 66 MHz, for about $600.

One of the things that has driven the prices down is that American Micro Devices (AMD), Cyrix, and several other companies have developed clone CPUs. Intel now has some competition.

The competition has forced prices down, and has also forced the companies to improve their products. Intel seemed perfectly happy with a 386 that operated at 33 MHz, until AMD introduced a 386 that operates at 40 MHz. Several other improvements have also been made. AMD reduced the required voltage for the CPU from 5 to 3 volts. The lower wattage reduces the amount of heat produced in the CPU.

Cyrix Corporation has developed a 486 CPU that's the same size as the smaller 386. You can remove a 386 CPU and install a Cyrix chip that gives you most of the speed and power of a 486. Cyrix and NexGEN are developing 586 CPU clones of the Pentium that will be less expensive than Intel's CPU. The competition is great for us—the consumers.

How is a CPU made?

Designing and creating a CPU or an integrated circuit is a very complex procedure. Basically, here's how it's done. A large, high-powered workstation and computer-aided design (CAD) software are used for the early design, which is then printed out on a very large piece of paper. Once the design is checked for accuracy, it's reduced by several magnitudes and photographed. The negative image is then transferred to a silicon die. Using acids and photo-engraving procedures and methods, portions of the die is etched away, leaving only the photographic image. Transistors and circuits are thus created.

The CPUs are etched into a thin slab of silicon about six inches in diameter. Several CPUs can be etched onto a single slab. The chips go through several stages of processing, at the end of which the individual CPUs are cut and separated. They're then tested and selected. Figure 4-2 shows a Pentium CPU, magnified several thousand times. The basic sections of the CPU are marked.

Built-in coprocessors

A considerable number of transistors on the 486 and Pentium are devoted to their built-in coprocessors. This makes them very fast for applications, such as spreadsheets and CAD programs, that can use a coprocessor. But there are many software applications that don't require a coprocessor. A coprocessor is useless unless your software applications are designed to use it.

Except for the 486DX, almost all motherboards and computers are sold without a math coprocessor. An empty socket is usually provided on the XT, 286, and 386 motherboards so you can add a coprocessor if you need it.

The 486DX CPU chip has 168 pins. Intel insisted that manufacturers of 486SX motherboards provide a 169-pin socket for a coprocessor. Intel then developed a 487SX coprocessor for the 486SX, which is actually a genuine 486DX with an extra pin. When plugged in, it disables the 486SX and takes over all the CPU and math coprocessor functions. The 487SX operates at the same frequencies as the 486SX: 16 MHz, 20 MHz, and 25 MHz. Rather than buying a 487SX, you'd be much better off buying an OverDrive chip to replace the 486SX.

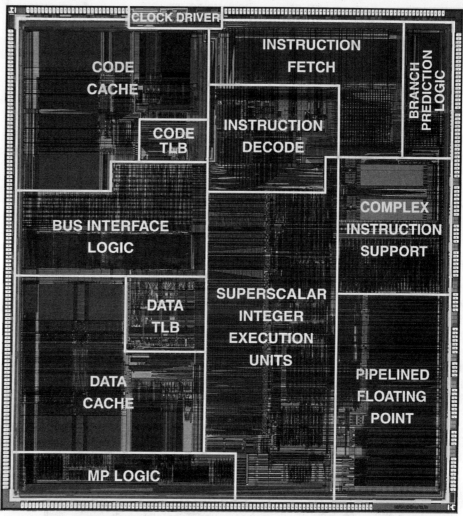

4-2 A Pentium CPU showing the basic sections.

The OverDrive

Once data is moved into the CPU, it might have to perform several instructions to process the data. Intel has developed OverDrive CPUs that can double the internal frequency of operations, which can increase the overall speed of a computer by 70% or more.

Intel's OverDrive CPU chips can be used with a 486SX or 486DX to double the internal frequency. (There isn't an OverDrive for the 486DX50.) In most cases, you just pull out the old CPU and plug in the new one.

The least expensive OverDrive currently lists for $249. It can take a 486SX-16, -20, or -25 and turn it into a 486SX-50. For a list price of $369, Intel offers an Over-

Drive that can turn the 486SX-25 into a 486DX2-50. The difference, of course, is that the DX2 has an internal math coprocessor.

An OverDrive CPU to upgrade a 486DX-33 to a 486DX2-66 lists for $499. Note that all quoted prices are current as of late 1994 and are provided for comparison only. By the time you read this, they should be lower. Also remember that street prices are always lower than list prices.

If you have a fax machine or a fax board, you can call Intel's fax-back line and have them fax you all the information you need about the various CPUs. Call their voice line at 800-525-3019 and follow the instructions. You'll probably want their fax-back catalog, item number 9010, which gives a brief listing of what's available. Item 9000 gives the list price of several of the products.

Check the ads in computer magazines for vendors who sell the OverDrive chip. Most vendors who sell motherboards also sell CPUs, though they might not advertise this fact. If you can't find a vendor, call Intel at 800-538-3373 and ask to be sent an Upgrade Guide, which will list the vendors in your area.

Upgrading a 486DX-25 to a 486DX2-50

I paid $4,450 for my first 486 motherboard. Keep in mind that this was in early 1989 when a dollar was worth a lot more than it is today. One reason it cost so much was because it was one of the first Micronics boards. It provided me with over five years of good service, but it operated at 25 MHz, which is very slow by today's standards.

Since I had so much invested in this motherboard and it was still running well, I decided it would be worthwhile to upgrade to the 50-MHz OverDrive chip. In late 1994, the Intel list price for the chip was $369. I bought it from a discount store for $299. Figure 4-3 shows the new 486DX2-50 OverDrive CPU and the original 486-25.

4-3 Upgrading a 486-25 to a 486DX2-50. Note the white dot in the lower left corner that indicates pin 1. That corner is also cut.

I ran a couple of basic tests before I switched the CPUs: Norton 7.0 Sysinfo and LandMark's System Speed Test 2.0. (LandMark's phone number is 800-683-6696.) There are later versions of both of these tests, but this is all I had at the time and it was good enough to give me an idea of any improvement.

Norton's Sysinfo compares the current CPU to that of an XT. For instance, a 286-12 is 8.9 times better than an XT, a 386-33 is 35.9 times better, and a 486-66 is 141.7 times better. Table 4-2 shows results of comparing system speed for both systems, using both programs.

**Table 4-2. Comparison of system speed
using both Norton Sysinfo and LandMark
(number of times faster than XT performance)**

	Norton Sysinfo		LandMark	
	CPU	Overall	CPU	FPU
25 MHz	54	39.5	83.56	204.5
50 MHz	106.7	74.4	167.7	408.06

Norton Sysinfo told me that the 25-MHz CPU was 54 times more efficient than an old XT. When I installed the OverDrive for 50 MHz, it said that it was 106.7 times better than an XT. The overall performance of a 25-MHz system was 39.6 times better, and that of a 50-MHz machine was 74.4 times better.

The LandMark test gave the 25-MHz CPU a rating of 83.56 and a floating point unit (FPU) rating of 204.5. The 50-MHz system rating was 167.15, and the FPU was 408.06.

As you can see, doubling the internal frequency to 50 MHz doesn't quite double the overall performance, but it's close. Of course, different programs and software will give you different results, which can range from a 50% increase up to over 90%.

Caution! Replacing the CPU is very simple, but you must take some precautions. Before handling the CPU or any chip, be sure to discharge yourself of any static electricity. Touch the metal chassis of the computer case or any metal object that's plugged in to discharge yourself.

It's also very important to make a diagram that shows the CPU orientation before you remove the CPU. The CPU has 168 pins and a small dot on the corner where pin 1 is. The corner is cut so it isn't sharp like the other three. The CPU can be plugged in backwards, so it's crucial to know where pin 1 is. It's a good idea to take a marking pen and put a mark of some kind on the motherboard for pin 1 before removing the CPU.

Since there are 168 pins, it can be a bit difficult to remove it. It's best to take a thin-blade screwdriver or knife to pry it up slightly around all sides before gradually lifting it up. The metal fillers for the openings on the back panel make a good tool for lifting out chips.

After the old CPU is removed, carefully plug in the new chip. You shouldn't have to set any jumpers or switches. It should work perfectly when you turn on the power.

As the prices come down, it should be less expensive to replace the motherboard than to replace the CPU. Before you replace your CPU, you might want to check out the prices of a completely new motherboard.

Testing and selection

When a batch of chips are processed, some chips might have defective transistors or circuits. The chips that aren't completely dead are tested for several specifications and parameters. Some of them will operate at a higher voltage, frequency, or temperature than others. They might also be tested to meet several other important specifications and criteria. CPU chips are separated and selected according to the tests they successfully pass. In a single batch they might have a few that can operate at 50 MHz, a few at 33 MHz, and some at 33 MHz or 25 MHz. Get the fastest one you can, even if you have to eat hamburger now and then instead of steak.

DX4 and P54C CPUs

At one time the etched lines connecting the internal circuits were as much as two or three microns wide. (A micron is a millionth of a meter. According to an international agreement in 1967, the term should be *micrometer*. Intel, and a lot of other people in the industry, still use the term *micron*.) The newer CPUs use lines that are usually less than 1 micron. The 486 uses lines that are .8 micron wide. The 486DX4 etched lines are .6 micron wide. The Pentium has also been redesigned to the smaller lines. Narrower lines means they can squeeze more transistors into a given area.

Most semiconductors on motherboards and CPUs are designed to use a 5-volt supply. The original Pentium and 486 used 5 volts, but there were problems dissipating the generated heat, which is about 15 watts for the Pentium, so the 486DX4s and the redesigned Pentium P54Cs will use 3.3 volts, which means less power. Instead of having to dissipate 15 watts, it will produce less than 10 watts and have much less of a heat problem.

Besides using less power, the chips will operate up to three times faster inside. The DX4s will operate at 75, 82.5, and 99 MHz. The P54C will operate at 100 MHz.

You can't just remove older CPUs and upgrade the motherboards with newer DX4 or P54C units. The CPUs are designed to use 3.3 volts, and old motherboards were designed for 5 volts. Applying 5 volts to a 3.3-volt unit would destroy it. Evergreen, at 503-757-0934, Bondwell, at 800-627-6888, Loranger International, at 814-723-2250, and several other companies have developed voltage regulator systems that allow a 3.3-volt chip to be used on an older motherboard. The voltage regulators are built into a socket that fits into the CPU socket, then the CPU is plugged into the regulator. Newer motherboards will have the 3.3-volt regulation built in.

Motherboard memory

A 386, 486, or Pentium motherboard should have sockets, or provisions, for the installation of at least 16MB of on-board RAM. Most of them will have provisions for between 16MB and 128MB. The majority of the motherboards will use single in-line memory module (SIMM) sockets, which allows for the most memory to be installed in the least amount of space. Today, very few, if any, motherboards use the older dual in-line package (DIP) memory chips. They require too much board real estate. You can install about 128MB of SIMM memory in the space that one megabyte of DIP memory would require. If you refer back to Fig. 3-1, the old XT motherboard has 640K of DIP chips in the lower left corner. The Pentium motherboard has four sockets for SIMMs. Up to 200 times more memory could be installed in those four Pentium SIMM sockets than in the 36 DIP sockets of the XT.

Before you order memory, make sure you get the right type for your motherboard. Get the right speed, memory size, and physical size. There are two types of SIMM configurations and sockets: 30 contacts and 72 contacts. Figure 4-4 shows a 4 × 36 16MB SIMM chip on the bottom and a 1 × 9 1MB chip on the top. The 72-contact SIMMs are usually designated as 1 × 36 (4MB), 2 × 36 (8MB), 4 × 36 (16MB), etc. Most systems require that you install memory in multiples of two.

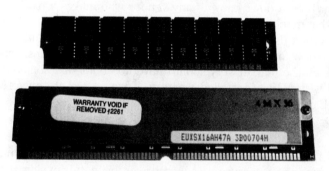

4-4
A 1 × 9 1MB SIMM module (top) and a 4 × 36 16MB SIMM (bottom).

Your motherboard will probably be sold without memory. Make sure you order the type and speed of memory that's required for your board. You can probably get by with 80 nanoseconds (ns) for a 20-MHz 486SX. For 25 MHz, you'll want 60 to 70 ns, and at least 60 ns for 33-MHz and faster systems.

It's very easy to install SIMMs. Just follow the documentation you receive with your motherboard and make sure you orient them properly when plugging them in. Most can be plugged in only one way. Notice that the left lower corner of the SIMMs in Fig. 4-4 are notched so they have to be plugged in properly. There are small holes in the ends of SIMMs that fit over small projections on the socket. When plugged in, a flexible metal latch locks them in. To remove them, just pull back on the metal latch.

If you aren't filling all the sockets, check your documentation. You might have to install memory in multiples of two (2MB, 4MB, or 8MB). The sockets are usually numbered. If you're installing only 2MB or 4MB, you'll have to plug them into the proper sockets. Areas of memory are designated as *banks*. Bank 0 must be filled first, then bank 1, 2, and finally 3.

You'll probably have to set some switches or jumpers on the motherboard to tell the system how much memory is installed. Again, your motherboard documentation should tell you how to do this.

DRAM

The primary memory used in PCs is dynamic random-access memory (DRAM). The older PCs reserved about one fourth of the motherboard area for memory chips, and the early boards used 64K chips. (64K is 64,000 bytes.) It took nine chips to make 64K, and that's all some motherboards had. They later developed 256K chips, and up to 640K was installed on some motherboards. Today there are 32MB single in-line memory modules (SIMMs) that let you install up to 128MB on a motherboard in less space than it took for the original 64K. If you refer back to Fig. 4-1, the four white slots at the bottom of this Micronics motherboard are for SIMM chips. The SIMM sockets can be located anywhere on different motherboards. The SIMM sockets on my Twin T Pentium motherboard shown in Fig. 3-3 are the four white sockets at the top right corner.

Note that the 386, 486, and Pentium can address up to 4 gigabytes (4GB), or 4,000,000,000 bytes of memory. (The prefix *giga* means billion.) The most common size of memory chip at this time is the 4MB SIMM. You would need 1,000 of these to make 4GB. At the present time, I don't know of any vendor who makes a motherboard that would accept that much memory. It's probably a bit more than you'll ever need. Most Pentium motherboards are designed to accept up to 128MB of RAM.

Several companies are now producing 16MB and 32MB SIMM DRAM chips, and 64MB SIMM chips will be on the market very soon. I have no doubt that someday we'll have motherboards with 1GB of installed memory. It would require only 16 64MB SIMMs to make 1GB of RAM.

Cache SRAM

When processing data, quite often the same information is accessed over and over again. Having to traverse the bus to repeatedly retrieve this data can slow the system down considerably.

The 486 has a small built-in 8K cache that contributes to its speed. But 8K isn't nearly large enough for some programs, so many motherboards have sockets for adding a very fast cache. This cache is usually made from static random-access memory (SRAM) and can be added in 32K increments, usually up to 512K or more. Refer back to Fig. 4-1, which shows 256K of SRAM cache memory chips at the top right corner. (SRAM is discussed in more detail in chapter 6.)

Write through and write back

After data is processed, it's returned to RAM. The older write-through systems simply send the data back to RAM and system operations are delayed while this takes place. The delay might be only microseconds, but if you're processing a lot of data, it can add up. The newer write-back systems keeps the data in the cache until there's a break in operations, then write the data to RAM.

Other motherboard chips

Besides the CPU and memory chips, there are several other chips and systems on the motherboard. The early PCs and the AT had a very large number of chips. I have an early 286 motherboard with one megabyte of memory on it. It has over 150 separate chips on it.

Chips and Technology, using very large-scale integration (VLSI), combined several motherboard chips into just a few chips. Other companies followed them so that today there are only a small number of chips on the motherboard.

The smaller number of chips means fewer solder connections, more reliability, more speed, less board real estate, and less cost. Some motherboards are now as small as one third the size of the original XT, and have only five or six large VLSI chips on them.

ROM BIOS

You don't have to worry about read-only memory (ROM) because you can't ordinarily change or alter it. ROM comes with the motherboard. The principal use of ROM in PCs today is for the basic input/output system (BIOS).

The BIOS chip is second in importance only to the CPU. Every time you turn your computer on, the BIOS does a power-on self test (POST). The BIOS checks all the major components to make sure they're operating properly. It also facilitates the transfer of data among peripherals. Many BIOS chips also have diagnostics and built-in utilities.

The BIOS performs its important functions under the control of firmware programs, which are similar to other types of software except that the ROM is actually made up of hundreds of transistors programmed to perform certain functions.

Most newer BIOS chips use flash memory, but until recently ROM BIOS programs were usually burned into electrically programmable read-only memory (EPROM) chips. With this type of EPROM, special devices are used to input a program into the ROM chip. As the program voltages pass through the chip, the transistors are turned on and off to match the input program. When voltage is applied to a normal transistor, it will turn on or off as long as the voltage is present. EPROM transistors are different from ordinary transistors. When EPROM transistors are turned on or off, they remain in that condition.

Fairly large programs and text can be stored on a ROM chip. The ROM BIOS for an early XT could be programmed onto a 64K ROM chip. The 486 ROM BIOS uses a 512K chip.

Companies that manufacture BIOS chips are constantly improving and adding new functionality to the BIOS. You can perform some useful upgrades to an older computer by just installing a new BIOS. I have a 386 computer in my office that I put together in early 1988. It has a 16-MHz CPU, which is very slow by today's standards. But it has served me well for all of these years. I recently decided to add a 250MB hard drive to it, but the largest hard drive the system would accept was 114MB. The BIOS had been written in 1988 and a 250MB hard drive was something few people could afford at that time.

New BIOS chips for the 386 system would cost about $50. I'm not sure that I'll upgrade the BIOS because the system would still run at 16 MHz. I could buy a new 386 motherboard that operates at 40 MHz for just a few dollars more.

The Micronics Pentium motherboard has BIOS in a flash memory chip. You can upgrade these chips by way of software from a floppy disk or even over a modem.

You'll soon see many other motherboards with flash memory BIOSs. It will become the industry standard.

Keyboard BIOS

The keyboard is a small computer in itself and has its own special BIOS chip on the motherboard. It's usually a long 40-pin chip located near the keyboard connector. You might not see this chip on some of the newer motherboards because many of them now integrate it into a VLSI chip. My Twin T Pentium motherboard has a keyboard BIOS chip, but it's integrated into a VLSI chip on the Micronics Pentium motherboard.

A scan code or signal is sent to the BIOS when a key is pressed and another signal is sent when the key is released. When two keys are pressed, it can detect which one was pressed first. It can also detect when a key is held down longer than normal, and it will start beeping at you. The last 20 keystrokes are stored in the keyboard memory and are continually flushed out and replaced by new keystrokes.

System configuration and CMOS

The CMOS system and batteries were discussed in chapter 2. When you install a hard drive, you have to tell the system configuration setup what kind it is, the number of heads and sectors, and other information. The configuration system also needs to be informed as to what kind of floppy drives you have. If you want to reset the time and date, you do it with the CMOS system setup.

The system configuration setup is stored in complementary metal oxide semiconductors (CMOS). These CMOS transistors use very little power, so there's a small battery mounted on the motherboard that can keep the transistors turned on to retain the date, time, and setup information—even when the computer is turned off.

Timing

A computer depends on precise timing. Several of the chips on a motherboard control the frequency and timing circuits. The timing is so crucial that there are usually one or more crystals on the motherboard that oscillate at a precise frequency to control the timing circuits. The crystals are usually in a small, oblong, shiny can. In Fig. 4-5 the pens point to a couple of crystal oscillator cans.

DMA

The direct memory access (DMA) system allows some processing to take place without having to bother the CPU. For instance, the disk drives can exchange data directly with RAM without having to go through the CPU.

IRQ

The interrupt request (IRQ) system is a very important part of the computer. It can cause the system to interrupt whatever it's doing and take care of the request. Without interrupts, nothing would get done. Even if the computer is doing nothing, it must be interrupted and told to perform a task.

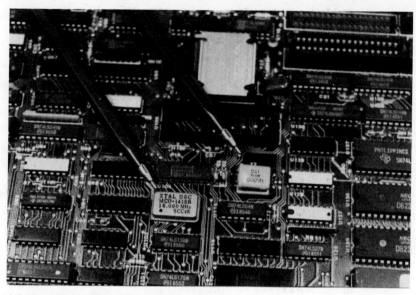

4-5 The pens point to a couple of crystal cans.

There are 16 IRQs, numbered from 0 to 15. Each input/output (I/O) device on the bus is given a unique IRQ number. Software can also perform interrupt requests. There's a priority system and some interrupts take precedence over others.

Sixteen IRQs might seem like a large number, but it isn't nearly enough. Several interrupts are reserved or used by the system, so they aren't available. It would be wonderful if the Pentium had about twice as many, but no such luck.

If you want to see how your system uses IRQs, if you have DOS 6.0 or later just type MSD (for Microsoft diagnostics). This command will not only let you look at your IRQs, it will tell you about most of the other important elements in your computer. Table 4-3 lists the 16 IRQs on my 486-66 system and how they're being used

As you can see, out of the 16 IRQs, 10, 11, 12, and 15 are available. IRQ5 is for LPT2, but since I don't have a second printer attached it could be used for another device, such as a mouse, sound board, or network card.

UARTs and serial ports

If your motherboard has built-in COM ports, you'll have one or two universal asynchronous transmitter-receiver (UART) chips somewhere on the board, but you might not be able to find them. These chips are integrated into VLSI chips on most of the newer motherboards. If your motherboard doesn't have built-in serial ports, then you'll have to get a plug-in board with these chips. Early chips had the designation 8250, and later chips were designated 16450 and 16550. Figure 4-6 shows an old plug-in card for a serial port taken out of an early Eagle computer. It has a single 8250 chip.

If the serial ports aren't built into the motherboard, they're usually integrated on a multi-input/output (multi-I/O) board. This board could have serial ports COM1 and COM2, printer port LPT1, a game port, and often a floppy disk controller and IDE

Table 4-3. The 16 IRQs on a 66-MHz 486 system

IRQ	Address	Description	Detected
0	OCO8:0103	Timer click	Yes
1	OCO8:0113	Keyboard	Yes
2	OA7D:OO57	Second 8259A	Yes
3	E939:1FAD	COM2: COM4	COM2
4	OA7D:0087	COM1: COM3	COM1
5	OA7D:OO9F	LPT2:	No
6	OA7D:OOB7	Floppy disk	Yes
7	OO7O:O6F4	LPT1:	Yes
8	OA7D:OO52	Real-time clock	Yes
9	FOOO:EED3	Redirected IRQ2	Yes
10	OA7D:OOCF	(Reserved)	
11	OA7D:OOE7	(Reserved)	
12	OA7D:OOFF	(Reserved)	
13	FOOO:EEDC	Math coprocessor	Yes
14	OA7D:O117	Fixed disk	Yes
15	FOOO:FF53	(Reserved)	

4-6 An old Eagle card for a single serial port. The long chip in the center is the 8250 UART.

hard disk interface. Some of the inexpensive multi-I/O boards are still using old 8250 chips. For fast modem transfers, you should have the 16550 UART. You probably won't be able to see it because it's integrated into a larger chip. You can determine what type is installed in your computer by invoking the MSD command. Just type

MSD at any prompt and use your mouse to click on COM ports. You'll see a vast amount of information about your computer.

The mouse, modems, fax boards, some printers, plotters, and several peripheral devices operate with serial data, which must be furnished over a single line with one bit following another. The computer operates with parallel data. It takes eight bits to make a character, so eight bits means eight lines and 16 bits means 16 lines. Obviously, this data can't be sent out over a modem or any other serial device. UARTs can take parallel data, transform it to serial data, and send it out. It can also receive serial data and transform it into parallel data.

Ordinarily, only two serial ports can be used and each requires a dedicated IRQ. COM1 uses IRQ4 and COM2 uses IRQ3. You might want to attach four or more different serial devices to your computer. It's possible to add two more ports, COM3 and COM4, but they must share the COM1 and COM2 IRQ lines (COM3 uses IRQ4 and COM4 uses IRQ3). There are some devices that are rather selfish, however, and don't like to share, and you need special software in order to use COM3 and COM4.

COM ports also have specific addresses in memory. COM1 uses 3F8h, COM2 uses 2F8h, COM3 uses 3E8h, and COM4 uses 2E8h. Life would be a whole lot simpler if only we had four or more dedicated IRQ lines for COM ports. Of course, you'd also need two more UART chips for the additional ports.

Architecture

The architecture of a computer refers to the overall design and the components it uses. The architecture is also concerned with the type of bus that's used. The bus is the internal pathways over which data is sent from one part of the computer to another. Eight-bit systems use 8-bit parallel paths, 16 use 16, 32 use 32, and 64 use 64. The flow of data over a bus is often compared to the flow of traffic on a highway. If there are only two lanes, it might be limited. Adding more lanes can vastly improve the flow of traffic.

ISA

IBM more or less abandoned the standard they established when they introduced their microchannel architecture (MCA) in 1987. There were far more IBM-compatible clone computers in existence than computers manufactured by IBM. Since IBM was now directing most of their efforts toward the MCA, the clone makers took over the standard and changed the name to ISA.

An ISA computer can be anything from the oldest and slowest XT up to the newest and fastest Pentium. The old XT used an 8-bit bus, which means that 8 parallel lines connected to the same pins on all the slot connectors for plug-in boards. When the 286 was being developed by IBM, it became apparent that an 8-bit bus was too slow and clearly inadequate. So they devised a 16-bit slot connector by adding a second 36-contact connector in front of the original 62-contact connector. This was a brilliant innovation. Refer back to Fig. 2-1, which shows an 8-bit ISA board on top and a 16-bit ISA board on the bottom.

Compatibility

There was about five billion dollars' worth of 8-bit hardware in existence at the time IBM introduced their 16-bit AT 286. But with the 16-bit connector, either an 8-bit or 16-bit board can be used in a 16-bit system. The industry loved it because it didn't make their present plug-in boards obsolete.

This downward compatibility still exists even with the fastest and most power-ful 486 and Pentium. But there's a price to pay for the compatibility. The CPU oper-ates over a special memory bus to communicate with RAM at the CPU's rated frequency. The 386 and 486 are 32-bit systems; the Pentium is a 64-bit system. The 386 and 486 communicate with the system RAM over a 32-bit bus, back and forth to memory. But the system can communicate only with its plug-in boards and periph-erals over a 16-bit bus. Even if the 486 operates at 66 MHz, the ISA I/O bus is limited to a speed of about 8 MHz and an I/O bus width of 16 parallel lines in order to be able to run all previous software and hardware.

MCA

IBM decided that the 16-bit ISA system was inadequate and designed a new sys-tem they called microchannel architecture (MCA), a 32-bit bus system for plug-in cards and memory. This wider bus was a much faster and more powerful system, but IBM also wanted it to be downward compatible with the available software, even if it wasn't compatible with the hardware. So the I/O speed from the plug-in boards and peripherals was still limited to 8 to 10 MHz.

Before introducing the MCA system, IBM had been losing a large share of busi-ness to low-cost clones, and had let the design of the original PC slip away from them. This time they very carefully patented everything about the MCA and kept most of the crucial specifications secret. They developed a machine that only they could manufacture and sell without any competition from the cloners.

The big problem was that the new MCA system couldn't use any of the available hardware. The connector contacts of the MCA boards were much smaller than those on the ISA boards. There was no way they could be used on ISA systems. New boards had to be designed for the MCA slots.

IBM was confident that the added speed and power of their new system would more than make up for the added expense. Besides, IBM had a very large and loyal following, especially among large corporations, most of whom had pretty deep pock-ets. But most ordinary buyers had to watch their budget. IBM computers have al-ways been expensive, and the new MCA PS/2 systems were even more expensive than the original IBM PCs. The boards needed for the MCA systems were also very expensive. There were millions and millions of clones in existence. Because of the large number of systems and the competition of the many vendors, the cost of a board for a clone was much less than that for a PS/2.

IBM is now a changed company. They have reduced the prices on most of their products. At one time you had to go through authorized dealers to buy any IBM product or for any repairs. They've now set up several direct-sale companies, and they'll sell you any of their products through mail order.

EISA

A group of IBM clone makers realized that IBM was right about needing a wider bus and more room for expansion and improvement, so they devised the extended industry standard architecture. This standard specified a new connector with almost double the number of contacts and added several new improvements to the ISA standard. Unlike the IBM MCA system, the EISA system was downwardly compatible with all previous hardware. The billions of dollars' worth of present boards could still be used with the EISA system, even the old 8-bit plug-in boards.

The standard contact on an ISA connector is .06 of an inch wide, and there's a .04-inch space between each contact. The EISA board was designed with a second set of contacts immediately below the ISA contacts. A connecting trace is placed between the ISA contacts for the lower set of EISA contacts. The EISA plug-in slot on the motherboard has two sets of contacts to match the contacts on the plug-in boards, and the EISA boards have cut-outs on the boards to match bars across the lower EISA section of the slot connector. When an ISA board is plugged in, the bars prevent it from being inserted deep enough to contact the EISA contacts. Figure 4-7 shows an EISA board.

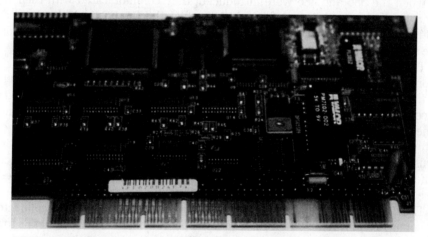

4-7 An EISA board. Note the edge connector. It has two sets of contacts, one that's equivalent to the ISA contacts and another set that extends between and below the ISA set.

Like the MCA system, the EISA system provides a 32-bit bus. Unlike the MCA, they wanted to remain downward compatible with earlier software and hardware. Therefore, the communication between the plug-in boards was still limited to a speed of 8 MHz.

Do you need an EISA?

Whether you need an EISA system depends on what you want to do with your computer and how much you want to spend. Several features have been created for the EISA. It's much faster and more powerful than an ISA board, and it can detect and automatically set up a board that's plugged in.

If you're running applications such as large spreadsheets, CAD programs, or any high-end application, then I would recommend the EISA type system. If you can afford it, even if you aren't running high-end applications, you might go ahead and buy an EISA system. Even if you don't actually need it at the moment, it feels good to have all that speed and utility available. You can never have a computer that's too fast or too powerful. So buy the biggest, most powerful, and fastest motherboard with the most goodies you can afford.

The VESA local bus

The PC bus has long been a bottleneck. The 8-bit bus at 4.77 MHz was okay for the XT. The 16-bit bus was a great leap forward when the 286 was introduced. The 286 CPU communicated with its RAM over a 16-bit memory bus at whatever speed the CPU operated at. But in order to remain compatible with previous hardware and software, the input/output (I/O) bus speed was locked in at 8 to 10 MHz.

When the 386 and 486 were introduced, they communicated with their RAM over a 32-bit memory bus at the speed of the CPU. But the I/O bus still operated on a 16-bit bus at 8 to 10 MHz. Some peripherals such as fast hard disks and monitors were slowed down considerably.

The Video Electronics Standards Association (VESA) developed a set of specifications for a new bus that eliminated some of the bottlenecks. The VESA local bus, or VL bus, was officially introduced on August 28, 1992. The VL specification added a second slot connector in line with the 16-bit slot connector. This solution is similar to the one used to move from an 8-bit to 16-bit slot, which was to add a second connector to the 8-bit slot connector to turn it into a 16-bit system. The system allowed the use of both 8-bit and 16-bit cards. The VL bus is quite similar; it adds a second connector in line with the 16-bit connectors so VL or 16-bit boards can be used in these slots.

The VL connector uses 116 miniature contacts, similar to the MCA connectors. The connector provides a 32-bit path from the plug-in boards and peripherals to the CPU. The VL bus is a direct extension of the CPU bus and runs at the same speed as the CPU. The VL bus increases the performance of a PC considerably, yet adds very little to the cost of the system. Figure 4-8 shows my combination ISA/EISA/VLB 486DX2-66. From the top, the fourth, fifth, and sixth slots are EISA connectors. Slots 6 and 7 have the additional VESA local bus connectors.

Figure 4-9 shows a 16-bit IDE hard disk interface and multi-I/O board on top, and a VLB IDE hard disk interface and multi-I/O board on the bottom. The difference is that the VLB board may be a bit faster than the standard 16-bit IDE board. Each of the boards can control two IDE hard drives, two floppy disks, serial ports COM1 and COM2, a parallel port LPT1 connector for the printer, and a set of pins for a game port or joystick. One of the COM ports can be accessed through the top connector on the back panel, and the other COM port through the 10 upright pins on the board. There are photos and instructions for connecting cables to these boards in chapter 7.

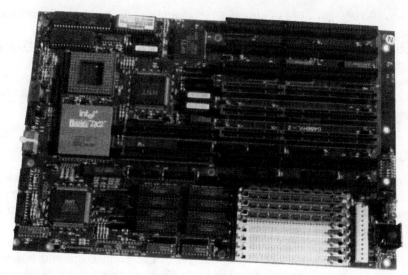

4-8 My 486DX2-66 motherboard with two VLB slots. This is a combination EISA-ISA-VLB motherboard. From the top, the 4th, 5th, and 6th slots are EISA bus connectors, and slots 6 and 7 have the additional VLB connectors.

4-9 Two IDE interface and multi-I/O boards. The longer board is also a VLB board.

Thousands of vendors have adopted the VL bus configuration. There's a lot of competition, so the cost of the VL bus plug-in boards is quite reasonable.

The VL bus is not a perfect solution. It allows only three connectors, which are ordinarily used for fast IDE hard disks, video adapters, and network interface cards (NICs).

The VL bus allows I/O communication over the 32-bit lines at the same speed as the CPU, but the other I/O components in the system are still relegated to the 16-bit bus at 8 to 10 MHz. Even the Pentium has this same standard ISA bus for I/O and peripherals in order to remain backward compatible.

Both the VL bus and the Intel peripheral component interconnect (PCI) systems can be used on the ISA, EISA, MCA, and Pentium motherboards. Some of the Pentium motherboards have both a VL bus and a PCI bus. The VESA VL 2.0 standard defines a 64-bit bus, which is backward compatible so it will still accept the 32-bit VL bus boards.

The Intel PCI bus

Intel introduced their peripheral component interconnect (PCI) local bus in July of 1992, a month before the VL bus was officially introduced. This local bus system can be used on the 386 and 486 systems, but it was designed primarily for the Pentium.

The VL bus connects directly to the CPU. The PCI bus is a bit different than the VL bus in that it's a separate bus. You can install it in line with a standard 16-bit connector or as a stand-alone connector. Many PCI bus connectors and boards are stand-alone, but boards designed for the VL bus system aren't stand-alone because they use both 16-bit VL bus pins.

Adding a plug-in board can often be frustrating. You might have to set several dip switches or jumpers so it doesn't conflict with the assigned interrupt request (IRQs), serial and parallel ports, and DMA channels of other plug-in boards.

One of the advantages of the PCI bus is that it's a plug-and-play system. It has an auto-configuration capability that will automatically configure a PCI add-in board. The original version of the VL bus is a "plug-and-pray" system. (Version 2 of the VL bus will be plug-and-play.) Another advantage of the PCI bus is that it allows up to ten connectors. For most practical purposes, however, the same three used in the VL system—hard disk, video, and network—are all that's currently needed.

One of the disadvantages of the PCI bus is that the VL bus has been in use for some time. There are thousands of boards and hundreds of vendors making and selling the VL bus board, but there currently aren't many PCI products available. Since there's very little competition and few products are available, the PCI boards are more expensive than the VL boards. Figure 4-10 shows a Pentium motherboard with three PCI slots, and Fig. 4-11 shows two monitor-adapter graphics-accelerator cards. A VLB card is at the top and a PCI card is at the bottom. Note that the cards are reversed. When looking from the front, the PCI cards have the components on the left side; the VLB card and most other ISA cards have the components on the right side.

Many experts think the PCI system is better than the VLB system. For the ordinary end user, however, there probably isn't that much of an advantage to buying a PCI system, especially when the new VL bus version 2 becomes available. At this time, most PCI products are more expensive than VLBs.

The PCI bus can be used with ISA, EISA, or MCA motherboards. There are three different PCI connectors: one for a 32-bit bus, one for a 3-volt 64-bit bus, and one for a 5-volt 64-bit bus. They can be installed as stand-alone connectors or at the end of the standard slot connectors, very similar to the VL bus connector system.

4-10 A Pentium motherboard. The three white slots near the top left are for PCI boards. The four slots at the lower edge are for SIMMs.

4-11 Two monitor adapters from Diamond Computer Systems: a VLB board on the top and a PCI board on the bottom.

Some think the PCI bus will eventually displace the VL bus, but the VESA local bus already has a fairly large installed base, and there's a lot of hardware available for it. The Intel PCI system hasn't yet been field-tested like the VESA bus; it might still have some bugs to be eliminated. Initially, the PCI motherboard cost about $100 more than a VL motherboard. Currently, it costs more to implement a PCI bus on a motherboard than a VLB, but eventually the prices will be about equal. We'll probably end up with two standards, the VL bus and the PCI bus.

ISA-EISA-VL-PCI combos

My 486DX-66 motherboard has four ISA slots, one ISA-VL slot, two EISA slots, and one EISA-VL slot. Several manufacturers have developed motherboards that have two or three EISA slots, two or more VL connectors, and the rest ISA slots. Or instead of the VL bus they may have two or three PCI connectors. There are a large number of motherboard variations now possible.

PCMCIA BUS

Many personal and desktop computers now have a PCMCIA slot. PCMCIA stands for the Personal Computer Memory Card International Association. The PCMCIA specification was originally developed to add memory to laptop and notebook computers, using credit-card-sized memory cards. You might ask why anyone would want a desktop computer with a PCMCIA slot. The answer is because there are now many devices and components besides memory that can be plugged into this slot. Dozens of new devices and components are being developed every day. A PCMCIA slot can be more useful than an extra slot on the motherboard. In order to change a board on the motherboard, you have to shut everything down, remove the cover, and install the new board. On a PCMCIA slot, if you want to use a modem just plug it in. You don't even have to shut off the power. After you've finished with the modem or fax, plug in an ethernet card, hard disk, sound card, SCSI interface, or any of the other available PCMCIA devices. A PCMCIA slot can add a vast amount of utility and expandability to a computer.

The PCMCIA headquarters, at 408-720-0107, has a book that lists most of the developers and their products. Greystone, at 408-866-4739, has developed Card-Dock, a PCMCIA adapter for desktop or tower computers. A CardDock can be mounted in a standard 5¼-inch bay and provides two slots for Type III cards. Figure 5-1 in the next chapter shows the CardDock adapter. An interface board is required for this adapter. Quatech, at 216-434-3154, also has several PCMCIA adapters that can be used with desktop computers. Figure 5-2 in the next chapter shows a Quatech adapter and interface board.

Built-in goodies

It's amazing how soon you can fill up all the available slots on a motherboard. One way to get around having to use plug-in boards is to have many of the functions built into the motherboard. My Twin T Patriot Pentium and most motherboards now have several built-in functions. One of the arguments against built-in functions is that they could become obsolete or defective. But, if necessary, on-board utilities can usually be disabled and replaced with a plug-in board. Here are some of the things that can be built in:

IDE interface

Many motherboards now have the IDE interface for hard disks and a floppy disk controller built into the motherboard. They have rows of pins protruding from the motherboard that accept the ribbon cables from the drives.

SCSI interface

Many Macintosh models have built-in SCSI interfaces, which is one of the reasons for their popularity. The PC industry has been lax in not following suit. SCSI is something that's essential, not only for multimedia, but for many PC applications. A few motherboard manufacturers are now including a built-in SCSI interface.

Serial ports

Mice, modems, and many other devices need a serial port. Some multifunction boards provide them, but it would be much simpler to have them built into the motherboard.

It's difficult to run many programs today without a mouse. A board for a bus mouse might have only two or three chips, but it requires a whole slot. It's very easy to incorporate a bus mouse interface into a motherboard.

Printer ports

There are very few computers that aren't tied to a printer of some sort. There are still a few printers that use a serial port, but most today use one of the two parallel ports, LPT1 or LPT2. Ordinarily, you'd have to buy a multifunction board that has a printer port on it, but it's easy to integrate the parallel ports into the motherboard.

Game ports

Many of the multifunction boards sold today have a game port for a joystick. With the increased interest in and popularity of multimedia, a game port has become almost mandatory.

Monitor adapter

Every computer needs a board or adapter to drive the monitor. Some motherboards have had built-in monitor adapters for some time. They're great for many applications. The main problem is that developers keep making the adapters faster and more and more complex, with better resolution and true colors. If your adapter is built-in, then you're stuck with whatever resolution and functions it provides. Most motherboards with built-in functions, however, have jumpers or switches that allow you to disable those functions and plug in a board.

Being stuck with an older monitor adapter might not be a problem for many applications. I'm still using 8-bit adapters on a couple of my older computers. I have other computers that use a 16-bit board, and my 486-66 uses a VESA local bus board. The various adapters all work fine for the applications the computers run.

Benchmarks

Benchmarks are tests designed to give a standard measure of performance, which you can use to predict how well and how fast a computer will run actual applications. There are many factors that affect the outcome of a benchmark test, some of which are the computer's CPU, architecture, design, system software, and hardware. There are several different benchmarks. Some are designed to test only a specific portion of a system.

MIPS

In Table 4-1, MIPS is an acronym for millions of instructions per second. Note that the XT can do only .75 and the Pentium can do 112, which is almost 150 times faster. We have truly come a long way since 1981.

The MIPS benchmark is good, but it doesn't measure all the capabilities of a CPU while it performs different tasks. A much better benchmark is one that measures the performance while running several actual applications. For instance, a 486SX can run number-crunching programs, but a 486DX that has a built-in floating-point math coprocessor would be much faster. A Pentium would be even faster because it can handle two instructions per cycle and also has a 16K built-in cache.

SPEC92

A group of organizations got together in January of 1992 and formed the Systems Performance Evaluation Cooperative (SPEC). They developed a suite of benchmark programs that effectively measure the performance of computing systems in actual application environments. The SPEC92 tests have become the industry standard, and are identified by the acronym SPEC. For instance, SPECint92 is a very effective benchmark to measure integer application performance and SPECfp92 measures floating-point performance.

Other benchmarks

An early benchmark was Norton's system information (SI), which came with Norton's utilities. It provided a measure for a system's throughput, including processing speed and the speed of some peripherals. Norton SI 1.0 is based on the original IBM XT, which has a CPU frequency of 4.77 MHz. Later systems are measured against this amount. My 486DX2-66 system measures 42.4, which means it's over 42 times faster than the original XT. The 66-MHz frequency of the 486 is actually a little over 13 times faster than the XT's frequency at 4.77 MHz, but the newer technology and operation of the CPU system yields over 42 times better performance.

There are several other benchmarks. Whetstone measures arithmetic operations, Dhrystones measures MIPS, and WinBench executes on top of Windows and gives WinMark measures. Other benchmarks have been developed by organizations such as Ziff-Davis Labs. They do a lot of testing for the system reviews in their various magazines.

Landmark Research, at 800-683-6696, has developed the Landmark benchmark, which, among other things, measures CPU operations. Landmark Research has also developed several diagnostic software tools, such as WinProbe and DOS for Windows.

iCOMP Index

The Intel comparative performance (iCOMP) index rating provides a simple relative measure of microprocessor performance. It isn't a system benchmark, but a test intended to help nontechnical end users decide which Intel CPU best meets their needs. The iCOMP is based on both 16- and 32-bit CPU performance processing integer, floating-point, graphics, and video performance. The higher the iCOMP index, the higher the relative performance.

Deciding what to buy

One of the first things you have to decide is which motherboard you want—or, if you're like me, which one you want at a price you can afford.

I subscribe to several computer magazines, most of which have articles and reviews of software and hardware. And of course they have lots of ads from stores that sell by mail. The ads give me a fairly good idea of the prices so I know what I can afford. Mail order is probably one of the better ways to purchase your parts, especially if you don't live near a large city.

Larger cities usually have a lot of computer stores. The San Francisco bay area and Los Angeles have hundreds. There are also computer swap meets every weekend. If I need something, I go to one of the swap meets and compare the prices at the various booths. I often take a pad along, write the prices down, then go back and make the best deal I can. Sometimes you can haggle with the vendors for a better price, especially if it's near closing time.

Upgrading a PC or XT

When it was first introduced in 1981, the XT was the hottest thing around. It was the best desktop computer you could buy. The XT is now obsolete, but there are a lot of people who ignore this fact and are still very productive with them. For some applications, such as word processing, they're as good as the fastest and most powerful 486 or Pentium. XT systems can also be used as a low-cost terminal on a local-area network (LAN).

The original PC and XT used the 8088 CPU, which had about 29,000 transistors and operated at 4.77 MHz. Computers perform their operations by moving blocks of data in precise blocks of time. The PC and XT can cycle 8-bit blocks of data at 4.77 million times per second. That sounds fast, but it takes eight bits to make a single byte, eight bits to create a single character of the alphabet, and a whole lot of bytes if you're using graphics. An XT can be painfully slow if you have to run a CAD program or a large spreadsheet.

Soon after IBM introduced the XT, clone makers introduced turbo XTs. They were souped up so they could be shifted into "high gear," up to 8 and even 10 or 12 MHz.

If you have an old 4.77-MHz XT you're in love with, there are several things you can do to jazz it up a little bit. Here are just a few suggestions. There are hundreds of 8-bit plug-in boards you can use with an XT to drive a color monitor or as an interface with a hand scanner, 2400-bps modem/fax board, or multifunction I/O board for COM ports, printer, and games.

The XT BIOS might not let you use 1.2MB or 1.44MB floppies, and it might not recognize hard disks above 32MB or so. Higher-density floppies and high-capacity hard disks are an absolute necessity nowadays. An XT will let you use them if you install a new BIOS, which would cost about $50. Or you can install a fairly large SCSI hard disk with an older 8-bit SCSI interface, even with the old BIOS. You can even install a CD-ROM drive and a sound card, but it will have to be one that uses the 8-bit system.

You can even attach a laser printer to an XT. In fact, in a large office network, it might be a good idea to dedicate an XT to drive a laser printer, which would free up other computers from having to wait for the printer. You can also use many new programs. If you're using an older version of DOS, it would help if you moved up to DOS 6.2.

Replacing the XT motherboard

The things you can add to an XT are limited. Even after you've added the new components, it's still an old, slow machine. You'd be much better off by replacing the motherboard. You can currently buy a 40-MHz 386SX motherboard for about $60, or you can spend a bit more and install anything up to a 486 or Pentium motherboard in your old XT.

You might have to spend a bit more, however. In addition to replacing the motherboard, you'll need at least 4MB of memory, which could cost up to $140. You might also need a new keyboard, which will cost from $20 to $40.

If you have an original true-blue IBM PC, it will have only five slots, which means the case or chassis has only five openings on the back panel. The XT has eight slots with eight openings in the back panel. Almost all motherboards now have eight slots. Your old PC case with the five openings in the rear panel won't accommodate the eight-slot motherboards. Some plug-in boards don't need to be accessed from the rear panel, but the spacing of the slot openings on the back panel won't match the boards you need to install, such as your printer, monitor adapter, mouse, and other peripherals. Your best bet is to scrap the old case and buy a new one. It will cost about $35 to $45 for a new case with a power supply. If you're in love with the IBM logo, just rip it off and glue it on the new case.

If you're upgrading an original IBM PC, you'll need a new power supply. The original PC had a puny 63-watt power supply; the XT and later models had 135- or 150-watt power supplies.

Replacing the motherboard is very simple, whether it's an XT, 286, 386, 486, or even a Pentium. At the time of this writing, my Pentium 60-MHz motherboard is only six months old, but it has already been made obsolete by the newer 100-MHz CPUs.

To replace a motherboard, just unplug the cables and plug-in boards, pull out the old motherboard, and slip in a new one. There are detailed instructions at the end of this chapter on how to do it.

Upgrading a PC or XT to a 286

I don't recommend this type of upgrade. A short time ago, converting an XT to a 286 was a very good upgrade, but the 286 is now obsolete. The IBM AT (advanced technology) uses the 80286, or 286, CPU. It has 125,000 transistors and is a 16-bit system. The original IBM AT operated at a very conservative speed of 6 MHz, but many of the 286 clones immediately boosted the speed up to 12, 16, and even 25 MHz.

A 286 CPU handles data in 16-bit chunks, twice that of the 8088. A 286 operating at 10 MHz would be more than four times faster than an XT operating at 4.77 MHz. Because it handles twice as much data per cycle, the 286 will still be twice faster even if the XT operates at the same 10 MHz.

The 286 was a great machine in its day; there are millions of them still in use and giving good service. Even though they're obsolete, some companies still manufacture 286 motherboards. For minor upgrades, there are hundreds of 16-bit boards and peripherals that can be added to a 286 to give you more utility. The trouble is that the 286 is still a 16-bit system; it's still very slow compared to most newer systems. A 286 can run Windows, but only in standard mode, and it can't take full advantage of Windows and many other newer software packages.

If you have an old 286, the best upgrade would be to replace the old motherboard. You can easily drop in a new 386SX, 386DX, 486SX, 486DX, or Pentium processor. You can use all your plug-in boards, keyboard, disk drives, and other peripherals. You'll also have to buy new memory chips. Depending on what you want to use your computer for, you should have a minimum of 4MB, or even 8MB.

Upgrading a PC or XT to a 386SX

If you want something inexpensive that offers many of the advantages of the larger systems, a 386SX will run any of the new software and can use any of the 16-bit boards and hardware. The 386SX is a low-cost version of the 386DX. It handles data in 16-bit chunks externally, but internally it processes data at a 32-bit rate. It operates at a frequency of 20 to 40 MHz. It can run all the software that the 386DX or 486 can run, just a bit more slowly.

Upgrading a PC, XT, or 286 to a 386DX

The 386DX systems use the Intel 80386 CPU, which has 275,000 transistors and can handle data in 32-bit chunks. The original 386 motherboards were the same size as the original 286 motherboards, and baby 386 motherboards using VSLI chips were developed that were about one inch longer but still fit in the XT case.

There are several options available for 386 motherboards. CPU speed, on-board RAM, cache memory, built-in serial and parallel ports, VGA monitor drivers, and other options are available on some motherboards. Of course, the more goodies you can get already built into the motherboard, the more open slots you'll have.

You'll still be able to use your old plug-in boards and peripherals, but you might need to buy a new keyboard and you'll definitely need to buy memory chips. Some of the 386DX motherboards have sockets for fast static RAM (SRAM) cache memory. You don't have to fill the sockets, but your system will operate much faster if you have a good cache.

There are lots of vendors who sell 386 motherboards. There are also hundreds of options, such as speed or frequency, cache, and amount of installed memory. What you plan to use your computer for should be a determining factor in what you choose.

Upgrading an XT, 286, or 386 to a 486SX or 497DX

Most of the original 486 motherboards were the same size as the standard AT, but now they're baby sized. Most of them have several built-in options, such as serial and parallel ports, monitor adapters, floppy controller, and IDE hard disk interface. In addition, 486 motherboards have sockets for a static random access memory cache.

The 486SX is the same as the 486DX except it might operate at a slower frequency and it doesn't have a built-in math coprocessor. Many programs don't need the math coprocessor. If you don't need it, then the 486SX motherboard is a good low-cost alternative to a 486DX. The 486SX costs less than a fast 486DX, but the 486DX will operate at 25 MHz to 66 MHz, much faster than the SX.

At one time a 486DX CPU cost more than $1,000. Depending on the speed or frequency of the CPU, they now cost as little as $200 to $500. These prices will come down even more very soon. I suggest that you choose the fastest one you can afford, either a 486DX2-66 or an even faster 486DX4.

As in all of the other upgrades, just pull out the old motherboard and install a 486DX motherboard.

Internal frequency vs. external frequency

Strange things happen when a circuit operates at high frequencies. In a low-frequency circuit, the effects of stray capacitance and inductance can usually be ignored. But it's a very big factor in high-frequency circuits, and the higher the frequency the more of a problem it becomes. It can be such a problem that a circuit won't operate at all.

It's very difficult and costly to devise high-frequency circuits. The distance between the components can be a problem. Even if the distance between components is only a half inch or so, at high frequency a large portion of the signal could be lost. The distance between transistors inside the CPU is very small. The capacitive and inductive effects are also small, so the frequency inside the CPU can be much faster than that in the external circuits.

Upgrading a 486SX CPU with the Intel OverDrive

The Intel OverDrive CPUs can be used to upgrade a 486SX. Just remove the 486SX chip and drop in the OverDrive. There are several different versions and speeds; get one that matches the external speed of your 486SX. The OverDrive uses the same technology as the 486DX2 and doubles the internal processing speed of the chip.

Upgrading a 486DX CPU to a 486DX2 CPU

The 486DX2 is similar to the 386SX in one respect. The 386SX handles data in 16-bit chunks externally, but processes it 32 bits at a time internally. The 486DX2 50 handles data at a speed or frequency of 25 MHz externally, but it processes data internally at a speed of 50 MHz. The 486DX2 66 handles data at 33 MHz externally, but processes it at a rate of 66 MHz internally.

Doubling the internal rate of processing doesn't double the overall speed. It increases the performance by about 70%. For instance, a 486DX2 will increase the overall speed of a 25-MHz system to an equivalent speed of about 40 MHz.

If you have a 486DX, you can remove the CPU and plug in a 486DX2. One of the problems is that the CPU alone could cost almost as much as a new motherboard with a DX2 CPU. But if you need more speed, then dropping in a new 486DX2 CPU might be the simplest and easiest way to go. The cost of the 486 CPUs are going down every day.

Upgrading to Blue Lightning

IBM has a license agreement with Intel that allows them to make their own 80x86 CPUs, but they went a step further than Intel did with their 486DX2 CPUs. IBM modified a couple of Intel CPUs so they operate internally at three times their normal frequency. The 25-MHz CPUs operate internally at 75 MHz and the 33-MHz chips operate at 99 MHz. Since IBM is affectionately called "big blue," it was only natural for them to name their new chips Blue Lightning.

One problem is that IBM isn't allowed to sell these chips on the general market, which would place them in competition with Intel. The Blue Lightning chips can be sold only as part of IBM products. However, there's nothing that prohibits IBM from developing a motherboard with these chips installed and then sell the motherboard to the general public. They also sell Blue Lightning as an upgrade to people who own PS/2s.

Upgrading to the DX4

Intel hasn't been sleeping all this time. They've also been tinkering with their CPUs to make them faster internally. They modified several of the chips so that they'd operate at frequencies of 75, 83, and 100 MHz. Like the Blue Lightning, their 25-MHz CPU will operate three times faster, at 75 MHz. The 33-MHz chip will operate two and a half times faster, at 82.5 or 83 MHz. The 50-MHz CPU can boost the internal frequency to 100 MHz.

Compared to the 486DX2, the 486DX4 CPUs have several important differences. The most important is that they now operate at 3.3 volts instead of the normal 5 volts. This means that you can't just replace an older 486 CPU with the newer 486DX4 unless you have a special socket or motherboard designed for the 3.3-volt supply. Some companies are designing special adapter sockets with a regulator that reduces the 5 volts to 3.3. The CPU will plug into this socket, then the special socket will plug into the motherboard socket.

Another difference in the 486DX4 is that it now has 1.6 million transistors instead of the original 1.2 million. Some of these extra 400,000 transistors increase the built-in cache from 8K to 16K. This larger cache and higher frequency makes this machine almost as powerful as the 60-MHz Pentium, but at a lower price.

Upgrading a 486 to the P24T

Many 486s have a large, empty 238-pin socket on the motherboard. If you look at my 486 motherboard, shown in Fig. 4-8, you'll see an empty socket just above the CPU. This socket, if it conforms to the Intel specifications, will let you install a P24T in the 238-pin zero insertion force (ZIF) socket. The P24T is actually a Pentium OverDrive chip, similar to the 486 OverDrive chips.

If you're wondering about the advantage of buying a P24T, Intel claims it will provide a 50% boost in performance over the 486DX2. Intel says it's one of the better ways to extend the life of a 486.

There are some disadvantages. The 486 motherboard was designed for a 486. The P24T cannot give you the full 64-bit bus of a Pentium, and the P24T still isn't available near the end of 1994. I have no idea how much it will cost. It might be better to just go ahead and buy a Pentium in the first place.

Another disadvantage is if you've already paid $300 to $400 for a 486 CPU. Now you have to pay even more for a P24T, which might not even be able to support burst reads and writes. I don't know for sure, but the P24T might not be worth the extra money.

Pentium CPU module upgrade

A few companies are manufacturing a Pentium CPU module that can be plugged into the 486 socket. The modules have an on-baord frequency crystal, but you're still limited to the 486 32-bit bus. You might also have to buy a new BIOS upgrade.

Only a few larger companies are making the Pentium CPU module, so it will probably be rather expensive. It might also be proprietary and operate only in certain computers.

Upgrading to the Pentium

It's as easy to upgrade an older computer to a Pentium as it is to upgrade it to a 386 or any other configuration. A new Pentium motherboard will give you all the advantages of a new Pentium, but it's much less expensive than buying a completely new system. The Pentium has 3.1 million transistors in its CPU; it's the most powerful CPU available for PCs. The Pentium is capable of performing 112 million instructions per second (MIPS). Some of the reduced instruction set computers (RISC) type CPUs are capable of over 100 MIPS. The DEC Alpha can do 150 MIPS, but the Pentium is the first complex instruction set computer (CISC) system that comes close to the RISC.

The Pentium can handle data over a 64-bit bus externally, but processes data in 32-bit chunks internally. Being able to handle 32-bit data internally makes it compatible with software written for the 32-bit 386 and 486 CPUs. The Pentium can operate at 60, 66, 90, and 100 MHz. The 66-MHz Pentium can process data about three times faster than a 33-MHz 486, and 150 times faster than the XT could process data ten years ago.

The powerful Pentium allows graphics and CAD programs to run much faster; it also allows for full-screen motion pictures. The Pentium is ideal for running the 32-bit Windows NT and OS/2 applications.

At this time, the price of a Pentium CPU chip is about $750 for 1000 lot orders. A motherboard with CPU might cost from $1,100 to $2,000. The 486 systems were about this expensive when first introduced. Within two or three years, the Pentium will sell for about what the 486 currently sells for. Some vendors are selling complete Pentium systems for as little as $2,500. Keep in mind that these prices are for comparison only; by the time you read this, the prices will probably be much lower.

Pentiums without CPUs

I've seen a lot of ads for 486 and Pentium motherboards for very low prices. Then somewhere in small print it says "without CPU." The CPU costs from $250 for a 486 up to $1,000 or more for a Pentium. You have to pay close attention to the ads. Some are rather misleading. In their defense, one reason some vendors don't list a price for the 486 and Pentium motherboard with a CPU is because there are several different CPUs and other options from which you can choose.

Upgrading to the PowerPC

The IBM reduced instruction-set computer (RISC) PowerPC uses the same basic components that all ISA complex instruction-set computers (CISC) use. The PowerPC motherboards are the same size as other baby motherboards and fit in the same size cases.

The PowerPC RISC machines are less expensive than the Pentium. At this time, the RISC CPU for the IBM PowerPC costs about $450, just half as much as a Pentium CPU. The PowerPC and other RISC machines also tend to be faster and more powerful than the Pentium but RISC machines require special software in order to run most DOS programs, so the overall operating cost could be a bit higher. The next chapter goes into more detail about this very important new PC.

Sources

The best place to look for any of the motherboards and components mentioned is in computer magazines. They're full of ads, and where you can get a good idea of what something should cost. If you live in a large city, there are probably computer stores and computer swaps once in a while.

If you can't get to a store or a computer swap, then order through the mail from the ads in computer magazines. Make sure to read the ads closely, however. The advertised price of many 486 motherboards is without a CPU. Almost all boards are also advertised without memory. See chapter 19 for more about mail order.

Upgrading to a new motherboard

Now that you've bought a new motherboard, you can easily install it in a few simple steps. The following basic procedures can be used for installing any of the motherboards.

Step 1: Know your CMOS setup.

This is very important! You must be able to tell the CMOS setup on your new system what type of hard disk drive you have. If you don't furnish all the proper information (type, number of cylinders, number of heads, and number of sectors), you might not be able to access the data on your hard disk.

If you don't have your system configuration written down somewhere, run your system CMOS setup to determine the data. Many older machines use several different methods to access the CMOS setup. If you have documentation, it should tell you how to access the setup mode. On most systems, you can press the Esc or Del key while the system is booting up. On some systems, if you hold down any key while it's booting up you'll be given an error message and told to press F1. This usually puts you into the setup mode. Run it and write down the type of drives; the number of cylinders, heads, and sectors; the landing zone; and any other information.

If you can't tell your new CMOS memory what kind of drives you have, you might not be able to install the drives with your new motherboard. And if you can't install your hard disk drives you won't be able to access any of the data on them.

Step 2: Back up your hard disks.

You might not need it, but you should stop and make a complete backup of your hard disk before you remove the old motherboard. You should always have a current backup; if you don't, shame on you. Chapter 10 discusses the reasons why you should have backups at all times.

Step 3: Mark and disconnect cables on the back panel.

The next thing to do is to shut off the power and disconnect the power cord and keyboard cable. There will probably be several other cables on the back panel of the PC. It's very easy to forget how and where things were plugged in, so it might be a good idea to use a felt-tip pen and put a distinctive mark on the cable connector and the board connector. When you get ready to plug the cables back into the new system, all you have to do is line up the various marks on the cables and board connectors. This ensures that every cable is plugged back into the same board. After you've marked all the cables, disconnect them.

Step 4: Remove the case cover.

Locate and remove the screws that hold the case or cover on. Most early systems have five screws on the back panel, one in each corner and one in the top center. The four screws that hold the power supply in place shouldn't be removed. Once the cover screws are removed, you can slide the cover off toward the front. Some of the newer cases have different screws to hold them on. You shouldn't have any trouble determining which ones.

Step 5: Make a diagram before disassembly.

Once the cover is removed, before doing anything else take a piece of paper and make a rough drawing of where each board is plugged in and any cable that's plugged into it. Then use a felt-tip pen to mark each cable and connector so you can match the cable and connectors back up to the same board. Some cables can be plugged in backwards or upside down. You can prevent this if you mark the connectors. Note in particular how the two connectors from the power supply are plugged into the motherboard. The four black wires are in the center. These two connectors must be connected to the new motherboard in the same way.

Most of the cables are ribbon cables from the floppy and hard drives to the controller. You should be able to leave the cables connected to the boards and just pull the boards out of the motherboard slot. You shouldn't have to remove any of the disk drives. Leave the cables plugged into the drives if possible.

Step 6: Remove all of the plug-in boards and cables.

The cables from the power supply are plugged into the motherboard, usually near the right rear corner of the motherboard. At the front there might also be several small wires for the front-panel light-emitting diodes (LEDs) and for the speaker. If these small wires and connectors aren't marked, take some masking tape and put labels on them. Your new motherboard will have similar pins for the connectors, but they might be in a different location.

Once you've removed all the boards and disconnected all the cables, look for a screw near the front center of the motherboard and another in the rear of the motherboard. Remove the screws, pull the motherboard to the left, and then lift it out. You might have to jiggle it a bit. The motherboard has grooved plastic stand-offs that slide into raised slots.

Step 7: Set switches and jumpers and install the motherboard.

You should have received some documentation with your new motherboard. Set any switches or jumpers to configure the system. Install any extra memory chips. Make sure you've installed all the plastic stand-offs in the proper holes, then drop the motherboard into the slots and push it to the right until it locks in place. Replace the screws in the front and back of the motherboard.

Connect all the front-panel LED wires and the speaker wires. The motherboard should have some markings to indicate where each small connector should be plugged in. You might have to refer to your documentation for some wires.

Next, connect the power-supply cables to the motherboard. Note that this connector can be plugged in incorrectly. When connected properly, the four black wires are in the center, adjacent to each other. The power-supply connector is usually two separate cables with six wires in each cable. They're sometimes marked P8 and P9.

If you have built-in systems on the motherboard, such as pins for IDE, a floppy controller, and COM ports, connect the proper cables to these pins. The motherboard should indicate which is pin 1. The flat-ribbon cables have a different colored wire on one side—either red, black, blue, or red stripes—that indicates pin 1. Make sure the cables are plugged in properly.

Step 8: Reinstall the boards.

Reinstall all your plug-in boards and reconnect any cables to the boards that were disconnected. Connect the monitor and keyboard. Plug in the power cord. Recheck all your connections to make sure everything is plugged in properly, then turn on the power. Make sure to try the system before you put the cover back on. This way if it doesn't work, it's fairly easy to check all the boards and cables to make sure they're installed correctly.

Step 9: Turn the computer on and boot up.

If you've reconnected everything correctly, the system should work. Depending on what type of BIOS you have, it will probably tell you that the time and date isn't set and give you an error message about your drives. Check your documentation for instructions on how to set the time and date, and how to tell the CMOS memory what type of floppy and hard drives you've installed.

If you did everything properly, then you shouldn't have any problems. If you have problems, check your documentation, all the cables, switches, and boards. If the problem remains, check chapter 19 for troubleshooting information.

Step 10: Reinstall the cover.

If everything works okay, put the cover back on.

5

Upgrading an
IBM PS/1 or PS/2

The PS/1 and PS/2 systems have a lot of goodies built into the motherboard. They have built-in floppy and hard disk controllers, monitor adapters, parallel and serial ports for printers, ports, and connectors for mice and other peripherals.

The PS/1 and some of the PS/2 machines were designed to be like the Macintosh. They had just about everything a home user could want, so there was no need to add anything. It was great for people who didn't want to bother about technology. All they needed to worry about was finding a wall outlet and plugging it in.

On the downside, IBM computers and components are usually much more expensive than clones. One reason is that the IBM PS/2s are similar to the Apple products in that they're a special, proprietary design. There are millions of clones that are all the same design. The competition and large number of clone users keep the costs down. Because of the much smaller PS/2 market, not too many companies design and develop components for these systems.

Automated manufacture

The integration of utilities on the motherboard makes it possible for IBM to manufacture the PS/1 and PS/2 systems almost entirely with automated equipment. The automation vastly reduces labor costs, but, unfortunately, IBM doesn't pass these savings along to the consumer. Someone estimated that it probably costs IBM less than $150 to manufacture a complete PS/2. That same computer will cost you over $1,500. But, of course, IBM has a lot of overhead. And even though it seems like IBM is making a lot of money selling a computer for a $1,350 profit margin, they lost several million dollars last year.

One good thing about automation is that the human factor, which can be responsible for many errors, has been almost eliminated. So the systems produced by IBM are very reliable.

Advantages of built-in utilities

It's great to have many utilities on the motherboard. All computers should have them. This integration reduces, or eliminates in some cases, the need for cables. Cables can be the source for many problems. Integration also reduces problems by reducing the number of solder joints and components. The more solder joints and components there are, the more chance for errors and failures.

Disadvantages of built-ins

There are also some disadvantages. If one of these utilities fail, then the entire motherboard might have to be replaced. The motherboard is usually the most expensive component in the system. On clone ISA systems, these utilities are often contained on plug-in boards. Most clone motherboards have eight slots available for plug-in boards. If one of these boards fail, it's fairly inexpensive to replace the single board.

Another disadvantage is that there are newer and better products being developed every day. For instance, there are new monitor adapter boards that are much better than the built-in systems on the older PS/2s. If you have an ISA system, you can easily replace and upgrade older boards with new Super VGA or XGA boards.

Replacing the motherboard

New PS/1s and PS/2s have been redesigned; they now have 386 and 486 systems. It's possible to order a new motherboard from IBM to replace your old one. If you wanted to, you could even upgrade to a 99-MHz Blue Lightning or even a PowerPC. Call IBM at 800-IBM-2YOU (800-426-2968) for Personal Systems. Or call their fax-back service at 800-426-4329. Ask for new user instructions, then Personal Systems documents.

Low-profile small computer cases

Another major disadvantage of the PS/2 is that IBM seems to be obsessed with making the computer case and system as small as possible. Only two or three expansion slots are provided in most of the systems. Even then, because the case is so small, some of the boards have to be mounted horizontally instead of vertically.

The original PS/1 was so small that it didn't have room for any expansion slots or even the power supply. So the power supply was mounted in the monitor system. Power supplies are one of the components that fail most often. If a PS/1 power supply fails, you might have to replace the whole monitor system. Newer systems have been changed.

Making the computer small also doesn't leave room for installing a CD-ROM or another hard disk. Today, CD-ROMs are an essential part of a computer. It's also essential today to have large-capacity hard disks.

One of the most important reasons for the early popularity of the IBM PC was the fact that it had a lot of room for expansion. There were thousands of plug-in boards, such as network interfaces, fax/modem cards, sound cards, and special graphics boards, that could be used to configure a computer almost any way imaginable. IBM realized that not leaving room for expansion was a serious mistake. They now provide larger cases with one or more expansion slots.

The first PS/1 used the 286 CPU. They now have models that use other CPUs, even the 486DX2-66.

PCMCIA

Just because PCMCIA cards are discussed in this chapter doesn't mean they can't be used in other systems. PCMCIA cards can be used in laptops, notebooks, desktops, towers, ISA, EISA, or MCA systems. They're a very easy way to upgrade a system.

IBM and several other companies have developed a series of PCMCIA cards that can be plugged into a PCMCIA slot. PCMCIA stands for Personal Computer Memory Card International Association. Originally, all cards were designed to add memory to laptop systems. There are now dozens of different cards and devices that can be plugged into these slots. Besides memory, there are now PCMCIA cards such as sound cards, SCSI interface cards, network interface cards (NICs), fax/modem cards, and hard disk drives.

Almost all laptop and notebook systems sold today come standard with PCMCIA slots, but many desktop systems also have them. To add PCMCIA to desktop computer, you can plug a special interface board into one of the motherboard slots. A cable assembly with a PCMCIA slot then plugs into the back of the board.

The original PCMCIA was type I, a thin credit-card-sized memory card, and the slot was 3.3 millimeter thick (.117 inches). Later, a type II design was added, which opened the slot to 5 mm or .195 inches. They've now added a type III specification, which is 10.5 mm or .4095 of an inch thick. The larger slots will accept any of the cards designed for the smaller slots. Toshiba has developed a type IV 16-mm (.624-inch) slot for some of their portables. Type IV hasn't yet been approved by the PCMCIA committee, but it should be by the time you read this.

Quatech, at 800-553-1170, Greystone, at 408-866-4739, and several other companies have developed PCMCIA slot systems that can be installed in an accessible bay on the front of a computer. Greystone's CardDock (see Fig. 5-1) fits in a standard 5¼-inch bay, and has either two or four slots. PCMCIA devices, like the one in Fig. 5-2, can then be plugged in or out just as if it were a floppy disk. Much like a floppy disk, you don't have to turn the power off to insert or unplug a PCMCIA card.

One of the advantages of being able to plug in or unplug a card is that you might have several cards and want to plug in just the one you need at that time. If you don't need your sound card all the time, you could remove it and plug in your fax/modem. You could do the same with the boards in a desktop, but you'd have to shut the system down, remove the cover, remove the board, and replace it with whatever you need. It's much easier to swap cards with a PCMCIA system.

If necessary, you can mount two or more PCMCIA slots for greater versatility. A PCMCIA slot is probably one of the better ways to expand a PS/2 or any other system.

5-1
A CardDock PCMCIA adapter from
Greystone.

5-2 A PCMCIA adapter and interface card from Quatech, Inc.

Card bus

The old ISA bus has some severe limitations. Many people think it should be updated and changed. There is currently a proposed fusion of the PCMCIA with the peripheral component interconnect (PCI) bus. Here are just a few of the things that might make such a system desirable: A PCMCIA/PCI would let the bus operate much faster, the cards could be inserted and removed without opening the computer case, and they'd be plug-and-play with no worry about IRQs or jumpers. In an article in *Electronic Engineering Times*, Ron Wilson says that it might just be the "next big thing (NBT)." One other thing he says that PCMCIA has going for it is that it has a "high cute factor."

One disadvantage to this system is that there are billions of dollars' worth of ISA boards in existence that won't be displaced overnight. But there's no reason why PCMCIA can't coexist with the ISA, EISA, MCA, PCI, and VLB bus systems.

Types of PCMCIA cards

There are several types of PCMCIA cards and devices. Here are just a few:

Memory

PCMCIA cards were originally developed to add extra memory to laptops and notebook systems, so there are a lot of memory cards available. The memory cards have flash memory, DRAM, or SRAM. Memory is available from 1MB up to 16MB.

Audio adapters

The IBM PCMCIA audio adapter provides 16-bit stereo sound to a system. It can be used for music and MIDI synthesis, presentation, and text-to-speech applications. The audio adapter has a built-in microphone and a line-out headphone jack. Creative Labs, DSP Solutions, Media Vision, New Media Corp., and Turtle Beach Systems all offer PCMCIA sound cards.

SCSI interfaces

Many of the companies listed previously also have SCSI PCMCIA cards that allow you to attach a CD-ROM, hard disk, or other SCSI device.

Hard disks

MiniStor, at 408-943-0165, and several other companies are now manufacturing 1.8-inch hard drives that can be plugged into one of the PCMCIA slots. MiniStor has a 260MB and 340MB drive in type III PCMCIA format. (These drives use Stacker data compression to achieve the high capacity.) Figure 5-3 shows a MiniStor drive for a PCMCIA slot.

Original PS/1s and PS/2s often came with a 30MB or 40MB hard disk. If you want to add a second hard disk, there's no room for one. A PCMCIA system can solve that problem.

5-3 A MiniStor hard disk designed for a PCMCIA slot. A disk this size can store up to 340MB.

LAN cards

IBM and several other companies have developed network interface PCMCIA cards for local-area networks (LANs). IBM has PCMCIA cards for infrared wireless network connections.

Fax-modem cards

IBM and several other companies have developed fax-modem cards. At the present time, most of these components are the older and slower modems and faxes, 2400 and 9600 bps. By the time you read this, several companies will probably have up-to-date fax-modem cards.

Docking stations

Greystone, at 408-866-4739, Zenith Data Systems, at 800-553-0331, Texas Instrument, at 800-848-3927, and several other companies have developed docking stations for notebooks. These are expansion boxes that have provisions for adding standard plug-in cards, bays for adding a floppy or hard disk, tape backup, and other ISA cards. There are no standards for docking stations, so there's a wide variation in the number of available slots, bays, expansion utilities, and capabilities. A portable computer can be attached to a docking station and have all the versatility of a large desktop computer. A docking station could also be used to expand the capability of some desktop computers.

PCMCIA sources

There are several PCMCIA devices available. Here are just a few of the companies who provide them:

IBM	800-426-0181
Quatech	800-553-1170
Transcend	800-886-5590
Creative Labs	408-428-6600
DSP Solutions	916-621-1787
Media Vision	510-770-8600
New Media Corp.	800-443-0550
Turtle Beach	800-645-5640
Kingston Tech	714-435-2600
MiniStor	408-943-0165
Texas Instruments	800-848-3927
Zenith Data	800-553-0331

PS/1 and PS/2 differences

IBM created a very large number of variations from the established standards with their PS/1 and PS/2 models, but some of the earlier models are just slightly different. IBM knew that not everyone would switch to the microchannel architecture (MCA) system, so PS/1 and the PS/2 model numbers 25 up through model 40 are ISA systems. These systems can use many of the available ISA boards that are available if they have any unused slots.

The PS/2 models 50 and up are strictly MCA systems. They can accept only MCA boards. Models 56 and 57 are 16-bit systems, and models 70 through 95 are 32-bit systems.

Differences in ISA and MCA

When IBM introduced the 16-bit AT, it was designed to address 16 megabytes of memory, so a total of 24 lines were needed. Several other new bus functions were also added to the AT bus. They needed the 62 pins already in use on the bus, plus several more for the new functions. They needed a larger connector, but a new connector could make all the hardware available at that time obsolete. Someone at IBM came up with a brilliant design. They simply added a second 36-pin connector in front of the standard 62-pin connector. The new connector readily accepted both 8-bit and 16-bit boards.

Later, when the 386 and 486 were developed, they still used the AT standard bus. Many of the early 386 and 486 ISA machines had a special 32-bit connector for plug-in memory boards. Almost all the motherboards today have sockets for 32-bit memory chips. Other than the 32-bit bus for memory, all the other I/O functions use the standard 16-bit AT bus.

In 1987, IBM introduced their new PS/2 line with microchannel architecture. This system added many new functions to the computer, but it also used a new bus system that was completely incompatible with older hardware. The new connector system was incompatible with the ISA system boards. For comparison, refer back to Fig. 2-1, which shows the edge connectors of an ISA board and an MCA board.

MCA offers some real advantages over the old original IBM standard. One of its excellent features is programmed option select (POS). MCA plug-in boards have a unique identification, or ID. When a board is plugged in, the bus recognizes it by its ID and automatically configures the board for use with the system interrupts, ports, and other system configurations. If there are any switches on the board, it will tell you how they should be set.

I recently spent almost a whole day trying to install a board that had three DIP switches and three different jumpers. The switches and jumpers had to be set so the board wouldn't conflict with the rest of the system. The three DIP switches alone had eight different possible configurations. The three different jumpers also had eight different possible configurations, and the two together totalled 64 possible combinations. Turning the computer off, setting the switches, then turning it back on and waiting for it to reboot between each combination could be awfully time-consuming and frustrating. I had a manual, but like most of them it was practically worthless. A PS/2 with MCA POS could have saved me all the time and frustration.

The MCA system was introduced in 1987, and some of the major players in the ISA world have finally recognized the importance of the programmed option select system. They've decided it's time to develop a similar system, and call it plug-and-play. The motherboards and plug-in boards that conform to this system will do about the same thing the POS system does. They'll automatically scan the boards already installed and then configure themselves for whatever IRQ or memory area is available. There are several boards that are already capable of this, and even more will be available shortly.

MCA offers several other very good features, such as bus arbitration. This is a system that evaluates bus requests and allocates time based on priority. This relieves the CPU of some of its burdens. The MCA bus is also much faster than the old AT bus. There are several other excellent benefits to MCA, but IBM is still the single source. There are a few third-party manufacturers, but because there's very little competition MCA boards cost much more than ISA boards.

Upgrade difficulties

Some PS/1 models have no slots at all for adding extra boards, and some later models have only one or two available slots. Most PS/2s have two or three available slots. There's a tremendous number of boards that could be used on these machines, but the small number of slots severely limits you. You'll have to make some tough decisions as to what to buy.

Except for a few third-party boards, IBM is the one and only authorized source for upgrades, replacements, and repairs. Since they have no competition, the parts and supplies are rather expensive. In contrast, there are thousands of dealers for ISA clone products. The heavy competition keeps the prices down.

Another reason that IBM products are more expensive than clone products is that there are a large number of distributors between the manufacturing plant and the expensive showrooms. Each distributor, or person who handles the product, gets a small piece of the pie. Many clone products go directly from the manufacturer to the dealer or end user.

In the last few years, IBM has lost a lot of money. In order to survive, they've taken a long hard look at the way the clone people do business. IBM has now eliminated many of their middlemen. They've now set up several companies for direct mail and distribution.

In the past, if you needed a replacement component, you had to take your computer to an authorized dealer for the necessary repairs. That policy has also changed. IBM will now sell you any component you need. Of course, they would still like to have you go to their authorized dealers, especially if the component is under warranty. But they no longer insist on it.

Upgrade components from IBM

IBM has a large number of upgrade components. For instance, you can buy the following PS/2 MCA 486 components:

- 487SX math coprocessor
- 486-25/50 processor upgrade (SX models only)
- 486DX2-50 processor upgrade (25-MHz SX models only)
- Enhanced 486 DX 50-MHz processor upgrade
- Blue Lightning 486 99-MHz CPU

You can order upgrade parts for any PS/1 or PS/2 model, but first you have to know what the part number is. IBM sells reference manuals for all their systems. These manuals are quite detailed and highly technical, and they probably contain more information than you need. They're also not free. For instance, IBM sells a separate manual for each model they manufacture, called *Guide to Operations and Quick Reference Manual Part Numbers and Prices*. There are different prices for each manual. The manual for model 25, part number 75X1051, sells for $28.75; the manual for model 25 286, part number 15F2179, sells for $42.50; the manual for model 60, part number 68X2213, sells for $54.25; and the manual for model 80, part number 15F2186, sells for $63.75. They have manuals for the XT, AT, and other systems. They even have manuals for the PCjr, part number 1502292, for a price of $23.25.

They also have *Hardware Maintenance Manual Part Numbers and Prices* manuals, and they offer libraries of the manuals for the various systems. These libraries cost from $150 up to $268. Here are some IBM telephone numbers:

Technical and service publications	800-426-7282
Authorized dealer locator	800-447-4700

IBM part number ID and lookup   303-924-4015
IBM general information   800-426-3333

You can use a credit card when ordering by telephone. I probably don't have to tell you that IBM is a very large company, spread out all over the world. There are hundreds and hundreds of different phone numbers, including a lot of 800 numbers. When you call, be prepared to listen to a string of recorded options. For PS/2 systems, probably the best number to call is 800-426-2968. There's also a help number, 800-772-2272.

Fax-back

The IBM Personal Computer Co. is located in Austin, Texas. They handle most of the parts for the PS/1 and PS/2 lines, and they have a fax-back system, which can be accessed at 800-426-4329. New users can order catalogs that list information and part numbers, and then call back and order what they need.

A word of caution, though—when I called, the automatic telephone answering device gave me a list of options. When it asked which catalog I wanted, I wasn't sure so I said all of them. It started sending me page after page after page, 82 in all. It used up all the paper I had in my fax machine. I know next time to be a bit more selective in my choices. If I had listened a bit more closely, I would have asked for new user instructions, which would have been four pages, including a navigation map, or menu of all the information in the system. The navigation map shows which steps to take to order any of the documents.

You'll probably want to order the list for Personal Systems, which is about 40 pages because it includes OS/2 machines, printers, LANs, monitors, adapters, and many other IBM products.

Clock tripler CPUs

IBM has an arrangement with Intel that allows them to manufacture CPUs identical to those made by Intel, but they're limited to making the CPUs for their own machines. IBM improved on the Intel 486 by tripling the internal clock speed and called it the Blue Lightning. Intel later introduced the 486DX4, which does the same thing.

IBM has developed an upgrade for those users who have PS/2 model 56 and 57 systems with a 20-MHz 386SX, 20-MHz 386SLC or 25/50-MHz 486SLC2. The CPUs in these machines can be replaced with the clock tripler upgrade CPU. At the present time, the processor card is priced at $535.

PS/1 and PS/2 parts and components

There are several small companies who now offer parts and components for PS/1 and PS/2 machines. Several dealers also buy used PS/2s. These used systems are then repaired, refurbished, and resold. Some systems that can't be easily repaired are stripped down and the parts are sold to anyone who needs them. They're usually sold for a price less than what IBM would charge for a new component. The parts are usually tested before shipping and a warranty is provided. I would have no problem with buying a used electronic part, but I wouldn't recommend buying a used mechanical part such as a disk drive.

Several magazines now carry ads from these companies. One of them is the *The Processor*, which is sent free to qualified subscribers. To get a free subscription request form, call 800-334-7443 or write to:

The Processor
P.O. Box 85518
Lincoln, NE 68501-9856

In order to qualify, you might have to exaggerate just a bit when filling out the form. I'm not telling you to lie, but people who say they make purchasing decisions for their company will usually get a free subscription. It's not likely that anyone will come out to your house to make sure you spend $50,000 or more for computer equipment each year. Here are just a few of the companies who advertised PS/2 components in a recent issue of *The Processor*:

Century Computer Marketing	310-827-0999
Computer Reset	214-276-8072
DakTech Company	800-325-3238
Federal Computer Exchange	404-642-2400
Gemini Parts	407-998-8735
Hartford Computer Group	708-934-3380
Selecterm	800-676-4944
Shreve Systems	800-227-3971

These companies will have almost any component or part you might need to repair or upgrade a PS/2. Call them for a list of their products.

At the present time, you won't see many ads for PS/2 parts in most larger magazines because the cost of an ad is based on the magazine's circulation. The larger the circulation, the higher the cost. There are many small companies who would like to advertise and let you know what they have, but the ad costs are prohibitive. As these small companies become more successful, you'll see their ads in the larger magazines.

Hard disk upgrades

Many companies offer larger hard disk drives. Manufacturers have vastly increased the capacity of hard disk drives without increasing their physical size. In some cases, they've more than doubled the capacity. Many of the early PS/2s were sold with 20MB to 30MB hard disks. It's very difficult to do any productive computing now with less than 200MB, and in some instances even 200MB isn't enough.

The main difference in the drives used in PS/2s and other systems is that PS/2s don't use cables. The IBM drives are plugged directly into a motherboard connector. They're mounted on a special "sled" that positions them so they mate correctly with the motherboard connector. The power lines and all data lines are in this one connector. The old MFM and RLL drives, and some other hard drives, have three different connectors and cables, a 34-wire flat-ribbon cable, a 20-wire ribbon cable, and a power cable.

Many companies offer direct replacement hard disks for the PS/1 and PS/2, and other companies offer special kits and controllers. Because it's an IBM machine, however, you can expect to pay up to twice as much as you'd pay for a hard drive for an ISA machine. I'm looking at a full-page ad in *PC Computing* for the Memory Super Source Company, at 800-457-6937. They have several PS/2 hard drives advertised, along with ads for hard drives for ISA PCs. For a 125MB IDE drive for a PS/2, they charge $414; a 130MB IDE drive for an ISA PC is $172. A 512MB IDE for a PS/2 costs $1043, and a SCSI for a PS/2 is $1204; a 540MB IDE for an ISA costs $413, and a SCSI for an ISA is $490.

This company also has microchannel IDE controllers or interfaces for sale at $169, and SCSIs at $179. You can buy an ISA IDE interface for less than $15, and a SCSI interface for $40 or more.

Hard cards

Several hard disk companies manufacture hard disk drives on plug-in cards. Kingston, at 714-435-2600, has a combination memory and hard card for PS/2s. This is a long standard card with the hard drive on one end and SIMM memory sockets on the other end that can accept up to 64MB of memory.

Here's information from a few ads from *Computer Shopper*, *Byte*, *PC World*, *Computer Reseller*, and *PC Week*:

Company	Phone	What they sell
Computer Techniques	407-453-8783	PS/2 hard drives
Compu.D	800-783-5783	Many PS/2 components
Data Solutions	714-637-5060	PS/2 hard drives
Dynamic Electronics	800-845-8228	Many PS/2 components
General Technics	800-487-2538	PS/2 hard drives
InterSolutions	800-666-0566	Many PS/2 components
jb Technologies	800-688-0908	PS/2 hard drives
MegaHaus	800-426-0560	PS/1 and PS/2 drives
Page Computer	800-886-0055	Many PS/2 components
Universal Memory	800-899-8518	PS/2 drives and memory

Memory upgrades

Many of the larger magazines carry ads for PS/1 and PS/2 memory upgrades. Almost every company who provides memory chips for other computers also provide them for the IBM systems. Here are just a few who provide PS/1 and PS/2 memory upgrades:

Altex Electronics	800-531-5369
AMT International	408-942-9695
PS International	800-444-1341
CitiTronics	818-855-5688
CyberTron Components	408-294-8700

I.C. Express   800-877-8188
L.A. Trade   800-433-3726
Microchip Company   800-848-9102
NECS   800-922-6327
PMP   800-424-1968
RSVPeripherals   800-554-7787
Source   800-535-5892
TDSI   408-287-4410
Worldwide Tech.   800-457-6937

BIOS upgrades

If you have one of the early PS/2 models 30 through 40, you might need to upgrade your BIOS. All the information regarding the BIOS system in chapter 7 applies to PS/2 ISA machines. Since they're ISA machines, they should be compatible with all other ISA machines, but they aren't.

I listed several BIOS suppliers in chapter 7, but only Unicore Software, at 800-800-2467, said their chips would work with a model 30 machine. All the other companies said their chips wouldn't work in a PS/2 system. It's a bit expensive, but your only source would seem to be IBM.

Many of the newer motherboard manufacturers install BIOS in flash memory. Then whenever it needs to be updated or upgraded, you can easily do so over a modem or by way of a floppy disk.

External drives

PS/2 systems are made so small that there isn't enough room to mount more than two drives. You can have two floppy drives or one floppy and one hard drive. They come with the 3½-inch floppy drive, but there might be times when you need a 5¼-inch drive. You'll probably also need a larger-capacity hard drive or a second hard drive, and you might want to install a CD-ROM drive or a tape backup system. But there's just no room in these systems.

Several companies have developed external drives for the PS/2. Many of them use a cable that can be plugged into the motherboard with a special connector. A cable is then run to the outside of the case for the drive.

Parallel port drives

Several companies have developed hard drives that can work off the printer's parallel port. The printer cable is unplugged and the cable from the drive is plugged into the port. If you intend to install the external drive permanently, most of them have a connector for the printer. When the printer is plugged into this connector, it operates as usual. Or you might just temporarily plug the external drive into the parallel port to download some files or back up your internal hard disk.

One company who offers these drives is the Pacific Rim Systems, 510-782-1013. Another company that provides external drives is MicroSolutions, 815-756-3411. They have 3½-inch and 5¼-inch floppy and hard drives that can be plugged into the parallel printer port. Axonix, at 800-866-9797, has small portable hard disks in 20MB, 40MB, 100MB, and 200MB capacities. Sysgen, at 800-821-2151, has portable hard drives that use the parallel port in several different capacities, from 40MB to 210MB. Kingston Technology, at 714-435-2600, also has several external hard drives that can be plugged into the parallel connector, in capacities from 52MB up to 240MB. Kingston has also developed several other upgrade components. Call them for a catalog.

SyQuest, at 800-437-9367, manufactures several hard disk drives with 88MB removable cartridges. They also have a model that attaches to the parallel port. These systems are great for backup, security, and transporting data.

External tape backup

There are several companies who provide tape backup systems that can be plugged into the parallel port, just like the hard drives previously mentioned. Sigen, at 408-737-3904, has several different tape drives that can be operated from the parallel port. Another company who provides portable tape backup systems is ADPI, at 513-339-2241.

External CD-ROM drives

CD-ROM drives are almost as necessary as floppy drives today. The PS/2 might not have the room to install a CD-ROM internally, but you can add one externally. Most companies who manufacture CD-ROM drives offer both internal and external models. Most of these drives use the SCSI interface. If you have a SCSI interface card, it probably has a connector on the back for attaching external devices, so connecting an external CD-ROM drive to a PS/2 can be fairly simple if you have a spare slot for the interface card. If you don't have a spare slot for a SCSI card, you might be able to install one through a PCMCIA slot.

You can buy a fairly good internal CD-ROM drive from $200 to $300. An external CD-ROM drive will cost from $100 to $200 more than an internal system. One reason for the extra cost is because external models need a built-in power supply.

Accelerator boards

An accelerator board is a card that has a 386 or 486 CPU and other associated circuitry on it. It can be plugged into a model 25, 30, or 40 and immediately transform the system into a much more powerful and faster machine. These boards can't give you all the benefits of the actual 386 or 486 machine, but they can give you most of it.

At one time an accelerator board was one of the better ways to upgrade a compatible clone system, but you can now buy a complete 386 or 486 clone motherboard for less than the cost of an accelerator board. Motherboards for PS/2 systems, however, must still come from IBM and they're still very expensive, so the accelerator boards are a very good alternative for upgrading.

Kingston has upgrade processors that can be used with all PS/2s, turning a PS/2 286 into a 386 and a 386 into a 486. The upgrade processors come with detailed, step-by-step installation instructions.

The Cyrix 486 CPU

Cyrix (214-994-8387) has a 486 CPU that's pin-compatible with the 386DX chip. Just remove the 386 CPU and plug in the Cyrix CPU. This chip also comes with a co-processor that plugs into the 387 socket, which will give you the coprocessing ability of a true 486DX system.

The Cyrix 486 CPU operates internally at 40 MHz, but it can be used in any 386DX system and also in the PS/2 386 systems. This upgrade provides almost all the power and functionality of a true 486DX 33-MHz system. The Cyrix 486 CPU costs about half as much as the Intel 486DX 33-MHz chip. It's the easiest and least expensive way I know of to upgrade to 486 power.

Processor upgrade modules

Kingston (714-435-2600) also has processor modules that can transform a 286 into a 386 or 486. These modules will operate in any of the ISA 286 PS/1 or PS/2 machines. The chips can be installed in most ISA clone machines and in the 286-based PS/2s. They use an Intel chip for the 386 and a Cyrix chip for the 486 conversion. This is a very easy upgrade; just pull off the cover, locate the 286 CPU, and plug in the new module.

Cumulus Corp., at 216-464-2211, and Evergreen Technologies, at 800-733-0934, are a few of the other companies who make processor modules for a 286 upgrade.

Installing a component in a PS/1 or PS/2

The PS/2 system requires very few tools to work on it. The plastic cases just snap together, so you can completely break down and take apart the entire system without any tools. By pressing plastic catches and latches, you can take apart the whole system, so it should be no problem to install or remove a component.

Troubleshooting

Troubleshooting PS/1 and PS/2 systems is no different than troubleshooting ISA systems. Even MCA systems are about the same when it comes to troubleshooting. There are several diagnostic programs that work on PS/2 as well as ISA systems.

POST cards

When a computer is first turned on, the BIOS checks the system. This is called a power-on self test (POST). If it finds a component or peripheral that isn't working properly, such as a stuck key on the keyboard or a nonresponsive floppy drive, it will give you an error code on the screen. (See chapter 20 for a listing of these codes.) Several companies have developed POST card diagnostic boards that are quite comprehensive.

Most POST cards, such as the POST-Probe from Micro 2000 (818-547-0125), come with a manual that explains all the codes and tests. The POST-Probe can be used on any ISA system, which would include models 25 through 40. It also comes with an adapter so it can be used with MCA models 50 and up.

The R.A.C.E.R. card from Ultra-X, at 800-722-3789, does everything the POST-Probe does, and in some cases more. Ultra-X has two different cards, one for ISA and one for MCA. Their cards are a bit less expensive than the POST-Probe. They claim that you can buy both of their cards for about what the POST-Probe costs.

Is an upgrade worthwhile?

Before you go to the trouble of upgrading a PS/2 system, do some research and add up the cost of necessary components. You might be better off buying a completely new system.

Apple, IBM, Compaq, and a few other companies go to great lengths to differentiate their products, but not necessarily in order to make them better. One reason they make them different is so you have to buy replacement parts from them.

6
CHAPTER

Memory

Memory is one of the most crucial elements of a computer. Computing as we know it would not be possible without memory. The PC uses two primary types of memory: ROM and RAM.

ROM

Read-only memory (ROM) is memory that cannot be altered or changed. The principal use of ROM in PCs is for the basic input/output system (BIOS). The BIOS contains routines that set up the computer when you first turn it on, and facilitates the transfer of data among peripherals.

ROM programs are usually burned into erasable programmable read-only memory (EPROM) chips. The ROM BIOS for an early XT could be programmed onto a 128K chip. The 486 ROM BIOS needs 512K of memory. It's possible to print out the programs stored in ROM. To give you some idea of how much 512K is, the entire text in some of my earlier books was less than 512K.

RAM

If you open a file from a hard or floppy disk, the files and data are read from the disk and placed in random-access memory (RAM). When you load in a program, be it word processing, spreadsheet, database, or whatever, you're working in the system RAM. If you're writing, programming, or creating another program, you're working in RAM. Actually, it's dynamic RAM, or DRAM. *Random access* means that you can find, address, change, or erase any single byte among several million bytes.

You can also randomly access any particular byte on a floppy or hard disk. In contrast, you can't randomly access data on a magnetic tape system because the data is stored sequentially. In order to find a particular byte, you'd have to run the tape forward or backward to the proper area.

Being able to randomly access memory lets you read and write to it immediately. It's somewhat like an electronic blackboard; you can manipulate data, calculate equations, enter more data, edit, search databases, or do any of the thousands of things that software allows you to do—all because you can access and change the data in RAM very quickly.

RAM is an essential element in a computer. Of course, if you're working on a large file you'll need a lot of RAM. If you're using Windows and you don't have enough RAM, some portions of the file might be loaded onto a special area of the hard disk and used as a swap file.

RAM volatility

An important difference in ROM and RAM is that RAM is volatile. That is, it will disappear if the machine is rebooted or if you exit a program without saving it. If there's a power interruption to the computer, even for a brief instant, any unsaved data in RAM is gone forever.

Get in the habit of saving your files to disk frequently, especially if you live in an area where there are power failures due to storms or other reasons. Many word-processing programs can be set to automatically save open files to disk at frequent intervals.

An uninterruptible power supply

If your data is crucial, you might consider using an uninterruptible power supply (UPS). Any data in RAM can quickly disappear if there's a power loss. If the power to the transistors that make up RAM is interrupted, all the transistors return to the 0 state. If you live in an area where there are frequent power outages, then it might be worthwhile to invest in an uninterruptible power supply.

How RAM is addressed

Each byte of memory has a separate address. The cells in the memory bank are like the "pigeon holes" for room keys in a large hotel, which are arranged in rows and columns so they correspond to each room on each floor. If the hotel had 100 rooms, you could have ten rows across and ten columns down, making it very simple to find any one of the 100 keys. Memory addressing is a bit more complicated, but with just 20 address lines, any individual byte out of one million bytes can be quickly accessed.

A byte is also called a *word*, so the old 8-bit XTs can address only one word at a time. The 16-bit 286 can address two words, the 32-bit 386 and 486 systems can address four words, and the 64-bit Pentium can address eight words at a time.

The CPU and RAM bus

The CPU is the brains of the computer. Almost everything that happens in a computer must travel over a bus path and go through the CPU.

Say you have a very fast and powerful Pentium. You probably have several plug-in boards and peripheral components that communicate with the CPU over a 16-bit bus at about 8 MHz. But data that moves between RAM and the CPU has its own special memory bus. Data moves back and forth on the bus between RAM and the CPU at the CPU speed or frequency. You might also have several components installed on a VL or PCI bus, which communicates with the CPU at the CPU frequency.

The amount of work a computer accomplishes depends on how fast it can process data. There can be billions of bits in a program, and it often takes a lot of shifting and adding and moving around to process the program. The faster the computer can handle these billions of iterations, the better.

One factor that determines the speed of a computer is the time that's spent shifting data back and forth between the CPU and RAM. The width of the path or bus between the CPU and the RAM is crucial in determining the operating speed of a computer.

The original PC had an 8-bit memory bus connected to the CPU. The bus was doubled to 16 bits for the 286 CPU. It was doubled again to 32 bits for the 386 and 486 CPUs. For the Pentium, the bus width is whatever the motherboard was designed for. It could be 32, 64, or even 128 bits. For a 128-bit bus, some designers have developed a 64-bit bus going in one direction to the CPU and another 64-bit bus returning from the CPU. Computer technology has come a long way in just a few short years.

The bus has been likened to a highway. If there are only eight lanes, it can be rather slow. Twice as many cars can get through on a 16-lane highway, and four times as many if there are 32 lanes. If there are 64 lanes, the traffic can really whiz along.

A brief explanation of memory

Computers operate on a binary system of 0s and 1s, or offs and ons. A transistor can be turned off or on to represent a 0 or 1. Two transistors can represent four different combinations: both off, both on, #1 on and #2 off, and #1 off and #2 on. A bank of four transistors can represent 16 different combinations. With eight transistors, there are 256 different combinations. It takes eight transistors to make one byte. With them you can represent each letter of the alphabet and each number and each symbol of the extended American Standard Code for Information Interchange (ASCII). With eight lines and a ground, the eight transistors can be turned on or off to represent any single one of the 256 characters of the ASCII code.

Each byte of memory has a separate address, similar to the "pigeon holes" discussed earlier. One megabyte of memory would require many more pigeon holes or cells, but with just 20 address lines and one ground line any individual byte can be quickly accessed. Actually it's 2^{20}, or 2 to the 20th power, which equals 1,048,576 bytes.

Programs that stay in RAM

Besides application programs that must be loaded into the 640K of RAM, there are certain DOS system programs that must be in RAM at all times. These are programs such as COMMAND.COM and the internal commands. There are over 20 internal commands, such as COPY, CD, CLS, DATE, DEL, MD, PATH, TIME, and TYPE. These commands are always in RAM and are available immediately. The CONFIG.SYS file and any drivers for your system are also loaded into RAM.

Terminate and stay resident (TSR) programs are also loaded into the 640K of RAM. These memory-resident programs, such as SideKick (which has now been revised and updated for Windows), will pop up any time you press a particular key combination key. Portions of RAM can also be used for a very fast RAM disk, buffers, and print spooling.

All these things contribute to the utility and functionality of the computer and makes it easier to use. But unfortunately, they take big bites out of the precious 640K of RAM. You might even end up with less than 400K for running applications after loading several memory-resident programs.

There are many application programs that won't run if you have less than 600K of free RAM. Some are now so large that they need up to 4MB in order to run properly. These programs are designed to run in extended or expanded memory.

Recent versions of DR DOS from Novell, Microsoft's MS-DOS, and IBM's PC DOS can now load much of the operating system and TSRs in upper memory. Upper memory is that 384K of memory above 640K. Several other memory management programs have been developed to help alleviate this problem. One excellent program is DESQview from Quarterdeck Office Systems, at 213-392-9701.

Motherboard memory

The XT motherboard can accept 640K of memory on the motherboard. The 286 and 386SX can accept up to 16MB on the motherboard, but many of them have sockets for only 4MB to 8MBs. You might be able to use 4MB chips on some of them, but on some you have to use a plug-in memory board for extra memory. This isn't usually a problem with most 386DX and 486 motherboards, some of which have SIMM connectors that will accept up to 128MB of DRAM.

The PC, XT, and AT bus

PCs and XTs use an 8-bit bus. AT systems, which include 286s, 386s, and 486s, use a 16-bit and 32-bit bus.

The 8-bit 8088 communicates with its RAM over a 20-line bus. With 20 lines, it's possible to address any individual byte in 1MB (2^{20} = 1,048,576 bytes of RAM). The 16-bit 286 communicates with its RAM over a 24-line bus, which allows it to address 16MB (2^{24} = 16,777,216 bytes). The 32-bit 386 and 486 CPUs communicate with their RAM over a 32-line bus. They can address 4 gigabytes (2^{32} = 4,294,967,296 bytes). A gigabyte is a billion bytes.

Although the 386 and 486 can address 4GB of RAM, without special software DOS won't let you access more than 640K. (Incidentally, 4GB of DRAM, in 1MB SIMM packages, requires 4,096 modules; you would need a fairly large board to install that much memory. It would also be rather expensive—at $35 per megabyte, 4,096 modules would cost $143,360.)

There are several programs that let you break the 640K barrier. But first a few basics about the different types of memory.

In its virtual memory mode, the 386 can address 64 terabytes, or 64 trillion bytes (64,000,000,000,000 bytes). This is the amount of data that can be stored on 3,200,000 20MB hard disks.

Virtual memory is a method of using part of a hard disk as RAM. Many large programs won't run unless the entire program resides in RAM, so you can load part of the program into available RAM and the rest of it into a virtual RAM section of the hard disk. Of course, having to access the disk for data can slow processing down considerably, but it's one solution. The virtual disk system must be implemented by the operating system.

If you have an older system with memory installed on plug-in boards, you know that these boards can slow a system down considerably. The 286 CPU can run as fast as 25 MHz, the 386DX 40 MHz, and the 486 100 MHz, but all these ISA systems communicate with plug-in boards and any other I/O devices over a 16-bit bus at about 8 MHz. One reason for this is for the systems to be compatible with the early boards and software.

If a 40-MHz 386 had to communicate with memory over a 16-bit bus at 8 MHz, it would be a terrible waste of speed. It would be like having a very fast car and driving around in second gear all the time.

386DX and 486 CPUs have a 32-bit bus that they use to communicate with memory. This means they can access and process data at the CPU speed. Memory boards are seldom used anymore.

Dual inline package (DIP)

Early DRAM chips had two rows of eight pins. They were bulky and used up a lot of motherboard real estate, and the 16 pins imposed limits on them. Later, 1MB DIPs were developed that had 18 pins. You won't find DIPs on motherboards very often now. They're used mostly for VGA adapters and special applications.

Single inline package (SIP)

Some older motherboards used SIP memory, which is similar to SIMMs except it has pins. Few if any motherboards use SIP memory now. Figure 6-1 shows a 1MB SIP module.

6-1 A 1MB SIP memory module.

Single inline memory module (SIMM)

Your computer motherboard probably has sockets for SIMMs. SIMMs are usually assemblies of 256K, 500K, 1MB, or 4MB miniature DRAM chips. There are usually nine chips on a small board that's usually plugged slantwise into a special connector. In some SIMMs, three of the nine chips are integrated into one, so they have only three chips. SIMMs require a very small amount of board real estate. Early PCs used dual in-line pin (DIP) chips with two rows of 8 pins, or 16 pins total, and they used up a lot of motherboard real estate.

It takes nine chips of whatever type of memory is designated. For instance, 64K requires eight 64K × 1-bit chips plus one 64K × 1-bit chip for parity checking. For 256K, you'll need eight 256K × 1-bit chips, plus one 256 × 1-bit chip for parity checking. Even with high-capacity SIMMs, it still takes nine chips to make up the designated memory. For 1 megabyte it takes eight 1,024K × 1-bit chips plus one 1,024K × 1-bit chip for parity. For a 4MB SIMM, it takes eight 4,096K × 1-bit chips, plus one 4,096K × 1-bit chip for parity. The same system is used even for the $n \times 36$ SIMM chips. Here is a brief chart:

64K = 64K × 1 bit + 64K × 1 bit for parity
256K = 256K × 1 bit + 256K × 1 bit for parity
1MB = 1024K × 1 bit + 1024K × 1 bit for parity
4MB = 4096K × 1 bit + 4096K × 1 bit for parity

Figure 6-2 shows two different 16MB 4 × 36 SIMMs. The module on the bottom has eight large 16MB × 1-bit chips and four smaller 4MB × 1-bit chips for the parity.

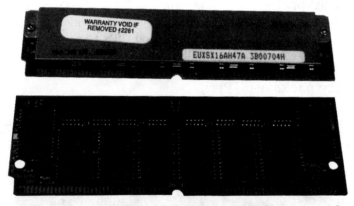

6-2 Two different 4 × 36 16MB SIMMs. The bottom module has eight large 16MB × 1-bit chips and four smaller 4MB × 1-bit chips for parity.

Figure 6-3 shows three different motherboards: a large standard 286 at the top left, a Pentium at the top right, and a small 386 at the bottom. To illustrate how much space DIP chips require, there are four rows of DIP chips in the top right corner of the 286, a total of 36 256K chips to make one megabyte. The four white SIMM 72 contact sockets on the right top corner of the Pentium motherboard can accept up to 128MB. The small 386 has four 30-contact SIMM sockets that can accept up to 64MB. Figure 6-4 shows a 30-contact 4MB SIMM assembly.

DIP chips are rather difficult to install. It's very easy to install them backwards in the socket or bend one of the pins so it doesn't make contact. Over a period of time, some DIP chips can actually creep up out of their sockets. In contrast, SIMM chips are very easy to install. They have a cutout on one end so they can be inserted only

6-3 286, Pentium, and 386SX motherboards. The top right corner of the 286 (top left) contains 36 256K chips to make 1MB. The four white slots on the Pentium (top right) will accept up to 128MB. The 386SX (bottom) has four slots that can accept up to 64MB.

6-4 A 4MB 30-contact SIMM assembly.

one way. Just lay the assembly slantwise in the socket, then push it to an upright position. There's a small hole in each end of the SIMM board, and a projection on the socket that fits in this hole when the SIMM is inserted in the socket. Spring-loaded clamps on each end lock the assembly in place. To remove the assembly, press on the clamps on each end.

Memory must be configured in banks. Most motherboards are designed for four banks: 0, 1, 2, and 3. Check the documentation that came with your motherboard. You must fill the lowest numbered bank before filling other banks. You must also install SIMMs in multiples of two. For instance, for 16MB you'd have to install two 8MB modules. The bank designations are often different on motherboards from different vendors. Some motherboards will designate bank 0 on one side of the socket assembly; others will designate the other side.

Caution: Although SIMM chips are so easy to install, it's possible to have a module that isn't seated properly. If this happens, the computer might not boot up. The screen will be completely blank with no error messages or any indication of a problem.

Before buying memory, check the type you need. Most older 386 and 486 motherboards have contact sockets for $n \times 9$ SIMMs, and some of the newer 486s and most Pentium motherboards have longer 72-contact SIMM sockets for the $n \times 36$ SIMMs. The $n \times 36$ SIMMs are sometimes called PS/2 or EISA modules. The $n \times 9$ SIMMs have only 30 contacts on each side; the newer $n \times 36$ SIMMs have 72 contacts on each side.

Don't even consider installing 1MB SIMMs. Many motherboards provide only four slots for memory, so if you install 1MB SIMMs you could install only 4MB of memory. You could probably get by with 4MB of RAM, but you'd be much better off installing at least 16MB. There are 16MB SIMMs available in the 30-contact size, so you could install 64MB in four sockets. The 1×36 SIMMs can give you 4MB in one 72-contact slot, and the 2×36 will give you 8MB in each slot. There are also 4×36 for 16MB and 8×36 for 32MB. You can install 128MB in just four slots by using 8×36 SIMMs. Figure 4-4 in chapter 4 shows a 72-contact 4×36 16MB SIMM board and a 1×9 30-contact 1MB SIMM. Figure 6-2 shows the two different 4×36 SIMMs I've installed in my Pentium machine, which give me 32MB of DRAM.

SIMMs will have speeds of 80, 70, and 60 ns. Buy the speed recommended by your documentation. A 60-MHz Pentium can use 70 ns or 60 ns, but a 70-ns SIMM will be a bit less expensive than a 60-ns SIMM. You can use 80-ns chips in some of the slower 25-MHz 486 systems, even those operating at 50 MHz, if they use an OverDrive DX2 CPU.

I suggest that you buy as much memory as you can afford. Memory is somewhat like money in that you can never have too much of it. Usually, you must have two SIMMs of the same type and capacity because memory is interleaved. If you intend to install 16MB of RAM, then you need to buy two 8MB modules. If you install a single module instead of the required two, the computer might not boot up. Interleaved memory is discussed in more detail later in the chapter.

Since memory comes in modules and is socketed, you can add as much as your motherboard allows. Memory chips sometimes fail. The BIOS does a power-on self test (POST) every time the computer is booted. During this test, all the memory chips are tested. MS-DOS 6.2 also does a more comprehensive memory test each time the computer is booted. If an assembly becomes defective, it's easy enough to replace it.

You might have to set some switches or install some jumpers to configure your motherboard to the amount of memory you install. Check the documentation that came with your motherboard.

Memory chip capacity

At the present time, 4MB DRAM chips are the largest generally available. Several companies, including IBM, are developing 16MB and 64MB DRAM chips, and 16MB chips should be on the market by the time you read this. The 64MB chips might take a bit longer.

The size and speed of a chip is usually printed on the top of the chip. For instance, a 256K chip at 150 ns might display the manufacturer's logo or name and some other data. But somewhere among all this would be the number 25615. The 15 indicates 150 ns (the zero is always left off), so a one-megabyte 100-ns chip might have the designation 102410.

Chips are usually arranged in banks or rows of nine. Almost all ISA computers use an extra ninth chip for parity checking. This chip checks and verifies the integrity of the memory at all times, and is usually the same type of chip as the eight that make up the bank. Macintosh systems don't use this chip and some experts say it's a waste of memory to use it on ISA systems.

The RAM in XTs and early 286s was usually located in the front left corner of the motherboard, and they all used DIP chips. To make 640K, most boards filled the first two banks, 0 and 1, with 256K chips, which would equal 512K. The next two banks, 2 and 3, were filled with 64K chips to make 128K. Thus the maximum of 640K was achieved.

Many early 286 and 386 systems filled all four banks with 256K DIP chips for a total of 1MB. Although the 286 was capable of addressing 16MB with special software, for most ordinary uses it was still limited to 640K. Boards that had the extra 384K could use it for a RAM disk, print spooling, or other extended memory needs with the proper software. Even the 386, 486, and Pentium are limited to 640K without special software that can take advantage of extended memory.

Prices

Table 6-1 lists some current advertised SIMM prices from a discount house. Keep in mind that memory prices are very volatile and fluctuate considerably; they might be a bit higher or lower than the prices quoted here. Also note that the price list is from a discount house, and prices at the average computer store will probably be higher. These prices, however, should give you some idea as to the differences in the cost of various types.

So say you use four banks of 70-ns 256K × 9-bit SIMMs to make 1MB of memory. At $10 each for the SIMMs, it would cost $40 for 1MB. It would take only one 70-ns 1MB × 9-bit SIMM to make 1MB, so this one megabyte of memory would cost only $35. And since it takes only one 70-ns 4MB × 9-bit SIMM to make 4MB, the cost would be $135, or about $34 per megabyte.

Table 6-1. Current memory prices

Chip	Price
80-ns 256K × 9-bit SIMM	$10
70-ns 1MB × 9-bit SIMM	$35
60-ns 1MB × 9-bit SIMM	$37
70-ns 4MB × 9-bit SIMM	$135
60-ns 4MB × 9-bit SIMM	$139
Four 70-ns 1MB × 36-bit SIMMs (4MB)	$148
Four 70-ns 2MB × 36-bit SIMMs (8MB)	$293
Four 70-ns 4MB × 36-bit SIMMs (16MB)	$559
Four 70-ns 8MB × 36-bit SIMMs (32MB)	$1175

Installing the chips

Now that you've bought your chips, you need to install them in the sockets on the motherboard.

One of the first things that you should do is discharge any static electricity you might have. This is especially important if you're working in a carpeted area. Touch a metal object, such as a lamp that's plugged into an outlet, to discharge yourself of any static electricity.

You can mix chips of different speeds in the same bank, such as 60 ns and 70 ns, but you'd be limited to the 70-ns speed. Don't use a chip slower than the speed of your CPU. You can't mix chips of different capacities, such as a 1 × 9 and a 4 × 9.

If you're using old DIP chips, they might have a small notch at one end or a round dot in one corner that indicates which end has pin 1. The socket has a matching notch or outline on the board to indicate how the chip should be plugged in. Ordinarily, all the chips on a board are installed or oriented in the same direction.

To install a DIP chip, set the leads in one side of the socket, then with a bit of pressure against that side line up the leads on the other side and press the chip in. Be careful not to bend the leads and check to make sure all the leads are inserted in the sockets. It's very easy for one to slip out unnoticed. If this happens, you'll have memory errors when you try to run the system.

If you're installing memory on a PC or XT, you might have to reset the DIP switch on the motherboard to reflect the amount of memory. Some older ATs have a jumper that has to be set.

To install SIPs, look for markings on the modules. On many of them, pin 1 is marked, and there's usually a corresponding mark on the motherboard sockets. The motherboard will probably also have markings for individual banks.

SIMM modules have a cutout on one end of the small board. It can be plugged only one way.

If you plan to add extra memory, be sure to get the kind and type for your machine, and make sure it's fast enough for your system. Check your documentation; it should tell you what speed and type of chips to buy.

More memory

Most people need more memory in their computers. For some applications, you might even need to buy several megabytes more. In the old days we got by fine with just 64K of memory. Many new programs, however, such as spreadsheets, databases, and accounting programs, require a lot of memory.

If you bought a new motherboard through mail order, you might have received it with 0K (which, as you probably know, doesn't mean "okay," but rather zero K of memory). The price of memory fluctuates quite a lot. Ads are sometimes made up and placed two or three months before the magazine comes out. Because of fluctuating prices, some vendors won't advertise a firm price for memory. Besides, if they included the price of the memory, it might frighten you away. They usually invite you to call them for the latest price. The good news for consumers is that memory prices are dropping every day.

Things to consider
before you buy memory

There are different types, sizes, speeds and other factors to consider before buying memory. You should buy the type that's best suited to your computer.

Dynamic RAM?

Dynamic RAM, or DRAM, is the most common type of memory used today. Each memory cell has a small etched transistor that's kept in a memory state, either on or off, by an electrical charge on a very small capacitor. Capacitors are similar to small rechargeable batteries. Units can be charged with voltage to represent a 1, or left uncharged to represent a 0. But those that are charged immediately start to lose their charge, so they must be constantly "refreshed" with a new charge.

Steve Gibson, the developer of SpinRite, compared "on" memory cell capacitors to small buckets with holes in the bottom. Buckets representing 1s are filled with water, which immediately starts leaking out through the holes, so they have to be constantly refilled. (You don't have to worry about filling the buckets that represent the 0s.) A computer might spend seven percent or more of its time just refreshing its DRAM chips.

Also, each time a cell is accessed, that small voltage in the capacitor flows through a transistor to turn it on. This drains the charge from the capacitor, so it must be refreshed before it can be accessed again. In the bucket of water comparison, when a cell is accessed, the bucket is turned upside down and emptied. So if it's a 1, it must be refilled immediately. Of course, it takes a finite amount of time to fill a bucket or place a charge on a capacitor. If the memory cell has a speed of 70 ns (nanoseconds, or billionths of a second), it could take 70 ns plus the time recycle (105 ns or more) before that cell can again be accessed.

Refresh and wait states

The speed of the DRAM chips in your system should match the speed of your CPU. You might be able to install slower chips, but your system would have to work with wait states. If the DRAM is too slow, a wait state has to be inserted. A wait state causes the CPU and the rest of the system to sit and wait while the RAM is accessed and then refreshed. Wait states can deprive your system of one of its greatest benefits, speed.

If the CPU operates at a very high frequency, it might have to sit and wait one cycle, or one wait state, for the refresh cycle. The wait state might be only a millionth of a second, or less, which doesn't seem like much time. But if the computer is performing several million operations per second, it can add up.

It takes a finite amount of time to charge up the DRAM, but some DRAM chips can be charged up much faster than others. For instance, the DRAM chips needed for a 4.77-MHz XT might take as much as 200 ns or billionths of a second to be refreshed. A 486 running at 25 MHz would need chips that could be refreshed in 70 ns or less time. Of course, the faster chips cost more.

The 66-MHz 486DX2 and 100-MHz DX4 can both use the same memory speed—about 60 ns. The CPU might be operating internally at 66 MHz or 100 MHz, but it still accesses the RAM at 33 MHz.

Interleaved memory

Most newer faster systems use interleaved memory to prevent having to insert wait states. The memory is always installed in multiples of two. You can install two banks of 512K, 2MB, 4MB, 8MB, 16MB, 32MB, 64MB, or 128MB of memory.

One half the memory is refreshed one cycle, then the other half. If the CPU needs to access an address that's in the half already refreshed, it's available immediately, which can reduce the amount of waiting by about 50 percent.

SRAM

Static RAM is made up of actual transistors that can be turned on to represent 1s or left off to represent 0s, and they'll stay in that condition until they receive a change signal. They don't need to be refreshed but they revert back to 0 when the computer is turned off or if the power is interrupted. They're very fast and can operate at speeds of 15 ns or less.

A DRAM cell needs only one transistor and a small capacitor, and takes up a very small amount of space. SRAM chips are assembled in a DIP-type package and require four to six transistors and other components, so they're physically larger and require more space than DRAM chips. SRAMs are also much more expensive than DRAM chips. Because of the physical and electronic differences, SRAM and DRAM chips are not interchangeable.

Your motherboard has sockets for SRAM chips. Many 486 motherboards had sockets for only up to 256K. You might have sockets for up to 1MB or more if you have a Pentium motherboard. My Twin T motherboard came with 512K of SRAM. 32K SRAM chips have 28 pins, but newer 64K SRAM chips have 32 pins. The SRAM sockets on my Twin T motherboard can accept 28-pin or 32-pin SRAM, so you could have the choice of installing 256K, 512K, or 1MB of SRAM. Using 32K SRAM chips, you'd need 16 chips for 512K.

Check your motherboard documentation for instructions on how they should be installed. Be careful because it's possible to plug them in backwards. Look for some indication on the motherboard as to which is pin 1. There should be a slight U-shaped indentation on the end of the chip that has pin 1. You might also have to set switches or install jumpers to configure your motherboard for the amount of SRAM you install.

Cache memory

A cache system can speed up computer operations quite a lot. When running an application program, the CPU often loops in and out of certain areas and uses portions of the same memory over and over. A cache system is usually made up of very fast memory chips, such as SRAM, that can store often-used data so it can be quickly accessed by the CPU.

The data that's moved back and forth between the CPU and RAM is composed of electrical on and off voltages, and electrons move at almost the speed of light. Still, it takes a finite amount of time to move a large amount of data. It takes even more time to access RAM, find the data that's needed, and then move it back to the CPU.

The computer can also be slowed down considerably if it has to search the entire memory each time it fetches some data. If often-used information is stored in memory, it can be accessed by the CPU very quickly. A good cache can greatly increase the processing speed.

The Pentium CPU has a built-in 16K cache in amongst its 3.1 million transistors. This cache helps considerably, but a good fast external cache can help speed things up even more. The speed and static characteristics of SRAM makes it an excellent device for memory cache systems.

Caution! Before handling your memory chips or any electronic components, discharge any electrostatic charge you might have built up. If you've ever walked across a carpet and gotten a shock when you touched a doorknob, then you know that you can build up static electricity. It's quite possible to build up 3,000 to 5,000 volts of static electricity in your body, so if you touch a fragile piece of electronics that normally operates at 5 to 12 volts you can severely damage it. Discharge this static electricity by touching any metal that touches the ground. The metal case of the power supply in your computer is a good ground if it's plugged into the wall socket. The power doesn't have to be on for it to connect to the ground. You can also touch an unpainted metal device or appliance that's plugged into a socket with a three-wire plug. Always discharge yourself before touching any plug-in board or other equipment where there are exposed electronic semiconductors.

Disk cache

Don't confuse cache memory with disk caching. Programs often need to access the hard disk while running. If a small disk cache is set up in RAM, the CPU can import the data from a RAM disk cache much more quickly than reading it from even the fastest hard disk. So a disk cache can help a program run much faster.

There are several commercial disk-caching programs, but MS-DOS 6.0 or later has SmartDrive, which lets you set up a disk cache in RAM.

Hit rate

A well-designed cache system could have a "hit rate" of over 90%, which means that each time the CPU needs a block of data it can find it in the nearby fast cache. A good cache system can increase a computer's speed and performance considerably.

486 cache

486 processors have a built-in 8K cache system, and 486DX4s and Pentium CPUs have two built-in 8K caches. These caches give the CPU about a 90% hit rate.

It takes a large number of transistors for a cache, even one as small as 8K. Cyrix built a 1K cache into their 486 clone, and claims that it gives them an 80% hit rate. Cyrix also left the coprocessor off their 486 clone, but packaged an external coprocessor with each CPU. By reducing the number of transistors, they reduced the size of their chip to be as small as a 386.

The Cyrix 486, along with the coprocessor, currently sells for $119, which is about $400 less than the equivalent Intel 486DX. Quoted prices are for comparison, and could be different by the time you read this.

CMOS

It takes very little power to keep a complementary metal oxide semiconductor (CMOS) alive. They're actually SRAM transistors that store your system setup. Several computer configurations, such as the time, date, type of disk drive, and other features that can be changed by the user, are stored in CMOS.

Take a pad and write down all the features stored in your CMOS setup. For instance, if you lose the data in CMOS and you don't know what type of hard drive is in the setup, you won't be able to access the data on your hard drive.

A lithium or rechargeable battery will keep data alive when the computer is turned off. If your computer isn't used for a long period of time, you might have to reset the time. If you have to reset the time quite often, you might need a new battery. Early IBM ATs used batteries that lasted only a couple of years. Most motherboards today have lithium batteries that last about ten years.

Clock rate

Computers operate at very precise clock rates because the CPU is controlled by timing circuits and crystals. The original PCs and XTs operated at 4.77 MHz, some 286 CPUs operate as high as 25 MHz, many 386s operate at 40 MHz, the 486DX2 runs as fast as 66 MHz, and the DX4 and Pentium can operate as fast as 100 MHz. AMD has a clone of the 486 that runs at 40 MHz, and they plan to triple the internal clock so it runs at 120 MHz. Intel has a preliminary version of their "next generation" machine, currently called P6, that they've demonstrated running at 150 MHz.

Many systems are just too fast for some components. Some computers are designed with built-in wait states so they can use slower memory, and some of the newer BIOS chips allow you to insert wait states. Wait states can cause a computer to operate 25 to 50 percent slower than one without wait states. For ordinary applications, this would probably amount to only a few billionths of a second, but for some applications it could add up and end up seeming like an eternity.

Table 6-2 will give you a rough idea of what speed chips you should buy for your system. These are only rough figures; your system might be designed to operate a bit differently. Check your system specifications and documentation or check with your vendor.

Table 6-2. Memory speed

CPU speed	Wait state	DRAM ns speed
4.77 MHz	0	200
6–8 MHz	1	120–150
6–8 MHz	0	100–120
8–10 MHz	1	100–120
8–10 MHz	0	80–100
10–12 MHz	1	100
12–20 MHz	1	80
16–25 MHz	0	70
25–33 MHz	0	60
40–50 MHz	0	40–53

The 640K limit

When DOS was first introduced in 1981, one megabyte of memory was an enormous amount, and most people believed it would always be more than satisfactory. After all, many CP/M machines were getting by fine with just 64K of memory. So DOS was designed to operate with a maximum of 1MB (actually, 1024K). Of this 1MB, 640K was used to run programs and applications and the other 384K was reserved for the BIOS, video control, and other special hardware control. This 384K is called *upper memory area* and is divided into blocks called *upper memory blocks*, or UMBs. Figure 6-3 is a diagram of how conventional memory is arranged.

Sometimes when I try to load and run a program, I get the error message "Not enough memory" or "Insufficient memory," even though I have 32MB of DRAM in my computer. I know the program I'm trying to run is less than 500K, so why can't I run it?

The reason is simple. If it's a DOS program, it can't handle extended memory and is limited to the 640K of conventional memory. But if the program is only 500K, why can't it run if there's 640K?

When you boot up your computer, COMMAND.COM and several other internal DOS commands are loaded into the 640K of conventional memory. In addition, any terminate and stay resident (TSR) programs are also loaded there. Any drivers for special devices listed in the CONFIG.SYS and AUTOEXEC.BAT, such as a fax-modem or a CD-ROM drive, are also loaded into conventional memory. After all this stuff is loaded, there might be less than 400K left. So if the program is larger than

400K, it won't run. Many programs and applications today are so large that they need 600K or more of RAM.

DOS internal commands and many TSRs stay in memory at all times because they need to be invoked with just a few keystrokes from any directory. There are about 75 DOS commands and about 30 of them are these instantly accessible internal commands, such as COPY, DEL, MD, CD, and TYPE. (In many of the early versions of DOS, these were all separate commands, but DOS now incorporates them into COMMAND.COM.) They're always loaded and immediately available. If you want to run one of the external commands, such as FIND or DISKCOMP, you have to go to the DOS directory and load them.

Tremendous improvements have been made in computer technology since the original PC. In spite of all of these improvements, however, we're still limited to the original 640K unless we have programs, such as Windows, that can take advantage of extra extended memory. One reason for this limitation is to make sure that computers remain compatible with and can still run all the software already created. Many people complain about the 640K barrier, but this backward compatibility is one of the foremost factors that has made the computer what it is today.

The 640K barrier isn't actually that much of a problem. Much of the reserved 384K of upper memory space is never needed by the system. MS-DOS and several other programs, such as DESQview, can load their internal commands, drivers, and TSRs into this unused 384K. In most cases, you can have over 600K in which to run your programs.

MS-DOS version 5.0 and later has a MEMMAKER command that can search the 384K of upper memory and find all the unused cracks and crannies. After that, every time you boot your computer it automatically loads most of the internal commands, drivers, and TSRs into upper memory. Windows, Windows NT, and IBM's OS/2 aren't limited to 640K. These systems will let you use all the RAM that's available, if needed.

Extended memory

Extended memory is memory that can be installed above one megabyte. The Pentium can address up to four gigabytes of extended memory. If it weren't for the DOS 640K limitation, it would be a seamless continuation of memory. Windows, Windows NT, and OS/2 2.1 can use extended memory. They can also use extended memory to run two or more programs at the same time, called *multitasking*.

Flash memory

Many people like to have a laptop or notebook computer for the times they're on the road. If you do buy one, make sure it has PCMCIA connectors for flash memory. Intel developed flash memory, which is similar to erasable programmable read-only memory (EPROM). It's also fairly slow compared to DRAM and SRAM, so it can't replace them.

Flash memory is often installed on small plug-in cards about the size of a credit card. The cards are ideal for use on laptop and notebook computers. When first introduced, these cards were quite limited in the amount of memory they could store, but there are ones now available that can store several megabytes. Flash memory, therefore, can be a good substitute for a hard disk on small notebook computers.

The Personal Computer Memory Card International Association (PCMCIA) adopted a standard for connectors so several products could be used with laptop and notebook computers. Most laptop and notebook computers now include the PCM-CIA connectors so flash memory and other peripherals can be installed.

There are several advantages of using PCMCIA cards rather than a hard disk in a laptop. A hard disk is a mechanical device, which will eventually wear out. PCMCIA flash memory is strictly electronic and should last several lifetimes. But it's still rather expensive and limited in the amount of memory it can hold. MiniStor, at 408-943-0165, has developed small hard disks that can be plugged into the PCMCIA connector.

Some companies are now incorporating the system BIOS into flash memory. Sometimes it's necessary to upgrade or update the BIOS in order to take advantage of new software and hardware, which can be rather expensive if you need to take the system apart and install the new upgrade. It's much easier to use a floppy disk to access and update a BIOS chip that's in flash memory.

Using flash memory and the PCMCIA standard, companies have developed other peripherals for laptop and notebook computers, things like high-speed modems and network adapters.

There aren't many more improvements that can be made to ISA, EISA, and MCA buses. Some engineers have suggested that PCMCIA might be the next logical step for the personal computer bus. In the future, you might find PCMCIA cards not only in laptop computers, but on desktop machines, automobiles, robots, all kinds of medical equipment, instruments, dozens of appliances, and many other applications not even imagined today.

VRAM

Video RAM chips are a bit different than DRAM chips. They're special memory chips used with monitor adapter cards.

Printer memory

Your printer probably contains a minimum amount of memory. Most printers require memory installed on special proprietary boards, and you can often add more printer memory for better printing speed.

Buying memory chips

Buying chips that are faster than what your system can use will only cost you extra money. It doesn't hurt to use faster chips, or even to intermix faster ones with slower ones, but make sure the memory chips you buy work with your system.

If you plan to upgrade the memory in an older system, you might have trouble finding older chips. Older systems used dual inline package (DIP) chips. Make sure that you buy only the type that will fit in your system. For instance, 64K and 256K DIP chips have 16 pins, the 1MB chips have 18. Some memory boards have interlaced 256K and 1MB sockets, so you can use either size chip. SIMM chips are the type used most often today, but you can't use a SIMM module unless your motherboard is designed for it.

Memory modes

There are two different memory modes: real and protected.

Real mode is the mode that uses the 640K of conventional memory. When an application is being processed, the program is loaded into RAM. The CPU uses RAM to process any input data. Computations, changes, or calculations are done in memory and then sent back to the disk, screen, printer, or other device. For most single-user applications, this processing is done in the standard 640K or less of RAM. Operating in the real mode doesn't cause much of a problem if you're running fairly small programs that can fit in available RAM. But if you're trying to update a spreadsheet that's 2MB in size, you're in trouble. It's like trying to put a gallon of gelatin in a quart bowl.

In protected mode, AT machines can run several programs at the same time. Each program runs in a 640K area of memory. In effect, this memory has a wall around it so it doesn't interfere with any other memory area.

DESQview

DESQview is an excellent program that lets you take advantage of the 386 and 486 virtual 8086 and 32-bit protected modes. It lets you run multiple DOS programs simultaneously, switch and transfer data between them, and run programs in the background. DESQview is very inexpensive; for more details, call 213-392-9701.

How much memory do you need?

This depends primarily on what you intend to use your computer for. For word processing or small applications, you can get by with 640K, but you should have at least 4MB, even better 8MB, if you expect to use Windows, large databases, or spreadsheets.

Having a lot of memory is like having a car with a large engine. You might not need that extra power very often, but it sure feels great being able to call on it when you do need it.

Building the
dream machine

This chapter is primarily about upgrading to a Pentium or building a PC from scratch. Upgrading an older computer to a Pentium is no more difficult than upgrading an XT to a 286. It merely involves removing the old motherboard and installing a new Pentium motherboard. You should be able to use most of your old components in the Pentium, but you'll probably need to buy new memory chips and perhaps a higher-capacity hard drive. Building or assembling a dream machine from scratch is no more difficult than assembling an XT or a 286. All PCs are very similar in the way they're assembled. They're all very simple.

Before looking at the Pentium in more detail, however, let's examine another kind of computer, called a RISC.

RISC hardware and software

A RISC (reduced instruction-set computer) might cost less to buy, but it costs more to operate because it requires special software and hardware. Software that's fed into a CPU is made up of electrical signals that cause certain transistors to turn on or off. Transistors in an Intel $80x86$ CPU are arranged differently than those in the Motorola $680x0$ CPU found in Apple products. The transistors in those CPUs are also arranged differently than those in RISC CPUs. Several companies make RISC CPUs, such as Motorola, DEC, and Sun, and the CPUs from these different companies are all different and incompatible.

Trying to use DOS and Windows software on Apple machines or RISCs is about like an English-speaking person trying to converse with an Italian who doesn't understand English. Of course, there are interpreters and translators who could help them understand one another. Some RISCs can use special emulation software to run software that has been designed for DOS and Apple products. Emulation software is like a translator. It intercepts the signals created by the DOS or Apple software and changes them into a form that can be used by the RISC CPU.

The disadvantage of using emulation software is that it slows the machine down, which defeats the purpose of using the faster RISC technology. Many software companies are recompiling their software so it will run on RISCs without emulation. Many developers are also writing new software just for RISC CPUs.

Another problem with RISCs is that not all of them understand the same language. The DEC, SUN, and the IBM-Apple-Motorola PowerPC RISCs all require their own different special software. Gertrude Stein wrote, "A rose is a rose is a rose." Unfortunately, a RISC is *not* a RISC is *not* a RISC."

The PowerPC

The PowerPC has some advantages and some disadvantages. Briefly, the advantages are:

Speed The name of the game is speed. Even if it's only a few microseconds, speed counts. RISCs can operate much faster than CISCs because of their ability to process more than one instruction at a time, but the Pentium is closing the gap. For some types of applications, the Pentium might even surpass a RISC.

The same hardware RISCs can use most of the same hardware used on CISCs, so there are billions of dollars' worth of hardware and peripherals, such as plug-in boards, modems, faxes, disk drives, CD-ROMs, and printers, that RISCs can readily use.

Low cost The cost for the PowerPC CPU is about half of that for a Pentium CPU. The bad news is that, since there's only one source and no competition, the price might go up. The good news is that it has caused Intel to become a bit worried and they've begun to lower the prices of the Pentium.

Now, here are the disadvantages:

No software There's currently very little software for RISCs. They can run only special software developed for that particular CPU. Some software, such as Windows NT, has been recompiled to run on the RISCs. There's also software that can translate DOS and Apple software to run on RISC CPUs. Several software companies are developing software, but it might be a while before it's available. IBM, Apple, and Motorola are currently developing RISC systems that can run DOS and Macintosh software.

Few vendors and no competition Very few companies are currently designing and manufacturing RISC motherboards, but hundreds of companies sell Pentium motherboards. IBM has said it will sell a PowerPC motherboard to anyone who wants one, but at this time IBM hasn't even made enough boards for its own use. By the time you read this, there should be some available; there should also be other vendors who have PowerPC motherboards.

The Pentium

The Pentium has 3.1 million transistors in its CPU. It's the most powerful CPU available for PCs; it's even more powerful than some minicomputers. The Pentium is capable of performing 112 million instructions per second (MIPS). Some RISC CPUs are capable of over 150 MIPS, but the Pentium is the first complex instruction-set computer (CISC) system that can do over 100 MIPS.

Some RISCs are less expensive than the Pentium. One reason is because the RISC CPU costs about $400. The Pentium CPU currently costs about $700 each if you buy at least 1,000 units. The cost is more if you buy in lesser quantities.

The 64-bit bus

Even though the Pentium is a 64-bit system, it can run all DOS software, even the old 8-bit software developed years ago. There have been thousands and thousands of programs written since the first PC was introduced in the early 1980s. Despite its power and speed, the Pentium can still run any of the software developed for the first PC.

Although early software will run on the Pentium, most of it doesn't take full advantage of Pentium power, so many software companies are now recompiling and modifying the older software to make it run better and faster on the Pentium.

Future software compatibility

Software always lags behind hardware developments. Not much software has even been developed to take full advantage of the 32-bit bus of the 386 and 486, so it will be a while before much software is available to take advantage of Pentium's 64-bit bus. But several companies are working overtime to develop it. For instance, Pentium's floating-point operations are about four times faster than the fastest 486, but there aren't many general business applications that can take advantage of this fact. You can expect several new and improved packages very soon.

External and internal processing

The Pentium can handle data over a 64-bit bus externally, but can process it only 32 bits at a time internally. Being able to handle 32-bit data internally makes it compatible with software written for 32-bit 386 and 486 CPUs. The Pentium CPU can operate at 60, 66, 90, and 100 MHz. Eventually, there will be 64-bit software that can take full advantage of the Pentium at its fastest speed.

The 64-bit bus allows 8 bytes of data at a time to be transferred back and forth to RAM. Operating at 66 MHz, the Pentium can transfer data at a rate of 8 bytes times 66 MHz, which equals 528MB per second. A 486 operating at 33 MHz over a 32-bit bus can transfer four bytes of data at a time, so 33 MHz times 4 bytes equals 132MB per second.

Even with a 64-bit bus, the DRAM might not be able to feed data to the CPU fast enough to keep it busy, so most systems will have a fast cache system. Cache RAM is made of static RAM, or SRAM, and is much faster than DRAM. Quite often a program causes certain parts of data to be looped in and out of memory. Cache memory stores this most-often used data and feeds it to the CPU very quickly.

The powerful Pentium allows graphics and CAD programs to run much faster. It can also run full-screen motion pictures. The Pentium is ideal for running 32-bit Windows NT and OS/2 applications. Since there aren't too many applications that can take advantage of a 64-bit bus, some companies have designed motherboards with a 32-bit bus.

What's in a name?

The next logical CPU name should have been 586, which is what a lot of people call it. But Intel was unable to copyright and protect the 386 and 486 names. It made Intel unhappy that clone makers could call their products by the same name, so this time they came up with a name they could copyright. They might not be able to prevent anyone from developing a clone of their Pentium, but they can prevent anyone from calling it a Pentium. (The word *pentium* is from the Greek word *pente*, meaning five.)

Many people ignore the name Intel hung on it, however, and call it what it should have been called, the 586. There are several companies who are busy developing compatible clones of the Pentium that will be called 586 CPUs.

It's well known that Intel is working on the next generation of CPUs, currently called the P6. There has been some speculation as to what they might eventually call it. The Greek word for six is *hex*, and the Latin word for six is *sex*. It's not very likely that Intel will call the next-generation CPU a hexium or sexium.

It doesn't matter what Intel names it, because most people will call it the 686. As Shakespeare wrote in *Romeo and Juliet*, "What's in a name? That which we call a rose by any other name would smell as sweet."

Intel wasn't able to copyright and protect the 486 name, but it has recently introduced the 486DX4. But they don't usually call it that; they call it the DX4, which they were able to copyright.

Why more power?

Computers work by using digital data in the form of 0s and 1s. To form a 0 or a 1 means that a transistor must turn off or on. Data usually has a very large amount of 0s and 1s. It takes 8 bits, or a single byte, of data to form a single character, such as an A or a B. The text in this book totals about a million bytes of data, which is a small amount compared to other types of data. A single color photo might require up to 25 times that.

The original PC operated at 4.7 MHz, and the Pentium can operate at up to 100 MHz. A Pentium speed of 66 MHz is only 14 times greater than the original 4.7 MHz, but because of design improvements it actually operates at over 300 times faster than the original PC. Eventually, the Pentium will operate at 150 MHz.

If you do nothing but simple word processing, then an original PC would be all you needed. But if you're processing graphics, large spreadsheets, or large databases, you'll need a lot more power and speed. Data that requires an hour or more for an XT to process might take less than a second for a Pentium. There are many PC applications, such as desktop video conferencing, multimedia, 3-D design, scientific modeling, speech and handwriting recognition, where the Pentium would be ideal. A company might be paying an engineer $60 an hour to design and process crucial data. If the engineer has to sit and wait for the computer to process the data, the company is wasting money. They're also wasting the engineer's time, which could be better spent doing productive work. In a situation such as this, a Pentium would pay for itself in a short time.

The Pentium is almost as powerful as some mainframes, yet it costs just a fraction of what a mainframe would cost. The Pentium is ideal for use as a network server.

Increased speed

Intel lists three ways to increase the speed of a CPU: add more transistors along with a cache, increase the clock speed or frequency, or increase the number of instructions executed per clock cycle.

The 486DX CPU has an 8K cache built in among its 1.2 million transistors. The Pentium has two 8K caches. The Pentium also has a new superscalar technology. The term *superscalar* means that the CPU architecture consists of more than one execution unit or pipeline. Superscalar technology enables the Pentium to process data simultaneously through two different pipelines. A *pipeline* is an arrangement of registers within the CPU, also called *execution units*. Each register performs part of a task, then passes the results to the next register.

Early CPUs required several clock cycles to execute a single instruction. The 486 can execute many of its instructions in a single clock cycle. The Pentium has the ability to execute two instructions in each of its two pipelines simultaneously in a single clock cycle, so a Pentium could possibly process four times as much data as a 486 in the same amount of time.

Figure 4-2 in chapter 4 shows the Pentium CPU and how the different sections are dedicated.

RISC vs. CISC motherboards

Although the RISC CPU might cost less than a CISC CPU, it might cost more for a RISC motherboard. The reason is that, at this time, there are few manufacturers who make RISC motherboards for end users. IBM, Motorola, and a few other companies are manufacturing them for original equipment manufacturers (OEMs). Since there isn't much demand at this time and little or no competition, the prices will remain fairly high for RISC motherboards.

There is, however, a great demand for Pentium motherboards and there are many manufacturers for OEMs and end users. At the present time, Pentium motherboards are being advertised for $1,200 to $1,500. I saw one advertised for $369, but of course it was without the CPU. Another company advertised 60-MHz CPUs for $573 and 66-MHz CPUs for $653. This means that you could buy a complete 60-MHz motherboard for $942 and a 66-MHz one for $1,022. Just six months ago, I paid $1,350 for my 60-MHz motherboard, and it was a very good deal at that time. Keep in mind that prices should be much lower by the time you read this, and the competition will keep the prices down.

The original PC and all PCs up through the Pentium are complex instruction-set computers (CISC). This means that the CPU has a set of instructions built into it. Whenever it's asked to perform a task, it has to sort through several hundred instructions to find the ones needed to accomplish the task. Having to sort through these instructions takes a finite amount of time, which slows down the CPU.

A reduced instruction-set computer (RISC) has to sort through less than half the number of instructions in order to perform a task. DEC has developed a RISC chip that has only 1.2 million transistors, and it's the fastest microchip in the world. Their Alpha AXP can perform 157 MIPS, while the Pentium with 3.1 million transistors can do only 112 MIPS.

IBM teamed up with Apple and Motorola to develop the RISC PowerPC CPU. It has 2.8 million transistors and can perform 100 MIPS. PowerPC is actually an IBM acronym for Performance Optimization With Enhanced RISC. (IBM is almost as prolific as the government in creating acronyms. When I worked for Lockheed, we had a large manual filled with government acronyms that had to be constantly updated to keep up with the new ones that were created daily.)

Which one should you buy?

So should you forget about the Pentium and buy a DEC Alpha or IBM-Apple-Motorola PowerPC RISC system? Right now, it's probably not a good idea. There are well over 50,000 programs available to run on the Pentium. These programs won't run on a RISC system unless they're translated or modified. If software has to be translated into a form that RISCs can understand, it will slow down considerably. Some programs are currently being recompiled. Windows NT can run on RISCs, and IBM and Apple are developing an emulation system that would allow a RISC system to use CISC software and vice versa. Just keep in mind that emulation will slow the system down.

The Pentium is currently the fastest and most powerful system that runs all existing PC software. Another big advantage of the Pentium is that there are well over 100 million PCs in use that are based on the Intel 80x86 architecture, the same as the Pentium. There are thousands and thousands of vendors competing for this PC market, which has made the market very competitive. This competition has also made the computer industry one of the few industries in the world where prices continually go down. The intense competition also causes manufacturers to continue to develop new and improved products.

DEC currently has no competition for its Alpha system; they're the sole supplier. The IBM-Apple-Motorola PowerPC is also a lone product with no competition. If a software developer can choose to develop a program that will run on 100 million machines, or use his time to develop a program that will run on a very limited number of machines, what system do you suppose he'll choose? The same thing is true for PC hardware designers and developers; they're all going to go with the greater opportunity for sales.

RISC systems have some advantages over the CISC systems, but it's highly doubtful that RISC systems will ever become as prevalent as CISC systems, at least not for a while. In the meantime, I suggest that you stay with the Pentium CISC systems.

Differences in CPUs

All CPUs are different. Ordinarily, software is written for a specific type of CPU. A computer works because the software gives instructions to the CPU. The CPU is the brains of any computer; it receives software instructions and then causes them to be carried out. The instructions, whether entered from disk, keyboard, or other peripheral, cause a unique digital voltage to be produced. If you press the letter A on the keyboard, it causes a dc voltage to be turned on and off to represent 1s and 0s for the decimal number 65, or 1000001. This voltage goes to the CPU and causes certain transistors to be turned on or off.

Since the Intel and Motorola CPUs are different, an instruction written for an Intel 80x86 CPUs would be handled quite differently than those written for a Motorola 680xx CPU. Software written for the 80x86 and that written for the 680xx are like two foreign languages. They can't understand the instructions unless they're written in their own native or machine language, which is why you can't take software written for a Macintosh and run it on a machine that has an Intel 80x86 CPU.

Cost

When it was first introduced, the price of the Pentium CPU chip was about $950 each, in quantities of 1,000. 486 CPUs were about this expensive when they were first introduced. Within two or three years, however, the Pentium CPU will sell for about what the fastest 486 CPU currently sells, about $400 each. The Chip Merchant, at 619-268-4774 x3, sells SIMMs and CPUs, and are now advertising a 90-MHz Pentium for $714. It will probably be less by the time you read this.

The first Pentium computer systems were rather expensive, at about $5,000 for a basic system and $10,000 or more for one with lots of goodies. Less than six months later, some systems were selling for less than $3,000. The lowered cost of the Pentium is causing some drastic cuts in the prices of 486 machines. Almost everybody can now afford a 486 system. And for many, the Pentium isn't that far out of reach.

At the present time, a 60-MHz Pentium CPU costs only a few dollars more than an Intel 100-MHz DX4 CPU. Even though the DX4 is faster, the Pentium can do more processing because it's superscalar, which means it can process two instructions at the same time. Although the CPUs cost about the same, the Pentium motherboard costs a bit more than the 486 motherboard because there are more 486 motherboards on the market and thus more competition.

Who needs a Pentium?

If you work with any of the following, you need a Pentium: multimedia applications, 3-D graphics, video applications, large-number crunching, a network server, and others. Minicomputers and mainframes were previously used for many of these. There are hundreds of scientific, business, and personal applications that can be handled best by the Pentium. A Pentium system can quickly calculate very complex financial equations, giving a Wall Street broker an advantage over anyone without a similar computer. Other applications are discussed in chapter 13.

Several companies are building high-end Pentium servers, and have designed special motherboards for the system. Most of these motherboards have eight expansion slots and allow for a maximum of 128MB of RAM. The ALR Evolution VQ/60 has 11 expansion slots and allows one gigabyte of RAM. Most systems have only five to eight drive bays; the ALR system has 13. You probably won't need a system like this.

I've had several computers. My first one was a Morrow with 64K of RAM and two single-sided 140K floppy disk drives. I built my next computer, an XT with 256K of RAM, double-sided 360K floppy drive, and 20MB hard disk drive. Since that time I've assembled several 286, 386, 486, and Pentium systems. I've always been amazed and quite happy with the differences and improvements in each newer system, but after I use the systems for a while I become rather indifferent and take them for granted, finding little faults here and there. It's somewhat like a new marriage after the honeymoon has worn off.

Before I built my Pentium, I used a 486DX2-66. It was fast, but there were times when I had to wait and twiddle my thumbs while it did its thing. I hate to wait. Even if it's only a few seconds, it seems like ages. If you're like me, you need a Pentium.

Another reason for owning a Pentium is the status. If you go to a computer user group and listen to the members talk among themselves, many of them boast about how big and powerful their system is. Writer Sebastian Rupley, in an article about the Pentium for *PC Computing*, used the term *technolust* to describe how some people felt about the Pentium. I think I might be one of those people.

To a computerphile, owning a big powerful Pentium system is probably about the same feeling a rich and famous person has in owning a Rolls Royce. And it's a whole lot less expensive.

Upgrading a 486

There are several ways you can upgrade a 486 to Pentium power, short of actually replacing the motherboard. One is with a P24T chip and the other is with a Pentium CPU module. Both are discussed in detail in chapter 4, under *Upgrading a 486 to the P24T* and *Pentium CPU module upgrade*.

Which Pentium motherboard should you buy?

There are several motherboard vendors, each one trying to differentiate his product from the others, so you have several choices. Which system you choose depends on what you want to use your computer for and how much money you want to spend.

An ISA, EISA, or MCA motherboard with either a VL or PCI bus, or combination of both might also have several on-board built-in options, such as serial and parallel ports, IDE and floppy drive interfaces, and a SCSI interface. You might also see a few of the low-profile motherboards with a single slot. I would avoid those if at all possible.

Sources for Pentium motherboards

Since there are several Pentium motherboard manufacturers, the competition will keep the prices fairly reasonable. I do a lot of my shopping by mail order. I look through computer magazines, such as *Computer Shopper, Byte, PC World, PC Magazine,* to compare prices and products. Several of them have a section near the back where the products are advertised during that issue. The items are categorized and grouped by product type, and include the page number for each ad so it's easy to find what you're looking for. This is a great help when you consider that *Computer Shopper* is often 1,000 pages long.

If you live near a large city, there will probably be several computer dealers in your city. You can ask them about components. Local dealers, however, might be a bit more expensive than mail order.

Again, if you live in a large city, there are probably computer swap meets every so often where local dealers meet at a large auditorium or fairgrounds and set up booths to sell their wares. Most of the dealers usually offer very good prices and discounts. You can go from booth to booth and compare prices and products. I often go to swap meets even if I don't need anything. There's usually a large crowd and lots of excitement in the air. It's almost like a circus.

Upgrading an older computer

If you have an older computer, you can easily upgrade it by installing a new Pentium motherboard. A new motherboard will give you all of the advantages of a new Pentium, but it'll be much less expensive than buying a completely new system. You should be able to use most of your old components because all PCs use the same basic components, other than the motherboard. If you're upgrading an old XT, you might not be able to use the keyboard. The 286 and all later models use a keyboard that looks just like the XT keyboard and even has the same connector, but it's electronically different. Keyboards are relatively inexpensive, costing from $10 to $50.

Upgrading to a Pentium motherboard

Step 1: Know your CMOS setup.

Important! You must be able to tell the CMOS setup on your new system what type of hard disk drive you have. If you don't furnish all the proper information (type, number of cylinders, number of heads, and number of sectors), you might not be able to access the data on your hard disk.

If you don't have your system configuration written down somewhere, run your system CMOS setup to determine the data. Many older machines used several different methods to access the CMOS setup. If you have documentation, it should tell you how to access the setup mode. On most systems, you can press something (Esc or Del) while the system is booting up. On some systems, if you hold down a key while the machine is booting up, it will give you an error and tell you to press F1. This usually puts you into the setup mode. Run it and write down the type of drives, number of cylinders, heads, and sectors, landing zone, and any other information that's given.

Step 2: Shut off the power and disconnect the cords and cables.

The next thing to do is to shut off the power and disconnect the power cord and the keyboard cable. There are probably several other cables on the back of the PC. It's very easy to forget how and where things were plugged in. Mark the various cables and cords, so when you're ready to plug them back into the new system you can match them up. This assures that every cable is plugged back into the correct place. After you've marked all the cables, disconnect them.

Step 3: Remove the case cover.

Locate and remove the screws that hold the case or cover on. Most early systems have five screws on the back panel, one in each corner and one in the top center. Don't remove the four screws that hold the power supply in place. Once the cover screws are removed, you can slide the cover off toward the front.

Step 4: Make a diagram before disassembly.

Once the cover is removed, before doing anything else take a piece of paper and make a rough drawing of where each board is plugged in and any cable plugged into it. Then use a felt-tip pen to mark each cable and connector so you can match them back up to the same board (like you did with the cords and cables on the back of the machine). Some cables can be plugged in backwards or upside down. You can prevent this by marking the connectors. Note in particular how the two connectors from the power supply are plugged into the motherboard. Note that the four black wires are in the center. These two connectors must be connected to the new motherboard in the same way.

Most of the cables are ribbon cables from the floppy and hard drives to the controller. You might be able to leave the cables connected to the boards and just pull the boards out of the motherboard slot. You shouldn't have to remove any of the disk drives. Leave the cables plugged into the drives if possible.

Step 5: Remove all the plug-in boards and cables.

The cables from the power supply are plugged into the motherboard, usually near the right rear corner of the motherboard. At the front there might also be several small wires for the front-panel light-emitting diodes (LEDs) and for the speaker. If these small wires and connectors aren't marked, take some masking tape and put labels on them. Your new motherboard will have similar pins for the connectors, but they might be in a different location.

Once you've removed all the boards and disconnected all the cables, look for a screw near the front center of the motherboard and another in the rear of the motherboard. Remove the screws, pull the motherboard to the left, and then lift it out. You might have to jiggle it a bit. The motherboard has grooved plastic stand-offs that slide into raised slots.

Step 6: Set switches and jumpers and install the motherboard.

You should have received some documentation with your new motherboard. Set any switches or jumpers to configure the system. Install any extra memory chips. Make sure you've installed all the plastic stand-offs in the proper holes, then drop the motherboard into the slots and push it to the right until it locks in place. Replace the screws in the front and back of the motherboard.

Connect all the front-panel LED wires and the speaker wires. The motherboard should have some markings to indicate where each small connector should be plugged in. You might have to refer to your documentation for some wires.

Next, connect the power-supply cables to the motherboard. Note that this connector can be plugged in incorrectly. When connected properly, the four black wires are in the center, adjacent to each other. The power-supply connector is

7-1 The power-supply connection to the motherboard. Note that the four black wires are in the center.

usually two separate cables with six wires in each cable. They're sometimes marked P8 and P9. Figure 7-1 shows the proper power-supply connection to the motherboard.

Step 7: Reinstall the boards.

Reinstall all your plug-in boards and reconnect any cables to the boards that were disconnected. Connect the monitor and keyboard. Plug in the power cord. Recheck all your connections to make sure everything is plugged in properly, then turn on the power. Make sure to try the system before you put the cover back on. This way if it doesn't work, it's fairly easy to check all the boards and cables to make sure they're installed correctly.

Step 8: Turn on and boot up the machine.

If you've reconnected everything correctly, the system should work. Depending on what type of BIOS you have, it will probably tell you that the time and date isn't set and give you an error message about your drives. Check your documentation for instructions on how to set the time and date, and how to tell the CMOS memory what type of floppy and hard drives you've installed.

Step 9: Reinstall the cover.

If everything works okay, put the cover back on and congratulate yourself for saving a bundle.

Building a PC from scratch

Rather than upgrading, you might decide to buy the components and assemble your own dream machine. There are a lot of advantages to building your own. You can definitely save a bundle if you shop wisely, and you can put only those components you really want in your computer. You can also control the quality of the components.

If you don't have enough money at the moment, you can buy the basic components and then buy the rest as you can afford it. There's one more very important reason why you should build your own: you'll gain valuable knowledge of your computer. You'll also have the pleasure and pride of having done it yourself.

Necessary components

The following sections list the necessary components; major components are discussed in detail in the various chapters. I recommend that you read those chapters before buying the components you need.

Case and power supply

Most cases come with a power supply. They're rather inexpensive, from about $35 for a desktop case to anywhere from $40 to $100 for various tower cases. There are mini-towers, medium towers, and full towers. I prefer the medium tower. It has all of the bays I need and plenty of room. It can sit upright on the desk or on the floor.

The case comes with a bag of screws for installing the disk drives and blank panels in the rear. It also has plastic stand-offs for the motherboard (see Fig. 7-2).

7-2
The bag of screws and plastic mounting hardware that comes with a case and power supply.

On old desktop cases, the switch for the power supply was usually a part of the power supply, and you had to reach around in back to turn it on. Most systems today have the switch on the front panel. You have to plug in four wires for the power switch (see Fig. 7-3). Figure 7-4 shows the switch with power lines connected, for illustration purposes only. You must first mount the switch on the control panel by pushing it into the opening from the outside. There are plastic locks on the switch that holds it in place. Then plug in the wires exactly as shown, otherwise you could have a direct short across 110-volt line. The approximate cost for a case and power supply is currently $45.

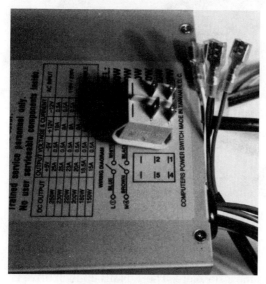

7-3
The switch for the power, and wires that must be connected.

7-4 This shows how the wires should be connected to the switch. The switch must first be mounted on the front panel and the wires plugged in the back.

Motherboard

Motherboards were discussed in general in chapter 4. This chapter discussed the Pentium in detail. I recommend the Pentium, but you can use any other motherboard. If you can't afford a Pentium or a 486, you can always buy a 386 motherboard for about $60 and then upgrade from the 386 to a 486 or Pentium. Figure 7-5 shows my Pentium motherboard from Twin T Distributors, at 703-352-4629. The approximate cost of a Pentium motherboard is currently $1,200.

7-5 My Pentium motherboard from Twin T.

Floppy disk drives

The 1.2MB 5¼-inch floppy drive is almost obsolete. The 1.44MB 3½-inch drive is much better in many ways, but there are still thousands of programs on 5¼-inch disks. You still need both drives. Some cases are limited in the number of bays they provide. Some of the older desktop cases had only two bays, accessible from the outside. So if you had two floppy disks you had no room to install a CD-ROM, a tape drive, or any other device. I recommend that you buy a combination drive, such as the one shown in Fig. 1-5 back in chapter 1. It has a 5¼-inch drive and a 3½-inch drive that are the same size, together, as a normal 5¼-inch drive. Floppy drives are discussed in chapter 8. The approximate cost of this type of floppy drive is currently $90.

Hard disk drives

I recommend two hard disk drives: either two IDE, two SCSI, or better yet an IDE and a SCSI. One of the main reasons for having two hard disk drives is so you can use one to back up the other. Hard disk drives fail, so it's important to maintain backups. It's very easy and fast to back up to a second hard drive.

If both drives are on an IDE or a SCSI interface, you could lose all of your data if the interface fails. If you have one on an IDE interface and one on a SCSI interface, the chances that both interfaces would fail at the same time is negligible. Figure 7-6

7-6 Two hard disk drives, a 540MB Maxtor IDE on the left and a Seagate 1.050GB SCSI on the right. They're both physically the same size.

shows the two hard drives I have in my Pentium. The drive on the left is a Maxtor 540MB IDE and the one on the right is a Seagate 1.050GB SCSI drive. The approximate cost for these two drives, at this time, is $1,000.

Disk drive interface

You can buy IDE interfaces for as little as $10, and many of them are also integrated with a multi-I/O board. It costs a bit more for a good fast VLB interface. Figure 7-7 shows a fast IDE interface with 2MB of DRAM for disk caching. This IDE board can control up to four IDE drives and four floppy drives, but it doesn't have the multi-I/O utilities of the less expensive boards.

7-7 A fast VLB IDE interface with 2MB of DRAM for disk caching.

Figure 7-8 shows my PowerSCSI! interface from Future Domain, at 714-253-0400. It can control floppy disk drives and up to seven SCSI devices. It's very easy to set up and use. The current approximate cost for a good IDE and SCSI interface is $350.

7-8 A SCSI interface card from Future Domain. It can control two floppy drives and up to seven SCSI devices.

Monitor

When choosing a monitor, buy the biggest and best you can afford. I bought a ViewSonic 21-inch monitor, which is shown in Fig. 7-9 alongside an old 13-inch monitor. The bigger screen makes a world of difference. The current approximate cost for this monitor is $1,700.

7-9 An early NEC 13-inch monitor (left) and 21-inch ViewSonic (right).

Monitor adapter

You must have an adapter to drive a monitor. You can buy one for as little as $40, but one with good resolution, good graphics, and speed will cost from $200 to $500. Figure 7-10 shows two very good monitor adapters from Diamond Computer Sys-

7-10 Two monitor adapters from Diamond, a VLB on top and a PCI on the bottom.

tems, at 408-736-2000. The one on top is the Viper VLB and the one on the bottom is the Viper PCI. They each have 2MB of video RAM (VRAM). The approximate cost at this time for one of these adapters is $250.

Keyboard

There are several ways to input data into a computer, one of the most common of which is with a keyboard. There are a lot of different keyboards, from $10 to $400. The current approximate cost for a keyboard is $40.

CD-ROM

It's almost essential now to have a CD-ROM drive on your computer. Many large software packages are being distributed on CD-ROM, and there's a world of information and entertainment available on CD-ROMs. Figure 7-11 shows my Toshiba CD-ROM drive attached to a Future Domain SCSI interface. A Seagate 1.050GB hard drive is also attached to this interface. The approximate cost for a double-speed CD-ROM drive at this time is $200, and about $400 for a quad-speed drive.

Sound card

Sound cards are also a necessity now. Figure 7-12 shows my CD-ROM connected to a Sound Blaster card. This CD-ROM drive is capable of playing sound from audio compact discs as well as from data CDs. Many sound cards come with a microphone and speakers. Their approximate cost at this time is $150.

7-11 A CD-ROM drive and a 1.050GB hard drive attached to a Future Domain SCSI interface.

7-12 A CD-ROM drive connected to a sound board.

Fax/modem

A fax/modem card is an absolute necessity in order to access bulletin boards, on-line services, and the Internet. They're now relatively inexpensive. Figure 7-13 shows my 14.4-Kbps SupraFAX modem. I paid $129 for it six months ago; it's now selling for less than $100. The approximate cost is currently $90.

7-13 A 14.4-Kbps fax/modem card.

Total cost

The approximate cost of this dream system would be about $5,115. Of course, there are several areas where you could save money. You could buy a 17-inch monitor instead of a 21-inch monitor to save about $800. You could also buy less-expensive disk drives, interfaces, and monitor adapters. The cost depends on what you want, how well you shop, and how much you want to spend.

Assembling the components

It's very easy to assemble computer components. All you have to do is plug them together. The boards plug into the slots on the motherboard, and there are only a few cables that connect the disk drives and power supply.

I usually assemble computers on a bench or kitchen table. If you use a kitchen table, put down several layers of newspaper, or something to protect the table. The motherboard and most other boards have very sharp component lead projections on the back, which can scratch and damage a surface.

I connect everything together and try it out. If there's anything wrong, it's very easy to troubleshoot the system on the table. After I'm satisfied that it works okay, I just move it all into the case. Here are some brief instructions and steps for assembly:

Step 1: Install the memory.

If you have SIMM memory, it's very easy to install. SIMM modules have a cutout on one end, so they have to be installed properly. Place the module into the socket on a slant, then push down and pull forward until the clamp locks them in. Check your documentation to make sure you install the memory in the proper banks.

Step 2: Connect the power supply to the motherboard.

The power supply is connected to the motherboard with two separate cables, usually marked P8 and P9. There are six wires in each connector, and it's possible to plug these connectors in backwards. Figure 7-1 shows the power-supply connection. When connected properly, the four black wires are adjacent to each other in the center.

Step 3: Connect ribbon cables to the floppy drives.

Figure 7-14 shows the ribbon cables you need. The cables on top with external connectors are for the COM ports and the printer port. You might not need these cables depending on the type of boards you have. All the ribbon cables have a different colored wire on one side, which indicates that those wires go to pin 1. Most of the connectors can be plugged in backwards. The boards that the cables plug into are also usually marked for pin 1. All you have to do is make sure the colored wire goes to the side with the pin 1 mark.

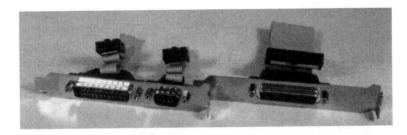

7-14 The cables on the top with the external connectors are for the COM and printer ports. The cable in the center is a 50-wire SCSI cable. The next one is a 40-wire IDE cable, and the one on the bottom is a 34-wire floppy disk cable.

The bottom part of the photo shows a SCSI cable that can be used to connect two devices. In the center is an IDE cable that can be used with two IDE drives. The ribbon cable on the bottom is for two floppy drives.

The 34-wire ribbon cable for the floppy drives has a connector on each end and one in the middle. The connector on one end has some wires that have been split and twisted. This connector goes to floppy drive A:. The connector in the center goes to drive B:. Just make sure that the colored wire goes to pin 1. Figure 7-15 shows a connector with pins. Some of the floppy drives might have an edge connector, such as the one shown in Fig. 7-16. Pin 1 might not be marked, but there's a slit between contacts 2 and 3, so you know pin 1 is on that side.

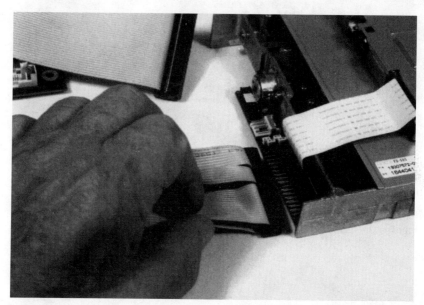

7-15 Connecting the cable to the floppy disk drive. The connector with the split and twisted wires goes to drive A: and the middle connector goes to drive B:. Make sure the side of the cable with the different colored wire goes to pin 1 of the connector.

The other end of the cable plugs into the set of floppy disk pins on the IDE multi-I/O board, or whatever board you're using. Just make sure the colored wire goes to the side marked pin 1 (see Fig. 7-17).

My Pentium motherboard has a built-in floppy and IDE controller, as well as a printer port and COM ports. The pins are clearly marked, so I just plug the floppy cable onto the motherboard pins (see Fig. 7-18).

Step 4: Connect the hard disks.

The connectors for a 40-wire IDE ribbon cable and 50-wire SCSI cable are quite similar. Figure 7-19 shows the connectors for a SCSI cable. Note the raised squares in the center of the connectors. The shell of the disk connector has a matching cutout, so these connectors have to be plugged in properly.

The other end of the IDE cable connector plugs into pins either on the motherboard or on a plug-in interface board. This end of the cable can be plugged in backwards, so make sure the colored wire goes to pin 1. If you intend to connect a second

7-16 A floppy drive with an edge connector. Note the slit between contacts 2 and 3. In this photo, you can also see the small round worm-screw motor that moves the heads from track to track.

7-17 Connecting an IDE cable to the interface board. This connector can be plugged in backwards. Look for an indication of pin 1 on the board and make sure that the colored wire of the cable goes to that side.

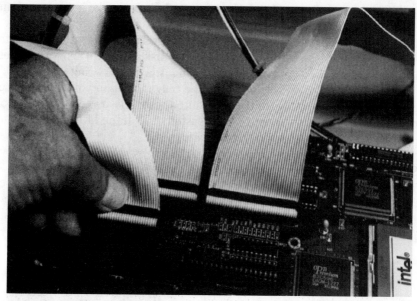

7-18 Connecting cables to a motherboard with built-in controllers and ports. This is my Twin T motherboard, with sets of upright pins for the printer, IDE drives, floppy drives, and two COM ports.

7-19
A close-up of the SCSI cable connectors. Note the square elevation in the center of the connector. There's a matching cutout in the shell around the board connector, so the connectors must be plugged in properly.

IDE drive to the middle connector, it must be configured either as the slave or master. There's a set of small pins that must be jumpered. Check your documentation.

The interface board for the SCSI cable has a shell that's keyed so the cable has to be connected properly. If you intend to connect more devices to the SCSI interface, each device must be configured by jumpers for a particular logical unit number (LUN). Check your documentation.

On a VLB board, the first four upright pins are for wires that go to the front-panel light-emitting diode (LED) that shows hard disk activity. When these wires are connected properly, the light will come on when the disk is being accessed. If you have a very quiet hard disk, this might be the only indication you have that something's happening. The two wires that plug into these pins are two different colors, and the pins might not be marked. Try the system first; if the LED doesn't come on, then try reversing the connection on the board.

Step 5: Connect power cables to the drives.

You should have four cables from your power supply for drives. Each cable should have a red wire, two black wires, and a yellow wire, and a small plastic connector that can be plugged in only one way. Plug a cable into each of the drives. Figure 7-20 shows a power cable being connected to an IDE hard drive.

7-20   Connecting a power cable to a hard disk.

If you have more than four drives in your system, you'll probably need a Y connector. This connector plugs into one of the power cables to give you two cables (see Fig. 7-21). If you have a 3½-inch drive or a combination 5¼-inch and 3½-inch drive, it might have a miniature connector. If so, you'll need an adapter. These adapters are usually included with the drive.

Step 6: Plug the boards into the motherboard slots.

Plug the SCSI interface board into one of the slots on the motherboard. If the IDE and floppy drive interfaces are built into the motherboard, then you don't have

7-21
A Y power cable to give an
extra connection.

to plug in a board. Plug in your monitor adapter and connect the monitor cable to it.
Plug the keyboard cable into the connector on the back of the motherboard.

Step 7: Check and turn on the power.

Check all your cable connections to make sure the colored wire goes to pin 1.
Make sure all the plug-in boards are completely seated. If everything seems to be
okay, then put a bootable floppy disk in drive A: and turn on the power.

Step 8: Install in the case.

If everything works okay, then turn off the power and install the components in
the case. You should have received a bag of hardware, including several white plastic
stand-offs for mounting the motherboard, with your case (refer back to Fig. 1-4 in
chapter 1). If you're mounting the system in a desktop machine, the case might look
something like the one in Fig. 1-3, also back in chapter 1. There are raised channels
in the floor and slots to accept the plastic stand-offs. Drop the motherboard so the
heads of the stand-offs fall into the wide portion of the slots, then push the board so
the narrow portion of the slot locks it in. Figure 7-22 shows the back of a motherboard
mounted in a tower case. Note the white heads of the plastic stand-offs in the slots.

7-22 The back of a motherboard installed in a tower case. Note the white heads
of the plastic standoff/retainers in the slots.

It might save you a bit of trouble to just remove the plug-in boards from the motherboard, and leave the cables connected to the boards and disk drives. You should have no trouble installing your hard disks in the bays.

You should also install your CD-ROM and fax/modem card at this time. Check your documentation and make sure to set any necessary jumpers or switches.

Step 9: Connect wires for the front-panel LEDs.

The front panel of your case has several wires that connect to pins on the motherboard. These wires go to light-emitting diodes (LEDs) that indicate power, turbo mode, and hard disk activity. There are also wires for the reset button and wires that connect the small speaker. There are usually markings on the motherboard, but you might have a bit of trouble tracing the wires back to each LED or switch. There are usually no markings on the wires.

LEDs are polarity sensitive. The motherboard might have a plus sign or a 1 near one of the pins. The wires are two colors, such as red and black, blue and black, green and white, or red and white. When there's a black or white wire present, it's usually the ground wire, and the other wire goes to pin 1. It won't hurt the LED to plug them in backward. If is doesn't work, plug them in the other way.

Step 10: Recheck and turn on the power again.

Recheck all the connections, then turn on the power to make sure it still works. If everything is still okay, turn the power off and install the case cover. Then go ask someone to pat you on the back and congratulate you. You deserve it.

8
CHAPTER
Floppy drives and disks

It's possible to run a PC with only floppy disk drives, but you'd be severely limited in the programs you could run, and it would take a whole lot of time. Floppy disks were all there were in the early days. Some PCs had only a single floppy drive and almost all the early drives used single-sided, 5¼-inch floppy disks that were 140K to 180K. It was a great leap forward when IBM introduced a PC with two floppy drives that could handle double-sided floppy disks. The floppy disks could be formatted to a whopping 180K on each side, for a total of 320K. Even if you were fortunate enough to have a PC with two floppy drives, doing any kind of computing involved an endless amount of disk swapping and it took forever to get anything done.

My first computer had two single-sided 140K drives. It was slow and required a lot of disk swapping. Floppy systems have come a long way since those early days. 140K systems were soon replaced with 320K double-sided systems, then 360K, then 1.2MB, 1.44MB, 2.88MB, and now even 21MB on a floppy disk.

Most programs today are very user-friendly. The more user-friendly they are, the larger they are. Today, most programs are shipped on 1.44MB disks in compressed form and they must be uncompressed before they can be used. Many programs require from 25MB up to 60MB or more to be installed and run. It would be impossible to run programs like these with a floppy disk system. With the low prices of hard disk drives today, I can't imagine anyone running a PC without a good high-capacity hard drive. If you're going to do any kind of productive computing, this is one of the better upgrades.

Floppy disks and floppy drives are a very important part of your computer. The majority of all software presently comes on floppy disks, although many companies now use CD-ROMs. No matter how you receive it, however, the software is usually copied to a hard disk.

Don't worry that the CD-ROM will replace the floppy disk. You can do many things with floppy disks that you can't do with a CD-ROM, such as making archive copies of small programs, backing up a hard disk, or moving a small program from one computer to another. The floppy system will be around for a long time.

How floppy drives operate

Computers rely to a large extent on magnetism. Magnetic lines of force are produced when voltage is passed through a coil of wire wrapped around a piece of iron. The amount of magnetism produced varies enormously on many factors, including the voltage level, number of turns of the wire, properties of the iron core, and the frequency of the voltage. Conversely, voltage is produced when a coil of wire is passed through a magnetic field. So voltage makes magnetism and magnetism makes voltage.

A floppy drive spins a disk much like a record player. The floppy disk is made from a type of plastic material called polyethylene terephthalate, which is coated with a magnetic material made primarily of iron oxide. It's similar to the tape used in cassette tape recorders. The drive head is basically a piece of iron with a coil of wire around it, shaped somewhat like a C. When voltage is passed through the coil of wire, a magnetic field is produced between the ends of the C. This small space is called the *gap*. The head records (writes) and plays back (reads) the disk much like the record/playback head in a cassette tape recorder. Figure 8-1 is an illustration of a read/write head.

There's a considerable difference in recording on a tape recorder and digital recording. When audio is recorded, sound waves cause a diaphragm in a microphone to vibrate. Attached to the diaphragm is a magnet that moves in and out of a coil of wire because of the sound vibrations. The movement of the magnet in the coil of wire generates a voltage that moves up and down, exactly matching the up and down vibration of the sound. This voltage is then amplified and fed to the tape record head. The record head responds with a voltage or current output that's a replica of the original sound. The varying current from the head magnetizes the tape with a duplicate of the original sound. When the tape is played back, as the magnetized image on the tape passes by the head it causes a voltage to be produced that's the same as the original sound. Of course, the voltage produced by the magnetism on the tape is very small, so it must be amplified.

Placing a small voltage on the base of a transistor turns it on and amplifies, or creates a much larger replica of, the small original voltage.

The voltages in a tape recorder are alternating current (ac), that is they vary. Most voltages used in computers are direct current (dc), usually 3 to 5 volts. Transistors, which act like switches, can turn the direct current on and off. When the current is on, it's a 1; when it's off, it's a 0. A transistor can be switched on and off millions of times per second.

When the head on a disk drive writes or records on the iron oxide surface, a pulse of electricity causes the head to magnetize that portion of track beneath the head. A spot on the track that's magnetized represents a 1; if the next spot of the same track is not magnetized, it represents a 0. When the tracks are read, the head detects whether each portion of the track is magnetized or not. If the spot is magnetized, it creates a small voltage signal to represent a 1, or a 0 if it's not magnetized.

Computers operate with a very precise clock rate, based on internal crystal oscillators. If the voltage remains high for a certain length of time, it can represent two or more 1s; if it's off for a certain length of time, it represents two or more 0s.

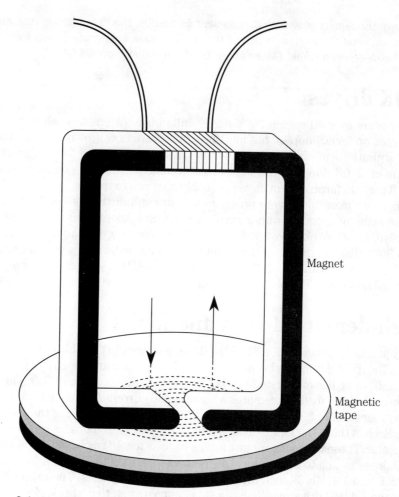

Magnet

Magnetic
tape

8-1 A representation of a read/write head on a floppy disk or tape recorder.

Floppy disks are divided into several concentric tracks, and each track is then divided into sectors. This system lets you find any particular item on the track. It's amazing to me that the head can find any one byte on a floppy disk that can have over a million bytes of information. It's even more amazing that the same system can find any one byte on a hard disk that can have as much as 2 billion bytes, or 2 gigabytes of data.

On a 1.2MB floppy disk, 80 tracks are laid down at the rate of 96 tracks per inch, so each track occupies ⅟₉₆ of an inch, or about .0104 inch. The record current that passes through the heads varies considerably. A strong current might even magnetize adjacent tracks. To prevent this, the actual recording part of the head is only about ⅛ as wide as the track width. There are two erase heads on each side and behind the record head that extend to the full width of the track. As the record head lays down the square waves that represent 1s and 0s, the erase heads trim any signal that exceeds the normal width of the track. These side erase heads form guard bands between each track. (More about tracks and disk formats later.)

360K drives

There are over 40 million 360K drives still in use. At one time all software was distributed on 360K floppies, but most programs have now grown so large that vendors distribute them on 1.2MB or 1.44MB disks in compressed form. If you need a program on 360K floppies, you might have trouble getting the company to supply them. If they do furnish them, it will probably cost you extra.

There are many shareware programs that are still distributed on 360K floppies because many of them are rather small. A short time ago, 1.2MB disks were rather expensive, but they now cost as little as 20 cents apiece, just a few pennies more than a 360K disk. So there really isn't much need for 360K drives or disks anymore. Since 1.2MB drives can read 360K disks, I recommend that you scrap your old drives and install new ones. The old 360K format has served us well, but it's now obsolete.

High-density drives and disks

By just looking at a 360K and 1.2MB drive, you wouldn't be able to tell which was which. The main difference between the two is magnetic and electrical differences. The 1.2MB drive has an Oersted (Oe) of 600, the 360K has an Oe of 300. The higher Oe means that the material requires a higher head current for magnetization.

In order to store 1.2MB on a floppy disk, 80 tracks on each side of the disk are laid down. Each of these tracks are divided into 15 sectors, and 512 bytes can be stored in each sector. These 80 tracks are just half as wide as the 40 tracks of a 360K disk. The 1.2MB drives switch to a lower head current when writing to the 360K format.

720K and 1.44MB 3½-inch drives also look very much alike. The main difference is that the 1.44MB drive usually has a small microswitch that checks for the square hole in the right rear corner of the 1.44MB disks. 1.44MB drives will read and write to the 720K format as well as to the high-density format. The 720K drive is also obsolete.

The all-media or combination floppy drive

If you decide to replace an obsolete 360K or a 720K drive, you might consider buying a combination drive. It's a rather inexpensive upgrade that can make life a lot easier. Most older systems don't have enough bays, and many desktop computers provide only three or four bays in which to mount drives. You might not have space to mount two floppy and two hard drives, a tape backup system, and a CD-ROM drive.

CMS Enhancements, 714-222-6316, noted this problem and created an all-media floppy drive by combining a 1.2MB and a 1.44MB floppy drive into a single unit. The 5¼-inch drive can handle 360K and 1.2MB floppies; the 3½-inch part can handle 720K and 1.44MB floppy disks. The combination drive requires only a single drive bay. Since the two drives can never both be used at the same time, there's no problem. They can even share most of the drive electronics. See Fig. 1-5 in chapter 1 for an example.

Teac, Canon, and several other companies are now manufacturing combination drives. Eventually, the 1.44MB drive will be replaced with the 2.88MB drive, which can handle 720K, 1.44MB, and 2.88MB floppies. This type of combination will become the standard. Combination drives currently cost about $100.

Disk drive motors

Disk drives have two motors. One drives the spindle that rotates the disk and the other, a stepping motor, or actuator, moves the heads back and forth to the various tracks.

Spindle motor

If you have an older computer, then you probably have a 5¼-inch 360K floppy drive, or maybe two such drives. If it's very old, they might be full height, or about 3½ inches high. If it's an original IBM machine, then they probably have a plastic or rubber O ring for a drive belt from the motor to the disk spindle. The O ring deteriorates and stretches with time. The speed of the disk is crucial; when the O ring stretches, the speed slows down and the spindle might not even turn at all.

I replaced an IBM 5¼-inch 360K floppy drive in 1985 because it kept giving me errors when reading floppies. It cost $425 for a new IBM drive. A 5¼-inch drive today costs about $45. I didn't realize it at the time, but I could have just replaced the O ring. Most newer drives use direct drive motors, where the spindle is just an extension of the motor shaft. Figure 8-2 shows an old IBM 360K drive on the left, a 1.2MB drive in the center, and a combination 3½-inch and 5¼-inch drive on the right.

The motors are regulated so the speed is usually fairly constant. The speed of the old 5¼-inch 360K floppy drive is 300 RPMs. A 5¼-inch 1.2MB drive rotates at 360 RPMs, even when reading and writing to a 360K disk. All 3½-inch floppy drives rotate at 300 RPMs.

Head actuator motor

The head actuator motor is electronically linked to the file allocation table (FAT). If a request is received to read data from a particular track, say track 20, the actuator motor moves the head, or rather heads, to that track. Floppy drives have two heads, one on top and one on the bottom. They're connected together and move as a single unit.

Several large companies manufacture floppy drives, such as Sony, Toshiba, Fuji, and Teac. Each company's prices are within a few dollars of the others. Most of them are fairly close in quality, but there might be minor differences. For instance, I have an older 1.2MB drive that's much quieter and operates much more smoothly than my combination drives.

On some older drives, a fairly large actuator stepping motor is used to position the heads. It's very quiet and smoothly moves the heads from track to track. It has a steel band around the motor shaft that moves the heads in and out.

8-2 Three floppy disk drives. The one on the left is an old IBM 360K drive with a rubber O ring to drive the spindle. The center is a 1.2MB drive, and the one on the right is a combination 3½-inch and 5¼-inch drive.

The actuator stepping motors on some drives are small cylindrical motors with a worm screw. The motors groan and grunt as they move the heads from track to track. Other than being a bit noisy, they usually work fine. Figure 7-16 back in chapter 7 shows a small round worm screw motor. You can see a bit of the worm screw that moves the heads in and out. Figure 8-3 shows a large square stepper motor in the bottom right corner. This is what moves the heads in discrete steps across the disk. There's a steel band attached to the shaft and heads of the stepper motor. If the software tells the motor to go track 15, it knows exactly how far to move the heads. If for some reason the steel band attached to the actuator motor shaft becomes loose or out of adjustment, the drive might not be able to find the proper tracks. If the hub of the disk you're trying to read has become worn or isn't centered exactly on the cone spindle, the heads might not be able to find a particular track.

If the heads in your disk drive are out of alignment, you can write and read on your own machine, because you're using the same misalignment to write and read. But another drive might have trouble reading a disk recorded with misaligned heads.

Floppy controllers

A floppy drive must have a controller to tell it when to turn on and when to go to a certain track and sector. In the early days, the controller was a large board full of chips. Later, some manufacturers integrated the floppy disk controller (FDC) onto the

8-3 A floppy drive that shows the square head motor in the bottom right corner. The spindle motor is the large round object. The pen is pointing to a set of pins that can be jumpered when more than two floppies are connected to the computer. Up to four floppies can be connected.

same board as the hard disk controller (HDC). These were large, full-length boards that were rather expensive, at about $250. Now, floppy drive controllers (FDCs) are usually built into a single VLSI chip and integrated with a hard disk controller or IDE interface. Now the FDC and the IDE hard disk interface are often built into the motherboard. These motherboards usually have a set of upright pins for the flat-ribbon cable connectors.

Older controller boards had an edge connector for the cable, and later boards had two rows of pins for the connector. Be very careful when plugging in the cable connector. Look for pin one on the board and make sure the different colored wire goes to that side. If the cable is plugged in backwards, the floppy disk won't work properly. If the cable is plugged in backwards and you try to boot up, the floppy drive will erase portions of the floppy disk's boot section. You'll no longer be able to boot up with the disk. I know this happens because I've made this stupid mistake. Fortunately, I had a backup boot disk.

Drive select jumpers

It's possible to have four different floppy drives connected to one controller. The floppies have a set of pins with a jumper so each drive can be set for a unique number. The pen in Fig. 8-3 points to this set of pins. The pins are labeled DS0, DS1, DS2, and DS3. Some manufacturers label them DS1, DS2, DS3, and DS4. The vast majority of systems use only two drives. These jumpers also let you determine which drive is A: and which one is B:. In most cases, you'll use them as they come from the factory and never have to worry about them.

Most drives come with the second set of pins jumpered, which means they're set for drive A:. If you install a second floppy drive, it will also have the second set of pins jumpered, just like the A: drive. Don't change it. Since the floppy cable has some twisted wires in it, the controller automatically recognizes it as drive B:. This can be confusing and you might not get any documentation at all with your drive. Fortunately, they usually work fine as received from the factory.

Combination drives usually have small jumper pins near the miniature power cable connector. They have two columns of pins, one for each drive. There are six pins in each column, and four pins in each column are jumpered. Again, you should never have to reset or bother with these pins. The two drives share a single controller cable connector. If you want to use the 5¼-inch drive as drive A:, then plug the end of the cable with the twisted wires into the cable connector. If you want the 3½-inch 1.44MB drive to be drive A:, then plug in the middle connector that has no twists. Again, fortunately, there's usually no need to move the jumpers. In Fig. 8-4, the pen points to the small white jumpers.

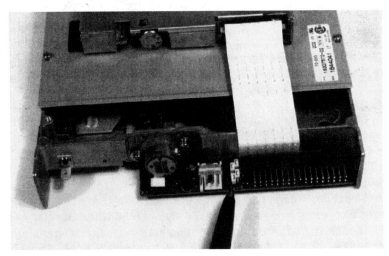

8-4 The pen points to the small white jumpers on a combination drive that can be used to configure each drive as A: or B:.

Extended-density drives

Several companies are now offering a 2.8MB 3½-inch extended-density floppy drive. The 2.8MB disks are barium ferrite and use perpendicular recording to achieve the extended density. In standard recording, the particles are magnetized so they lie horizontally on the disk. In perpendicular recording, the particles stand vertically on end for greater density.

ED drives require a controller that operates at 1 MHz. Other floppy controllers operate at 500 KHz. Several companies are now integrating the ED controller with the other floppy controllers. ED drives are downward compatible and can read and write to 720K and 1.44MB disks. ED drives and disks are still rather expensive, but the prices will come down eventually.

The virtual drive

DOS reserves the letters A and B for floppy drives. If you have only one drive, it can be both A: and B:. For instance, you can give the command COPY A: B: and the drive will copy whatever is in the drive into RAM, then prompt you to insert another disk in the same drive. Of course, you could have specified COPY A: A: with the same results.

Very-high-density drives

The floppy technology continues to advance. Several new higher-capacity drives and disks are now available. Insite, at 408-946-8080, developed a very-high-density (VHD) 3½-inch floppy disk that can store over 20 megabytes of information.

One of the problems that had to be overcome in VHD drives was that of tracking. A 3½-inch floppy drive has very little trouble reading and writing to the 135 tracks per inch (TPI) of the standard 3½-inch disk, but 20MB requires many more tracks much closer together. Head positioning must be very accurate to find and lock onto the various tracks.

To solve the head-positioning problem, Insite developed a special laser optical system. Since the drive used a combination of optical and floppy systems, they called it *floptical* drive. They use a laser beam to etch optical servo tracks onto the disks, and a layer of magnetic material is then laid down over the etched servo tracks. When reading or writing to these special disks, a laser beam that controls the head location locks onto the servo tracks, which provides very accurate reading and writing to the data tracks. The Insite drive has a head with two different gaps, so it's capable of reading and writing to the 20MB format as well as the 720K and 1.44MB formats. Figure 8-5 shows the 20MB Insite drive on the left with a standard 3½-inch drive on the right.

Disk compression systems such as Stacker can be used with these disks to store about 40MB on each disk. This system is great for making backups. You can also use a floptical system to make crucial data secure. You can remove and lock up the disk that contains the important data.

Iomega Corporation, at 801-778-1000, and several other companies are now also manufacturing floptical drives. Look in the computer magazines such as *Computer Shopper* and *PC World* for ads and current prices.

Bernoulli drives

Iomega Corporation has a high-capacity Bernoulli floppy disk system, which allows you to record up to 150MB on special 5¼-inch floppy disks. Using Stacker com-

8-5
An Insite floptical
20MB floppy drive on
the left and a standard
3½-inch drive on the
right.

pression software, the 150MB floppy will hold 300MB. With a Bernoulli drive, you need never run out of disk space. You can use a Bernoulli instead of or in conjunction with a hard disk.

Bernoulli disks spin much faster than a standard floppy, which forces the flexible disk to bend around the heads without actually touching them. This is in accordance with the aerodynamics principle discovered by the Swiss scientist Daniel Bernoulli (1700–1782). Bernoulli floppy disks spin at 2,368 RPMs. The ordinary floppy spins at 300 RPMs. In order to keep the Bernoulli from flexing too much at the high speed, it's placed between two steel plates.

The Bernoulli system stores data on only one side of the disk. For lower-capacity systems, a single floppy is used; for the higher-capacity disks, two floppy disks are sandwiched together and each is recorded on the outer side. The average seek time for a Bernoulli system is 32 ms, compare to 15 ms for better hard drives.

Since the floppies can be removed and locked up, they're an excellent security tool. They're also a way to make backups of your hard disks. You can back up 300MB in just seconds with a Bernoulli. It would take hours using floppy disks and a lot of intensive swapping of disks.

Look in computer magazines for ads and current prices, or call Iomega for brochures and your nearest dealer.

Data compression

Data compression can double your disk capacity. One of the most popular compression programs is Stacker from Stac Electronics (800-522-7822). Microsoft released MS-DOS 6.0 and 6.2 with a compression utility called DoubleSpace, and Stac

Electronics complained that the software infringed on their product. The complaint was settled and Microsoft bought a portion of the rights for Stacker. The two companies are now partners. DR DOS 7.0 comes with SuperStor as one of its utilities. IBM PC DOS also has a compression utility.

At one time, data compression wasn't completely trustworthy, but bulletin boards have been using it for years with very few problems, and backup programs use compression so fewer disks are needed. Compression has matured and is now reliable, and compression programs are fast and transparent to the user.

With Stacker and AddStor, you can double the size of any floppy disk. Stacker works great on VHD 20MB floppies and Bernoulli disks. I've used the Stacker systems for several years, since version 1.0, and have never had any problems. Compression can be the least expensive way to double your disk space, hard or floppy. More about data compression in the next chapter on hard drives.

Differences between floppy disks

360K 5¼-inch and 720K 3½-inch disks are called double-sided double-density disks (DS/DD); 1.2MB 5¼-inch and 1.44MB 3½-inch disks are called high-density disks (HD). 3½-inch disks are usually marked, but 5¼-inch disks usually have no markings. They look exactly alike, except that 360K disks usually have a re-enforcing ring or collar around the large center hole, and high-density 1.2MB disks don't have the ring. Some 360K disks have a white collar or ring, but most new disks have a black ring.

One major difference between 720K and 1.44MB disks is that high-density 1.44MB disks have a small square hole on the same side of the disk as the write-protect hole and 720K don't. The 3½-inch drive has a small media sensor microswitch that protrudes upwards. If it finds a hole on that side of the disk, it knows it's a 1.44MB disk. If there's no hole, it's treated as a 720K disks.

On 3½-inch disks, the write-protect hole has a small black slide that can be moved to cover it. Another small microswitch on the drive protrudes upward and checks the hole when the disk is inserted. If the hole is covered, the switch is pressed down, allowing the disk to be written on. If the hole is open, the switch protects the disk so it can't be written to or erased.

This 3½-inch write-protect system is just the opposite of the system used by 5¼-inch disks. They have a square notch that must be covered with opaque tape to prevent writing to or unintentionally erasing the disk. (Incidentally, you must use opaque tape. The 5¼-inch system uses a light to shine through the square notch. If the detector in the system can see the light through the notch, then it can write on the disk. Some people have used clear plastic tape to cover the notch with disastrous results.)

You might at some time want to make a copy of a 720K disk and all you have are 1.44MB disks. Or you might want to use a 1.44MB disk as a 720K disk. You can cover the hole with any kind of tape and it will format as 720K.

Table 8-1 shows some of the differences in various types of floppy disks. Notice that the maximum number of root directories is the same for 720K, 1.2MB, and

1.44MB disks. 2.88MB disks have four times the capacity of 720K disks, yet allow only 16 more root entries. This means that you can enter 224 different files on a 1.2MB disk, but not a single file more, even if you have hundreds of bytes of unused space. The reason is that DOS file allocation was designed for this limited number of files. There is, however, an easy way around the problem. Just create subdirectories, like those on a hard disk. Just use the MD (make directory) command. If necessary, you can even make sub-subdirectories.

Table 8-1. Capacities of various floppy disks

Disk size	Tracks per side	Sectors per track	Unformatted capacity	System use	Available to user	Max. dirs.
360K	40	9	368640	6144	362496	112
1.2MB	80	15	1228800	14898	1213952	224
3½"	80	9	737280	12800	724480	224
3½"	80	18	1474560	16896	1457664	224
3½"	80	36	2949120	33792	2915328	240

360K and 1.2MB

Although 360K and 1.2MB disks look exactly alike except for the hub ring on 360K disks, there's a large difference in their magnetic media formulation. Several materials, such as cobalt or barium, can be added to the iron oxide base to alter the magnetic properties. Cobalt is added to increase the Oersted (Oe) of high-density floppy disks. Barium is used for 2.88MB extra-high-density (ED) disks.

Oe is a measure of the resistance of a material to being magnetized. The lower the Oe, the easier it can be magnetized. 360K disks have an Oe of 300, and 1.2MB disks have an Oe of 600. 360K disks are fairly easy to magnetize or write to, so they require a fairly low head current. 1.2MB disks are more difficult to magnetize, so a much higher head current is required. A 1.2MB system can switch the current to match whatever type of disk you're using.

If you place a 360K floppy in a 1.2MB drive and type FORMAT, it will try to format it as a 1.2MB disk, but it will find several bad sectors, especially near the center where the sectors are shorter. These sectors will be marked and locked out. The system might report that you have over a megabyte of space on a 360K disk. I wouldn't recommend that you use such a disk for any important data. The data is packed much closer together when it's recorded as 1.2MB. Since the 300 Oe of the 360K disks is so easy to magnetize, nearby data might be affected. The data could migrate, eventually deteriorate, and become unusable.

720K and 1.44MB

3½-inch disks have several benefits and characteristics that make them superior to 5¼-inch disks. A 720K disk can store twice as much data as a 360K disk in a much smaller space. A 1.44MB can store four times as much as a 360K disk in the same small space.

3½-inch floppy disks have a hard plastic protective shell, so they're not easily damaged. They also have a spring-loaded shutter that automatically covers and protects the head opening when they aren't in use.

3½-inch systems are much more accurate than the 5¼-inch systems in reading and writing. 5¼-inch drive systems have a cone-shaped hub for the large center hole in the disks. When disks are used for any length of time, the hole can become stretched or enlarged. If the disk isn't centered exactly on the hub, the heads won't be able to find and read the data. 3½-inch floppies have a metal hub on the back, which make them much more accurate, even though the tracks on 3½-inch systems are much closer together.

It's possible to insert a 5¼-inch floppy upside down, backwards, or sideways. When I first started using computers, I inserted a floppy that had original software on it into a drive. I waited for a while and nothing happened. Then I got the error message "Not ready error reading drive A: Abort, Retry, Fail?" I panicked. I thought for sure I had destroyed the software. I finally discovered that I had inserted the floppy upside down. I was still scared that I had damaged the disk, so I did what I should have done when I first got the program. I made a backup of the disk. The software was still okay.

You can't actually damage a disk by inserting it upside down, but you can't read it because the small hole that tells DOS where track one begins is on the wrong side when it's inserted upside down. And of course you can't write to it or format it because the write-protect notch is on the other side.

3½-inch disks are designed so they must be inserted properly. They have arrows at the left top portion of the disks that indicate how they're to be inserted into the drive. They also have notches on the back that prevent them from being inserted upside down.

720K 3½-inch disks have an Oe of 600 to 700, 1.44MB disks have an Oe of 700 to 720, and the Oe of extra-high-density 2.88MB disks is about 750.

Disk format structure

Tracks

Before you can use a disk, you must format it, which consists of creating concentric tracks on each side of the disk. If it's a 360K disk, each side is marked or configured with 40 tracks, numbered from 0 to 39. If it's a 1.2MB, 720K, or 1.44MB disk, each side is configured with 80 tracks, numbered from 0 to 79.

The tracks have the same number on the top and bottom of the disk. The top is side 0 and the bottom is side 1. When the head is over track 1 on the top, it's also over track 1 on the bottom. The heads move as a single unit to the various tracks by a head actuator motor or positioner. When data is written to a track, as much as possible is written on the top track, then the head is electronically switched and it continues to write to the same track on the bottom side. It's much faster and easier to electronically switch between the heads than to move them to another track.

Cylinders

If you could strip away all the tracks on each side of track 1 on side 0 and track 1 on side 1, the disk would be very flat, but it might look like a cylinder. So if a disk has 40 tracks, such as a 360K disk, it also has 40 cylinders; 1.2MB and 1.44MB disks have 80 cylinders.

Sectors

Each track is divided into sectors. Each track of a 360K disk is divided into nine sectors, each track of a 1.2MB disk is divided into 15 sectors, each track in a 720K disk is divided into nine sectors, each track in a 1.44MB disk is divided into 18 sectors, and each track in a 2.88MB disk is divided into 36 sectors.

Each sector can contain 512 bytes. Multiplying the number of sectors by number of bytes per sector by the number of tracks by two sides gives you the amount of data that can be stored on a disk. For instance, a 1.2MB disk has 15 sectors, times 512 bytes, times 80 tracks, times two, or $15 \times 512 \times 80 \times 2 = 1{,}228{,}800$ bytes. The system uses 14,898 bytes to mark the tracks and sectors during formatting, so there are actually 1,213,952 bytes available on a 1.2MB floppy. Figure 8-6 shows how the tracks and sectors are laid out on a disk.

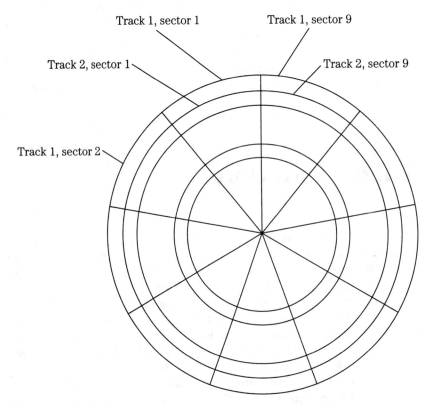

8-6 A diagram showing how tracks and sectors are laid out on a disk.

Clusters or allocation units

DOS allocates one or more sectors on a disk and calls it a *cluster* or *allocation unit*. On 360K and 720K disks, a cluster is two sectors. On 1.2MB and 1.44MB disks, each allocation unit is one sector. Only single files or parts of single files can be written into an allocation unit. If two different files are written into a single allocation unit, the data would become mixed and corrupted.

File-allocation table (FAT)

During formatting, a file-allocation table (FAT) is created on the first track of the disk. This FAT acts like a table of contents for a book. Whenever a file is recorded on the disk, it's broken up into allocation units. The head looks in the FAT to find empty units, then records the parts of the file in any empty units it can find. Part of a file might be recorded in sector 5 of track 10 and part in sector 8 of track 15. Then the computer records the location of all the various parts of the file in the FAT. Using the FAT, your computer can erase or add to parts of a file without changing the entire disk.

TPI

The 40 tracks of a 360K disk are laid down at a rate of 48 tracks per inch (TPI), so each of the 40 tracks is ⅟₄₈ of an inch wide. The 80 tracks of a high-density 1.2MB disk are laid down at a rate of 96 TPI, so each track is ⅟₉₆ of an inch, and the 80 tracks of a 3½-inch disk are laid down at a density of 135 TPI, or .0074 inch per track.

Read accuracy

5¼-inch disks have a 1⅛-inch center hole. The disk drives have a spindle with a conical hub that comes up through the center hole in the disk when the drive latch is closed. This centers the disk so the heads can find each track. The plastic material the disk is made from is subject to environmental changes and wear and tear. The conical spindle might not center each disk exactly, so head to track accuracy is difficult with more than 80 tracks. (If you have trouble reading a disk, it might be off-center. Try removing and reinserting it). Most 360K disks use a reinforcement hub ring, but it probably doesn't help much.

If your drive consistently has trouble reading your disks, especially those recorded on another machine, the heads might be out of alignment. The steel band or worm screw of the actuator motor that moves the heads might have slipped or become worn, so the actuator or head positioner can't move the heads to the proper track. It's possible to realign the heads, but it's time-consuming and expensive. Computer service time can cost $100 or more per hour; it would probably be much less expensive to scrap the drive and buy a new one.

3½-inch disks have a metal hub on the back, which is used to center the disks. The tracks of 3½-inch floppies are narrower and greater in density per inch. But because of the metal hub, the head-tracking accuracy is much better than that of 5¼-inch systems.

Differences between floppy and hard disks

Hard disks have very accurate and precise head-tracking systems. Some hard disks have a density of 3,000 or more tracks per inch, so much more data can be stored on a hard disk.

Floppy disks have a very smooth, lubricated surface and they rotate at a fairly slow 300 RPMs. Magnetic lines of force deteriorate very fast with distance, so the closer the heads, the better they can read and write. Floppy heads are in direct contact with floppy disks.

Hard disks rotate at speeds from 3,600 to 7,200 RPMs. The heads and surface would be severely damaged if they came in contact at this speed, so the heads "fly" over the surface of each disk, just a few millionths of an inch above it.

Floppy disks are quite a bit less expensive than hard disks. 1.2MB high-density disks sell at discount houses for as little as 21 cents, 25 cents if preformatted. 1.44MB disks sell for 35 cents, 39 cents if preformatted. There are several discount mail-order stores where you can get some real bargains in floppy disks. Check the computer magazines for ads.

Formatting

It's possible to use almost any version of MS-DOS, even old 1.0, but if you aren't using one of the later versions you're handicapping yourself and your computer. If you're using an older version of MS-DOS or any other DOS, it's one of the best upgrades you can make.

If you're using an older version of DOS but have upgraded to a 1.2MB A: drive, type FORMAT A:/4 to format a 360K disk. To format a 1.2MB disk, just type FORMAT A:. If you insert a 360K disk and type FORMAT A:, it will try to format it to 1.2MB and will probably find several bad sectors. To format a 720K disk in a 1.44MB B: drive, type FORMAT B:/F:720. To format a 1.44MB disk, just type FORMAT B:.

The FORMAT command in newer versions can take a very long time to start because it searches the floppy disk, saving any information on the disk. If you decide later that you want to unformat the disk, just type UNFORMAT. For most cases, however, you won't want to unformat a disk, especially if it's one that has never been formatted before. You can speed up the formatting process by typing FORMAT A:/U. This performs an unconditional format. If a disk has been formatted before, you can type FORMAT A:/Q., which gives you a quick format by just erasing the first letter of the files in the file-allocation table of the disk.

The MS-DOS manual doesn't give you too much help with the FORMAT command. The on-disk help is much better. If you have trouble with the FORMAT command, just type HELP FORMAT. If you need help with any command, just type HELP and then the name of the command.

I recently needed to boot my computer from a floppy disk with the minimum number of boot files. After I had booted up, I tried to make a new bootable floppy by typing FORMAT A:/S and got the error message "General failure reading drive A. Abort, Retry, or Fail?" I tried another floppy and got the same message. This is a message you often get when a disk is bad, but I couldn't believe that several disks were bad. I then tried the FORMAT command without the /S and it format-ted immediately. After it was formatted, I had no trouble invoking the SYS com-mand to transfer the operating system. I was a bit puzzled at first as to why it would give me a general failure error when I tried to format the disk with /S. I fi-nally figured out that when the system is normally booted up, it loads several files into memory. These files weren't present on the minimum disk I had booted up from and therefore weren't loaded into memory, so I couldn't make a bootable disk with all the system files on it.

Formatting .BAT files

Here are some batch files that save me a lot of time in formatting disks. End each line by hitting the Enter key. The ^Z indicates the end of the file, and you make it by pressing F6, or Ctrl–Z.

```
COPY CON FM36.BAT
FORMAT A:/4/U
^Z

COPY CON FM12.BAT
FORMAT A:/U
^Z

COPY CON FM72.BAT
FORMAT B:/F:720/U
^Z

COPY CON FM14.BAT
FORMAT B:/U
^Z
```

With these batch files, I then type just FM36 for a 360K disk, FM12 for a 1.2MB disk, FM72 for a 720K disk, and FM14 to format a 1.44MB disk. The /U tells DOS to go ahead and do an unconditional format and not to waste time reading the disk and saving data. Keep in mind that the commands in these .BAT files apply to latest ver-sions of MS-DOS and DR DOS.

How to install drives

To install your drives, you'll need a Phillips-head and standard screwdriver. (It helps if they're magnetized, but be careful if you're using magnetized tools around your floppy disks. They can partially erase or damage them.) You might also find it helpful to have a pair of long-nosed pliers.

Step 1: Set any switches or jumpers.

You should have received some sort of documentation with your drive. It might have jumpers that must be set depending on the type of system you have. Check the documentation and, if necessary, set the jumpers before you install the drive. In most cases you can use the drive as it comes, with the factory default settings.

There are exceptions. I once overlooked the setting of a jumper on one of the 3½-inch drives I had installed in one of my 386 machines. It seemed to work fine, but if

I typed DIR to display the disk's directory, then removed that disk, inserted another, and did another DIR, it would display the same directory from the first disk. The other drive on my system worked fine, so I knew something was wrong with the new drive. I finally found that one of the jumpers needed to be set to something other than the factory default setting.

The documentation that comes with most drives and other components is often very poorly written and organized, and you might have trouble understanding it. Your dealer might not even be able to help you, especially if you bought it from a mail-order house. This is a good reason to belong to a good user group. Such a group can be a tremendous help if you have problems.

Step 2: Install an expansion frame if necessary.
All older cases had bays for 5¼-inch drives. 3½-inch drives are much smaller than the old standard 5¼-inch drives, and many newer cases have small bays or provisions for mounting them. But if you have an older case, you might need to buy an expansion bracket that allows the drive to be mounted in any standard 5¼-inch drive bay. An expansion bracket will probably cost from $3 to $5. Figure out what type of case you have and order the expansion bracket when you order the drive.

Four screws usually mount the drive to the bracket. For some older cases, you might have to install plastic or metal slide rails on each side of the bracket assembly.

Step 3: Remove the cover.
You're now ready to install the drive in the system. The first thing to do, of course, is to unplug the power. If you have one of the older standard cases, remove the cover by removing each of the screws in the four corners of the back panel. There's usually one more screw in the top center of the back panel. Slip the cover off. If you have one of the tower cases, there are usually three screws on the back, along each side. The edges of the front part of the cover fit under the panel. Remove the screws from the back, pull the cover back slightly, and lift it off.

Once the cover is off, make a rough diagram of the cables—how and where they're connected. Pay close attention to the position of the colored wire on each ribbon cable. Now you can remove your old drives. If you're going to use the same controller, leave the cable plugged into it.

Step 4: Mount the drives.
Mount the drives in the chassis. If they're not to be mounted with slide rails, there are several holes on the sides of the drives and the bay. Line the holes up and insert screws. Make sure to use only the proper screws; if they're too long, they could damage the drive. Don't overtighten the screws. The metal is very soft and it's very easy to strip the threads.

Step 5: Reconnect the cables.
The flat ribbon cable to the drives should have three connectors. The connector on one end will have a split and twist in some of the wires. This connector goes to drive A: (see Fig. 8-7). The connector in the middle goes to the B: drive. If you have two drives, whichever one has the connector on the end with the twist is drive A:.

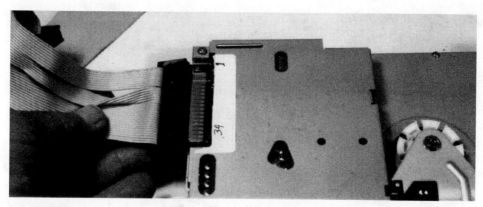

8-7 Connecting a floppy drive. Note the twist in the wires to this end connector, which makes this the A: drive.

The middle connector goes to the B: drive, and the connector on the other end plugs into the controller card or upright pins if the motherboard has a built-in controller.

Caution! The connectors can be plugged in backwards. Note that the edge connector on the drives has a narrow slit between contacts 2 and 3. That end of the board has contact number 1, the colored wire on the ribbon cable that goes to pin 1 of the connector. You might also see a number etched on the board. All the even numbers of the contacts are on top of the board, and the odd numbers are on the back. You might see a small number 2 near the narrow slit and a 34 on the other end.

The drive shown in Fig. 8-8 is a combination 5¼-inch and 3½-inch drive, so it needs only one cable connection. The configuration shown makes the 5¼-inch drive

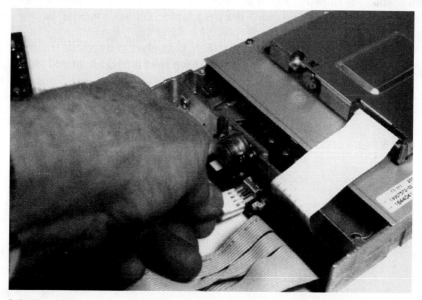

8-8 The cable connector with the split goes to drive A:. This photo shows a combination drive.

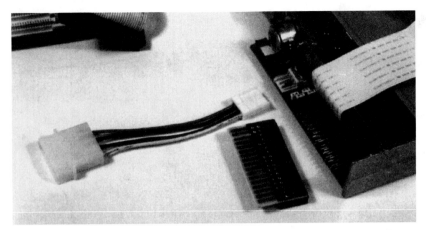

8-9 An adapter for a miniature power connector, used for some floppies. These adapters are usually included with the drive.

the boot drive. To make the 3½-inch drive the boot drive, just connect the middle connector. There are a set of small white jumpers you can set to configure the drives almost any way you want to. It's up to you to decide which one to make drive A: and drive B:. I usually make my 5¼-inch drive the A: drive.

The power to the drives is supplied through a four-wire cable. This cable can be plugged in only one way. Refer to Fig. 7-20 in the previous chapter.

Some 3½-inch and combination drives use a miniature power connector. Some newer power supplies have this miniature connector. If yours doesn't, you'll have to use an adapter, as shown in Fig. 8-9. Most drives that have the miniature connector come with the adapter. If you didn't get the adapter, call your vendor, or you can always buy one at your local computer store for about $3.

After you've installed your drives, try them out before you replace the cover. Format a blank disk, write a file to the disk, and then read it back. It should work fine.

9
CHAPTER

Choosing and installing
a hard disk

Lengthy books have been written about hard disks, but even an entire book can't cover all the questions you might have about hard disks. Because hard disk drives are such an important part of your system, this is one of the longest chapters in this book. This chapter covers some hard drive basics, different types of hard drives, and installing them in your computer. It also explains how to format and configure hard disks once they're installed.

The IBM term for hard disk drives is direct-access storage devices (DASD, pronounced *dazdee*). They're also called "winchester drives." (The IBM plant that developed the first hard drives is located near the Winchester House in San Jose, California, built by the widow of the famous inventor of the Winchester .30-.30 repeating rifle. The first IBM hard disk had 30 tracks and 30 sectors per track, so someone hung the name Winchester on it. You don't hear it too often nowadays, but for several years all hard drives were called Winchester drives.)

Floppy and hard disk similarities

A hard disk is similar to a floppy disk in some respects. Floppy disks are a single disk and hard drives are an assembly of one or more rigid disks. Hard disks platters are coated with a magnetic plating, similar to that of floppy disks. Depending on the capacity, there can be several disks on a common spindle. A motor turns the floppy spindle at 300 RPMs; a hard disk spindle will turn from 3600 RPMS up to 7200 RPMs.

Read/write heads are placed on the top and bottom of each disk. On floppy disk systems, the head actually touches the disk; on a hard disk system, the head "flies" just a few millionths of an inch above the disk on a cushion of purified air. If the head touches the disk at the high speed at which it turns, it would cause a *head crash*, which could destroy the disk, the head, and all the data on the disk.

Tracks and sectors

Like the floppy disk, the hard disk is formatted into several individual concentric tracks. A 360K floppy has 40 tracks on each side; a high-capacity hard disk has 3,000 or more tracks. Also, like the floppy, each hard disk track is divided into sectors, usually of 512 bytes. But the 360K floppy system divides each track into nine sectors and a hard disk system will divide each track into as many as 84 sectors.

Clusters and allocation units

A sector is only 512 bytes, but most files are much longer than that, so DOS lumps two or more sectors together and calls it a *cluster* or *allocation unit*. If an empty cluster is on track 5, the system will record as much of the file as it can there, then move to the next empty cluster, which could be on track 20. DOS combines sectors into allocation units depending on the capacity of the hard disk. For a 100MB disk, DOS combines four sectors, or 2048 bytes, into each allocation unit; for a 200MB disk, each allocation unit is composed of eight sectors, or 4,096 bytes.

File-allocation table

The location of each part of the file and which cluster it's in is recorded in the file-allocation table (FAT) so the computer can find it. Usually, the larger the hard disk partition the more sectors are assigned to each allocation unit.

A 500MB hard disk would actually have 524,288,000 bytes. Dividing this number by 512 to find the number of actual sectors gives you 1,024,000 sectors. If each allocation unit is made up of four sectors, there would be only 256,000 of them; if eight sectors were used, then DOS would have to worry about the location of only 128,000 allocation units. If DOS had to search through 1,024,000 entries in the FAT each time it accessed the hard disk, it would slow things down considerably. The FAT is updated and rewritten each time the disk is accessed.

I have a 500MB hard disk that's divided into three logical disks, 100MB and two 200MB. The 100MB disk uses four sectors per allocation unit, so it has 51,219 allocation units. The 200MB disk uses eight sectors per allocation units, so it has 51,283 allocation units, about the same number as the 100MB disk.

The FAT is very important. If it's damaged or erased, you won't be able to access any of the data on the disk. The heads just wouldn't know where to look for the data. The FAT is usually written on track 0 of the hard disk. Because it's so important, a second copy is also made near the center of the disk so if the original is damaged, it's possible to use the copy.

Cylinders

Just like the floppy, each same-numbered track on the top and bottom of a disk is called a cylinder. Since a hard disk can have ten or more platters, the concept of cylinders makes more sense when applied to hard disks. Incidentally, some BIOS chips in older computers might not allow you to install a hard disk that has more than 1,024 cylinders and 63 sectors, which is about 504MB. It's possible to install a disk larger than 500MB, however, by using special driver software. A new IDE ATA specification is being developed to overcome this limitation. It's discussed in more detail later in this chapter. The specification should be available by the time you read this.

Head actuators or positioners

Like the floppy disk drive, a head motor or head actuator moves the heads from track to track. The head actuator must move the heads quickly and accurately to a specified track, then detect the small variations in the magnetic fields in the specified sectors. Some of the less expensive and older hard disk drives use a stepper motor similar to that used in floppy disk drives to move the head from track to track. Most newer hard disks use a voice-coil motor, which is much smoother, quieter, and faster than the stepper motor.

The voice coil of a loudspeaker is made up of a coil of wire that's wound on a hollow tube attached to the material of the speaker cone. Permanent magnets are then placed inside and around the outside of the coil. Whenever a voltage is passed through the coil of wire, it causes magnetic lines of force to build up around the coil. Depending on the polarity of the input voltage, these lines of magnetic flux are either the same or opposite the lines of force of the permanent magnets. If the polarity of the voltage causes the lines of force to be the same as the permanent magnet, then they'll repel each other and the voice coil will move forward. If they're opposite, they'll attract each other and the coil will move backwards.

Some of the better and faster hard disks use voice-coil technology with a closed-loop servo control. They usually use one surface of one of the disks to store data and track locations. Most specification sheets list the number of heads on a drive. If you see one that has an odd number of heads, such as 5, 7, or 9, it uses a head and disk surface for servo information. Since all the heads are on the same spindle, they all move as one. When the servo head moves to a certain track and sector, the other heads follow. Feedback information from the closed servo loop positions the head on the exact track very accurately.

Figure 9-1 shows a couple of Seagate hard drives with the cover removed to show the heads and disks. The voice-coil actuator is the section in the lower left corner of the drive. It can quickly and accurately swing the arm and head to any track on the disk.

Timing

Everything a computer does depends on precise timing. Crystals and oscillators are set up so certain circuits perform tasks at specific times. These oscillating circuits are usually called *clock circuits*. The clock frequency for the standard modified frequency modulation (MFM) method of reading and writing to a hard disk is 10 MHz per second.

To write on a disk during a one-second period, the voltage might turn on for a fraction of a second, then turn off for the next period of time, then back on for a certain length of time. The head sits over a track that's moving at a constant speed. Blocks of data are written or read during the precise timing of the system clock. Because the voltage must be either positive or zero (two states) in order to write 1s and 0s, the maximum data transfer rate is only five megabits per second for MFM, just half of the clock frequency.

9-1 Two Seagate hard drives with the cover removed to show the heads and disks.

RLL systems transfer data at a rate of 7.5 megabits per second, and some ESDI drives have a transfer rate of 10 megabits/second or more. (Note that these figures are bits; it takes 8 bits to make one byte.) SCSI and IDE systems can have a transfer rate of 10 to 13 megabytes or more, so a SCSI or IDE system that can transfer 10 megabytes/second is eight times faster than a 10-megabit/second ESDI.

You've probably seen representations of magnetic lines of force around a magnet. The magnetized spot on a disk track has similar lines of force. To read the data on the disk, the head is positioned over the track and the lines of force from each magnetized area cause a pulse of voltage to be induced in the head. During a precise block of time, an induced pulse of voltage represents a 1 and the absence of an induced pulse represents a 0.

Pulses of voltage through the head cause a magnetic pulse to be formed, which magnetizes the disk track. When reading the data from the track, the small magnetic changes on the recorded track cause voltage to be produced in the heads. It's a two-way system: Forcing voltage through the heads causes magnetism to be produced, and bringing a magnetic field into the area of the head when reading causes voltage to be produced. Figure 8-1 in the previous chapter shows how a head operates.

Head spacing

The amount of magnetism placed on a disk when it's recorded is very small. It must be small so it doesn't affect other recorded bits or tracks near it. Magnetic lines of force decrease as you move away from a magnet by the square of the distance, so you want to have the heads as close to the disk as possible.

On a floppy disk drive, the heads actually contact the disk. This causes some wear, but not very much because the rotation is fairly slow and the plastic disks have a special lubricant and are fairly slippery. However, the heads of hard disk systems never touch the disk. The fragile heads and the disk would be severely damaged if they made contact at a speed of 3,600 to 7,200 RPMs. The heads fly over the spinning disk, just millionths of an inch above it. Hard disks are sealed and the air inside is purified. The air must be pure because the smallest speck of dust or dirt can cause the head to crash. You should never open a hard disk.

Disk platters

The surface of hard disk platters must be very smooth. Because the heads are only a few millionths of an inch away from the surface, any unevenness could cause a head crash. Hard disk platters are usually made from aluminum, which is nonmagnetic, and lapped to a mirror finish. They're then coated or plated with a magnetic material. Some companies are now using tempered glass as a substrate for platters.

The platters must also be very rigid so the close distance between the head and the platter surface is maintained. Early 5¼-inch hard disks had to be fairly thick to achieve the necessary rigidity. Being thick, they were heavy and required a fairly large spindle motor and lots of wattage to move the large amount of mass.

If a platter is smaller, it can be thinner and still have the necessary rigidity. If disks are thinner, then more platters can be stacked in the same area. Smaller disks also need less power and smaller motors. With smaller-diameter disks, the heads don't have to travel as far between the outer and inner tracks, which improves the access time tremendously.

Avoid any sudden movement of the computer or any jarring while the disk is spinning because it could cause the head to crash onto the disk and damage it. Most newer hard disk systems automatically move the heads away from the read/write surface to a "parking area" when the power is turned off.

I worked for Ampex Corporation during the early 1970s. They developed one of the first hard disks for military use, which was 16¼ inches in diameter and ¼ inch thick. It could store 1.5MB on each side, for a total of 3MB. Figure 9-2 shows this large hard disk on the left. In the top center is a 5¼-inch disk that can store over 200MB. The upper right disk is a 3½-inch platter that can also store over 200MB. The two bright discs in the lower portion of the photo are CD-ROMs. The larger one can store over 600MB and the smaller one about 250MB.

Several companies are now manufacturing 2½-inch and 1.8-inch drives. IBM has developed a new 2½-inch drive they call model DVAA. It can store 810MB on three 2½-inch platters. One way they're able to store more data is with a new formatting technique called no ID-sector formatting. The ID sector information is stored in solid-state memory mounted on the integrated circuit board. Hewlett-Packard makes a 1.8-inch hard disk that stores 20MB. To give you a perspective, Fig. 9-3 shows the size of 1.3-inch, 1.8-inch, and 2-inch hard disk platters.

9-2 The large disk was an early AMPEX hard disk that could store 1.5MB on each side. The smaller disks are a 5¼-inch, 3½-inch, and two CD-ROMs.

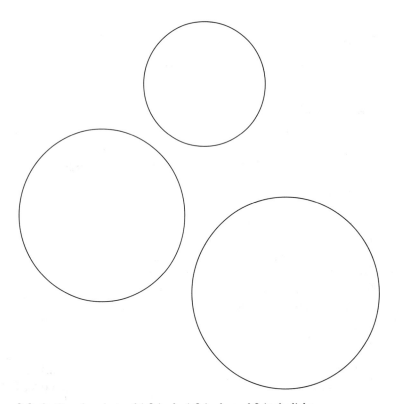

9-3 Outline drawings of 1.3-inch, 1.8-inch, and 2-inch disks.

Many companies also manufacture small drives to fit in the type-III PCMCIA slots (discussed in chapter 5). Many smaller hard disks are used in laptop computers, printers, cameras, and automobiles. A great number of automobile functions, such as fuel use, automatic transmission, brakes, air conditioning, and headlights, can be controlled by a computer and a small hard disk.

Rotational speed and recording density

As the disk spins beneath the head, a pulse of voltage through the head causes the area of the track that's beneath the head to become magnetized. If this pulse of voltage is turned on for a certain amount of time and then turned off for some amount of time, it can represent the writing or recording of 1s and 0s. The hard disk spins much faster than a floppy, so the duration of the magnetizing pulses can be much shorter and at a higher frequency.

The recording density depends to a great extent on the changes in magnetic flux. The faster the disk spins, the greater the number of possible changes are. This allows much more data to be recorded in the same amount of space.

Note that the recording density, or bits per inch (bpi), changes from the inner tracks to the outer tracks. The reason for this is that the speed at which the inner tracks pass beneath the heads is faster than that of the outer tracks.

The overall drive speed is another way of increasing the amount of storage. Old MFM drives spun at 3,600 RPMs; newer drives have a rotational speed of between 6,300 and 7,200 RPMs. One big factor in the amount of data that can be recorded in a given area is the frequency of the changing zeros and ones and the speed of the disk. The higher the speed of the disk, the higher the recording frequency can be.

Of course, the rotational speed of the disk is also one of the factors that determines the seek, access, and transfer time. If you want to access data on a certain track, the faster the disk rotates the sooner that sector will be available for reading.

Physical size

One of the first hard drives I ever owned was a full-height 10MB drive, which was over 3¾ inches high, 6 inches wide, and 8 inches deep. Original full-height floppies were the same size. Later, half-height drives were developed for both hard and floppy disks.

Old drives were physically large and clunky and operated at a very slow 100 ms. They were also expensive. A 20MB hard disk could cost as much as $2,500. And that was back in the days when $2,500 was worth at least twice what it is today. You can buy a 2GB hard disk today for less than $1,500. A modern 2GB drive is only 1 inch high, 4 inches wide, and 6 inches deep, yet it has 100 times greater storage capacity, operates ten times faster at about 10 ms, and is $1,000 less expensive than a large 20MB drive was ten years ago. If you weren't around in those early days, you can't begin to appreciate the advances in the industry. We've come a long way.

How they can make smaller drives

One of the reasons manufacturers can make smaller hard disks is because they've developed thinner disks and better plating materials, motors, and electronics.

Zone-bit recording

There are several reasons why old hard drives were physically so much larger than newer drives. Old MFM drives divided each track into 17 sectors. A track on the outer edge of a 5¼-inch platter would be over 15 inches long if it were stretched out. You can determine this by using the simple formula for pi times the diameter. So pi, or 3.14159, × 5.25 is 16.493 inches in length. A track on the inner portion of the disk might only be 1.5 inches times pi, or 4.712 inches in length. The MFM system divided each track into 17 sectors, no matter whether it was 16 or only four inches long.

You should obviously be able to store more data in the longer outer tracks than in the short inner tracks, which is exactly what newer drives do. One reason newer drives can be made so much smaller with so much more capacity is that they use zone-bit recording (ZBR). The platters on the Maxtor 540MB drive are divided up into eight different zones.

Zone 1 has shorter inner tracks, and 48 sectors per track. The number of sectors per track becomes larger as the zones move outward to the longer tracks. The outer zone, 8, has 87 sectors per track.

The Quantum Lightning series of IDE drives divides the disks into 15 different zones. The inner zones have 64 sectors per track and the outer zones have 128 sectors per track. Compare this to a 360K floppy, which has nine sectors per track and only 40 tracks per side. The Quantum 730MB has 1,416 tracks on each side of each disk.

Factors to consider when choosing a hard drive

There are many different types and capacities of disks to choose from. Of course, what you choose depends on what you need to do with your computer and how much money you want to spend.

Capacity

When you consider capacity, buy the biggest you can afford. You might have heard of Mr. C. Northcote Parkinson. After observing business organizations for some time, he formulated several laws. One law says that "work expands to fill up available employee time." To paraphrase Mr. Parkinson: "Data expands to fill up available hard disk space."

Don't even think of buying anything less than 200MB. Better yet would be 500MB. New software has become more and more friendly and offers more and more options. Most basic application programs you'll need, such as spreadsheets, data-bases, CAD programs, and word processors, will each require 10 to 30 megabytes of disk storage space. Windows NT requires about 80MB.

Most major hard disk drives are fairly close in quality and price. I recommend that you buy the highest-capacity drive you can possibly afford. Hard disk drives are now selling for less than one dollar per megabyte.

Speed or access time

Speed or access time is the time it takes a hard disk to locate and retrieve a sector of data. This includes the time it takes to move the head to the track and read the data. For a high-end, very fast disk, this might be as little as 9 milliseconds (ms). Some older drives and systems required as much as 100 ms. An 85-ms hard drive might be fine for a slow XT, but a 28-ms drive might not be fast enough for a 386. For disk-intensive uses, a 15-ms or better IDE or SCSI system would be advisable.

Early drives

I'll briefly discuss some of the old, obsolete drives for those who still own one. I don't expect many people will install old MFM drives; after all, that would be a downgrade, not an upgrade. Even if someone offers to give you an old MFM drive, I recommend that you install a newer IDE or SCSI instead. Here are some of the factors that should influence your decision:

MFM

The modified frequency modulation (MFM) system is an early standard method for disk recording. In the early 1980s, Seagate Technology developed the ST506/412 interface for MFM, and it became the standard. This method formats several concentric tracks on a disk like those laid down on a floppy disk. MFM systems divide the tracks into 17 sectors per track, with 512 bytes in each sector. They usually have a transfer rate of five megabits per second. The MFM method can be used with drives from 5MB up to several hundred megabytes.

Older MFM drives are rugged and reliable, but they're physically large, slow, and limited in capacity. Like 360K and 720K drives, they're as obsolete as the Model T Ford. And like the Model T, old MFM drives will get you there if you have the time and don't need much capacity.

The head actuator used in most MFM drives is a stepper motor. It makes a loud clunking noise as it steps the heads in discrete movements from track to track. Some people like this feature, because they can hear that something is happening. Many newer hard drives have voice-coil head actuators, which make very little noise as they move smoothly from track to track. It's often difficult to determine if anything is happening unless you look at the disk activity LED on the front panel.

Since MFM drives are obsolete, no major companies currently manufacture them. About the only place to find one is from companies who rebuild and refurbish hard drives. Even a used refurbished MFM drive will cost almost as much as a new IDE drive with three or four times the capacity.

RLL

The run-length limited (RLL) system is a modification of the MFM system. RLL drives, when used with an RLL controller, formats the disk to 26 sectors per track, which allows for the storage of 50% more data than the 17 sectors per track on an MFM drive. They also have a transfer rate of 7.5 megabits, 50% faster than MFM. Not all drives are capable of running RLL. Seagate places an R after the model number to denote RLL drives.

Except for being just a bit faster and storing 50% more data, RLL drives are about the same as the MFM types. They're obsolete.

ESDI

The enhanced small-device interface (ESDI, pronounced *ezdy*), is another modification of the MFM system. Most ESDI drives are usually over 100MB, a very large capacity at the time they were made. Today, 100MB is much too small.

ESDI drives can be formatted to 34 sectors or more per track, so they can store more than twice as much data as the 17 sectors of standard MFM drives. They have a very fast access speed, usually 15 to 18 ms, and a data transfer rate of 10 to 15 megabits or more per second.

Perstor

Perstor developed a special controller similar to RLL controllers. Where RLL systems allowed 26 sectors per track, Perstor controller divided each track into 31 sectors. I used a Perstor system for several years with no problems, but like other MFM systems Perstor drives are obsolete. The company is no longer in business.

Controllers

When the computer directs data to be read from or written to the hard disk, the heads quickly move to the proper tracks and sectors. One reason early MFM type drives were so slow is that the electronics in the controller board weren't able to keep up with the disk. Many of them used a system of reading a sector into the controller electronics and then skipping the next several sectors while the electronics digested the data it had just received. The data was then passed on and the controller was free to accept more data. The systems would read one sector and then let two, three, or as many as six sectors pass before reading another sector. This was called *interleaving*. Of course, an interleave of 2:1 was much faster than an interleave of 6:1. The interleave had to be set when the drive was low-level formatted.

Controllers were usually made by companies other than the ones who manufactured the hard drives. Some controllers performed better than others, and some hard drives performed better than others. If the interleave was set too high, it could cause errors; if set too low, then you'd have a performance penalty in wasted time. It was often difficult to find the optimum interleave. In the late '80s, new controllers were developed that allowed interleaving of 1:1 on most MFM hard drives.

Hard disk controllers also act as interfaces to the computer. Whenever any device is attached to a computer, it must go through some sort of interface, port, or I/O device. The edge connector of the plug-in controller board connects to specific contacts on the bus. These contacts provide voltage signals that control the disk head actuators. The controller also makes contact with the bus data signal lines, which transfers the data to the proper area.

Newer IDE and SCSI hard drives have built-in controller electronics. You no longer have to worry about low-level formatting and interleave settings, but you still need an interface between the hard drive and the computer. IDE interfaces and the SCSI host adapters are discussed later in this chapter.

Replacements for obsolete drives

Seagate and most other manufacturers have stopped producing almost all MFM, RLL, ESDI, and some early SCSI drives, and Seagate has published a list of replacements for their out-of-production drives. Originally, Seagate produced several versions of each model number or family. For instance, ST138 is a 32MB MFM drive, ST138A is a 32MB IDE drive, ST138R is a 32MB RLL drive, and ST138N is a 32MB SCSI drive.

Here's a partial listing of some of the Seagate out-of-production drives and Seagate's suggested replacements: If you have a model ST125, 138, 151, or 157, they suggest replacing it with an ST351A/X. This is an IDE 42MB drive that's smaller and faster than any of those it replaces. You'll have to pull out the old MFM controller card and replace it with an IDE interface. For the ST177, 277, 296, 1096, and 1100 families, they suggest ST3120A, a 106MB IDE drive.

I suggest you ignore Seagate's suggestions. The drives they suggest are much too small. Today, you'll need at least 200MB to do any productive computing. If you're going to replace a drive, get the very highest capacity you can afford.

Adding a second MFM or RLL hard disk drive

If you're using an older hard disk, you're probably running out of disk space. If you have only one hard disk, you can add another one. If you're considering adding another hard disk, you should get one that's the same type as what you already have, which could be a problem if you have an old MFM or RLL disk because they're no longer being manufactured.

If you can find an old MFM or RLL hard disk, it's fairly simple to install it. You should have a 34-pin flat-ribbon cable that's similar to the floppy disk cable, and it should have a connector in the center such as the one on the floppy cable. Plug it in so the red or colored wire on the edge of the cable goes to pin one on the drive. You'll also have a 20-wire ribbon cable for the data lines. Make sure it's plugged in so the side of the cable with the colored wire goes to pin 1. Plug the other end of this cable into the controller board. Again, make sure that pin 1 and the colored wire are in agreement.

You might have to install jumpers on a set of pins to tell the system that this is a second drive. The pins might be located near the rear of the drive close to the edge connectors for the ribbon cables. The pen in Fig. 9-4 points to the pins for drive num-

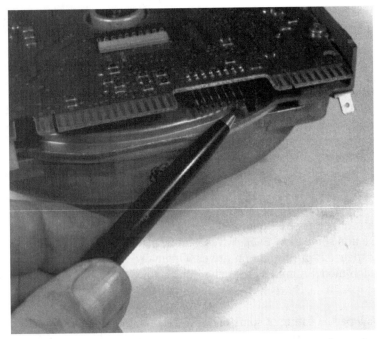

9-4 Pins on an old MFM drive that must be jumpered to configure for drive numbers if more than one drive is connected.

ber configuration. There might be designations on the board for the pins, such as DS0 or DS1. The first hard drive is drive 0 and the second drive is drive 1.

Some hard disk 34-wire ribbon cables have a twist near the end connector that's similar to the twist in the floppy drive cables. (Although the cables are similar to those for floppy disks, they aren't interchangeable because different wires are twisted.) If the cable has a twist, then both drive 0 and drive 1 are jumpered as drive 0. If the cable is straight through for both connectors, then one drive is jumpered as drive 0 and the other as drive 1. Check your documentation.

Terminating resistors

Hard drives have small plug-in resistor packs that are used for termination. Terminating resistors help to balance the electronic circuits on disk drives. You need only one terminating resistor pack. The resistor pack should be removed from the second hard disk, or one on the middle connector, and it should be left in place on the first drive, or one on the end connector. The terminator is actually a group of eight small resistors. Different companies used different configurations, but the pack is usually a flat package with pins that plug into a socket. Figure 9-5 shows a resistor pack on an old MFM drive. The location of the resistor pack might not be the same on different drives. Check your documentation for the location of the resistor pack. Once the drive is installed, it might need to be low-level and high-level formatted.

9-5 A terminating resistor pack on an old MFM drive. If two drives are installed, the resistor pack should be removed from the drive on the middle connector.

A better upgrade—SCSI

Rather than installing a second obsolete MFM or RLL drive, a much better upgrade would be to install a fairly high-capacity SCSI drive. Since it's installed with drivers, it won't conflict with the MFM drive in memory or IRQ addresses.

IDE or AT drives

The most popular drives today are those with integrated drive electronics (IDE). They're sometimes called ATA (advanced technology attachment) drives because they were first developed for use on the 286 AT. The drives are similar to SCSI drives in that all their controller electronics are integrated on the drive. You don't need a controller card such as those required by the older MFM, RLL, and ESDI drives, but you do need an interface. The interface might be a plug-in card or a set of upright pins on the motherboard.

Figure 9-6 shows an early Seagate 3½-inch 80MB IDE drive on the right. On the left is a Maxtor 540MB IDE drive. The 80MB drive is 1½ inches high. The newer 540MB drive is only 1 inch high. Figure 9-7 shows an old Seagate 5¼-inch 40MB MFM drive on the left, and a Seagate 3½-inch 1.050 SCSI drive on the right. The SCSI drive is only 1 inch high, the same size as the 540MB drive in Fig. 9-6.

Enhanced IDE ATA-2

The BIOS in some systems cannot recognize a hard disk with more than 1,024 cylinders, so you don't see many IDE drives larger than 540MB. An ANSI committee

9-6 An early Seagate 3½-inch 80MB IDE drive on the right and a much smaller 3½-inch 540MB IDE drive on the left.

9-7 An old Seagate 40MB MFM drive on the left and a Seagate 1.050GB SCSI drive on the right.

is working on a new set of standards for both IDE and SCSI devices. The new enhanced IDE ATA-2 standard will be able to go beyond 1,024-cylinder limitation. If your system BIOS doesn't recognize the larger-capacity IDE drives, your vendor can usually supply you with software drivers. It's better, however, install it as a 500MB drive with 1,024 cylinders, which will actually be 528MB because each megabyte is 1,048,576 bytes. You'll lose about 12MB, but that's rather insignificant compared to the 528MB you'll have.

The new enhanced IDE ATA-2 is somewhat similar to SCSI. It supports up to four devices, including CD-ROMs. Of course, the CD-ROMs must be designed to operate off the IDE ATA-2 interface. The new specification also allows data transfer up to 13.3 megabytes per second. The present IDE has a transfer rate of 4.3 megabytes per second.

The enhanced IDE ATA-2 requires hardware adjustments to the motherboard and the BIOS so it can recognize the new system. The new adapters and hard drives also need new connectors and cables. You might also need special operating-system software support.

In January of 1994, Phoenix Corp. published a set of their BIOS specifications for the enhanced IDE ATA-2 system. By the time you read this, most other major BIOS companies will also have developed new BIOS specifications.

Fast ATA IDE drives

Seagate has developed a fast ATA IDE system. Standard IDE drives have a transfer rate of 4 to 8.3 megabytes per second (MB/sec). The fast ATA IDE drives can operate from 11.1 to 13.3 MB/sec. Standard SCSI drives operate at 5 MB/sec, and fast SCSI drives operate at 10 MB/sec. Fast ATA IDE drives maximize and accelerate data transfer on any system. These drives can vastly improve the processing of full-motion video and other multimedia applications.

To take advantage of a fast ATA IDE system, you'll need the fast ATA host adapter and fast ATA drives. The prices shouldn't be much more than those for standard IDE drives and adapters. Fast ATA IDE drives will work with VL bus and PCI systems, and on any ISA or EISA system.

Some have accused Seagate of confusing the public. They say that their fast ATA specification covers only speed, which is just one aspect of the new enhanced ATA IDE standard. But Seagate says that the fast ATA standard can be used on any system without a major overhaul.

Seagate, at 408-438-8111, was one of the first to develop fast ATA IDE drives, but several other companies are now offering them. To find out more about the specification and drives, fax Tim Sutton of Seagate at 408-438-4127.

Installation configuration

If you're installing only a single IDE drive, it will probably be very simple. The drive should have jumpers set at the factory that make it drive 1, or the master drive. Check your documentation and the jumpers, then just plug the 40-pin cable into the drive connector, and the other end into a board interface or a set of pins on the motherboard. You must make sure that the colored side of the ribbon cable goes to pin 1 on the drive and on the interface.

If you're installing a second IDE drive, you might have some problems. You'll need to set some jumpers so the system will know which drive to access. Figure 9-8 shows the small-configuration jumper pins on a Maxtor drive. Your drive might be different. When two IDE drives are installed, the IDE system uses the term *master* to designate the C: or boot drive and the term *slave* to designate the second drive. You'll have to place small jumpers on the drives to configure them. They usually come from the factory config-

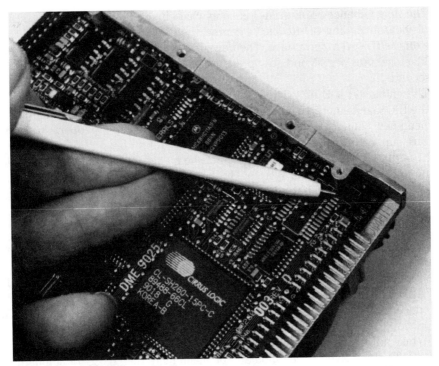

9-8 The pen points to the small-configuration jumpers on a Maxtor drive. You must set your jumpers to configure for a second IDE drive.

ured as a single drive. If you install a second drive, you'll have to set the jumpers properly. If the drives aren't configured properly, you'll get an error message telling you you have a hard disk or controller failure, and you won't be able to access the drives. Unlike MFM drives, you don't have to set any termination resistors on IDE drives.

There were no standards for early IDE drives. Different manufacturers used different designations and sometimes different functions for the pins, so it could be difficult or even impossible to install and configure two early IDE drives in a system. If you have one of the early IDE drives and want to install a second drive, it must either match your first drive or at least be made by the same company.

Later, a group of IDE manufacturers got together and agreed on an IDE standard specification. They called the specification common access method AT attachment, or CAM ATA. Almost all IDE drives now conform to this specification. You should have very little trouble connecting drives made by different companies or drives of different capacities if they conform to the CAM ATA specification.

Most later IDE models have three sets of pins for jumpers to configure the drive as a single drive, master, or slave. The pins might be marked as DS, SS, or SP.

Some early Conner IDE drives, such as the 100MB CP3104, used the designations ACT, C/D, and DSP for the pins. For a single drive, ACT and C/D must be jumpered. For a master and slave drive, jumper ACT, C/D, and DSP on the master and remove all jumpers from the slave. Some other early Conner IDE drives, such as

CP3204, used pin designations E-1 and E-2. For a single drive, jumper pins E-2; for a master, jumper E-1 and E-2. Then remove all jumpers from the slave.

Some older Seagate IDE drives, such as the ST1057A, ST1102A, and ST1144A, have numbered jumpers. Pins 3 and 4 are jumpered for the master and pins 5 and 6 are jumpered if a slave is present. You might have trouble with these and some other drives if you try to install them in a machine that has an older BIOS, made before 1990.

Some drives have pins that can be jumpered so they're read-only. This is similar to write-protecting a floppy, and could be used on a hard disk with data you wanted to never be changed or written over.

You should have received some documentation with your drive. If you don't have the configuration information, call the company or dealer. Here are technical support numbers for some of the more popular companies:

- Conner Peripherals has technical support at 408-456-3388, a BBS at 408-456-4415, and fax-back information at 800-426-6637.
- Maxtor Corp. has technical support at 800-262-9867. They also have a BBS at 303-678-2222 for 2,400 bps or 303-678-2020 for 9,600 bps. Set your modem for 8 data bits, one stop bit, and no parity.
- Quantum Corp. offers free technical support at 800-826-8022. They also have a fax-on-demand system. If you call 800-434-7532 from your fax machine, they'll send you documentation and configuration specifications for all their products. When you call, ask for their product catalog, which lists all available documents by number. You can review the catalog and order whatever document you need. Quantum also has a BBS, at 408-894-3214.
- Seagate Technology Corp. has technical support at 800-468-3472, and a bulletin board with a technical desk reference file that lists most of their hard disk configurations. The number for their BBS is 408-438-8771. Set communications software for 8 bits, no parity, and one stop bit (8-N-1). The Seagate BBS also has some free software you can download. FINDTYPE and FINDINIT can make installation of AT drives easier.
- Western Digital offers technical support at 800-832-4778. They also have a BBS for 2,400 bps at 714-753-1234, one for 9,600 bps and up at 714-753-1068.

Table 9-1 shows the specifications and configurations for three of Quantum's more popular Lightning IDE drives. Figure 9-9 is a diagram of the printed circuit board (PCB) assembly for those drives, and Table 9-2 lists the jumper options. Table 9-3 shows the specifications and configurations for some of Quantum's older drives.

IDE interface board

IDE drives need only a very inexpensive interface to connect with the bus. Figure 9-10 shows a VLB IDE interface card, which is also a multi-I/O card. It has an interface for the IDE drives, floppy disk controller, parallel printer ports, and two serial ports. An IDE interface/multi-I/O card can be plugged into any of the eight slots. I try to install board as close to the drives as possible so the cables won't drape over other boards.

Since the interface is so simple, some vendors have designed motherboards with a built-in interface (a set of pins on the motherboard). A single cable can be plugged into these pins to control two IDE drives. This saves the cost of a controller and also one of your slots. Many motherboards also have a built-in controller for floppy drives. A set of pins similar to the hard drive connector pins is provided.

Table 9-1. A configuration and specification chart for some Quantum IDE drives

	Lightning 365AT	Lightning 540AT	Lightning 730AT
Logical cylinders	976	1,120	1,416
Logical heads	12	16	16
Logical sectors/track	61	59	63
Total number logical sectors	714, 432	1,057,280	1,427,328
Capacity (formatted)	365.7MB	541.3MB	730.8MB
Nominal rotational speed (rpm)	4,500	4,500	4,500
Number of disks	1	2	2
Number of R/W heads	2	3	4
Data organization:			
Zones per surface	15	15	15
Tracks per surface	3,658	3,658	3,658
Total tracks	7,316	10,974	14,632
Sectors per track:			
Inside zone	64	64	64
Outside zone	128	128	128
Total user sectors	714,432	1,057,280	1,427,328
Bytes per sector	512	512	512
Number of tracks per cylinder	2	3	4

Table 9-2. Jumper options on the drive PCB

CS	DS	SP	Description
0	0	0	Slave drive. Compatible with drives using the PDIAG line to handle master/slave communications.
0*	1*	0*	Master drive (or single drive). Uses DASP to check for the presence of a slave.
0	1	1	Master drive (in PDIAG mode). Uses the SP jumper to determine whether a slave is present, without checking DASP.
1	0	X	Slave or master drive, depending on the state of the quantum cable select signal (pin 28) at the AT-bus connector.
			If the cable select signal is set to 0 (grounded), then the drive is configured as if DS were 1, described earlier. If the cable select signal is set up to 1 (high), then the drive is configured as if DS were 0, described earlier.

Note: In Table 9-2, a *0* indicates that the jumper is removed; a *1* indicates that the jumper is installed. The asterisk (*) indicates factory default settings.

Courtesy Quantum Corp.

Table 9-3. Configuration data for some of Quantum's older IDE drives

Parameter	40	ELS 42	LPS 52	80	ELS 85	LPS 105	120	LPS 120	ELS 127	LPS 127	170	ELS 170	LPS 170	210	LPS 240	LPS 270	LPS 340	425/425i	LPS 525	LPS 540
Formatted capacity (MB)	42	42	52	84	85	105	120	122	127	127.9	168	170	170.1	209	245	270	342.6	426	525	540
Logical cylinders	965	968	751	965	977	755	814	901	919	919	968	1011	1011	873	723	944	1011	1021	1017	1120
Logical heads	5	5	8	10	10	16	9	5	16	16	10	15	15	13	13	14	15	16	16	16
Logical sectors per track	17	17	17	17	17	17	32	53	17	17	34	22	22	36	51	40	44	51	63	59
Write precompensation	0	0	0	0	0	0	0	0	0	0	0	0	0	0	0	0	0	0	0	0
Landing zone	965	968	751	965	977	755	814	901	919	919	968	1011	1011	873	723	944	1011	1021	1017	1120
Sectors per drive	82,029	82,280	102,171	164,058	166,090	205,561	234,454	238,765	249,968	249,968	329,134	333,630	334,290	408,574	479,349	528,640	667,260	833,136	1,025,136	1,057,280

Note: If you do not have a drive type with the exact logical specifications listed in Table 9-3, choose a user definable drive type or any drive type that does not exceed the total capacity of the drive.

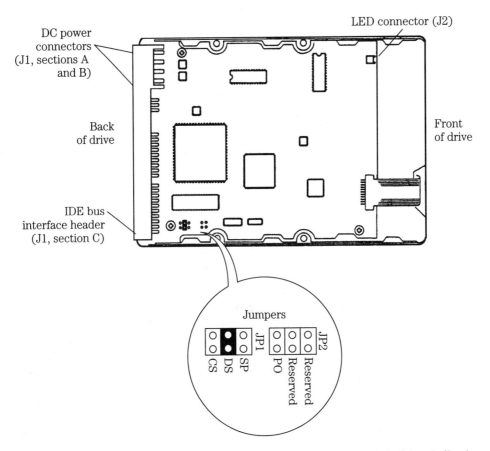

DC power connectors (J1, sections A and B)

LED connector (J2)

Back of drive

Front of drive

IDE bus interface header (J1, section C)

Jumpers

JP1
CS DS SP

JP2
PO Reserved Reserved Reserved

9-9 The printed circuit-board assembly for the 365/540/730AT hard disk drive, indicating jumper options.

9-10 A VLB IDE hard disk interface and multi-I/O board.

When plugging the connector into the pins for floppy and hard drives, be very careful to locate pin 1 on the board and plug the cable in so the colored wire goes to the pin-1 side. If you plug the cable in backwards, you could damage some of the built-in electronics on the hard disk.

IDE drives cost less than a dollar per megabyte, which is a bit less expensive than SCSI drives. One major difference is that the IDE interface might cost nothing if it's built-in, or as little as $10 for a low-cost one that can also control two floppy drives. There are more expensive IDE interfaces, such as the VESA local bus (VLB) or Intel Peripheral Component Interchange (PCI) bus. Some of these interfaces might have up to 2MB or more of a RAM cache, which can vastly accelerate hard disk operations. Of course, the extra memory will add to the cost of the interface.

SCSI

Most companies who manufacture IDE drives also make identical SCSI models. The built-in electronics on the two drives are very similar, except one has a SCSI adapter. SCSI stands for small computer system interface and is pronounced *scuzzy*. The *small computer* part of the name was to distinguish it from the big iron mainframes that ruled the computer world when the drive was first introduced.

At the time it was introduced, desktop PCs were proliferating and there was a real need to connect various peripherals to these PCs, but there wasn't a standard among PCs. You can imagine the problems in trying to devise a standard to work with several nonstandard machines. In addition, it would have to work with several different peripherals from different companies. Devices that conform to the SCSI standard have most of their controller functions built into the device.

A SCSI board can interface up to seven different intelligent devices to a computer. SCSI devices are called *logical units*, and each device is assigned a logical unit number (LUN). The devices have switches or jumpers that must be set to the proper LUN. You might see a reference that states that the SCSI can handle up to eight units. This is because the interface board is actually counted as a logical unit.

It's possible to install up to four different interface boards in a PC. You could install seven different SCSI units on each of the four interface boards, so it's theoretically possible to run 28 different SCSI devices from a PC. The different devices could be two or more SCSI drives, one or more CD-ROM drives, a scanner, a tape backup unit, or any other scuzzy product.

Besides handling up to seven scuzzy products, many interface boards also have a built-in controller for two floppy drives. Most hard drive manufacturers don't manufacture controllers. In many cases, you buy a drive from one manufacturer and a controller from another manufacturer. IDE and SCSI drives have most of the disk-controlling functions integrated onto the drive, which makes a lot of sense because the control electronics can be optimally matched to the drive. The electronics still require an interface card to transmit the data in 8-bit parallel back and forth to the disk, much like a parallel printer port. Because it can handle 8 bits of data at a time, it can have very fast transfer rates. MFM, RLL, and ESDI drives are serial systems and transfer data one bit at a time over the lines.

Most companies manufacture equivalent SCSI and IDE hard drives that are physically the same size. They both use the same type of zone-bit recording and rotational speed. The only difference in the two is the on-board electronics.

SCSI systems need a host adapter, or interface card, to drive them, and SCSI interfaces are rather complex. Some older systems were very difficult to set up. Some newer systems are of the plug-and-play (PNP) variety and are very easy to install. Figure 9-11 shows a SCSI interface from Future Domain that was developed for the Intel PCI system. Similar SCSI interfaces have been developed for the VLB bus.

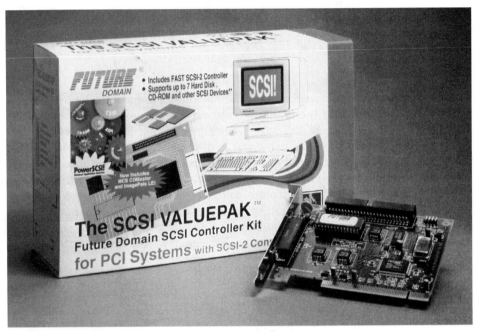

9-11 A PCI plug-and-play SCSI interface from Future Domain.

Some new SCSI adapters are fairly expensive and might cost from $50 up to $250. Some of the more expensive SCSI adapters have been designed for the EISA system. Figure 9-12 shows four different SCSI interface adapters.

SCSI drivers

Most hard drives require that you enter the drive type into the CMOS setup. The setup lists several drive types and describes the hard disk characteristics. The setup allows only two drives and they must be the same type, such as two IDE, ESDI, RLL, or MFM drives, but you can add up to 28 SCSI drives or devices along with the other two drives in your CMOS setup. The SCSI interface has its own drivers, so it doesn't have to be entered into the CMOS setup.

The SCSI interface is actually a bus. An interface card can support up to seven different devices in a daisy-chain configuration. Up to four SCSI interface cards can

9-12 Four different SCSI interface adapters.

be installed in a PC and each interface, which is actually a SCSI device, can support up to seven other SCSI devices—so as many as 28 different devices can be attached. However, DOS will let you install only up to 24 of these devices. You can't have more because it would use up all the letters in the alphabet. DOS reserves the letters A and B for floppy drives and C for the first hard disk. DOS can then assign the other 23 letters for additional hard drives, CD-ROMs, backup tape machines, scanners, and other SCSI devices.

Apple Computer has been promoting SCSI for some time. When they designed the Macintosh, it was a closed system; there were no slots for adding extra boards or peripherals. So they added a SCSI chip to the motherboard, or, in Apple Language, a *logic board,* so external SCSI devices could be plugged into a socket on the back panel without having to plug in an interface board.

A few years ago, SCSI didn't seem to be very important to the ISA world. Open ISA PCs usually had enough slots to accommodate most needs. Besides, the SCSI devices were usually more expensive and there weren't that many products available. Most importantly, the SCSI standard wasn't well established or observed and it was often difficult to install a SCSI device.

Times change. Now there are several good reasons to use a SCSI. There have been several revisions to the SCSI standard. It's now quite easy to use, and there are even plug-and-play systems available. There are also several good SCSI products available at a cost that's very close to that for IDE and other proprietary devices.

It was sometimes difficult to set up some early SCSI devices, especially if you were trying to daisy-chain two different devices to a single interface. SCSI devices must have a special driver, and manufacturers provided different drivers for their own devices. Often, drivers from one company wouldn't work with an interface from another company. You sometimes had to buy a separate SCSI interface to match the SCSI device. This served to defeat one of the better features of SCSI.

Advanced SCSI programming interface

The advanced SCSI programming interface (ASPI) is a set of standards first developed by Adaptec, one of the foremost companies in the design of SCSI products. The ASPI standard has been widely accepted by most other manufacturers. You still need a separate driver from each manufacturer for individual devices, and the drivers are set up in your CONFIG.SYS file. Then the ASPI driver is installed in CONFIG.SYS. If the device drivers are software-compatible with the ASPI specification, then the ASPI driver controls the other drivers. It's much easier to install SCSI devices that comply with the ASPI standard.

Corel, at 800-836-7274, has one of the best drawing and graphics programs available. They've also developed one of the best programs for installing SCSI devices. CorelSCSI is ASPI software that supports hundreds of SCSI devices. It makes it very easy to daisy-chain up to seven devices and install the software drivers. CorelSCSI supports hard drives, removable hard drives, CD-ROM drives, CD-ROM jukeboxes, DAT tape drives, QIC tape drives, WORM and magneto-optical hard drives, and other SCSI devices.

An industry committee has designed another SCSI specification, called common access method (CAM). It's primarily for use with OS/2 applications.

Host adapter sources

You should be able to find several sources for SCSI host adapters or interfaces in computer magazine ads and computer stores. One of the first companies to develop SCSI adapters was Adaptec, at 408-945-8600. Future Domain, at 714-253-0400, has also been in the forefront. Both of these companies supply necessary driver software for almost all SCSI products along with their adapters.

There are many different manufacturers of SCSI host adapters and many different models. There are SCSI adapters for ISA, EISA, VLB, PCI, and MCA systems. Some adapters have one or more megabytes of cache memory, and some adapters have a built-in floppy controller on the board. There are 8-bit, 16-bit, and 32-bit SCSI adapters. Many of the newer adapters are plug-and-play and are very easy to install.

Of course, the price of the adapters varies considerably, depending on factors such as brand name, amount of cache, built-in goodies, and whether it's an 8-, 16-, or 32-bit bus. Both Adaptec and Future Domain manufacture almost any type of adapter you could want.

Fast SCSI-2 and wide SCSI-2

SCSI-1 as defined in 1986 is an 8-bit bus with a transfer rate of 5 MHz. In 1992, ANSI added the SCSI-2, which allows data transfer rates up to 10 MHz. It's backward compatible so it supports SCSI-1 devices.

Wide SCSI-2 is a 16-bit bus that allows twice as much data to be transferred. The transfer rate can be as high as 20 MHz, but few if any devices have been developed at this time that can achieve this high rate. This specification will also allow as many as 16 devices, counting the host adapter. The wide SCSI-2 has a 68-pin connector.

SCSI ID

Since you can have as many as seven devices attached to a host adapter, each device is given its own unique number. There's usually a set of jumpers or switches you can set to assign a number to the unit. The lowest-numbered units have priority. Ordinarily, the hard disk is given number 0, although you can assign any number not used by another device.

Cables and connectors

The standard SCSI cable is a 50-wire flat-ribbon cable. The standard connectors are Centronics, but some devices have a miniature connector. Most devices have two connectors in parallel for attaching and daisy-chaining other devices. I have a Future Domain host adapter that has a miniature connector for external devices. In order to attach my Epson 800 Pro scanner, I had to buy a cable with the miniature connector on one end. It cost almost $40. I found out later that there are adapters for this purpose that cost about $5.00. Try some of the cable companies that advertise in *Computer Shopper* and other computer magazines.

Not all the 50 wires in a flat-ribbon cable are needed for data exchange. Many are ground wires placed between the data wires to help keep the data from being corrupted. Better and more expensive cables are round cables with twisted and shielded wires. This type of cable might be necessary for distances greater than six feet.

You should be aware that the advertised price of a SCSI device usually doesn't include an interface or cables; it might not even include any software drivers. Be sure to ask about these items whenever you order a SCSI device.

Frame adapters

If you're upgrading an older computer and installing newer hard drives or 3½-inch floppy drives, you might need to buy an expansion frame adapter. The bays in older computer cases were made for full-height and half-height drives. There are inexpensive frames you can buy that lets you install a smaller drive in a larger bay.

Drive capacities

Some IDE drives are currently limited to about 540MB, but under the new specification they'll be able to match SCSI capacity. SCSI drives can be up to 2GB or more. And, of course, you can daisy-chain up to seven of them from one interface and have up to four interfaces in a PC. Theoretically, you could have up to 28 drives in one PC, but DOS allows only 24. The letters A and B are reserved for floppy drives, but you can have one hard disk for each of the remaining letters of the alphabet. This would probably be a little more disk space than the average home office or small business would need, but some large businesses need this much and more.

One reason to have two or more drives is that you can use one to quickly back up another. This can be a simple way to implement a RAID system. RAID is an acronym for redundant array of inexpensive disks. Most businesses that handle crucial data use a RAID system of some sort.

Removable disk drives

There are several companies who manufacture removable disk drives. One of the most popular type is a Bernoulli.

Bernoulli drives

Iomega (801-778-1000) is no doubt the best-known company for removable disk drives. They first began with a 20MB floppy cartridge, then 40MB, then 90MB, now they have a 150MB removable drive.

I discussed Iomega Bernoulli drives in chapter 8 because technically they're floppies. But they can be used instead of or in combination with a hard drive system. Iomega provides drives that operate with three different types of interfaces: SCSI, IDE, and a proprietary interface. With a SCSI interface, you can have two standard hard drives and up to seven Bernoullis or other SCSI devices.

Bernoulli drives are the same size as the old standard half-height drives, so they can be mounted in a standard sized bay. Iomega also manufactures drives for external use. Since you also need a power supply and cables, the external units are more expensive.

One disadvantage of the Bernoulli system is that it's a bit slower than the newer hard disks. Another is that it's somewhat limited in storage capacity compared. One big advantage is that you don't have to worry about a Bernoulli drive crashing. If the head comes into contact with the soft floppy disk, it will cause little or no damage.

Bernoulli disk cartridges are very sturdy. They have a 1000-G rating, which means you could drop them about eight feet with no damage. The cartridges are ideal for shipping data through the mail. Unless the mailman runs over the cartridge with a truck, the data should arrive intact.

SyQuest drives

SyQuest, at 800-437-9367, has several models of removable hard disk cartridges. Each cartridge is actually a single hard disk platter. SyQuest uses zone-bit recording (ZBR) on some of their disks. The maximum SyQuest cartridge capacity is currently 270MB, but you can use data compression to double it.

For the increased capacity, SyQuest uses ZBR to divide the disks into zones. A 105MB disk is divided into two zones. The outer, longer tracks are divided into 52 sectors per track, with 512 bytes per sector. The inner-zone tracks are divided into 72 sectors per track, but each sector is only 256 bytes. This is unusual because almost all systems use 512 bytes per sector.

SyQuest has 60MB and 80MB 1.8-inch removable drives that can be used in PCMCIA type-III slots. They also have both external and internal drives that operates off a SCSI adapter. Read the ads carefully; some vendors advertise the drives at a very low price, but they don't come with a controller card.

Parallel port hard drives

SyQuest and other companies have parallel port models that can be used with laptop computers, PS/2s, or any computer with a parallel port. These drives are great for backup, removal and security, and data transport.

I discussed these systems in chapter 5; please refer back to that chapter for a listing of some of the companies. The drives come in several capacities, from 20MB to over 300MB. They're great for backup or adding a second hard drive. Since these drives plug into the computer's only parallel port, they usually provide a parallel port connector for the printer.

JTS drives

JTS Corp., at 408-747-1315, has the largest-capacity hard drives of any of the removables: 250MB, 360MB, and 540MB. Their drives are not only the largest, they're among the least expensive. JTS Corp. was formerly Kalok, and now call their products K-Stor drives. Kalok was one of the first companies to manufacture hard drives with very few parts and components.

JTS removable hard drives are ideal for backup purposes. It can take several hours to back up a 100MB disk to tape, but you can back up the same disk to another hard disk, such as a JTS, in just seconds. Unlike some other removable hard drives, JTS removable cartridges are a complete, sealed hard drive with heads and electronics. The cartridges are only one quarter inch high. With a few cartridges, you could store your most important data in a safe place to prevent damage from accidental erasure, fire, or theft.

PCMCIA drives

MiniStor, at 408-943-0165, and several other companies have 60MB to 340MB 1.8-inch drives that fit in type-III PCMCIA slots. The MiniStor 340MB hard disk is actually a 170MB disk that uses Stacker 4.0 data compression to double the capacity. (Of course, you can use data compression programs, such as Stacker, to double the capacity of any disk.) MiniStor disks are ideal for laptop and notebook computers that have PCMCIA slots. Many desktop computers are now installing PCMCIA slots. The small plug-in PCMCIA hard disks are much smaller than floppy disks, can store an enormous amount of data, and are very fast. Of course, they're ideal for security, backup, and transfer of data—and they have all the advantages of removable drives (listed later in this chapter).

The PCMCIA specification allows you to insert or remove a card or hard disk without having to shut off the power to the main system.

Magneto-optical drives

Magneto-optical (M-O) drives are a combination of magnetic and optical technologies. Magnetic disks, especially floppies, can be easily erased. Over a period of time, the data on a magnetic disk—hard or floppy—gradually deteriorates. Crucial data must be renewed about every two years.

If magnetic material has a high coercivity, or a high resistance to being magnetized, it will also resist being demagnetized. (Coercivity is measured by oersteds, Oe). The higher the Oe, the more current that's needed to magnetize the area. A large amount of current might magnetize a large area of the disk. In order to pack more density, the magnetized area must be very small.

The Oe of a material decreases as it's heated. Most materials have a Curie temperature whereby the Oe can become zero. By heating the magnetic medium with a laser beam, a very small current can be used to write data to the disk. The heated spots cool very quickly and regain their high coercivity. The disks can be easily written over or changed by heating up the area again with the laser beam.

The most popular M-O drives at this time have a capacity of 128MB and 256MB. M-O disks have a minimum lifetime of more than ten years without degradation of data.

Recordable CD-ROMs

There are several companies who now offer drives that can record CD-ROMs. When first introduced, the recordable drives cost up to $10,000. There are some that are available today for less than $3,500.

A blank CD-ROM can hold up to 600MB of data. This is a great way to backup or archive data and records that should never change. And the blank discs cost less than $20 each, so if you want to change some of the data, just change the data and record it onto another disc.

Unlike magnetic media that deteriorates or can be erased, CD-ROMs should last for many, many years. CD-ROMs are discussed in more detail in chapter 15.

WORMs

A write once, read many (WORM) drive is a laser system similar to the recordable CD-ROM. One difference is that it uses a larger disk and can store much more data. Another is that there are no standards for the system. Several companies manufacture proprietary systems that are incompatible with other systems. WORM systems are also much more expensive than CD-ROM systems.

Advantages of removable disk drives

Security
You can put information on a removable hard disk that you don't want certain people to see. You can put sensitive data, such as company design secrets or personal employee data, on a removable disk, remove the disk, and lock it up for security. After all, you wouldn't want just anyone seeing the boss's salary or personal phone number.

Unlimited capacity
With enough cartridges, you'll never have to worry about running out of disk space. If you fill one cartridge, just pop in another and continue.

Fast backup

One reason people don't like to back up their data is that it's usually a lot of trouble and takes a lot of time, especially if you're using a tape backup system. It might take several hours to back up a large hard drive onto tape, but only seconds or minutes to back up the same data onto a removable drive. A big advantage of removable cartridge backup is that the data can be randomly accessed; a tape backup must be accessed sequentially. If you want a file that's in the middle of the tape, you must run through the tape to find it.

Moving data to another computer

If you have two or more computer systems with the same type of removable drive, you can easily transfer large amounts of data from one machine to another. It's possible to send data on a cartridge through the mail to another location that has the same type system.

Multiple users of one software copy

Most people don't bother to read the license agreements that come with software, and who can blame them. They're often several pages long, in small type, and filled with lawyer jargon. Essentially, most of them simply say: "You are granted the right to use one copy of the enclosed software on a single computer."

But suppose you have several computers in an office. Some of the people do nothing but word processing most of the time, and others run databases or spreadsheets. Occasionally, these users might need to use one of the other programs for a short time. If they all have standard hard disks, then you'd need additional copies of all the software used on the computers. Some programs cost more than $1,000, so if you have several computers in an office, providing individual packages for each machine can be quite expensive.

If these computers had removable disks, then you could install a program on a disk and use the disk in different machines.

Disadvantages of removable disk drives

Limited cartridge capacity

Many removable cartridges have a capacity of only 40MB to 88MB, which might not be enough to store all the data that you need to operate some of today's large programs. And if you have several removable disks, there will always be times when you need to access a file that's on the other disk. Of course, you can use data compression with removable disks as easily as with hard disks.

Cost of cartridges

Another disadvantage is that removable drives might cost a bit more than a standard hard drive. A cartridge will cost from $70 to $100. But if you consider that with enough cartridges the capacity is unlimited, the cost is quite reasonable. M-O disks are about the least expensive of all removable disks, but the initial cost of the drive itself is much higher than other kinds of hard disk drives.

Need for accessible bays

If you intend to buy an internal system, you'll need to access it from the front panel. If you have a system that has a limited number of bays that are accessible from the outside, it could be a problem. Some desktop cases have only four bays: two accessible bays for floppy disk drives and two internal bays for hard disks. If your system doesn't have enough bays, you might consider buying a larger case, perhaps a tower case. A case and power supply will cost from about $35 to over $100 for a large tower case with a 325-watt power supply. Many tower systems have from five to eight bays. It's very easy to transfer a system from one case to another. The main component to be transferred is the motherboard. Refer back to chapter 4 for motherboard installation steps. Of course, you can always buy an external drive with removable disks, but it will cost a bit more than an internally mounted drive.

Access speed

Still another disadvantage is that some removable drives are a bit slower than most standard hard drives. The M-O drives are especially slow because it takes time to heat the area with the laser. But if you don't mind waiting a few milliseconds, it shouldn't be too much of a problem.

Hard cards

At one time hard cards were quite popular, but not many companies make them today. Hard cards are hard disks on plug-in cards, where the disk is on one end of the card and the controller is on the other. They're less than an inch thick and easily plug into any slot on your motherboard. They make it very easy to add a second hard disk to your system. It's often difficult and expensive to find a hard disk for PS/2 systems because they use a different type of connection than all other systems. Hard cards, however, can be easily installed in any open slot in the PS/2. Here are some sources for hard cards:

- Kingston Corp. at 714-435-2600
- Quantum Corp. at 408-894-4000
- Megahaus at 800-786-1185

Data compression

You can double the capacity of all the hard drives previously mentioned by using data compression. MS-DOS, IBM's PC DOS, and DR DOS all come with disk compression utilities. Stacker, from Stac Electronics at 619-431-7474, has one of the most popular stand-alone compression utilities. Some people worry about data compression, but I've never had any problems with Stacker. I had some problems with the compression program included with MS-DOS 6.0 (DoubleSpace), but Microsoft and Stac Electronics are now partners and MS-DOS 6.22 contains a new compression program that uses the same technology as Stacker. Using data compression is certainly less expensive and easier than installing a second or larger hard disk.

Mean time between failures (MTBF)

Disk drives are mechanical devices. If used long enough, every disk drive will fail sooner or later. Manufacturers test their drives and assign them an average lifetime, or mean time between failures (MTBF) figure ranging from 40,000 to 150,000 hours. Of course, the larger the figure the longer they should last (and the more they cost). These are average figures, much like those quoted for a human lifespan, but lifetimes vary greatly in length. Likewise, some hard disks die very young and some older ones become obsolete before they wear out.

I have difficulty in accepting some manufacturers' MTBF figures. For instance, to put 150,000 hours on a drive, it would have to be used eight hours a day, every day, for over 51 years. If they operated a drive for 24 hours a day, 365 days a year, it would take over 17 years to put 150,000 hours on it. Since hard drives have been around for only about ten years, I'm pretty sure no one has ever done a 150,000-hour test on a drive.

Installing a hard disk drive

Following are the steps to install a hard disk. If you're installing a hard disk in one of the older cases, you might have to buy an expansion frame. The bays in the older cases were made for 5¼-inch drives. Most of the drives sold today are 3½-inch, so most newer cases have bays for 3½-inch drives. If you have one of the older cases, order the expansion frame at the same time you order your drive.

Step 1: Remove the cover.

Find and remove the screws that hold the cover on. Unplug the power cable. Older cases have five screws on the back panel, one in each corner and one in the top center. There are other screws on the back panel that hold the power supply and connectors in place. *Do not* remove these screws. When the screws that hold the cover on are removed, the cover can be slid forward and off.

Newer tower cases also have screws on the back panel along each side that hold the cover on. When these screws are removed, the cover can be pulled toward the rear, then lifted off.

Step 2: Check the instructions, then set jumpers and switches.

Check the documentation that came with the disk and set any required jumpers. Unless you're installing a second hard disk, you might not have to set any.

Step 3: Install the disk in a bay.

Place the drive in a bay and use the screws to secure it. If it's one of the small 3½-inch drives, you might have to use an expansion frame to mount the drive in a standard 5¼-inch bay. Most newer cases have both 3½-inch and 5¼-inch bays.

If you're installing an AT, 286, or 386 hard drive, first check the instructions to see if there are any jumpers that should be set. If you're installing the drive in an older case, you might have to install slide rails on the drives. There are several holes in the sides of the disk. The easiest way to determine which ones to use is to try them. The tapered end of the rail should go toward the rear. Insert the disk in the bay and check the fit. If you're lucky and have started them in the right holes, then install the rest of the screws in the rails.

Step 4: Install the controller and cables.

Now that you have the drives installed, you need to check any instructions that might have come with your controller or interface card. Set any switches and jumpers as necessary. Plug the board into an empty slot, preferably one near the disk drives so the cables won't have to be draped over other boards. The power cables for the drives are four-wire cables from the power supply. They can be plugged in only one way.

MFM drives Now attach the cables to the drives. For old MFM drives, there are two flat-ribbon cables, one with 20 wires and the other with 34. One edge of the cable has a different colored wire to indicate pin 1. It's possible to plug the connector in backwards. The disk drive edge connectors have a slit in the board between pins 2 and 3; the colored wire goes to this side of the connections.

If your controller can handle both floppy drives and the hard disk, you'll have one 34-wire ribbon cable from the floppies and one from the hard disk. The controller will have two sets of pins for the attachment of the 34-wire cable connectors. Your controller instructions should tell you which cable goes to which row of pins. Ordinarily, the row of pins in the center will be for the hard disk, and the one toward the rear will be for the floppy.

The connectors can be plugged in backwards, so be sure to check the board for a small number 1 or some indication as to which is pin 1. Then plug the connector so the colored wire goes to that end. If the pins are in a horizontal row, pin 1 will usually be oriented so it's facing the front. If the row of pins is vertical, then pin 1 is usually toward the top of the board. Once you determine the orientation of one connection, all the others should be the same.

There are also two sets of 20-wire pins. The row closest to the 34-wire hard disk connector is for hard disk number 1. If you install a second hard disk, the 20-wire cable will plug into the second set of pins, those usually toward the bottom if oriented horizontally or toward the front if vertical.

IDE and SCSI drives If you're installing an IDE drive, you'll have a single 40-wire cable; for SCSI it will be a 50-wire cable. In most drives, the cable can be plugged in only one way. If the IDE interface is built into the motherboard, you might have only a set of upright pins. There will usually be a set of pins nearby for the floppy disk drives. These connections can be plugged in backwards. You have to determine which is pin 1 and orient the cable connector so the colored wire goes to that side.

Check your documentation. SCSI drives need to have a switch or jumper set for their ID number. IDE drives must also have jumpers set to configure the drive as master or slave.

Step 5: Install a second hard disk (optional).

You never know when a hard disk will fail. You should always have a current backup. You can back up the information on a hard disk to another hard disk in just seconds. The probability that both drives will fail at the same time is quite small.

The need for storage is seldom satisfied. Even if you have a disk with a gigabyte of storage, you'll soon be trying to store two gigabytes of data on it. A second hard drive can help.

I don't recommend adding an old obsolete MFM drive, but if you insist it's fairly easy to add a second one. Most MFM controllers can control two hard disks, and some will let you use different types and sizes. Others will control a second drive only if it's the same type and size as the first one.

You should have some sort of documentation for your drive that tells you what switches or jumpers to set. Follow any instructions that came with the drive.

The second drive should have a terminating resistor pack, which you'll need to remove. Only drive C: should have a terminating resistor pack. Figure 9-5 shows a hard disk with a terminating resistor pack and Fig. 9-4 shows the configuration pins. These pins can be jumpered so the disk can be configured for drive number 2. If you have a ribbon cable with no twisted wires at the end connector, this should go to disk 1, which should have its pins jumpered for disk 1. (Note: Some systems call the first disk 0 and the second disk 1.)

The 34-wire ribbon cable has a connector on each end and one near the center. This cable might have some twisted wires at the end connector and look very much like the cable used for floppy drives. If the cable has a twist, drive 1 and the drive 2 will both be jumpered as drive 2. Again, you should have received some instructions with your drive.

You might be very limited in the size of the drive you install on an XT, older 286, or 386. Some older BIOS chips never heard of some of the drives that are available today, which is just one more reason to throw out the old XT motherboard and install a 386 or 486.

All the back panel slots should be covered with blank panels. The fan in the power supply should draw air only through the vents in the front of the computer. It then passes this air over the components to cool them. If there are additional openings in the case, it cuts down on the efficiency of the cooling system.

Step 6: Boot from a floppy.

Once the drives are installed and connected, you can turn on the power and boot up the computer from a floppy disk in drive A. Besides the system files for booting up, the floppy should have the FDISK and FORMAT command on it. Caution! Never boot up with a floppy disk version that's different from the DOS version used to format the hard disk. There is a short boot record on the hard disk. If you use a different version to boot up, you might lose all the data on the disk.

Step 7: Run the setup routine and enter drive information.

Enter the drive type into your CMOS setup table. You won't be able to access or do anything with your hard drives until you tell your system what type drive you have, which is determined by the number of cylinders, heads, sectors, and all the other information necessary for that drive. In the early 1980s, IBM determined that there were only 15 different types of hard drives available. This information was put into a standard table and included in the BIOS of IBMs and all compatible clones. But pretty soon different type drives were being developed. The first 15 types remained standard, but as new types were introduced each BIOS manufacturer produced different tables. It soon reached the number 46. There are now hundreds of different types. Most setup routines allow you to enter type 46 or 47 and then type in data for any drive that doesn't fit any of the listed types.

Table 9-4 lists a Type 1 drive, with 306 cylinders, 4 heads, and 17 sectors per track for a total of 10MB. A Type 3 has 615 cylinders, 6 heads, and 17 sectors per track for a total of 30MB. The table provides the statistics for some MFM drives from three of the major BIOS manufacturers.

Table 9-4. MFM hard disk drive types and specifications from three major BIOS manufacturers

	AMI BIOS				
Type	Cyls	Heads	LandZ	Sects	MB
1	306	4	305	17	10
2	615	4	615	17	20
3	615	6	615	17	31
4	940	8	940	17	62
5	940	6	940	17	47
6	615	4	615	17	20
7	462	8	511	17	31
8	733	5	733	17	30
9	900	15	901	17	117
10	820	3	820	17	20
11	855	5	855	17	35
12	855	7	855	17	50
13	306	8	319	17	20
14	733	7	733	17	43
15	(Reserved)				
16	612	4	663	17	20
17	977	5	977	17	41
18	977	7	977	17	57
19	1024	7	1023	17	59
20	733	5	732	17	30
21	733	7	732	17	43
22	733	5	733	17	30
23	306	4	336	17	10
24	925	7	925	17	54
25	925	9	925	17	69
26	754	7	754	17	44
27	754	11	754	17	69
28	699	7	699	17	41
29	823	10	823	17	68
30	918	7	918	17	53
31	1024	11	1024	17	93

32	1024	15	1024	17	127
33	1024	5	1024	17	42
34	612	2	612	17	10
35	1024	9	1024	17	76
36	1024	8	1024	17	68
37	615	8	615	17	41
38	987	3	987	17	25
39	987	7	987	17	57
40	820	6	820	17	41
41	977	5	977	17	41
42	981	5	981	17	41
43	830	7	830	17	48
44	830	10	830	17	69
45	917	15	918	17	114
46	1224	15	1223	17	152
47	(User defined)				

Award BIOS (First 15 types same as AMI BIOS)

Type	Cyls	Heads	LandZ	Sects	MB
16	612	5	663	17	20
17	977	5	977	17	41
18	977	7	977	17	57
19	1024	7	1023	17	59
20	733	5	732	17	30
21	733	7	732	17	43
22	733	5	733	17	30
23	306	4	336	17	10
24	977	5	976	17	41
25	1024	9	1279	17	76
26	1224	7	1223	17	71
27	1224	11	1223	17	112
28	1224	15	1223	17	152
29	1024	8	1023	17	68
30	1024	11	1023	17	93
31	918	11	1023	17	84
32	925	9	926	17	69
33	1024	10	1023	17	85
34	1024	12	1023	17	102
35	1024	13	1023	17	110
36	1024	14	103	17	119
37	1024	2	1023	17	17
38	1024	16	1023	17	136
39	918	15	1023	17	114
40	820	6	820	17	41

Table 9-4. Continued

Phoenix BIOS (First 15 types same as AMI and Award BIOS)

Type	Cyls	Heads	LandZ	Sects	MB
16	733	3	733	17	19
17	965	5	965	17	41
18	965	10	965	17	82
19	977	5	977	17	42
20	615	8	615	17	42
21	820	4	820	17	28
22	820	6	820	17	42
23	612	4	612	17	21
24	872	7	872	17	5
25	872	8	872	17	60
26	(Reserved)				
27	(Reserved)				
28	(Reserved)				
29	(Reserved)				
30	(Reserved)				
31	(Reserved)				
32	(Reserved)				
33	615	4	615	26	32
34	615	6	615	26	48
35	745	4	745	26	40
36	733	3	733	26	30
37	733	2	733	26	48
38	733	7	733	26	67
39	820	4	820	26	43
40	820	6	820	26	64
41	799	5	799	26	64
42	782	2	782	26	20
43	782	4	782	26	41
44	782	6	782	26	61
45	745	4	745	28	42
46	776	8	776	33	102
47	1148	4	1148	36	83

For most BIOS manufacturers, the drive table will be the same for the first 15 drives that IBM standardized. But from 16 on up, it's every man for himself. For instance, the AMI BIOS lists a drive with 925 cylinders and 7 heads for type 24. The Award BIOS lists a drive with 977 cylinders and 5 heads for type 24. The Phoenix BIOS lists a drive with 872 cylinders and 7 heads for type 24. You must know what type of BIOS you have when entering the drive type.

The BIOS must also know the number and type of floppy drives you have, the time, the date, type of monitor, and other information. The setup routine asks several questions, then configures the BIOS for that configuration. This part of the BIOS configuration is in low-power CMOS semiconductors and is on all the time. Even when the computer is turned off, a small battery on the motherboard supplies power for the CMOS semiconductors.

The setup usually allows you to enter only two drives, C and D. But you can have two very large drives that are divided into smaller partitions. So your D drive might be a part of the hard disk that also contains your C drive, so ignore the designation for drive D. Enter the information for your first drive, the C drive; then enter the information under the D drive for your second drive. The CMOS setup would be less confusing if it asked for information about hard drive number 1 and then number 2, instead of C and D.

To enter the drive type information, turn on your system and press the necessary key or keys to access the setup routine. Different vendors use different keys. You can access the AMI setup during bootup by pressing the Delete key. Some systems require you to press the Esc and Delete keys or some other combination during bootup. Your motherboard documentation should tell you which keys to press. If you don't have your documentation, you might be able to access the setup by holding down one of the keys on the keyboard during bootup. The system will beep at you and say that you have a keyboard error. It will then usually give you the option of pressing F1 to access the setup routine.

Once you've accessed the setup, enter the data for your drive. If your drive type isn't in the BIOS table, choose one that's close to your type. Try to find a type with the same number of heads. You can format the drive with a lesser number of heads and cylinders, but not more than the drive supports. Of course, you won't be using the entire capacity of the drive. It's possible to format a hard disk for a smaller capacity, but not larger than what it is.

IDE cylinder limitations

Under the IDE specification at this time, you're limited to 1,024 cylinders. The new IDE specifications will overcome this limitation.

540MB IDE disks are the most popular currently. A friend of mine just bought a Maxtor 546MB disk. The documentation that came with it said that it had 1,060 cylinders, 16 heads, and 63 sectors per track. When he entered those figures into the CMOS setup and invoked the FDISK command to partition the disk, the partition information said that he had only 17MB of available space. When he called Maxtor's excellent support line, at 800-2-MAXTOR, he was told to ignore the figure of 1,060 cylinders and input 1,024. The partition information then showed that he had 504MB. DOS rounds off figures and counts one megabyte as one million bytes. Actually, one megabyte is equal to 1,048,576 bytes, so 504 times 1,048,576 is equal to 528,482,304 bytes.

Evidently, the 17MB that DOS displayed when 1,060 cylinders was entered was the difference between 1,024 and 1,060 cylinders. Actually, it would be a bit more than 17MB (1060 – 1024 = 36 cylinders × 63 sectors × 512 bytes per sector × 16 heads = 18,579,456). Not having access to the 18MB is probably better than using special software.

I recently bought a Quantum 540MB drive. The documentation said that it had 1,120 cylinders, 16 heads, and 59 sectors per track. When I called the Quantum support number, they said to ignore the 1,120 and input 1,024. They also said to ignore the 59 sectors and input 63.

IDE systems use a universal translation scheme. You can input almost any number into the CMOS table as long as the number of cylinders times the number of sectors doesn't exceed the capacity of the disk. Of course, you can't input more than 1,024 cylinders and 63 sectors at this time.

Caution! Write your drive type down somewhere. (In fact, you should have a copy of all of your CMOS setup.) If you have data on your hard drive and for some reason you remove the drive or your on-board CMOS battery goes completely dead, you won't be able to access your hard drive unless you tell the CMOS setup exactly what type it is.

Why format?

Formatting organizes the disk so data can be stored and accessed easily and quickly. If the data weren't organized, it would be very difficult to find an item on a large hard disk. I have about 3,000 files on my two hard disks. Those files are on tracks and sectors that are numbered. A file-allocation table (FAT) is set up to record the location of each track and sector on the disk.

A brief analogy would be that of developing a piece of land. The developer would lay out the streets and create blocks. He would then partition each block into lots and build a house on each lot. Each house would have a unique address. A map of these streets and house addresses would be filed with the city. A track would be analogous to a street, and a sector number would be similar to a house number.

The FAT is similar to an index in a street atlas or a book. When a request is sent to the heads to read or write to a file, it goes to the file-allocation table, looks for the location of that file, and goes directly to it. The heads can find any file or part of any file quickly and easily.

Formatting isn't something you do every day, and can be rather difficult in some cases. One reason that disks don't come from the manufacturer preformatted is that there are so many options. If you have a 540MB hard disk, you'll probably want to divide or partition it into two or three different logical disks.

One reason they didn't preformat old MFM drives is because there were so many different controller cards. Controller cards are usually designed so they'll operate with several different types of hard disks, so most have DIP switches that you must set to configure your particular hard disk. Usually some documentation comes with the hard disk controller. Like most other manuals and documentation, the instructions are sometimes difficult to understand, especially if you're a beginner.

Low-level formatting

A floppy disk is formatted in a single procedure, but a hard disk requires two levels of format, at a low level and then a high level.

You should have received some sort of documentation with your hard disk and controller. A low-level format is already performed at the factory for most hard drives, especially SCSI and IDE drives, but the low-level data recorded on a hard disk might deteriorate with time. There are several programs that can check MFM and RLL drives and reformat them if necessary. Two of them are Spin-Rite (714-362-8800) and Disk Technician (619-274-5000). These programs don't work with SCSI, IDE, and some other nonstandard disks.

Caution! Never try to low-level format IDE and SCSI drives unless you have specially designed software for that purpose. One company who provides diagnostic software that works with IDE drives is Micro-2000, at 818-547-0125. Their Micro-Scope diagnostic software can low-level format IDE drives. It can also perform several other diagnostic tests on hard drives and all floppy drives. It can read write and edit data on any track of a floppy or hard drive, and can check the IRQ assignment of devices in the event of a conflict.

If an MFM hard disk has been low-level formatted, you can type FDISK and it will allow you to partition the disk. If it doesn't allow you do an FDISK, then you probably need to do a low-level format. If it hasn't been formatted, use whatever software or instructions you received with the disk.

Using the DEBUG command

With many MFM and RLL controllers, you can use the DOS DEBUG command to invoke the low-level format. Type DEBUG and when you see the hyphen, type G=C800:5. The following message will be displayed: "This is a FORMAT routine. It will DESTROY any existing data on your disk! Press <RET> if you wish to continue or <ESC> to abort."

If you press Return, it will ask you several questions. One is if you want to input any bad sector data. It's almost impossible to manufacture a perfect hard disk. The disk usually comes with a list of bad sectors that the manufacturer discovered during his testing. If they're very bad your controller might detect them, but if they're marginal it might not. When you input the list of bad sectors, DOS marks them so they're not used. As much as 100K or more space might be in bad sectors, but it will be a small percentage compared to the disk's overall capacity.

Utility programs for low-level formatting

Some controllers won't let you use the DEBUG command to do a low-level format. Several utility programs can do it for you:

Check-It	800-531-0450
Disk Technician	619-274-5000
DOSUTILS	800-752-1333
QAPlus	408-438-8247
Micro 2000	818-547-0125
SpinRite	714-362-8800

High-level formatting and FDISK

If the low-level format has been done, you can then proceed to the high-level format. Boot up from your floppy disk drive with a copy of DOS and type DIR C:. If you see the message "Invalid drive specification," put a copy of DOS that has the FDISK command on it in drive A: and type FDISK. If you're using MS-DOS 6.2 or later, the following message will be displayed:

```
MS-DOS Version 6.2
Fixed Disk Setup Program
Copyright Microsoft Corp. 1983, 1993
FDISK Options
Current Fixed Disk Drive: 1
Choose one of the following:

1. Create DOS partition or Logical DOS Drive
2. Set active partition
3. Delete Partition or Logical DOS Drive
4. Display partition information
5. Change current fixed disk drive (Option 5 is only displayed if you
have more than one drive).

Enter choice: [1]
Press ESC to exit FDISK
```

If you choose 1 and the disk hasn't been prepared, a screen like this will come up:

```
Create DOS Partition or Logical DOS Drive
Current Fixed Drive: 1
Choose one of the following:

1. Create Primary DOS partition
2. Create Extended DOS partition
3. Create logical DOS drive(s) in the Extended DOS partition

Enter choice: [1]
Press ESC to return to FDISK Options
```

If you want to boot from your hard drive (I can't think of any reason why you wouldn't want to), then you must choose 1 to create a primary DOS partition and make it active.

DOS 3.3 and earlier could handle only hard disks up to 32MB. If you bought a 40MB hard disk, you could use only 32MB of it unless you used special software such as DiskManager. DOS 4.0 and later versions allows very large partitions, up to 2 gigabytes.

I would recommend not making a partition of more than 200MB. If there are several partitions on a disk and one of them fails, you might be able to recover the data in the other partitions. If your disk is one large partition and it fails, you might not be able to recover any of the data, especially if the FAT is destroyed. Central Point's PC Tools and later versions of DOS can be set up to make a mirror image of the FAT. If the primary FAT is destroyed, you can still use the mirror image.

DOS uses all the letters of the alphabet for disk drives. It reserves A and B for floppy drives and C for the boot drive. So if you have a very large disk, you can make up to 23 logical partitions, or drives D: through Z:.

Using FDISK can be a bit confusing. The manual that comes with MS-DOS 6.2 is no help at all. MS-DOS has on-disk help for all its commands; just type HELP and the command name (don't bother with HELP FDISK). Microsoft Press is a division of Microsoft that primarily publishes books about how to use Microsoft software. If their manuals were well written, you wouldn't need to buy an extra book to learn how to use the software. If I were a suspicious or distrustful person, I might think that Microsoft manuals were poorly written so you'd have to buy some of their books on the software.

In order to make several partitions, you must first choose option 2 to create an extended DOS partition. It will tell you how much space is available, which will be the entire drive. You can't partition the drive at this point. Accept the figure given for the entire drive. If you try to partition the drive at this point, whatever you choose will be all that you can use. For instance, if you have a 500MB drive and you try to divide it into two 250MB partitions, it will figure that the entire drive is to be only 250MB and you won't be able to use the other 250MB. You must tell it to use the 500MB that's available. Press Esc to return to the options, then choose option number 3, Create Logical DOS Drives in Extended DOS Partition. You can now divide this partition into as many drives as you want.

After completing the FDISK options, return to drive A: and high-level format drive C:. Because you want to boot off this drive, you must also transfer the system and hidden files to the disk as it's being formatted, so you must use /S to transfer the files. Type FORMAT C: /S and DOS will display the following message:

```
WARNING! ALL DATA ON NON-REMOVABLE DISK DRIVE C: WILL BE LOST!
Proceed with Format? (Y/N)
```

If you press Y, the disk light will come on and you might hear the drive stepping through each track. After a few minutes, it will display:

```
Format complete
System transferred
Volume label? (11 characters, ENTER for none)
```

You can give each partition a unique name or volume label if you want. You can test your drive by doing a warm boot (press Ctrl–Alt–Del). The computer should reboot. Now that drive C: is formatted, if you have other partitions or a second disk, format each of them.

Master boot record refresh

Occasionally, you might not be able to boot from drive C after formatting it. I recently had this problem. I tried everything I could think of. I reformatted the drive three times and checked the cables, jumpers, and CMOS setup several times, but it still wouldn't boot. I could boot from floppy drive A, access C, write to it and read from it, but it wouldn't boot. I wasted several hours before I finally called Maxtor. One of their technicians, Gary Anderson, told me to run FDISK/MBR. The system booted up like a charm. Evidently, when the system was transferred from drive A to C, it was somehow damaged or incomplete.

MBR is an undocumented utility in the FDISK command that stands for master boot record. When you boot up, the BIOS reads the master boot record, the extended boot record (EBR), the DOS boot record (DBR), the file-allocation tables (FATs), and the root directory. It then begins the process of loading necessary operating firmware and software. Invoking the command FDISK/MBR refreshes the master boot record. (For what it's worth, I have dozens of books on DOS and I've never seen the FDISK/MBR mentioned in any of them.)

Fragmentation

If a disk has just been formatted, all files are recorded contiguously, in sectors near each other. After you've used a hard disk for a while, you've probably written, erased, and modified several files. Parts of these files are likely to be located all over the disk; in other words, they're fragmented. The computer can find all the parts of these fragmented files, but it might have to do a lot of searching. This can slow the overall speed of the disk considerably.

You could do a complete backup of your hard disk, high-level reformat it, then restore all your files. But that would take a lot of time and be quite a bit of trouble. Most utility programs mentioned earlier can defragment a hard disk without having to reformat it. MS-DOS 6.0 and later has the utility DEFRAG, which is licensed from Symantec's Norton Utilities.

An excellent utility program that everyone should have is PC Tools, available almost everywhere. If you can't find it, call 503-690-8088 for the nearest distributor. Of course, no one should be without Norton Utilities. This program can be used for defragmentation and has dozens of other essential tools. Frequently defragmenting your disk is the next best thing to upgrading to a faster disk.

Renewal of low-level format

There are several things you can do to improve the performance of an old drive. If it's very old, you could be losing data now and then. When a hard disk is low-level formatted, bits of data are recorded to indicate the beginning of each track and each sector. The head reads this information when data is recorded to or read from a track.

Every time a file is worked on, it's read from the tracks and placed in RAM, where it can be manipulated and changed. This data is then recorded back onto the disk. So the file data on a track might be erased and rerecorded many times, but the track and sector data isn't usually rewritten. Over a period of time, this magnetic track and sector information can deteriorate and become weak.

In order to remedy the problem, you can use a program such as Steve Gibson's SpinRite III to repair and renew the format. This program does a nondestructive format by moving data from one track to another, then repairing that track, then moving the data back. The program does a very thorough test of the entire disk and might take hours to complete, so it's best to run it at night or when the computer isn't in use.

Sources

Local computer stores and computer swap meets are a good place to find a hard disk. You can at least look them over and get some idea of the prices and what you want. Mail order is also a very good way to buy a hard disk. There are hundreds of ads in many computer magazines. Check the list of magazines in chapter 19.

10
CHAPTER

Backing up: disaster prevention

Making backups is a chore that most people dislike, but if your data is worth anything at all, you should be backing it up. You might be one of the lucky ones and never need it, but there are thousands of ways to lose data. Data can be lost due to a power failure or a component failure in the computer system. In a fraction of a second, data that might be worth thousands of dollars—that took hundreds of hours to accumulate and is impossible to duplicate—could be lost forever. Yet many unfortunate people don't back up their precious data. Most of these people are those who have been fortunate enough not to have had a major catastrophe. Just as sure as there are earthquakes in California, if you use a computer long enough, you can look forward to at least one unfortunate disaster. But if your data is backed up, it doesn't have to be a catastrophe.

By far, most losses are the result of just plain dumb mistakes. I've made lots of mistakes in the past and, no matter how careful I am, I'll make mistakes in the future. When the poet said "to err is human," he could have been talking about me—and possibly thee.

Write-protect your software

When you buy software, make a copy of the program and store the original in a safe place. If you ruin the copy, you can always make a new copy from the original. But the very first thing you should do, before you even make a copy, is write-protect the original floppies. It's very easy to become distracted and accidentally write on a program disk. The vendor might give you a new copy, but it would probably mean weeks of waiting and a lot of paperwork.

If you're using 5¼-inch floppies, cover the square write-protect notch with a piece of opaque tape. Don't use clear tape. The drive focuses a light through the square notch, and if the light detector can sense the light it will allow the disk to be written on and erased. If the notch is covered with opaque tape, the disk can be read but not written on or erased. Some vendors now distribute their programs on diskettes without the square notch (so they're permanently write-protected).

If you are using 3½-inch floppy disks, move the small slide on the left rear side so the square hole is open. The 3½-inch write protect system is just the opposite of the 5¼-inch system. The 3½-inch system uses a small microswitch. If the square hole is open, the disk can be read but not written on or erased. If the slide is moved to cover the square hole, the diskette can be written on, read or erased.

It takes less than a minute to write-protect a diskette, but it could save months of valuable time.

Protect your original floppies

Your original program disks should be protected from dirt and dust, especially 5¼-inch floppies. There's a simple, easy way to protect them; just seal them in plastic Ziploc baggies.

Make sure not to place the originals near any magnetic source. Also, don't expose them to excessive heat (for instance, by leaving them in a closed car on a hot summer day). I ruined a half dozen disks one day by leaving them in a closed car where the sun could hit them.

.BAK files

There are functions in many word processors and some other programs that creates a .BAK file each time you alter or change a file. The .BAK file is usually just a copy of the original file before you changed it. You can call a .BAK file up, but you might not be able edit it or use it unless you rename it. Usually, just changing the .BAK extension is all that's necessary. WordStar and several other word processors can be set up to automatically save any file you're working on at certain times, when there's no keyboard activity. If there's a power outage or if you shut the machine off without saving a file, chances are that there's a backup of it saved to disk.

Unerase software

Anyone who works with computers for any length of time is bound to make a few errors. One of the best protections against errors is to have a backup. The second best protection is to have a good utility program, which can unerase a file or even unformat a disk. When a file is erased, DOS goes to the FAT and deletes the first letter of the filename. All the data remains on the disk unless a new file is written over it. If you've erased a file or formatted a disk in error, do *not* do anything to it until you've tried using a recover utility.

There are several unerase and undelete utilities, such as Norton Utilities from Symantec Corp. at 408-253-9600, PC Tools from Central Point Software at 503-690-8090, and DOSUTILS from Ontrack Computer Systems at 800-752-1333. To restore erased files, most utilities ask you to supply the missing first letter of the filename.

MS-DOS delete protection

Erasing or deleting files by mistake is so common that Microsoft licensed the undelete technology from one of the major utility companies and included an UNDELETE command in MS-DOS 5.0 and later versions. MS-DOS 6.0 and later versions have an enhanced undelete system that offers three levels of protection: sentry, tracker, and standard undelete.

Sentry is the highest level of protection. It creates a hidden directory, SENTRY, to record copies of deleted files. If you decide later that you want to undelete a file, it's just copied back to its original directory. To invoke the sentry level of undelete for a current drive, at the DOS prompt type UNDELETE /S. You can also place this command in your AUTOEXEC.BAT file so it runs each time you boot up. You can specify that one or all of your drives are to be protected.

Sentry can use up to seven percent of your disk to store deleted files. If this limit is exceeded, it will purge the oldest files to make room for newly deleted files. Besides disk space, this type of undelete requires 13.5K of your 640K conventional memory.

Tracker provides protection by using a hidden file named PCTRACKER.DEL. This command records the location of deleted files and allows you to undelete a file only if it hasn't been written over by another file. Delete Tracker also requires 13.5K of conventional memory, but it requires very little hard disk space.

The standard UNDELETE command is immediately available from any DOS prompt. It allows you to recover a file only if you haven't written over it, and doesn't require any resident memory or disk space. To find out more about UNDELETE, type HELP UNDELETE at any DOS prompt.

Early versions of MS-DOS made it very easy to format your hard disk in error. If you happened to be at your C: prompt and typed FORMAT, it would immediately begin to format your hard disk and wipe out everything. Later versions won't format unless you specify a drive letter. Early versions of DOS would also let you copy over another file. If two files were different but you told DOS to copy one to a directory that had a file with the same name, the original file would be gone forever. MS-DOS 6.2 now asks if you want to overwrite the file.

Jumbled FAT

The all-important file-allocation table (FAT) was discussed in chapters 8 and 9. The FAT keeps a record of the location of all the files on a disk. Parts of a file might be located in several sectors, but the FAT knows exactly where they are. If for some reason track 0, where the FAT is located, is damaged, erased, or becomes defective, you won't be able to read from or write to any of the files on the disk.

Because the FAT is so important, programs such as PC Tools and Norton Utilities let you make a copy of the FAT and store it in another location on the disk. Every time you add or edit a file, the FAT changes, so these programs make a new copy every time the FAT is altered. If the original FAT is damaged, you can still get your data by using the alternate FAT.

Norton Utilities is an excellent utility software package. If you accept the defaults when installing Norton Utilities 8.0, it adds a line to your AUTOEXEC.BAT file that causes Norton to scan your disk and analyze the boot record, file-allocation table, directory structure, and file structure and check for lost clusters or cross-linked files. It then reads the FAT and stores a copy in a different place on the hard disk.

Reason for smaller logical drives

Early versions of DOS wouldn't recognize a hard disk larger than 32MB. DOS can now handle a hard disk with capacities up to 1 gigabyte or more. You could have a very large drive C:, but if this large hard disk crashed, you might not be able to recover any of its data. DOS allows you to use the FDISK command when formatting your disk to divide it up into as many as 24 logical drives. If you divided a disk into several smaller logical drives and one of the logical sections failed, you might be able to recover data in the unaffected logical drives.

A very fast way to back up is to copy data from one logical drive to another. This type of backup is very fast and very easy, but it doesn't offer the amount of protection of a separate hard drive. Still, it's much better than no backup at all.

Head crash

The heads of a hard disk "fly" over the disk just a few millionths of an inch from the surface. They have to be close in order to detect the small magnetic changes in the tracks. The disk spins at 3,600 RPMs on some older drives and up to 7,200 RPMs on some of the newer drives. If the heads touch the surface of a disk spinning this fast, it can scratch it and ruin the disk.

A sudden jar or bump to the computer while the hard disk is spinning can cause the heads to crash. Of course, a mechanical failure or some other factor could also cause a crash. You should never move or bump your computer while the hard disk is running.

Most newer disks have a built-in "park" utility. When the power is removed, the head is automatically moved to the center of the disk where there are no tracks.

The technology of hard disk systems has improved tremendously over the last couple of years, but they're still mechanical devices. And as such they will wear out, fail, or crash.

I've worked in electronics for over 30 years and I'm still amazed that a hard disk works at all. It's a most remarkable mechanical device, made up of several precision components. The mechanical tolerances must be held to several millionths of an inch in some devices, such as the head and the distances between tracks. The magnetic flux changes are minute, yet the heads can detect them easily and output reliable data.

Despite all the things that could go wrong with a hard disk, most are quite reliable. Manufacturers quote mean time between failure (MTBF) figures of several thousand hours, but these figures are only an average so there's no guarantee that a disk won't fail in the next few minutes. Newer hard disks, however, are much better than the early ones. I had several old hard disks fail on me.

Despite the MTBF claims, hard drives do fail. There are lots of businesses who do nothing but repair hard disks that have crashed or failed. A failure can be frustrating and time-consuming, and it can make you feel utterly helpless. In the unhappy event of a crash, depending on its severity, it might be possible to recover some of your data, one way or another.

Crash recovery

There are some companies who specialize in recovering data and rebuilding hard disks. Many of them have sophisticated tools and software that can recover data if the disk isn't completely ruined. If it's possible to recover any data at all, Ontrack Computer Systems, at 800-752-1333, can probably do it. There are several others. Look in computer magazine ads.

Recovery services can be rather expensive, but if you have crucial data it's well worth it. It's a whole lot cheaper, however, to have a backup.

Preventing hard disk failures

During manufacturing, the hard disk platters are coated or plated with a precise layer of magnetic material. It's almost impossible to manufacture a perfect platter. Most hard disks end up with a few defective areas. When the vendor does the low-level format, these areas are detected and marked as bad. Then they're locked out so that they can't be used. But there might be areas that are borderline and aren't detected. Over time, some of these areas might change and therefore lose some of the data written to them.

Several companies manufacture hard disk utilities that perform rigorous tests on the hard disk and can detect any borderline areas. If there happens to be data in an area that's questionable, these programs can usually move the data to another safe area.

The SCANDISK command in MS-DOS 6.2 basically does what some stand-alone utilities do. It performs a surface test of the hard disk, reports on any questionable areas, and then moves any data from those areas to safer areas. It then marks the questionable areas as bad. These bad areas are listed in the FAT just as if they were protected files that can't be written to or erased.

Disk Technician from Prime Solutions, at 619-274-5000, is a much more sophisticated and comprehensive program than ScanDisk. You can set it up to automatically check your hard disk every time you boot up. It can detect errors, recover data, and relocate data that's in danger.

SpinRite from Gibson Research, at 714-362-8800, has been around for over seven years. SpinRite was developed by Steve Gibson, who writes a very interesting column for *InfoWorld*. Version 3.1 is a complete data recovery and disk repair system. It can read and recover most data from both hard and floppy disks that DOS tells you is unreadable. It analyzes and tests the disks for surface defects and moves endangered data to safe areas. SpinRite can work with most types of hard disks and disk-compression systems. There are a few nonstandard systems it can't work on: Atlas mass-storage devices, Awesome I/O cards, Expanz! disk expander cards,

Iomega and Bernoulli box devices, Konan mass-storage devices, PerStor controller cards, and Tallgrass data-storage systems. There are also a few nonstandard programs SpinRite is incompatible with.

The SpinRite user manual is about the briefest of any that I've ever seen. It's only 30 pages with very brief instructions and several screen shots. But don't let the brief manual fool you; you don't really need a lot of instructions. It's a robust program and has extensive help on disk.

Why some people don't back up and why they should

Here are a few of the lame excuses why some people don't back up their software:

Don't have the time

This is not a good excuse. If your data is worth anything at all, it's worth backing up. It takes only a few minutes to back up a large hard disk with some of the newer software.

Too much trouble

It can be a bit of trouble unless you have an expensive tape automated backup system or a second hard disk. If you back up to floppies, it can require a bit of disk swapping, labeling, and storing. But with a little organizing, it can be done easily. If you keep all of the disks together, you don't have to label each one. Just stack them in order, put a rubber band around them, and use one label for the first one of the lot.

It *is* a bit of trouble to make backups. But if you don't have a backup, consider the trouble it would take to re-create your files from a disk that has crashed. The trouble it takes to make a backup is infinitesimal compared to that.

Don't have the necessary disks, software, or tools

If you use floppy disks, depending on the amount of data to be backed up and the software used, it might require 50 to 100 disks. But it might take only a few minutes and just a few disks to back up only the data that has been altered. In most cases, you can use the same disks the next day to update the files.

Failures and disasters happen only to other people

People who believe this are those who have never experienced a disaster. There's nothing you can say to convince them. They just have to learn the hard way.

Outside of ordinary care, there's little you can do to prevent a general failure. It could be a component on the hard disk electronics or in the controller system, or any one of a thousand other things. Even things such as a power failure during a read/write operation can cause data corruption.

Theft and burglary

Computers are easy to sell, so they're a favorite target for burglars. It would be bad enough to lose a computer, but many computers have hard disks that are filled with data that's even more valuable than the computer.

Speaking of theft, it might be a good idea to put your name and address on several of the files on your hard disk. You might also want to scratch identifying marks on the back and bottom of the case, and write down the serial numbers of your monitor and drives. I heard a story where a man took a computer to a pawn shop. The dealer wanted to see if it worked, so he turned it on. A name came up on the screen that was different from the name the man had given him. He called the police and the man was arrested for burglary. The owner of the computer was very happy to get it back. He was also quite fortunate.

Another good idea is to store your backup files in an area away from your computer. This way there's less chance of losing both computer and backups in case of a burglary or fire. You can always buy another computer, but if you had a large database of customer orders, files, and history, how could you replace that?

An article in a recent *Information Week* magazine says that PC theft has increased 400% since 1991. Not only have PCs been stolen, there have been several brazen break-ins to steal microchips. They reported that a shoebox full of microchips could sell for as much as $75,000. (As a comparison, a shoebox full of cocaine would sell for only about half that much.) The chips could be easily sold and installed in computers and no one would ever know because there was no way of identifying a stolen chip from one that was legitimate. Because so many microchips are being stolen, Intel has now begun to stamp serial numbers on CPUs.

Archives

Another reason to back up is for archival purposes. No matter how large a hard disk is, it will eventually fill up with data. Quite often, there are files that are no longer used or used only once in a great while. I keep copies of all the letters I write on disk. I have hundreds of them. Rather than erase the old files or old letters, I put them on a disk and store them away.

Data transfer

It's often necessary to transfer a large amount of data from one hard disk on a computer to another. It's quite easy and fast if you use a good backup program. You could make several copies of data, company policies and procedures, sales figures, and other information to several people in a large office or company. The data could easily be shipped or mailed to branch offices, customers, almost anywhere.

There are times when a disk recorded on with one computer can't be read by another computer. SpinRite can alleviate this problem in most cases.

Types of backup

There are two main types of backup: image and file-oriented. An image backup is an exact bit-for-bit copy of the hard disk, copied as a continuous stream of data. This type of backup is rather inflexible and doesn't allow for separate file backup or restoration. The file-oriented backup identifies and indexes each file separately. With this type of backup, you can easily back up and restore a separate file or directory. It can be very time-consuming to have to back up an entire 40MB of data or more each day, but with a file-oriented system, once a full backup has been made, it's necessary to make only incremental backups of those files that have been changed or altered.

DOS stores an archive attribute in each file directory entry. When a file is created, DOS turns the archive attribute flag on. If you back up the file with DOS BACKUP or any of the commercial backup programs, the archive attribute flag is turned off. If the file is later altered or changed, DOS turns the attribute back on. At the next backup, you can have the program search the files, look for the attribute flag, and back up only those that have been altered or changed since the last backup. You can view or modify a file's archive attribute by using the DOS ATTRIB command.

There are several very good programs on the market that let you use a 5¼-inch or 3½-inch disk drive to back up your data. Again, you should have backups of all your master software so you don't have to worry about backing up that software every day. Since DOS stamps each file with the date and time it was created, it's easy to back up only those files that were created after a certain date and time.

Once the first backup is made, all subsequent backups need to record only data that has been changed or updated. Most backup programs can recognize whether a file has been changed since the last backup. Most of them can also look at the date that's stamped on each file and back up only those within a specified date range. So it might take only a few minutes to make a copy of new or changed files, and it's usually not necessary to back up your programs. You *do* have the original software disks safely tucked away, don't you?

BACKUP.COM

Early versions of MS-DOS included BACKUP and RESTORE programs that was very slow and rather difficult to use. MS-DOS 6.0 and later versions have MS-BACKUP for DOS and BACKUP for Windows that are fast and easy to use. MS-DOS's backup program can now compete with some of the commercial backup programs. With MSBACKUP and Windows BACKUP, you can make full, incremental, or differential backups. DR DOS and IBM PC DOS also have backup commands that are as good as or better than the MS-DOS commands.

You can also use the MS-DOS XCOPY command for backup, using several switches (a switch is a / followed by a letter that specifies a particular setting for the command). For instance, XCOPY /A will copy only those files that have their archive attribute set on. It doesn't reset the attribute flag. XCOPY /M will copy the files and then reset the flag. When a disk on A: is full, you merely have to insert a new floppy and hit F3 to repeat the last command. This will continue to copy all files that haven't been backed up. XCOPY /D:06-15-94 will copy only those files created after June 15, 1994. There are several other very useful switches you can use.

Check your MS-DOS, DR DOS, or PC DOS manuals for more details on backup. All these systems have built-in on-line help for all commands.

MSBACKUP, Windows BACKUP, and XCOPY can't be used with most tape backup systems. Tape backup systems usually have their own proprietary backup software. The following sections list just a few commercial backup programs; there are many others.

Fastback

Fastback from Fifth Generation Software, at 504-291-7221, was one of the first commercial backup programs. It was the fastest backup program available when it was first introduced in the early 1980s. I still have a copy of version 1.0. Fastback is now owned by Symantec, and they've discontinued the Windows version but will continue to market the DOS version.

Norton Backup for Windows

Norton Backup for Windows 3.0 from Symantec, at 800-441-7234 or 503-334-6054, is very easy to use. It also supports most tape and SCSI drives. Norton Desktop for Windows combines Norton Backup for Windows plus other Norton Utilities.

PC Tools Backup 2.0 for Windows

PC Tools Backup 2.0 for Windows from Central Point Software, at 800-964-6896 or 503-690-8088, is one of the few backup programs that can check for viruses. Central Point Software is now also a part of Symantec, which gives Symantec three of the most popular backup programs in existence. They will continue to market them separately for the time being.

Back-It 4 and Back-It 2.0 for Windows

Back-It 4 and Back-It 2.0 for Windows, from Gazelle Systems at 800-786-3278 or 801-377-1288, are very good, inexpensive backup programs. Back-It for Windows 2.0 has a current list price of $50. The program also checks for viruses.

XTree

XTree, from XTree at 805-541-0604 (now a division of Central Point Software), is an excellent shell program for disk and file management. It has several functions that make computing much easier. You can use it to easily copy files from one directory or disk to another. I often use it to make backups when I have only a few files.

Tape systems

There are several tape backup systems on the market. Tape backup is easy, but it can be relatively expensive—$250 to over $500 for a drive unit and $10 to $20 for the tape cartridges. Some of them require you to use a controller that's similar to the disk controller. So they'll use one of your precious slots, although some SCSI systems can be daisy-chained to a SCSI controller. Unless the tape drives are external, they'll also require one of the disk-mounting areas. Since it's used only for backup, it will be idle most of the time.

There are tape systems that run off the parallel port. These systems don't require a controller board that takes up one of your slots, and you can use them to back up several different computers by simply moving the system from one computer to the other. Figure 10-1 shows a tape backup system that works off a parallel port connector.

10-1 A parallel-port, quarter-inch, cassette-tape (QIC) backup system.

Like floppy disks, tapes have to be formatted before they can be used. But unlike a floppy disk, it can take over two hours to format a tape. You can buy tapes that have been preformatted, but they cost quite a bit more than unformatted tapes.

Tape systems are very slow, so the backups should be done at night or during off hours. Most systems can be set up so the backup is done automatically. If you set it to auto, you won't have to worry about forgetting to back up or wasting the time doing it.

One big disadvantage of tape systems is that they record data sequentially. If you want to find a file in the middle of the tape, the system has to search from the beginning until it finds it. Since disk systems have random access, they're much faster to access than tape.

DAT

Several companies offer DAT systems for backing up large hard disk systems. DAT systems offer storage capacities as high as 1.3 gigabytes on a very small cartridge, and use helical scan recording that's similar to video recording. DAT tapes are four millimeters wide, which is about .156 inch.

Removable disks

One of the better kinds of data backup and data security is to back up to a disk that can be removed and locked up. There are several different systems and companies that manufacture such systems. Most of these drives were discussed in chapter 9.

Floptical systems

Several companies are now offering floptical systems. A floptical drive is the same size as a standard 3½-inch drive, and they can read from and write to standard 3½-inch floppies as well as very high-density 3½-inch 20MB floppy disks. One of the problems with high-density floppy disks is maintaining accuracy when moving the heads to the proper tracks for reading and writing. 20MB floppies have a servo track that has been etched onto the floppy by a laser. The drive locks onto this laser track to control the heads. With 20MB floppies, you can use Stacker or other compression systems so you can store about 40MB.

Bernoulli drives

The Bernoulli systems from Iomega use a 5¼-inch floppy disk cartridge. They call them Bernoulli systems because the drives conform to the Bernoulli effect, the aerodynamic principles discovered by Daniel Bernoulli in the late 1700s. Iomega floppy drives can spin at almost the speed of a hard disk and the floppy drive heads don't touch the floppy disk because of the Bernoulli effect.

Iomega has several different models and disk compression can be used with the floppies, so their 150MB floppy can actually store about 300MB. These drives can be used instead of a hard drive for most purposes.

SyQuest Corp. drives

SyQuest Corp. manufactures drives with removable disks that can store up to 270MB. Of course, data compression can be used to almost double this amount of storage.

JTS Corp. cartridges

JTS Corp. has removable hard disk cartridges with a capacity as great as 540MB. The cartridge is .5 inch thick, 4 inches wide, and 5.75 inches long. The cartridge is a sealed unit, complete with heads and some of the necessary electronics, and they're very fast at 8.3MB/sec. Cost per megabyte is less than most other systems. This system is ideal for fast backups, security, transporting data to other areas, multimedia applications, and anything that requires a fast, large-capacity hard disk.

Magneto-optical drives

Magneto-optical (MO) drives are rather expensive, but the removable cartridges are available at a low cost. They're a good choice for use as a normal hard drive and for backup.

Recordable CD-ROMs

When they first came out, recordable CD-ROM systems were very expensive, at up to $10,000. Some companies now selling them for less than half that amount, and the prices are still dropping.

If you have a lot of data that needs to be permanently backed up, a CD-ROM can store over 600MB. Unlike magnetic systems, the data on a CD-ROM cannot be changed or altered. If the data needs to be changed, just record it on another disc. At this time, the blank discs cost about $20 each, but the price will soon come down to within a few dollars each.

Second hard disk

The easiest and fastest of all backup methods is to have a second hard disk. It's very easy to install a second hard disk. IDE interfaces will control two hard drives, and you can add as many as seven hard drives to a SCSI interface.

A very good system is an IDE drive for the C: boot drive and one or more SCSI drives. The chances are very good that both systems won't become defective at the same time. So if you store the same data on both systems, it should offer very good RAID-like protection.

RAID system

RAID is an acronym for redundant arrays of inexpensive disks. There's some data that is absolutely essential. In order to make sure it's safe, it's written to two or more hard disks at the same time. Originally, five different levels were suggested, but only three levels—1, 3, and 5—are in general use today.

RAID 3 requires two or more parallel hard disk drives and a single parity drive. Parity is a communications technique used to detect data errors. The computer adds up the number of bits and can detect if there's a data error in any drive. Parity information is stored on a dedicated drive and is used to reconstruct missing data. RAID 5 requires two or more parallel hard disk drives, but parity is interleaved with the data so a separate parity drive isn't required.

Some RAID systems allow you to "hot swap," or pull and replace a defective disk drive without having to power down. You don't lose any information because the same data is written to another hard disk drive.

To prevent data losses due to a controller failure, some RAID systems use a separate disk controller for each drive. A mirror copy is made of the data on each system, called *duplexing*. Some systems use a separate power supply for each system, and all systems use uninterruptible power supplies.

RAID systems are essential for networks or any other area where the data is crucial and must absolutely be preserved. But no matter how careful you are and how many backup systems you have, you might occasionally lose data through accidents or some other act of God. You can add to backup systems to make them more failsafe, but eventually you'll reach a point of diminishing returns.

Depending on how much you spend for it and how well it's engineered, a system should be system fault tolerant (SFT), that is it will remain fully operational regardless of component failures.

Uninterruptible power supply

You can have the most sophisticated backup system ever designed, but if you have a power failure or brown-out you could lose a lot of valuable data. In areas where there are frequent electrical storms, it's essential to have an uninterruptible power supply (UPS). A basic UPS is a battery that's constantly charged by a 110-volt input voltage. If the power is interrupted, the battery system takes over and continues to provide power long enough for you to save any data in RAM, then it shuts down.

Several companies manufacture quite sophisticated UPS systems for almost all types of computer systems and networks. For a single user, you need only a small system. A network or several computers will require a system that can output a lot of current. Here are just a few of the companies:

Acme Electric Corp.	716-968-2400
American Power Conversion	800-788-2208
Best Power Technology	800-356-5794
Deltec Corp.	619-291-4211
Sola Electric	800-289-7652
Tripp-Lite Mfg.	312-329-1777

Again, if your data is worth anything at all, it's worth backing up. It's much better to be backed up than to be sorry.

11
CHAPTER

Monitors

You can't beat quality. Good monitors usually last a very long time. I'm still using an early NEC Multisync color monitor that's almost 10 years old on one of my computers. I first used it on one of my old XTs with a digital adapter, but NEC was ahead of most monitor manufacturers and included a switch so it could be used with analog input. Almost all monitors today are analog. It would be difficult to find a monitor that accepts digital input.

I recently bought three low-cost color monitors, via mail order, for systems I set up for my grandchildren. Two of the three monitors failed within several weeks. Although the vendors replaced them, the small amount of money I saved on the price was more than offset by the cost and trouble of packing them up and sending them back, and not being able to use the computers while waiting for the replacements. I still think you can get some real bargains through mail order, but be careful to buy high-quality merchandise.

It's possible to run some applications on a monochrome monitor, but most applications look much better in color. I spend a lot of time at my computer and most of that time I'm looking at the monitor. I like color, so even if I'm just doing word processing, I want color. A lot of people feel the same way. The monochrome monitors are now obsolete; it's difficult to even find a dealer who sells them today.

There are many different types of monitors with many different qualities and, of course, many different prices.

Monitor basics

Here are just a few basics to help you understand how a monitor operates.

The CRT

A monitor is similar to a TV. The main component is the cathode-ray tube (CRT), or picture tube. In some respects, the CRT is like a dinosaur that's left over from the vacuum tube era. Before the silicon age of semiconductors, vacuum tubes operated almost all electronic devices. Like all vacuum tubes, CRTs use enormous amounts of power and generate a lot of heat.

Vacuum tubes have three main elements: the cathode, grid, and plate. These elements correspond to the emitter, base, and collector of the transistor. In a vacuum tube, the cathode is made from a metallic material that causes electrons to be boiled off when heated. The filament is made from resistive wire similar to that used in light bulbs. Also, very much like light bulbs, the filaments burn out, which will cause the tube to fail. Burned-out filaments is the single greatest cause of failure in vacuum tubes. The filaments of computer CRTs are designed a bit better now, so they don't burn out as often as they did in the early days.

If a positive direct current (dc) voltage is placed on the plate of a vacuum tube, the negative electrons boiled off from the heated cathode will be attracted to the plate. A control grid is placed between the cathode and plate. If a small negative voltage is placed on the grid, it will repel the negative electrons and keep them from reaching the plate. Zero voltage or a small positive voltage on the grid will let them go through to the plate. As the analog voltage swings up and down on the grid, it acts as a switch that allows a much larger voltage to pass through the vacuum tube. A voltage as small as a millionth of a volt on the grid of a vacuum tube can create a much larger exact voltage replica on the output of the plate.

With the proper voltages on the emitter, base, and collector, a transistor operates much like a vacuum tube, as a switch or an amplifier. Figure 11-1 shows how a vacuum tube can take a small signal and amplify it. A vacuum tube might be quite large, requires a lot of space and energy and produces a lot of heat. Figure 11-2 shows how a transistor can amplify the same signal, but it requires much less power and space. If you refer back to the Pentium keyring in Fig. I-1, there are 3.1 million transistors in that small area. If you had 3.1 million vacuum tubes, it would fill a large warehouse.

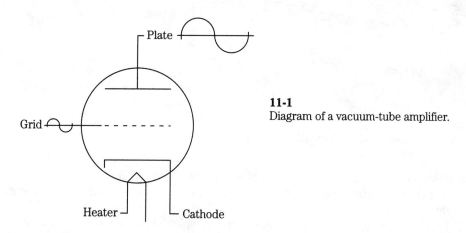

11-1
Diagram of a vacuum-tube amplifier.

Figure 11-3 is a diagram of a basic CRT. Like the vacuum tube, the CRT has a filament that heats up a cathode to produce electrons. It also has a grid that can shut off the passage of electrons or let them pass through. The corresponding plate of the CRT is the back of the picture screen, which has about 25,000 volts on it to attract

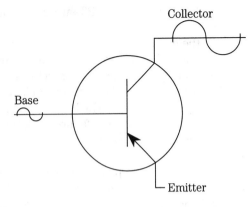

11-2
Diagram of a transistor amplifier.

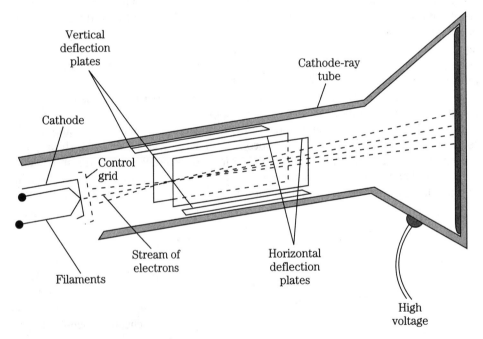

11-3 Diagram of a basic cathode-ray tube (CRT).

the electrons from the cathode. The back of the screen has a phosphor coating. Because of the high attracting voltage, the electrons slam into the coating and cause it to light up and glow.

   This produces a very thin beam of electrons, which acts like a piece of iron in a magnetic field. If four electromagnets are placed around the neck of the CRT, one on top, one on the bottom, and one each side, the beam of electrons can be directed to any area of the screen by varying the polarity of the voltage fed to the electromagnets. If you wanted the beam to move to the right, you'd increase the plus voltage on the right magnet. If you wanted the beam to move up, you'd increase the plus voltage on the top magnet. With these electromagnets, you can move the beam to any spot on the screen.

The small input signal voltage on the grid of the CRT turns the electron beam on and off to cause portions of the screen to light up. You can cause the beam to move and write on the screen just as if you were writing with a pencil. Alphabet characters or any kind of graphics can be created in an exact replica of the input signal.

Present-day CRTs are like dinosaurs. Many laptop and notebook computers have excellent color screens that use transistors. The active-matrix screen uses thousands of transistors to light up each individual pixel. Other, less costly systems are being developed. Eventually we'll have large, low-energy, flat screens that can produce a high-resolution picture. Even television CRTs will be replaced with flat screens that can be hung on a wall.

Monochrome vs. color

In a monochrome TV or monitor, there's a single "gun" that shoots the electrons toward the back of the screen. Color TVs and monitors are much more complicated than monochrome systems. During the manufacture of color monitors, three different phosphors—red, green, and blue (RGB)—are deposited on the back of the screen. Usually a very small dot of each color is placed in a triangular shape. If you use a magnifying glass and look at a color monitor or color TV, you can see the individual dots.

The different phosphors used to make color monitors are made from rare earth elements. They're designed to glow for a certain period of time after they have been hit by an electron beam.

In a color TV or monitor, there are three guns, each shooting a beam of electrons. The electrons from each gun have no color, but each gun is aimed at a particular color—one to hit only the red dots, one the blue dots, and one the green dots. They're very accurately aimed, so they converge only on their assigned color dots. To make sure the beams hit only their target, they must go through the holes of a metal shadow mask. Being hit by stray electrons causes the shadow mask to heat up and the heat can cause fatigue and loss of focus. Many newer monitors use shadow masks made from invar, an alloy that has good heat resistance. By turning the guns on or off to light up and mix the different red, green, and blue dots of phosphor, any color can be generated.

Sony Trinitron monitors and TVs use a system that's a bit different. Its three guns are in a single housing and fires through a single lens. Instead of a shadow mask, the Trinitron uses a vertical grill. The Trinitron system was actually invented in this country, but no one in the TV industry was interested until Sony adopted it.

Dot pitch

If you look closely at a black-and-white photo in a newspaper, you can see that it's made up of small dots. There will be a lot of dots in the darker areas and fewer in the light areas. The text or image on a monitor or a television screen is also made up of dots very similar to those of a newspaper photo. You can easily see these dots with a magnifying glass. The more dots and the closer together they are, the better the resolution. A good high-resolution monitor will have solid, sharply defined characters and images.

The more dots and the closer together they are, the more difficult it is to manu-facture a CRT. The red, blue, and green dots must be placed very accurately and uni-formly in order for their specific electron beam to hit them. Most standard monitors have a dot pitch of .28 millimeters (mm). Better monitors have dots that are as close together as .24 mm. Some low-cost color monitors have them from .39 mm up to .52 mm. Such monitors might be all right for playing games, but they wouldn't be very good for anything else.

Pixels

Resolution is also determined by the number of picture elements (pixels) that can be displayed. A *pixel* is the smallest unit that can be drawn or displayed on the screen. It can be turned on or off with a single bit, but it might take several bits per pixel to control the intensity and color depth.

The following figures relate primarily to text, but the graphics resolution will be similar to the text resolution. Most monitors are designed to display 80 characters in one row or line across the screen. By leaving a bit of space between each row, 25 lines of text can be displayed from top to bottom. The old color graphics adapter (CGA) monitor could display 640×200 pixels. If you divide 640 by 80, you'll see that one character will be eight pixels wide. There can be 25 lines of characters, so $200 \div 25 = 8$ pixels high. So the entire screen has $640 \times 200 = 128,000$ pixels. The EGA monitor has 640×350 pixels, so each cell has eight pixels wide and 14 pixels high. The Video Electronics Standards Association (VESA) chose 640×480 for the VGA standard and 800×600 for the Super VGA (SVGA) standard. SVGA has $800 \div 80 = 10$ pixels wide and $600 \div 25 = 24$ pixels high. Many newer systems are now capable of $1,024 \times 768$, $1,280 \times 1,024$, $1,664 \times 1,200$, and more. With a resolution of $1,664 \times 1,200$, you'd have 1,996,800 or almost 2 million pixels that could be lit up. We've come a long way from the 128,000 pixels possible with CGA.

Painting the screen

To put an image on the screen, the electron beam starts at the top left corner. Under the influence of the electromagnets, it's drawn across to the right of the screen lighting up a very thin line as it moves. Depending on what the beam is de-picting, it will be turned on and off by the grid as it sweeps across the screen. When the beam reaches the right side of the screen, it is turned off and sent back to the left side. It drops down a bit and begins sweeping across the screen to paint another line. On a TV set, it paints 262.5 lines in ⅟₆₀ of a second. These are all the even-numbered lines. It then goes back to the top and interlaces the other 262.5 odd-numbered lines in between the first 262.5. It does this fairly fast, at a frequency of 15,750 Hz. (15750 ÷ 60 = 262.5). So it takes ⅟₃₀ of a second to paint 525 lines. This is called a *frame*, so 30 frames are written to the screen in one second.

When you watch a movie, you're seeing a series of still photos, flashed one after the other. Due to our persistence of vision, it appears to be continuous motion. It's this same phenomenon that allows us to see motion and images on our television and video screens.

Horizontal scan rate

Obviously, 525 lines on a TV set, especially a large screen, leaves a lot of space in between the lines. If there were more lines, the resolution could be improved. At the time this is being written, the FCC and the TV industry are trying to decide on a standard for high-definition TV that would have from 750 to about 1,200 lines at 30 frames per second. At 750 lines, it would paint 375 lines in $\frac{1}{60}$ of a second and 750 in $\frac{1}{30}$ of a second. For 750 lines, the horizontal frequency would be 22,500 Hz. For 1,200 lines the horizontal frequency would be 36,000 Hz.

Vertical scan rate

The time it takes to fill a screen with lines from top to bottom is the *vertical scan rate*, also called the *refresh rate*. The phosphor coating might start losing some of its glow after a period of time unless the vertical scan refreshes it in a timely manner. Some multiscan, or multifrequency, monitors can have several fixed or variable vertical scan rates. VESA specifies a minimum of 70 Hz for SVGA and 72 Hz for VGA systems.

Interlaced vs. noninterlaced

Higher scan frequencies require that the adapter have more precise and higher-quality electronics. The monitor must also be capable of responding to higher frequencies, which of course is more expensive to manufacture. To avoid this higher cost, IBM designed some of their systems with an interlaced horizontal system. Instead of increasing the horizontal frequency, they merely painted every other line across the screen from top to bottom, then returned to the top and painted the lines that were skipped—the same system used on TV sets. Theoretically, this sounds like a great idea. But practically, it doesn't work too well because it causes a flicker that can be very irritating to people who have to work with this type of monitor for very long.

The flicker isn't readily apparent, but some people have complained of eye strain, headaches, and fatigue after prolonged use of an interlaced monitor. If you use an interlaced monitor for only short periods of time, then it probably won't be a problem.

Some companies make models that are interlaced in some modes and noninterlaced in other modes. Most companies don't advertise the fact that their systems use interlacing, and some use the abbreviation N/I for their noninterlaced adapters. Interlaced models are usually a bit lower in price than the noninterlaced. You can ask vendors what system is used.

Multiscan

Multiscan monitors can accept a wide range of vertical and horizontal frequencies, which makes them quite versatile and flexible. Most early multiscans could accept both digital and analog signals. If you had an older EGA or even a CGA adapter card, it would work with it. Almost all monitors sold today are analog.

The VGA system introduced by IBM on their PS/2 systems in 1987 didn't use a multiscan adapter and monitor. The system operated at a fixed frequency. A multiscan design costs more to build, so many low-cost VGAs are designed to operate at a single fixed frequency. They aren't as versatile or flexible as the multiscan, but the resolution can be as good.

Many companies manufacture monitors with multiple, fixed frequencies. Again, they aren't quite as flexible as the true multiscan, but they can cost less. I use a 19-inch Sampo TriSync, which has three different frequencies and it does everything I need it to do.

Some of the large 19- to 30-inch multiscan monitors can sell for as little as $250 and more than $3,500.

Adapter basics

You can't just plug a monitor into your computer and expect it to function. Just as a hard disk needs a controller, a monitor needs an adapter to interface with the computer. Computer monitors are a bit different than a TV screen. A TV set usually has all of its controlling electronics mounted in the console or case, and it's assembled and sold as a single unit. A computer monitor might have some electronics within its case, but its main controller, the adapter, is usually on a plug-in board on the PC motherboard. This gives you more versatility and utility because you can use different or specialized adapters.

Several manufacturers make monitor adapters, so there's quite a lot of competition. This has helped keep the prices fairly reasonable. Most monitors can operate with several different types of adapters. Some adapters cost as little as $40, some more than $1,000. Some monitors cost as little as $200 and some more than $3,000. It would be foolish to buy a very expensive monitor and an inexpensive adapter, or vice versa. Try to match the capabilities of the monitor and the adapter.

The early IBM color graphics adapter (CGA) standard for monitors used the same 15,750-Hz horizontal frequency rate used by the TV industry. The resolution was terrible for close work, such as computer-aided design (CAD). Later, the enhanced graphics adapter (EGA) standard used a horizontal frequency of 22,500 Hz for a much better resolution. The standard horizontal frequency for video graphics array (VGA) monitors is 31,500 Hz. The Super VGA (SVGA) and extended graphics array (XGA) standards can have several fixed or variable horizontal frequencies as high as 100 KHz.

Note that CGA and EGA systems are obsolete. I mention these type of monitors for historical and comparison reasons only. A few companies still offer them for sale, but I wouldn't recommend that you buy one.

Most monitor adapters have text character generators built onto the board, which is similar to a built-in library. When you send an A to the screen, the adapter goes to its library and sends the signal for a preformed A to the screen. Each character occupies a cell made up of a number of pixels. The number of pixels depends on the resolution of the screen and the adapter. In the case of CGA, if all the dots within a cell were lit up, there would be a solid block of dots eight pixels wide and eight pixels high. When the A is placed in a cell, only the dots necessary to form the outline of an A are lit up. It's very similar to how characters are formed by a dot-matrix printer.

With the proper software, a graphics adapter allows you to place lines, images, photos, various text fonts, and almost anything you can imagine on the screen. Almost all adapters sold today have both text and graphics capability.

The original IBM PC came with a green monochrome monitor and monochrome display adapter (MDA) that could display text only. Hercules immediately saw the folly of this limitation, so they developed the Hercules monographic adapter (HMGA) and set a new standard. It wasn't long before IBM and a lot of other companies were selling similar MGA cards that could display both graphics and text. These adapters provide a high resolution of 720×350 pixels.

IBM then introduced their color monitor and color graphics adapter (CGA). CGA is a digital system that allows a mix of red, green, and blue dots. The adapter has a cable with four lines, one each for red, green, and blue, and one for intensity. This allows two different intensities for each color, on for bright or off for dim. So there are four objects, each of which can be in either of two states, or two to the fourth power (2^4). Therefore, CGA has a limit of 16 colors.

The EGA system has six lines and allows each of the primary colors to be mixed together in any of four different intensities, so there are 2^6 or 64 different colors it can display.

The video graphics adapter (VGA) can easily handle a resolution of 640×480, and Super VGA (SVGA) can handle 800×600 and as high as $1,280 \times 1,024$.

Analog vs. digital

Almost all monitors and adapters sold today are analog systems. Until the introduction of the PS/2 with VGA, most displays used digital systems and they have severe limitations.

Digital signals are of two states, either fully on or completely off. The signals for color and intensity require separate lines in the cables. As stated previously, it takes six lines for the EGA to be able to display 16 colors out of a palette of 64. So digital systems are obsolete.

The analog signals that drive the color guns are voltages that are continuously variable. It takes only a few lines for the three primary colors. The intensity voltage for each color can then be varied almost infinitely to create as many as 256 colors out of a possible 262,144. To display more than 256 colors requires a true color adapter.

Graphics chips

There are hundreds of video adapters on the market and they have many different features, but there are three main types of adapters. The type of adapter depends primarily on the type of graphics chip used.

The dumb frame-buffer chip sent everything to the CPU for processing, which slowed the system down because it had to traverse a 16-bit I/O bus back and forth to RAM at a speed of 8 MHz. These chips were used in older VGA cards. If you don't mind waiting, these cards are fairly inexpensive, from $50 to $100.

Accelerator boards

Fixed-function cards have accelerator chips with several built-in graphics functions. Because they have built-in functions, they can handle many Windows graphics tasks without having to bother the CPU. Since they don't often have to go back and forth to the CPU over the I/O bus at the slow speed of 8 MHz, they're usually much faster than the dumb frame-buffer chip. There's a wide price range for these cards. Examples of the graphics chips used in these cards are S3 86CXXX, IIT AGX014, and ATI 68800. Some that have a limited fixed function cost as little as $50.

Another type of adapter has its own coprocessor chip on board, such as the Texas Instruments 34010 or the Hitachi HD63483. By using an on-board coprocessor, it saves having to traverse the 16-bit bus back and forth to the CPU, which also frees up the CPU for other tasks. Coprocessor boards are usually more expensive than any other type of boards.

Video memory

Having memory on the adapter board saves having to go through the bus to conventional RAM. Some adapter boards even have a separate plug-in daughterboard to add more memory. With older dumb frame-buffer cards, even with a lot of memory, the adapter had to go back and forth over the 16-bit bus to communicate with the CPU and many applications, especially under Windows, could be painfully slow. An accelerator card with a lot of on-board memory and a local bus system can speed up the processing considerably.

It's possible to use 8-bit boards to display color images in 256 colors, but these type of boards are obsolete. You'd be much better off using a 16-bit board. Better yet would be a VESA local bus (VLB) or a peripheral component interconnect (PCI) bus. You should have at least 1MB of memory to display 256 colors in 1,024×768 resolution. Of course, the more colors displayed and the higher the resolution, the more memory is required. Displaying 64,000 colors at 1,024×768 resolution requires 2MB, and 24-bit true color takes about 4MB.

Graphics speed can slow down if the graphics have to be pulled off a hard disk. You can speed up the process a bit if you have at least 8MB of RAM with a 2MB Smart-Drive disk cache. Even better is 16MB of RAM with a 4MB SmartDrive disk cache.

Adapter memory

Many high-resolution adapters have up to 4MB or more of video RAM (VRAM) on board. VRAM chips look very much like the older DRAM DIP chips, but they're not interchangeable with DRAM. DRAM chips have a single port; they can be accessed or written to through this port. VRAM chips have two ports and can be accessed by one port while being written to in the other. This makes them much faster and a bit more expensive than DRAM. Some less expensive adapters use DRAM.

Many less expensive adapter boards are sold with only 512K of DRAM or less, and they often have empty sockets for adding more memory. Some cards have space to install as much as 40MB of DRAM. It's not likely that you'd need that much for ordinary use. It is very easy to install the memory chips in the sockets; just be sure that you orient them properly. They should be installed the same way as other memory on the board. Make sure all legs are fully inserted in the sockets.

If you expect to do any high-resolution graphics, then you should have a minimum of 1MB of VRAM on the adapter, but 2MB would be even better.

SVGA colors

The number of colors an SVGA card can display is dependent on the resolution. Here are the numbers for a low-cost SVGA: 16.7 million colors at 640 × 480, 64,000 colors at 800 × 600, and 16 colors at 1,280 × 1,024. Of course, there are adapters that can display a much greater number of colors than those listed above, but they're also more expensive.

True colors

Most standard, low-cost VGA cards are capable of displaying only 16 colors. True colors or pure colors requires video boards with a lot of fast memory, a coprocessor, and complex electronics. *True color* means that a video board can drive a monitor to display a large number of shades in separate, distinct hues. It's also very expensive. Remember that a pixel can be turned on or off with a single bit, but for color intensity or shades and depth, it might take several bits per pixel. A good adapter for true color might cost more than the monitor. Table 11-1 is a brief listing.

Table 11-1. True color

Bits	Shades	Depth
4 (2^4)	16	
8 (2^8)	256	
15 (2^{15})	32,768	5:5:5
16 (2^{16})	65,536	5:6:5 or 6:6:4
24 (2^{32})	16.7 million	8:8:8

Depth

True color usually refers to displays with 15-, 16-, or 24-bit depths. *Depth* means that each of the individual red, green, and blue (RGB) color pixels has a large amount of information about each color. The 15-bit system has five bits of information for each of the three colors. The 16-bit system has six bits for red, six bits for green, and four bits for blue, or a combination of 5:6:5. The 24-bit system has eight bits for each color. Table 11-2 will give you an idea of how much memory is needed for the various resolutions and colors.

Table 11-2. Memory and resolution

Bits/pixel	Color	640 × 480	800 × 600	1024 × 768
4	16	150K	234K	386K
8	256	300K	469K	768K
16	35,536	600K	938K	1.536MB
24	16,777,216	900K	1.406MB	2.304MB

Dithering

If a board doesn't have enough power to display the true colors, it might use dithering to mix the colors in order to give an approximation.

Dithering takes advantage of the eye's tendency to blur colors and view them as an average. A printed black-and-white photo uses all black dots, but several shades of gray can be produced depending on the number of black dots per inch. A mixture of red and white dots will create a pink image. Dithering intersperses pixels of various colors to create a gradual color transition.

VL-bus and PCI bus adapters

Old XT motherboards had an 8-bit bus. The 286 and all systems after have a 16-bit input/output (I/O) bus. Many 486 and Pentium motherboards have either a VESA local (VL) bus or an Intel peripheral component interconnect (PCI) local bus. The VL-bus and PCI-bus adapters are much faster than older graphics and accelerator boards because they have a 32- or 64-bit path that's used to directly communicate with the CPU. This direct path also allows them to communicate at the CPU speed or frequency. Older I/O systems were limited to the 8-or 16-bit bus and thus a speed of 8 MHz, no matter how fast the CPU was.

Some Windows, most graphics, and many other applications require a lot of interaction with the CPU, so many true color adapters are made for motherboards with a VL-bus connector.

The 32-bit VL bus and the PCI bus were both proposed at about the same time in 1991 and standards were adopted in mid-1992, but the VL bus was a lot simpler and less expensive to integrate onto the motherboard. There were many VL-bus motherboards and adapters on the market for well over a year before the PCI bus was introduced. Many people believe that the PCI system will eventually be the bus of choice, but there are still many more VL bus adapters and motherboards available than there are PCI. VL-bus systems are also a bit less expensive than PCI systems.

There are both 32-bit and 64-bit PCI-bus motherboards. By the time you read this, there will also be 64-bit VL-bus motherboards available. It's difficult to say which system you should choose. There are a few differences between them, and the differences aren't that great.

The VESA local bus is limited to three slots, and the VL-bus connector is added to the end of a standard slot on a motherboard. This is similar to the IBM solution to adding 16-bit slots to 8-bit slots. So you can use any 8-bit or 16-bit card in VL-bus slot, but if it isn't a VL-bus card you won't get the advantages of the local bus.

Adapters that have their own coprocessor on board might be as fast as the VL-bus or PCI-bus adapters. The disadvantage is that they're usually more expensive.

Figure 7-11 in chapter 7 shows Diamond's VL-bus and PCI-bus adapters. They're both about equal in speed and color reproduction, and are about the best that you can buy.

Adapter sources

There are hundreds of adapter manufacturers. I hesitate to mention models because each manufacturer has dozens of models with different features and resolutions, and they're constantly designing, developing, and introducing new models. Table 11-3 lists only a few manufacturers who offer high-end adapters.

Table 11-3. Manufacturers of high-end adapters

Company	Model	Bus	Telephone
Artist Graphics	WinSprint 900	ISA, VL	800-627-8478
ATI Tech.	UltraPro	ISA, VL	416-756-0718
Boca Research	SVGAXx	ISA, VL	407-997-6227
Diamond Computer	Viper	ISA, VL, PCI	408-736-2000
Genoa Systems	Windows VGA	ISA, VL	408-432-9090
Matrox Electronics	MGA	ISA, VL, PCI	514-685-2630
Micronics Company	MVC8000LB	VL	510-651-2300
Number Nine Corp.	#9GXE	ISA, VL, PCI	800-438-6463
Orchid Tech.	Fahrenheit	ISA, VL	800-767-2443
STB Systems	PowerGraph	ISA, VL	214-234-8750
Western Digital	Paradise	ISA, VL	800-832-4778

Most of the companies listed in Table 11-3, and many others, have both PCI and VL boards. They might also have boards in the EISA configuration for both PCI and VLB. Call the vendor and ask for specification sheets. Some low-cost boards use standard DRAM for on-board memory. DRAM might be a bit slower than VRAM because it can't be accessed while being refreshed. VRAM has two ports, and can be refreshed from one port while being accessed at the other port. The system is similar to the interleaving of main DRAM, where one half can be accessed while the other half is being refreshed. If you're going to use your Pentium for high-end graphics, make sure the adapters use VRAM and can display up to 16.7 million colors.

Adapter software

Most adapter cards will work with any software you have. But many adapter vendors provide special software drivers that are necessary for high-resolution and speed with certain applications. Make sure the adapter has drivers for all popular graphics software.

VGA-to-video adapters

Several companies have developed special VGA adapters that can transform VGA output to a television signal. This National Television Standards Committee (NTSC) signal can then be recorded on a VCR or displayed on a TV screen. These adapters can be used to create excellent presentations or for computerized special effects.

The U.S. Video Company, 203-964-9000, has several adapters. Their TVGA card can drive a monitor up to 1024 × 768 and output NTSC signals. They also have several other cards for special effects. Other companies who have similar products are Jovian Logic Corp. at 415-651-4823 and Willow Peripherals at 212-402-0010.

Choosing a monitor

The primary determining factor for choosing a monitor should be what it's going to be used for and the amount of money you have to spend. If you can afford it, buy a large 21-inch monitor with super high resolution and a good SVGA board to drive it. I bought a ViewSonic 21-inch low-radiation monitor and a Diamond Viper VLB graphics accelerator adapter. I paid a little less than $2,000 for the monitor and adapter system, and it's worth every penny.

The screen size of a monitor can be very misleading. The stated size is a diagonal measurement, but there's a border on all four sides of the screen. The reason for this border is because the screen is markedly curved near the edges on all sides; the curve can cause distortion so the areas are masked off and not used. The usable viewing area on a 14-inch monitor, therefore, is about 9.75 inches wide and about 7.75 inches high.

If you expect to do any kind of graphics or CAD/CAM design work, you'll definitely need a good large-screen color monitor with very high resolution. A large screen is almost essential for some types of design drawings so as much of the drawing as possible can be viewed on the screen at one time.

You'll also need a high-resolution monitor for close tolerance designs. For instance, you might draw two lines to touch on a low-resolution monitor and they'd look fine, but when the drawing was magnified or printed out the lines might not even be close to one another.

Most monitors are wider than they are tall, called *landscape*. There are others that are taller than they are wide. These are called *portrait* monitors. Some 19-inch and larger landscape monitors can display two pages of text side by side if the software allows it.

Most desktop publishing (DTP) applications produce black-and-white print and illustrations, so high-resolution paper-white monochrome monitors might be all you need for these applications. These monitors can usually display several shades of gray. Many of these monitors are portrait and have a display area of 8½ × 11 inches. Instead of 25 lines, they have 66 lines, which is the standard for an 11-inch sheet of paper. Many have a phosphor that lets you have black text on a white background so the screen looks very much like the finished text. Some of the newer color monitors let you switch to pure white with black type.

What to look for

If possible, go to several stores and compare various models. Turn the brightness up and check the center of the screen and the outer edges. Is the intensity the same in the center and the outer edges? Check the focus, brightness, and contrast with text and graphics. There can be vast differences even in the same models from the same manufacturer. I've seen monitors that displayed demonstration graphics programs beautifully, but weren't worth a damn when displaying text in various colors. If possible, try it out with both text and graphics.

Ask the vendor for a copy of the specifications. Check the dot pitch; for good high resolution it should be no greater than .28 mm, and even better would be .26 mm or .24 mm. Also, check the horizontal and vertical scan frequency. For a multiscan monitor, the wider the range the better. A good system should have a horizontal range of 30 KHz or better. The vertical range should be 45 Hz or higher.

Bandwidth

The bandwidth of a monitor is the range of frequencies its circuits can handle. A multiscan monitor might accept horizontal frequencies from 15.75 KHz up to about 75 KHz and vertical frequencies from 40 Hz up to about 90 Hz. To get a rough estimate of the bandwidth required, multiply the resolution pixels times the vertical scan or frame rate. For instance, for a Super VGA, or VESA standard, monitor: 800 × 600 × 60 Hz = 28.8 MHz.

But systems require a certain amount of overhead for things such as retrace, which is the time needed to move back to the left side of the screen, drop it down one line, and start a new line. So the bandwidth should be at least 30 MHz. If the vertical scan rate is 90 Hz, then it's the following: 800 × 600 × 90 = 43.2 MHz, or at least a 45-MHz bandwidth. A very high-resolution monitor would require a bandwidth of 1600 × 1200 × 90 = 172.8 MHz, or about 180 MHz, counting the overhead. Many very high-resolution units are specified at a 200-MHz video bandwidth. Of course, the higher the bandwidth the more costly and difficult to manufacture.

Controls

You might also check for available controls to adjust the brightness, contrast, and vertical/horizontal lines. Some manufacturers place them on the back of the computer or some other difficult-to-access area. It's much better if they're on the front so you can see what the effect is as you adjust them.

Glare

If a monitor reflects too much light, it can seem like a mirror and be very distracting. Some manufacturers coat their screens with a silicon formula, some etch the screen, and some tint them to cut down on the amount of reflection. If possible, try out a monitor under various lighting conditions. If you have a glare problem, several supply companies and mail-order houses offer glare shields that cost from $20 to $100.

Cleaning the screen

The 25,000 volts of electricity hitting the back of a monitor's face creates a static attraction for dust, which can distort and make the screen difficult to read. Most manufacturers should provide instructions on cleaning the screen. If you have a screen that has been coated with silicon to reduce glare, don't use any harsh cleansers on it. Usually, plain water and a soft paper towel will do fine.

Tilt-and-swivel base

Most people sit their monitor on top of the computer. If you're either short or tall, have a low or high chair, or work at a nonstandard desk, the monitor might not be at eye level. A tilt-and-swivel base allows you to position the monitor to best suit you. Many monitors now come with this base. If yours doesn't have one, many specialty stores and mail-order houses sell them for $15 to $40.

Several suppliers also offer an adjustable arm that clamps to the desk, with a small platform for the monitor to sit on. The arm can swing up and down and from side to side. This kind of arrangement can free up a lot of desk space. These adjustable arms cost from $50 to $150, but might not be suitable for the heavy large-screen monitors.

Monitor radiation

Almost all electrical devices emit very low-frequency (VLF) magnetic and electrical fields. There have been no definitive studies proving that this radiation is harmful, and the emissions are sometimes so weak that they can hardly be measured. However, the Swedish government has developed a set of guidelines to regulate the strength of emissions from video display terminals (VDTs).

Several people in this country are also concerned that VDT radiation might be a problem, so many monitor manufacturers now add shielding to control the emission. If you're worried about VDT emissions, look for monitors that are certified to meet MPR II specifications. Incidentally, if you use a hair dryer, you'll get much more radiation from that than from a monitor.

Green monitors

Monitors use from 100 to 150 watts of energy. The EPA Energy Star program demands that the energy be reduced to no more than 30 watts when not being used.

I sometimes sit in front of my monitor for 10 or 15 minutes doing research, or more likely with writer's block. All this time the monitor is burning up a lot of energy. New monitors that meet Energy Star specifications go into sleep mode when there's no activity, where they use very little energy. A small amount of voltage is still applied to the monitor, and it comes back on-line almost immediately.

None of my monitors comply with the Energy Star specification, but I save energy by using the PC ener-g saver from NEI, at 800-832-4007 (see Fig. 11-4). I plug my monitor and printer into it and, using software that comes with the unit, set it to shut off power to the units if there's no keyboard activity. You can set the time interval for no activity from just a few seconds up to several minutes. As soon as any key is pressed or the mouse is moved, the monitor comes back on. It comes back to the same place where you were working when it shut down. To reactivate the printer, just send it a print command.

Software for monitor testing

If you're planning to buy an expensive high-resolution monitor, you might want a program called DisplayMate for Windows, from Sonera Technologies at 908-747-

11-4 The PC ener-g saver, which help you conserve monitor and printer power.

6886. It's a collection of utilities that can perform several checks on a monitor. It lets you measure the resolution for fine lines, the clarity of the image, and the distortion, and it has gray scales, color scales, and a full range of intensities and colors. The software can actually help you tweak and fine-tune your monitor and adapter. The setup will also help you set your optimum values. If you plan to spend $1,500 or so for a monitor, it could be well worth it to test the monitor first.

Monitor resources

A monitor is a very important part of your computer system. I couldn't possibly tell you all you need to know in this short chapter. One of the better ways to keep up on this ever-changing technology is to subscribe to several computer magazines, several of which are listed in chapter 18.

12
CHAPTER

Input devices

Before you do anything with a computer, you must input data. There are several ways to do so: via keyboard, disk, modem, mouse, scanner, barcode reader, voice recognition, or fax. This chapter will discuss a few of the ways to send data to a computer.

Keyboards

By far the most common way to get data into the computer is with the keyboard. For most common applications, it's impossible to operate the computer without a keyboard.

The keyboard is a most personal connection with your computer. If you do a lot of typing, it's very important that you get a keyboard that suits you. Not all keyboards are the same. Some have a light mushy touch, some heavy. Some have noisy keys; others are silent with very little feedback.

A need for standards

Typewriter keyboards are fairly standard. There are only 26 letters in the alphabet and a few symbols, so most QWERTY typewriters have about 50 keys. I've had several computers over the last few years, however, and every one of them has had a different keyboard. The letters of the alphabet aren't ever changed, but some very important control keys, like Esc, Ctrl, and PrtSc, \, function keys, and several others are moved all over the keyboard.

IBM can be blamed for most of the changes. The original IBM keyboard had the very important and often-used Esc key just to the left of the 1 key in the numeric row. The 84-key keyboard moved the Esc key over to the top row of the keypad, and the tilde (~) and grave (`) key was moved to the original Esc position to the left side of the 1. The IBM 101-key keyboard moved the Esc back to its original position.

IBM also decided to move the function keys to the top of the keyboard above the numeric keys (probably so they could expand them from 10 to 12 keys). This can be quite frustrating, however, for anyone who memorized the function keys for various options. The keys are also much harder to access all the way at the top of the keyboard than they are directly to the left of the letter keys.

There are well over 400 different keyboards in the U.S. Many people make their living by typing on a keyboard, and many large companies have systems that count the number of keystrokes employees make during their shifts. If an employee fails to make a certain number of keystrokes, then he or she can be fired. Can you imagine the problems if that person has to frequently learn a new keyboard? I'm not a very good typist in the first place, and I have great difficulty using different keyboards. There definitely should be some sort of standards.

Figure 12-1 shows three keyboards, each of them with different key arrangements. The keyboard at the top is a Focus FK 5001. It is the one that I use most often; it has the all-important function keys at the left of the keyboard where they're most handy for WordStar and WordPerfect users. It also has a duplicate set of function keys along the top. This keyboard also has a separate keypad on the right. It also has a slot at the top of the keyboard for holding program templates, and even comes with several templates: those for WordStar, WordPerfect, Microsoft Word, Lotus 1-2-3, and dBASE IV. These templates have all the basic commands and are very helpful. The keyboard in the center has a built-in trackball. Its keys are also positioned differently than the others.

12-1 Three keyboards, all with different key arrangements.

Innovation, creating something useful and needed that makes life better or easier, is great. That type of innovation should be encouraged everywhere. But many times changes are made just for the sake of differentiation without adding any real value or functionality to the product. This applies not only to keyboards, but to all technology. IBM hasn't introduced a new keyboard design in the last couple of years. Dare we hope that we have the most recent design that will last a while?

How does a keyboard work?

The keyboard is actually a computer in itself; it has a small microprocessor with its own ROM. The electronics of a keyboard eliminates the bounce of the keys, can determine how long to hold a key down for repeat, can store up to 20 or more keystrokes, and can determine which key was pressed first if you press two at a time.

In addition to the standard BIOS chips on your motherboard, there's a special keyboard BIOS chip. Each time a key is pressed, a unique signal is sent to the BIOS. This signal is a direct-current voltage that's turned on and off a certain number of times, within a definite time frame, to represent zeros and ones.

Each time a 5-volt line is turned on for a certain amount of time, it represents a 1; when it is off for a certain amount of time, it represents a 0. In ASCII, if the letter A is pressed, the code for 65 will be generated: 1 0 0 0 0 0 1.

Reprogramming key functions

You can use various software to change the standard keyboard keys to represent almost anything you want them to. One thing that makes learning computers so difficult is that every program uses function keys and other special keys in different ways. You might learn all the special keys WordPerfect uses, but then if you want to use Microsoft Word or any other word-processing program, you'll have to learn the special commands and keys it uses.

Major word processing, spreadsheet, and other programs will let you set up macros. A macro is like a mini-program; it lets you record a series of keystrokes, such as your name and address, or even a series of commands, such as those to save and print the current file. Then you can either generate the keystrokes or repeat the commands whenever you want to just by pressing one or two keys.

Keyboard sources

Keyboard preference is strictly a matter of individual taste. Key Tronic, of Spokane, at 509-928-8000, makes some excellent keyboards. They're the IBM of the keyboard world; their keyboards have set the standards. Key Tronic keyboards have been copied by the clone makers, even to the extent of using the same model numbers.

Quality keyboards use a copper-etched printed circuit board and keys that switch on and off. The circuitry is designed so the keys don't bounce; that is, when a key is depressed, it makes contact only once. Quality keyboards have a small spring beneath each key to give them uniform tension.

Key Tronic offers several models. On some they even let you change the springs under the keys to a different tension. The standard is two ounces, but you can configure the key tension to whatever you like: 1, 1.5, 2, 2.5, or 3. They also let you exchange the positions of the Caps Lock and Ctrl keys. Key Tronic keyboards have several other functions, which are described in their manual. Call them for a copy.

Many less-expensive keyboards are of very poor quality and workmanship. Instead of an copper-etched printed circuit board, many use a piece of plastic and conductive paint for the connecting lines. Instead of springs beneath each key, they use a rubber cup. The bottom of each key is coated with a carbon conductive material. When the key is depressed, the carbon allows an electrical connection between the painted lines. Despite the poor quality, the keyboards work fairly well.

Key Tronic lost a lot of their market share to low-cost clones. They now also produce a low-cost keyboard that's competitively priced with the clones. I was surprised and pleased at how well the keyboard feels and operates. Figure 12-2 shows one of the keys on the Key Tronic keyboard being lifted up to show the rubber cup beneath. The key caps are held in place by plastic hinges, which are a part of the key cap.

12-2 A low-cost Key Tronic keyboard. One of the plastic key caps is raised to show the rubber cap below.

I recently saw new clone keyboards being sold at a swap meet for $10 each. The keyboards looked very much like the Key Tronic 101-key keyboard, but the assembly snapped together instead of using metal screws. They also had several other cost-saving features. But there's quite a lot of electronics in a keyboard. I don't know how they can possibly make a keyboard to sell for $10. At that price, you could buy two or three of them and, if you ever had any trouble with one, you could just throw it away and plug in a new one.

There are several keyboard manufacturers with hundreds of different models. Prices range from $10 to over $400. Look through any computer magazine.

Specialized keyboards

Several companies have developed specialized keyboards, several of which are listed in this section.

Quite often, I need to do some minor calculations. The computer is great for calculations. Several programs, such as SideKick and WordStar, have built-in calculators, but most of the programs require that the computer be accessing a file. A keyboard that's available from Shamrock, 800-722-2898, and also from Jameco, 415-592-8097, has a built-in solar-powered calculator where the number pad is located. The calculator can be used whether the computer is on or not.

Focus Electronic Corp., 818-820-0416, has a series of specialized keyboards. They have keyboards with function keys in both locations, extra * and \ keys, and several other goodies. Their FK-9000 has a built-in calculator with a small battery. Their FK-5001 keyboard has eight cursor arrow keys (see Fig. 12-3). With these keys, you can move the cursor right or left, up or down, and diagonally toward any of the four corners of the screen. You can also vary the speed of the cursor movement by using the function keys. These eight cursor keys will do just about everything a mouse can do.

12-3 A Focus 5003 keyboard.

Besides their standard keyboards, Key Tronic has developed a large number of specialized ones. Instead of a keypad, one has a touch pad. This pad can operate in several different modes. In one, by using your finger or a stylus, you can move the cursor much the same as with a mouse. It comes with templates for several popular programs, such as WordStar, WordPerfect, and Lotus 1-2-3.

Another Key Tronic model has a bar-code reader attached to it. This can be extremely handy if you have a small business that uses bar codes. This keyboard would be ideal for a computer in a point-of-sale (POS) system.

Carpal tunnel syndrome

Businesses spend billions of dollars each year for employee health insurance. Of course, the more employee injuries the more the insurance costs. Carpal tunnel syndrome (CTS) has become one of the more common problems. CTS, also referred to as RSI, or repetitive strain injury, causes pain and/or numbness in the palm of the hand, the thumb, and index and ring fingers. The pain might radiate up into the arm, and any movement of the hand or fingers could be very painful. CTS is caused by pressure on the median nerve where it passes into the hand through the carpal tunnel and under a ligament at the front of the wrist. Either one or both hands may be affected. Many employees are asking for workers' compensation insurance and taking companies to court because of RSI. It has become a serious problem.

CTS most commonly affects people who use their hands and arms for repetitive motion, like typing on a computer keyboard or using a bar-code scanner for long periods of time. Keying in data is a very important function in the computer age, and it's the job of many employees. When people who use a computer get CTS, it's usually caused by the way they hold their wrists while typing on the keyboard. There are several pads and devices to help make typing more comfortable and keep your wrists in the proper position. I have a firm foam rubber pad that's the length of the keyboard, about four inches wide, and three quarters of an inch thick. I can rest and support my wrists on this pad and still reach most of the keys.

Before the computer revolution, thousands and thousands of people sat at a typewriter eight or more hours a day typing on keyboards similar to computer keyboards. Yet there were few, if any, cases of CTS or RSI ever reported. It's a disorder that has become prevalent only in the last few years. It could be that typewriter keyboards have more slant and were usually placed at a different height. Another factor might be that the typewriter limited a typist's speed and repetition. A computer data input worker might do 13,000 keystrokes per hour.

Key Tronic, at 509-923-8000, has an ergonomic keyboard that breaks in the middle, and each half can be elevated from the center. The center can then be separated and angled to fit the angle of your hands. You can separate the B and N keys by as much as an inch or more, while the Y and T keys could be touching (see Fig. 12-4). The elevation and angle should help prevent CTS and RSI. The keyboard is a bit ex-

12-4 The Key Tronic FlexPro keyboard. It splits and can be elevated in the center to help prevent CTS and RSI.

pensive, but it costs a lot less than having to go to a doctor for a painful operation that might not be successful. The other alternative is to rest your hands and miss several months of work. If you work for a large company, they might save money by installing these ergonomic keyboards.

Ergonomixx, at 703-771-1047, has the MyKey keyboard, which can help prevent CTS and RSI. This keyboard has a built-in trackball and a very unusual set of function keys in a round circle (see Fig. 12-5).

12-5
The MyKey keyboard. Its shape can
help prevent CTS and RSI.

Dalco Electronics, at 800-445-5342, has a less expensive ergonomic keyboard, which is angled to fit the way the hands sit on the keyboard. Unlike the Key Tronic system, it's a single flat unit, but you could put something under the back of the keyboard to elevate the height to suit you.

Another thing to help prevent carpal tunnel syndrome (CTS) and repetitive strain injury (RSI) is to use a foam rubber pad in front of the keyboard for a wrist rest. Many vendors give them away at shows like COMDEX. Figure 12-6 shows one that Borland gave away. It seems to help.

Keyboard covers

There are special plastic covers that you can place over your keyboard to protect it against spills, dust, or other environmental hazards. There are some places, such as the floor of a manufacturing area, where a cover is absolutely essential. Most are made from soft plastic that's molded to fit over the keys. They're pliable, but they'll slow down any serious typist.

12-6 A foam rubber wrist rest to help prevent CTS and RSI.

Several companies manufacture custom covers, including CompuCover, at 800-874-6391 and Tech-Cessories, at 800-637-0909. There are well over 400 different keyboards used in the U.S., and there are probably over 4,000 different types worldwide. These companies claim they can provide a cover for most of them. The average cover costs about $25.

In an emergency, or if you don't want to spend money for a cover, you can use cling-type plastic wrap. It works well and it could be less expensive.

Mouse systems

One of the biggest reasons for the success of the Macintosh is that it's easy to use. With a mouse and icons, all you have to do is point and click. You don't have to learn a lot of commands and rules. A person who knows nothing about computers can become productive in a very short time. The DOS world finally took note of this and began developing programs and applications such as Windows for the IBM and compatibles.

Dozens of companies are now manufacturing mice. Many programs have been developed that can be used without a mouse, but they operate much faster and better with a mouse. To be productive, a mouse is essential for Windows, CAD, paint, and graphics programs.

Some mice cost more than $100, but you can now buy very good ones for less than $10. What is the difference in a mouse that costs $100 and one that costs $10? The answer is $90. The mouse in Fig. 12-7 cost $8.00 at a swap meet. It came with drivers and utilities on a 3½-inch floppy disk, and also a mouse pad. It does just about everything most people would need from a mouse. After all, how much mouse do you

12-7
A mouse that costs $8; it's all
you need for most work.

need just to point and click? Of course, if you're doing high-end drafting and designing, then you probably need one that's a little better.

Standard mice

The vast majority of mice today use a small round rubber ball on the underside of the unit that contacts the desktop or mouse pad. As the mouse is moved, the ball turns. Inside the mouse, two flywheels contact the ball, one for horizontal and one for vertical movements. The flywheels are mounted between two light-sensitive diodes. The flywheels have small holes in the outer edge. As they turn, light shines through the holes or is blocked where there are no holes. This breaks the light up into patterns of 1s and 0s. You don't need a grid for this type of mouse, but you do need about a square foot of clear desk space to move the mouse about. The ball picks up dirt so it should be cleaned often.

Optical mice

Some older mice used optics with an LED that shined on a reflective grid that formed small squares. As the mouse was moved across the grid, the reflected light was picked up by a detector and sent to the computer to move the cursor.

For a design that demands very close tolerances, the spacings of the grid for an optical mouse might not provide sufficient resolution. You might be better off in this case with a high-resolution mouse that uses a ball. This type of mouse system is practically obsolete now. If you have one of these older types, you might consider upgrading to the ball type.

Mouse interfaces

You can't just plug in a mouse and start using it. The software must recognize and be able to interface with the mouse, so mouse companies have developed software drivers that allow their mouse to operate with various programs. The drivers are usually supplied on a disk. Microsoft's mouse is the closest there is to a standard, so most other companies emulate the Microsoft driver. Most mice today come with a small switch that allows you to switch between Microsoft or IBM emulation. If the switch isn't in the proper position, it won't work.

Some older mice systems required a voltage, usually 5 volts. They often came with a small transformer you could plug into your power strip. You no longer have to supply power for a mouse. They draw all the power they need from the serial port.

A mouse requires one of your serial ports in order to connect to the computer, which could cause a problem if you already have two serial devices using COM1 and COM2.

Microsoft, Logitech, and several other mouse companies have developed a bus mouse. It interfaces directly with the bus and doesn't require the use of one of your COM ports, but it does require the use of one of your slots and IRQs. Most mouse systems come with several software packages and drivers that allow the mouse to be used with several programs.

PS/2 computers have a built-in pointing-device interface on their motherboard. The connector looks much like those used on the ISA clone machines, but it's wired differently. Many clones have also built the mouse interface into their motherboards. Some of them use the IBM socket. If you buy a mouse, depending on what type of system you have you might have to buy an adapter.

A mouse plugs into a serial port. The serial ports on some systems use a DB25 type socket connector with 25 contacts. Others use a DB9 socket with nine contacts. Many mice now come with the DB9 connector and a DB25 connector adapter. Figure 12-8 shows a mouse with an adapter. Note that the DB25 connector looks exactly like the DB25 connector used for the LPT1 parallel printer port except the serial port connect is a male connector with pins and the LPT1 printer port is a female connector with sockets.

What if you need a male cable and all you have is a female cable (or vice versa)? You can buy a DB25 "gender bender" adapter. Figure 12-9 shows a couple of gender benders. The one on the right is part of a test unit. It has LEDs that light up when there's a signal present in the line. Or you can purchase an extension to connect two similar cables. There are all kinds of combinations available. Cables to Go, at 800-225-8646, has just about every cable and accessory you'd ever need. Dalco Electronics, at 800-445-5342, also has many types of cables, adapters, and electronic components.

Before you buy a mouse, check what type of serial port connector you have and order the proper type. You can buy an adapter for about $3.

Loading the mouse driver

When you buy a mouse, you must usually load the software driver into the system before the mouse will operate. The file for many of the software drivers is fairly small. I usually just install the mouse driver file in the root directory, C:\, then put a

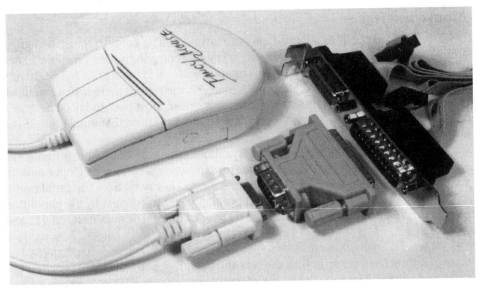

12-8 A mouse with a DB9 to DB25 connector adapter.

12-9
A couple of gender-bender adapters. The one on the right is part of a test unit. It has LEDs that light up if a signal is present.

line in my AUTOEXEC.BAT file to load it each time the system boots up. When you install Windows, it asks what kind of mouse you have. It will then automatically load the mouse driver each time you load Windows.

Trackballs

A trackball is a mouse turned upside down. Like older mice, older trackball systems required a voltage from a transformer or other source. Newer trackballs don't require an outside source of power, and like the new mice they also require a serial port or a slot if they're a bus mouse.

Instead of moving the mouse to move the ball, you move only the ball with your fingers. The balls in trackballs are usually larger than the balls in mice, so it's possible to have better resolution. They're often used with CAD and crucial design systems.

Since trackballs are stationary, they don't require as much desk space as ordinary mice. If your desk is as cluttered as mine, then you definitely need a trackball.

Several companies manufacture trackballs; look through the computer magazines for advertisements.

Keyboard/trackball combinations

Several companies have keyboards with a trackball built into the right-hand area. (Some are reversible for left-handers.) This gives you benefits and capabilities of a mouse without using up any desk real estate. Most trackballs are compatible with standard Microsoft mouse systems. As shown in Fig. 9-1, from back in chapter 9, the middle keyboard from Chicony has a built-in trackball.

Touch screens and light pens

Some fast-food places now have a touch screen with a menu of several items. You merely touch the item that you want and the order is transmitted to the kitchen. The same type of system is sometimes found in kiosks in shopping malls and large department stores. The touch system is accurate, saves time and money, and is convenient.

Using a touch screen is similar to pointing and clicking a mouse. On most of them, a frame is installed on the bezel of the monitor. Beams of infrared light crisscross the front of the monitor screen. Most monitors are set up for 80 columns left to right and 25 rows from top to bottom of regular text. Columns of beams originate from the top part of the frame and pass to the bottom frame. Rows of beams originate from the left portion of the frame and pass to the right frame. If one of the beams is interrupted by an object, such as a finger or pencil, the computer can determine which character happens to be in that portion of the screen.

Joysticks

Joysticks are used primarily for games. They're serial devices and need an interface. Many multifunction boards that have COM ports also provide a game connector for joysticks. Joysticks are fairly reasonable, selling from $10 to $30. There are usually several ads for them in magazines such as *Computer Shopper*.

Digitizers and graphics tablets

Graphics tablets and digitizers are similar to a flat drawing pad or drafting table. Most of them use some sort of pointing device that can translate movement into digitized output for the computer. Some are very small and some are as large as a standard drafting table. Some cost as little as $150 and some will run you over $1,500. Most of them have a very high resolution, are very accurate, and are intended for precision drawing.

Some tablets have programmable overlays and function keys, and some will work with a mouse-like device, a pen light, or a pencil-like stylus. The tablets can be used for designing circuits, CAD, graphics design, freehand drawing, and even text and data input. The most common use is with CAD software.

Most tablets are serial devices, but some of them require their own interface board. Many are compatible with the Microsoft mouse systems.

CalComp, at 800-932-1212, has developed several models. These tablets use a puck that's similar to a mouse except it has a magnifying glass and cross-hairs for very high resolution. They manufacture both corded and cordless pucks. Call CalComp for a brochure and more information.

Signature capture

It's very easy to generate a fax with a computer, but most letters and memos need a signature. Inforite, at 800-366-4635, has a small pad and stylus that lets you input a signature into a file (see Fig. 12-10). You can then attach the signature to a fax or other documents. With the Inforite system, you can add notes, comments, or drawings to electronic documents.

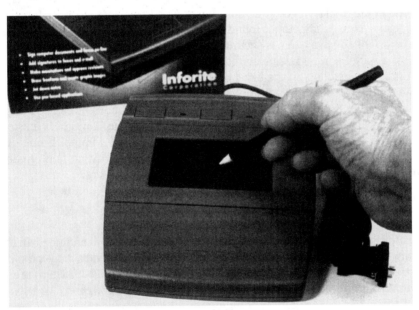

12-10 The Inforite pad that lets you capture your signature and store it on a hard disk or add handwritten data to a computer file.

Pressure-sensitive graphics tablets

Several companies have developed pressure-sensitive tablets. Wacom has developed several different models that use an electromagnetic resonance system with a special stylus that requires no wires or batteries. The tablet has a grid of embedded wires that can detect the location of the stylus and the applied pressure. The tablet senses the amount of pressure and will draw a thin or heavy line in response. You can use this system with different graphics programs to create sketches, drawings, designs, and art.

This type of pad could also be very useful in a psychologist's or psychiatrist's office. Certain words might evoke tension, stress, or other emotions. The doctor could ask a patient to write down certain words, such as mother, wife, husband, boyfriend, or girlfriend. If the doctor was sitting in front of a computer screen, he could tell which words had an emotional content. If a patient disliked someone, he would put more pressure on the pen when writing that name. This could help the doctor zero in on the problem.

Most businesses aren't allowed to use a polygraph when hiring people, but many of them would sure like to. In many cases, once a person has been hired, it's very difficult to get rid of them. It would be much better if the employer could determine who might be a problem ahead of time.

A pressure-sensitive tablet could be used in personnel offices when interviewing someone. A questionnaire sheet could be placed over the pad. As the applicant answered the questions, different pressures would be used. It would be fairly obvious which areas were answered truthfully and in which areas there may have been a bit of fudging. If the questionnaire was designed properly, it could be almost as good as a polygraph. The system could also be used by police forces and in many other areas.

Of course, there are a lot of people who would object to this type of tool, and there are some who would abuse it and use it improperly. But with the proper software and if used properly, I think it would do more good than it would harm. Here are some of the companies who manufacture pressure-sensitive tablets:

Wacom Technology	800-922-6613
Communication Intelligence	800-888-9242
Kurta Corp.	602-276-5533
Summagraphics	800-337-8662

Call the companies for brochures or more information.

Scanners and optical character readers

Most large companies have mountains of memos, manuals, documents, and files that must be maintained, revised, and updated periodically. Several companies now manufacture optical character readers (OCR) that can scan a line of printed type, recognize each character, and input that character into a computer just as if it were typed in from a keyboard. A beam of light sweeps across the page and the characters are determined by the absorption and reflection of the light. One problem with early scanners was that they could recognize only a few different fonts, and they couldn't recognize graphics at all. The machines today have much more memory and the technology has improved so better scanners can recognize almost any font or type.

One difference between a fax machine and a scanner is that when you send a printed page through a stand-alone fax machine, it scans the whole page and generates a digital, graphic copy of the page. When a printed page is scanned, it's transformed into electronic text that can be manipulated. You can use a word processor to revise or change the data, then print it out again.

Once printed matter is stored in a computer, you can search it very quickly for any item. Many times I've spent hours going through printed manuals looking for certain items. If the data had been in a computer, I could have found the information in just minutes.

Optical character readers have been around for several years. When they first came out, they cost from $6,000 to more than $15,000. They were very limited in the character fonts they could recognize. Vast improvements have been made in the last few years. Many full-page scanners are now fairly inexpensive, starting at about $500. Some hand-held ones cost as little as $100. I have a good hand-held scanner from Caere, at 408-395-7000 (see Fig. 12-11). There are times when it's all I need to input an item. The more expensive models usually can recognize a large number of fonts and graphics.

12-11 A hand-held scanner and interface.

Flat-bed scanners

Although my hand-held scanner is a very good tool, there are times when I need to be able to scan text as well as graphics. I also need to scan color once in a while.

There are a large number of color scanners available. I looked at several of them before I decided to buy an Epson 800C Pro color scanner (see Fig. 12-12). It has OCR and graphics software so I can scan almost anything and enter it into my computer.

The Epson scanner came with a SCSI interface card, a six-foot cable, and a standard Centronics 50-pin connector. I didn't need the interface card since I already had a Future Domain PowerSCSI, which was already installed in my Pentium computer and was driving my 1.05GB hard disk and Toshiba 3401 CD-ROM drive. The problem was that my Future Domain PowerSCSI has a high-density miniature 50-pin connector and the cable that came with the scanner has the much larger standard Centronics 50-pin connector. I looked through a couple of computer magazines and tried to find a company that had an adapter, but had no luck. I finally bought a cable from

12-12 An Epson ES 800C flat-bed color scanner.

JDR Microdevices, at 800-538-5000. This cable has the miniature high-density connector on one end and the standard Centronics connector on the other.

I now have an extra SCSI interface that's worth about $150 and a cable that's worth about $40. I could probably have saved this money if I had checked several sources before I bought the scanner.

What to look for when buying a scanner

What to look for depends on what you want to do with your scanner, and of course how much you want to pay. There are several manufacturers of scanners and hundreds of different models, types, resolutions, bus types, and prices. A monochrome scanner is fine for text, and many monochrome scanners are relatively inexpensive. They'll recognize text and graphic images in up to 256 different shades.

If you're buying a color scanner, there are a lot more options to consider. Some of the lower-priced ones might have to make three passes—one each for red, green, and blue. For each pass, the light is sent through filters that can recognize 256 levels of red, green, or blue.

Less expensive color scanners can read a resolution of only 300 or 400 dots per inch (dpi), but they often use interpolation software that fills in the spaces between the dots to give two or three times the true resolution. As you'd expect, some ads list the interpolated resolution in large letters and the true resolution in small letters (if it's mentioned at all).

The more expensive color scanners can do it in one pass, and some of them scan at a true 24-bit color depth to yield 16.7 million colors. That means that there can be eight bits of color information about each of the red, green, or blue colors.

Try to find a system that conforms to the twain specification. Twain isn't an acronym; it's just a word for an application programming interface (API) specification that was jointly developed by Aldus, Caere, Eastman Kodak, Hewlett-Packard, and Logitech. Twain helps to eliminate some of the device drivers such as those necessary for every printer.

Some less expensive scanners use a proprietary interface board. It's much better to buy one that uses the SCSI interface.

There are many manufacturers of scanners. Look in any of the computer magazines listed in chapter 19. You'll see many advertisements for all types of keyboards, scanners, mice, and other input devices. Some of the magazines, such as *PC Computing* and *Computer Shopper*, have a separate product listing in the back pages. It's a great help, but they list only those products advertised for that month in their magazine.

Of course, there are many good products whose manufacturers can't afford the high cost of magazine ads. If you live in a larger city, there are local computer stores and computer swaps, both of which can be a very good source.

OCR software

The OCR capabilities of a scanner allow it to recognize each character of a printed document and input that character into a computer just as if it were typed in from a keyboard. Once the data is in the computer, you can use a word processor to revise or change the data, then print it out again.

Faxes are received as graphical documents. It requires a lot of disk space to store the graphical information, but a scanner can convert it to text, which takes up much less disk space. Some OCR software, such as WordScan Plus from Calera, can work with a large number of different scanners. It can even recognize degraded text by reading it in context, and has a large internal dictionary that helps in this respect. It yields excellent OCR accuracy.

Several companies have developed advanced software to work with their scanners and, in some cases, those manufactured by other companies. Here is a brief list of the companies who have OCR software:

Caere Corp. (OmniPage Professional)	800-535-7226
Calera Corp. (WordScan Plus)	800-544-7051
Logitech Corp. (Catchword Pro)	510-795-8500
Ocron, Inc. (Perceive)	408-980-8900
Recognita Corp. (Recognita Plus)	408-241-5772

Some fax software, such as WinFax PRO from Delrina at 408-363-2345, can intercept an incoming fax and convert it into digital characters.

Business-card scanners

If you depend on business cards to keep in contact with prospective buyers or for other business purposes, you might have several rolodexes full of cards. You could take each card and enter the information into your computer database, but there's an easier way. Some companies have developed card scanners that can read the information off a business card and enter it into a computer.

At this time they're still a bit expensive, but if you depend on business cards they're well worth it. Like most computer products, the prices will come down very soon. Here are four of the companies that offer business card scanners:

CypherTech, Inc. (CyperScan 1000)	408-734-8765
Microtek Labs (Scan-in-Dex)	800-654-4160
Cognitive Technology (Cognitive BCR)	415-925-2367
Pacific Crest Tech. (CardGrabber)	714-261-6444

Large-sized scanners

Houston Instruments specializes in manufacturing plotters. They've developed a scanning head for one of their plotters that can scan a large drawing, digitize the lines and symbols, then enter them into a computer. The drawing can then be changed and replotted very easily.

Installing a scanner

Most scanners come with a plug-in board and software drivers, and most of them are serial type devices, so they require the use of one of your serial ports and one of your motherboard slots. You have set switches or jumpers to configure the board so it doesn't conflict with other devices in your system.

As you can see, two serial ports per machine just aren't enough. We also need more than eight motherboard slots. There are boards that can provide more ports and there are motherboards that have up to 12 slots, but they're rather expensive.

Voice recognition

Another way to input data into a computer is to talk to it. Of course, you need electronics that can detect the spoken words and turn them into digital information a computer can use.

Early voice-recognition systems were very expensive and also very limited. One reason was that the voice technology required a lot of memory, but the cost of memory has dropped considerably in the last few years and the technology has improved in many other ways. Eventually, voice-recognition technology will replace the keyboard for many applications.

Voice technology involves "training" a computer to recognize a word spoken by a person. When you speak into a microphone, the sound waves cause a diaphragm, or some other device, to move back and forth in a magnetic field and create a voltage that's analogous to the sound wave. If this voltage is recorded and played through a good audio system, the loudspeaker will respond to the amplified voltages and reproduce a sound identical to the one sent to the microphone.

A person can speak a word into a microphone, which creates a unique voltage for that word and that particular person's voice. The voltage is fed into an electronic circuit, and the pattern is digitized and stored in the computer. If several words are spoken, the circuit will digitize each one of them and store them. Each one will have a distinct and unique pattern. Later, when the computer hears a word, it will search through the patterns it has stored to see if the input word matches any one of its stored words.

Of course, once the computer is able to recognize a word, you can have it perform some useful work. You could command it to load and run a program, or perform any of several other tasks.

Because every person's voice is different, a computer wouldn't ordinarily recognize the voice of anyone other than the person who trained it. Training the computer might involve saying the same word several times so the computer can store several patterns of the person's voice. Some new systems recognize the voices of people who haven't trained the computer.

Uses for voice recognition

Uses for voice recognition include letters, reports, and complicated business and technical text. Voice recognition can be used by doctors, nurses, lawyers, reporters, loan officers, auditors, researchers, secretaries, and business executives—in manufacturing, language interpretation, and writing.

Computer voice recognition is very useful whenever you must use both hands to do a job, but still need a computer to perform certain tasks. One area where voice recognition is used extensively is in military jet fighter planes. They move so fast that the pilot doesn't have time to manipulate computer keys because both hands are usually busy. The pilot can have the computer do hundreds of jobs by just telling it what he wants done.

Voice recognition is also useful on production lines where people don't have time to manually enter data into a computer. It can also be used in a laboratory where scientists look through a microscope and can't take their eyes off their subject to write down the findings or data. There might be times when the lighting is kept too dim to type data into a computer. In other instances, someone might be several feet from a computer and still be able to input data through the microphone line or even with a wireless microphone. The person might even be miles away and be able to input data over a telephone line. Voice recognition can help many people who have physical limitations become productive and independent.

An excellent use of voice recognition is for doctors. Instead of writing out a patient's history, they could speak and record it into a computer. And instead of writing prescriptions, they could record them into a computer and then have them printed out. Many pharmacists have become quite proficient in deciphering most prescriptions, but there are still times there have been mistakes because of the indecipherable handwriting of the doctor. If prescriptions were printed out, it might even save a few lives.

Not only doctors have bad handwriting. Mine becomes almost indecipherable when the temperature goes down. Many executives issue a lot of memos and orders, but many have the same handwriting problem I have. I'm thankful I can use a computer instead of writing, but many executives don't know how to type on a computer. However, most of them are very good at talking. If they had a computer to talk to, they could probably manage to issue a lot more executive memos and orders.

It's true that any executive who deserves the title should have a good secretary who can take dictation and then type out the memos and letters. But many companies are going through some difficult times. It's possible that some executives might have the title but not all the perks. A voice-recognition system is rather inexpensive today. Such a computer system would cost a lot less than a good secretary.

The Carnegie Mellon Institute is working on a system to allow, for instance, an English-speaking person to call a German-speaking person and for both parties to understand each other. The spoken English would be translated into German and the spoken German would be translated into English. The system would recognize the spoken word and then use computerized speech recognition to translate it for the parties. So the parties would actually be talking to a computerized mechanical interpreter. Similar systems are being developed for Japanese and other foreign languages.

The same type of system could be built into small hand-held foreign-language interpreters. Speak an English word into the machine and it would give you the equivalent spoken foreign word.

Many luxury automobiles now come with cellular phones that have voice-activated dialing. This lets the driver keep his eyes on the road while the number is being dialed.

At one time I didn't think car phones were necessary, but if you live in the Los Angeles area you can spend hours sitting in traffic jams on the freeways. If you have a cellular phone, you can at least do a bit of business while sitting there. Some people have even installed fax machines in their cars.

Computer designers are constantly looking for new ways to differentiate and improve their products. In the very near future you can be sure that many of them will come out with systems that have built-in voice recognition.

Chips that use very large-scale integration (VLSI) are combining more and more computer functions onto single chips, and they're making computers smaller and smaller. We now have some very powerful computers that can fit in a shirt pocket. One of the big problems is that there isn't room for a decent keyboard. To fit all the necessary keys on a keyboard, they have to be very small. You can use only a single finger to type on the keyboards of these miniaturized computers and, even then, if your fingers are very large you might end up pressing two keys at once. A solution is to build in voice recognition so the keyboard isn't needed.

Limitations to voice recognition

For most voice-recognition systems, the computer must be trained to recognize a specific discrete individual word, so the computer's vocabulary is limited to what it's trained to recognize, the amount of memory available, and the limitations imposed by the software and hardware. There are many basic systems available today that are very good at recognizing discrete words, but when we speak many words tend to run together. There aren't many systems around that can recognize continuous speech.

Another problem is homonyms, or words that are pronounced the same and sometimes spelled the same, but have different meanings. For instance, him and hymn are pronounced the same but have very different meanings. Another instance is the words to, too, and two. Many people misspell and confuse the words there and their, your and you're, and it's and its. Also, many words have several meanings, such as set, run, round, date, and many, many others.

One solution to this problem is software and hardware with enough intelligence to recognize not only the words themselves but their meaning, due to the context in which they're used. That, unfortunately, requires more intelligence than some human beings have.

Replacing the keyboard?

Even with the wrist supports and other aids, CTS is still a major problem. Millions of dollars could be saved if the keyboard could be replaced with voice-recognition technology. Realistically, we probably won't be able to completely eliminate the keyboard for at least several years, but we're getting closer.

The rate of data input can be speeded up considerably with voice input. The average typist can type about 60 words per minute. (Counting the errors I make, I can do only about half that.) We can speak at a much faster rate. There are some people who speak faster than I can listen—which is one of the problems with computers.

Every spoken word can be derived from just 42 phonemes. Several companies are working on systems that will take a small sample of a person's voice that contains these phonemes. Using the phonemes from this sample, you could train a computer to recognize any word you speak. A system such as this could help eliminate the keyboard.

There are several large companies, such as Kurzweil, IBM, Microsoft, WordPerfect, WordStar, and DeScribe, who are working on voice-recognition products. The object linking and embedding (OLE) sound recorders and drivers in Windows 3.1 lend a standardization that will help speed the development of complex voice recognition.

IBM has done a considerable amount of research to develop the IBM Speech Server Series products. Customers can access up to 20,000 words in an active vocabulary. Speech Server accepts spoken words at a rate of 70 words per minute, faster than most people can type. These products are designed primarily to run on high-end OS/2 and RISC machines. You can get more information about the IBM Speech Server Series by calling 800-772-2227.

A fairly small company, Dragon Systems, at 617-965-5200, has developed some very sophisticated voice-recognition products. IBM has licensed Dragon Systems' technology for inclusion and distribution in some of their products, and they've licensed Dragon Systems' Dragon Talk->To Plus and DragonDictate-7K. These systems run on DOS, Windows 3.1, and OS/2 2.1. Dragon Talk->To Plus is a fairly low-cost, simple system. DragonDictate-7K allows you to have a customized dictionary of up to 7,000 words, and is a bit more expensive. Microsoft has also licensed Dragon Systems' technology for inclusion in their Windows Sound System. This system contains Voice Pilot, which provides voice command and control of a system.

The technology is advancing, and digital signal processing (DSP) is going to help speed up the development. The 115 million instructions per second (MIPS) power of the Pentium will also help speed up the development of voice-recognition technology and the ultimate elimination of the keyboard.

Security systems

The voice of every person is as distinct and different as fingerprints. Voice prints have even been used to convict criminals. Since no two voices are alike, a voice-recognition system could be used to practically eliminate the need for keys. Most automobiles already have built-in computerized systems. You can be sure that sometime soon you'll see autos that have a voice-recognition system instead of ignition keys. Such a system could help reduce the number of car thefts and carjackings.

A voice-recognition system could also be used anywhere that required strict security. If they installed voice recognition at Fort Knox, they could probably eliminate many of their other security measures.

Basic systems

Verbex Voice Systems, at 800-275-8729, has developed a fairly sophisticated system that can make the keyboard almost obsolete. Their Listen for Windows uses special software and a 16-bit plug-in board with a digital signal processor (DSP) on it. After a bit of training, this system can recognize continuous speech. Of course, it still isn't perfect, so there are times when you have to slow down and pronounce discrete words and make corrections for words the system doesn't understand. Call Verbex for more information and current pricing.

Covox, 503-342-1271, has a less expensive voice-recognition system that also recognizes discrete words. Voice Master is an 8-bit plug-in bus card. Voice Master, System II is an external system that plugs into the parallel port. Voice Master can practically replace the keyboard, and it works with most major word processors.

The software is loaded as a terminate-and-stay-resident program (TSR) that requires about 20K. When the "hot keys" (the two shift keys) are pressed, a menu pops up. You then type in the command or macro you want performed, then say the command or name for the macro three times. This trains the software to recognize the command. Up to 1,023 commands or words for a macro can be stored. The internal Voice Master bus card and the parallel-port Voice Master, System II both come with headset microphones.

An advantage of the parallel-port System II is that it doesn't require you to open your computer. It also doesn't require the use of a precious slot. You can use it on notebook and laptop computers, or any ISA computer that has a parallel port. The Voice Master system is priced fairly low. Call Covox for current prices.

Computers and devices for the handicapped

Several computer devices have been developed that can help disabled people live better lives. There are devices that allow blind, deaf, quadriplegic, and other disabled people to communicate. There are special Braille keyboards and keyboards with enlarged keys for blind people. The EyeTyper from the Sentient Systems Technology of Pittsburgh, PA has an embedded camera on the keyboard that can determine which key the user is looking at. It then enters that key into the computer.

Words Plus of Sunnyvale, CA has a sensitive visor that can understand input from a raised brow, head movement, or eye blink.

Speaking Devices Corp., 408-727-5571, has a telephone that can be trained to recognize an individual's voice. It can then dial up to 100 different numbers when the person tells it to. The same company has a tiny earphone that also acts as a microphone. These devices would be ideal for people who cannot use their hands.

Several organizations can help in locating special equipment and lend support. If you know someone who might benefit from the latest technology and devices for the handicapped, contact these organizations:

AbleData	800-344-5405
Accent on Information	309-378-2961
Apple Computer	408-996-1010
Closing the Gap, Inc.	612-248-3294
Direct Link for the Disabled	805-688-1603
Easter Seals Systems Office	312-667-8626
IBM National Support Center	800-426-2133
American Foundation for the Blind	212-620-2000
Trace Research and Development Center	608-262-6966
National ALS Association	818-340-7500

Most of these organizations will be glad to accept your old computers. Of course, you can write it off your income tax as a donation. You'll be helping them and yourself.

13
CHAPTER

Communications

Telephones are an important and sometimes crucial part of our lives. By adding a modem to your computer, you can communicate over telephone lines with anyone else in the world who also has a computer and a modem. Many modem boards are now integrated with fax capability, and a fax/modem might not cost much more than just a modem. Communicating by fax is fast and efficient.

Reaching out

There are over 100 million personal computers installed in homes and businesses worldwide. About half of them have a modem or some sort of communications capability. This is one of the most important abilities of a computer.

You can use a telephone to communicate with any one of several million people anywhere in the world. Likewise, if you have a computer with telecommunications capabilities, you can communicate with several million other people who have computers. You can access over 10,000 bulletin boards in the U.S. and take advantage of electronic mail, faxes, of-up-to-the-minute stock market quotations, many data services and databases, and a large number of other online services, such as home shopping, home banking, and travel agencies.

For some types of work, you can use a modem and work from home, called *telecommuting*. It's a whole lot better than commuting by car, possibly several hours a day, and sitting in traffic jams. Unfortunately, communicating by computer isn't as easy as talking on a telephone. Computers are still just dumb pieces of machinery and will do only what they're told. To get them to do what you want, you must tell them exactly what you want them to do. But newer technologies and advances are making it easier.

The area of communications covers a wide range of activities and technologies. Several books have been written just about single sections of this wide-ranging technology. Just a small part of it will be discussed in this chapter.

The Internet

One of the hottest topics at the moment is the Internet, also called the "information superhighway." The Internet started as a government project in 1973 with the Advanced Research Projects Agency (ARPA), an agency of the Department of Defense (DOD). It was a network designed to facilitate scientific collaboration in military research among educational institutions. ARPAnet had some similarities to peer-to-peer networking, and allowed almost any system to connect through an electronic gateway.

It's now possible to access the Internet from CompuServe (800-848-8990), America Online (800-827-6364), Delphi (800-695-4005), and many, many other services. Currently, however, Delphi is the only service that offers full Internet access; the others just let you use the e-mail. Many books have been written about the Internet. Three very good ones, published by Osborne/McGraw-Hill at 800-227-0900, are *Internet Essentials and Fun List*, *Internet, the Complete Reference*, and *The Internet Yellow Pages*. If you're just getting started, *Internet, the Complete Reference* will help you immensely. It has over 800 pages of information about getting on the net, and addresses and numbers of hundreds of local, state, national, and international access gateways. There are valuable, helpful hints on almost every page.

Millions of people access the Internet. There's something there for everyone: encyclopedias, up-to-the-minute news, people chatting with one another, online romance, and X-rated photos and talk. You can post notes or send e-mail. If you don't know where to find something, you can use Gopher, Archie, Veronica, and Jughead to search for you. These comic-book characters are search software that can help you find almost anything on the net.

The vast majority of people are good and honest, but when you get this many people communicating with one another, there are always a few who will try to take advantage of others. Just be careful.

Modems

A modem is an electronic device that allows a computer to use an ordinary telephone line to communicate with other computers also equipped with a modem. *Modem* is a contraction of the words *modulate* and *demodulate*. The telephone system transmits voice and data in analog voltage form. Analog voltages vary continuously up and down. Computer data is usually in a digital voltage form. Digital signals are a series of on and off voltages. When the voltage is on for a certain period of time, it represents a 1. When it's off, it represents a 0.

A modem takes digitized bits of voltage from a computer and modulates, or transforms it into analog voltages in order to transmit it over the telephone line. At the receiving end, a similar modem demodulates the analog voltage, transforming it back into a digital form.

Transmission difficulties

Telephone systems were originally designed for voice and have a very narrow bandwidth. A person with perfect hearing can hear 20 cycles per second, or 20 Hz, all the way up to 20,000 Hz. For normal speech, however, we use only from about 300 Hz to 2000 Hz.

A telephone's analog voltages are subject to noise, static, and other electrical disturbances. Noise and static take the form of analog voltages, as do most electrical disturbances, such as electrical storms and pulses generated by operating electrical equipment. The analog noise and static voltages are added and imposed on any data voltages being transmitted. The mixture of static and noise voltages with data voltages can corrupt and severely damage the data, and the demodulator might not be able to determine which voltages represent data and which are noise.

Baud rate

The problem of static and electrical noise interfering with data transmission, and the state of technology at the time, limited the original modems to about 5 characters per second, or a rate of 50 baud.

The term baud comes from the French inventor Emile Baudot (1845–1903). Originally, the baud rate was a measure of the dots and dashes in telegraphy, but is now defined as the actual rate of symbols transmitted per second. For lower baud rates, the measurement is essentially the same as bits per second (bps). Remember that it takes eight bits to make a character. Just as periods and spaces separate words, you must use one start bit and one stop bit to separate on/off bits into characters. A transmission of 300 baud would mean that 300 on/off bits were sent in one second. For every eight bits of data that represent a character, you need one bit to indicate the start of the character and one bit to indicate the end of the character. You then need another bit to indicate the start of the next character, so counting the start/stop bits it takes 11 bits for each character. If you divide 300 by 11, you get about 27 characters per second (cps).

Some of the newer technologies, however, actually transmit symbols that represent more than one bit, so for rates of 1,200 and higher the bps and baud rate can be considerably different and the term *bps* should be used.

There have been some fantastic advances in modems. A couple of years ago 2,400-bps systems were the standard, but today they're obsolete. The industry has leaped over 4,800- and 9,600-bps systems to 14.4-Kbps systems. These units incorporate the V.42bis compression standard, which allows them to use 4:1 data compression and thus transmit at 57,600 bps.

Several companies have developed modems that will transmit at 16.8 Kbps, 19.2 Kbps, and 28.8 Kbps. At the time of this writing, there are no standards to support these higher frequencies. A standard of sorts is called the V.fast class. Hayes and several other manufacturers are actively promoting V.fast even though it hasn't yet been made a standard. The proposed new standard will be called V.34. By the time you read this, the V.34 standard should be approved. Hayes claims they can transmit at

230,400 bits per second by using their enhanced Optima compression technology. Table 13-1 lists modem types and uncompressed transmission rates.

Table 13-1. Uncompressed transmission rates for several modems

Modem	Transfer rate
V.32bis	14.4 Kbps
V.32terbo	19.2 Kbps
V.fast	28.8 Kbps
V.34	28.8 Kbps

When communicating with another modem, both the sending and receiving unit must operate at the same bps (transmission rate) and use the same protocols. Most faster modems are downward compatible and can operate at slower speeds.

Ordinarily, the higher the transmission rate the less time it takes to download or transmit a file, but this might not always be so because at higher speeds more transmission errors are encountered. In case of errors, parts of the file, or even the whole file, might have to be retransmitted. However, if you transmit data frequently, a high-speed modem can quickly pay for itself. We sure have come a long way since that early 50-baud standard.

How to estimate connect time

You can figure the approximate length of time it will take to transmit a file by calculating the cps. Just divide the transmission rate by 10. For instance, a 2,400-bps transmission would be 240 cps. Look at the directory and determine the number of bytes in the file, divide the number of bytes in the file by the cps, then multiply that figure by 1.3 for the start/stop bits to get a final approximation. For instance, to find the time it would take to transmit a 40K file at 2,400 bps, use the following equation: $40,000 \div 240 = 167$ seconds $\times 1.3 = 217$ seconds, or 3.6 minutes. If you transmitted the same 40K file with a 14.4-Kbps modem, it would be $40,000 \div 14,400 = 2.78$ seconds $\times 1.3 = 3.6$ seconds. High-speed modems can save you a lot of money in telephone charges.

Data compression

Besides using a faster transmission rate, another way to reduce phone charges is to use file compression. Bulletin boards have been using a form of data compression for years. There are several public-domain programs you can use to squeeze and unsqueeze data. Newer modems take advantage of compression using the V.42bis standard for 4-to-1 compression. Using 4-to-1 compression, a 14.4-Kbps modem can send 57,600 bits per second. With a 14.4-Kbps modem and 4-to-1 compression, the same 40K file that took 3.6 minutes when transmitted at 2,400 baud could be sent in less than one second.

2,400-bps modems are obsolete but many companies still advertise and sell them. Many companies now sell 14.4-Kbps fax/modems for less than $100. Considering the telephone rates for long distance, it might be worthwhile to buy a high-speed modem. I have a perfectly good Intel 2,400-bps modem with a 9,600-bps fax, but I replaced it with a SupraFAX V.32bis fax/modem, a combination 14.4-Kbps modem and fax board from Supra Corp., at 506-967-2400. Figure 7-13 in chapter 7 shows my SupraFAX V.32bis modem.

Besides the phone line charges you have to pay, major online service companies such as CompuServe, Dataquest, and Dow Jones News/Retrieval charge for connect time to their service. The connect time is much less with a high-speed modem, but in order to keep their revenue up, some companies charge a bit more for access via high-speed modem.

Protocols

Protocols are procedures that have been established for exchanging data, along with instructions that coordinate the process. Most protocols can sense when data is corrupted or lost due to noise, static, or a bad connection and automatically resend the affected data until it's received correctly.

There are several protocols, but the most popular ones are kermit (named for Kermit the frog), x-modem, and y-modem. The protocol transmits a block of data along with an error-checking code, then waits for the receiver to send back an acknowledgment. It then sends another block and waits to see if it got through okay. If a block doesn't get through, it's re-sent immediately. Protocols such as z-modem and hyperprotocol send a whole file in a continuous stream of data, with error-checking codes inserted at certain intervals. They then wait for confirmation of a successful transmission. If the transmission is unsuccessful, then the whole file must be resent.

Both sending and receiving modems must use the same protocol and transmission rate. You can't send a file at 14.4 Kbps to someone who has only a 2,400-bps modem, but faster modems are able to shift down and send or receive at lower speeds.

ITU recommended standards

The communications industry is very complex, so there haven't been many real standards. There are, however, many different manufacturers and software developers who, of course, want to differentiate their hardware or software by adding new features. So you might not be able to communicate with someone else who isn't using the same features or is using a nonstandard modem.

A United Nations standards committee was established to help create worldwide communications standards. If every country had different protocols and standards, it would be very difficult to communicate. The committee was originally called the Comite Consulatif Internal de Telegraphique et Telephone (CCITT), but has now been changed to International Telecommunications Union (ITU). The committee has representatives from over 80 countries and several large private manufacturers, and makes recommendations only. Companies are free to use or ignore them, but more and more companies are now adopting the recommendations.

All ITU recommendations for small computers have a V or X prefix. The V series is for use with switched telephone networks, which is almost all of them. The X series is for systems that don't use switched phone lines. Revisions or alternate recommendations have bis (second) or ter (third) added.

The V prefixes can be a bit confusing. For instance, a V.32 modem can communicate at 4,800 or 9,600 bps with any other V.32 modem. A V.32bis modem can communicate at 14,400 bps. The V.32bis standard is a modulation method, not a compression technique.

The V.42bis standard is a method of data compression and a system of error checking. A V.42bis modem can communicate with another V.42bis modem at up to 57,600 bps by using compression and error checking. A higher number following the V doesn't necessarily mean the modem operates at a higher speed. Table 13-2 lists some of the V standards for modems.

Table 13-2. ITU V standards

Speed	Standard
300 bps	Bell 103/V.21
1,200 bps	Bell 211A/V.22
2,400 bps	V.22bis
4,800 bps	V.32
9,600 bps	V.32
14.4 Kbps	V.32bis
28.8 Kbps	V.42bis

Modem error-checking and correction protocols

Besides the V specification, you might see modems advertised with several other labels. Here are a few:

MNP

MNP stands for Microcom networking protocol. Microcom has developed a series of ten different protocols, MNP 1 to MNP 10, that work so well that most of the industry has adopted them. MNP 1 to MNP 3 were early modem protocols. MNP 4 through MNP 10 deal with sending data in packets with advanced error detection, error correction, and data compression. The MNP protocols are usually programmed into ROM chips on the modem.

LAPM

LAPM stands for link access procedure for modems, and provides error control between modems that use LAPM. This is a part of the V.42 specification for 2,400-bps and 9,600-bps modems. When the modems try to connect, they first try to establish the LAPM protocol. If they can't connect with this protocol, they'll then try the MNP protocol. If that doesn't work, they'll drop down to the normal connection.

Communications software

In order to use a modem, it must be driven and controlled by software. There are dozens of communication programs you can use. CrossTalk (404-998-3998) was one of the earlier modem programs. There's also a CrossTalk for Windows. ProComm Plus from DataStorm, at 314-474-8461, is an excellent communications program. Qmodem is another very good program. At one time both ProComm and Qmodem were low-cost shareware programs, and were among the most popular communication programs available. Both are now commercial programs. Qmodem was one of the early shareware programs developed by John Friel. He called it the "Forbin Project." A few years ago, the Forbin Project was taken over by Mustang Software, at 805-873-2500.

Both ProComm and Qmodem have been updated to work under Windows. Qmodem can even handle your fax communications. Mustang Software also provides software for setting up bulletin boards. If you'd like to start your own BBS, contact them for the details.

One of the most comprehensive communications programs is WinComm PRO, from Delrina at 800-268-6082. It operates under Windows and handles both modem and fax communications. You can use it to access all the online services as well as other modems, and you can even set it up as a mini-BBS, setting up passwords and access privileges and letting other users log on to your computer. Since it works under Windows, you can use a mouse to point and click on the many icons and buttons. WinComm PRO is much like plug-and-play software in that it can automatically detect and avoid port conflicts. Call Delrina and ask for a brochure. It's one of the best communications packages available.

If you buy a modem or modem/fax board, many companies include a basic communications program. You can still get copies of communications shareware from bulletin boards or from any of the several companies who provide shareware and public-domain software. Just remember that shareware is *not* free. You can try it out, but if you like it and continue to use it the developers ask you to register the program and send in a nominal fee. For this low cost, they'll usually provide a manual and some support.

Basic types of modems

There are two basic types of modems: the external desktop and the internal. Each type has some advantages and disadvantages.

Both external and internal models have speakers so you hear the phone ringing or a busy signal, but the internal modem might have a very small speaker you might not be able to hear. Some external models have a volume control for the built-in speaker.

Internal modems are built entirely on a board, usually a half or short board. The good news is that it doesn't use up any of your desk real estate, but the bad news is that it uses one of your precious slots. It also doesn't have the LEDs to let you know the progress of your call. Of course, not being able to see the LEDs flashing might not be that important to you. The only thing most people care about is whether it works or not. The fewer items to worry about, the better.

Even if you use an external modem, if your motherboard doesn't have built-in COM ports you'll need an I/O board that requires the use of one of your slots for a COM port.

External modems can cost up to $100 more than an equivalent internal modem, and they require some of your precious desk space and a voltage source. They also require a COM port to drive them.

Modem LEDs

Most external models have LEDs that light up and let you know what is happening during your call. Here are some of the LEDs and the abbreviations for their functions:

Carrier Detect (CD)

This means your modem has detected a carrier signal from another modem, whether the modem is calling you or you've called the other modem.

Clear to Send (CS)

This light will flash when your computer signals the other computer that it can send more data.

Error Checking (EC)

This indicates that the communications link uses an error-checking protocol.

High Speed (HS)

This light indicates whether the modem is able to send at a high speed. If the light isn't on, then it's operating at a low speed. Some newer modems have numeric indicators for the speed, such as 12, 24, 48, or 96.

Modem Ready (MR)

This indicates that the power is on and the modem is ready to operate.

Off Hook (OH)

Off Hook means that the phone is "off the hook" and the telephone circuit is open. The OH light will stay on for as long as the connection lasts.

Received Data (RD)

Received Data indicates that data is being received from another modem.

Request to Send (RS)

This light comes on when your computer's serial port controls the data flow.

Send Data (SD)

The SD light comes on when the computer sends data to the modem. Both the SD and RD lights should be on when data is being sent. If either or both stop flashing, it means that no data is being sent.

Terminal Ready (TR)

This light comes on when the modem receives a signal from the computer terminal indicating it's ready to send or receive.

Hayes compatibility

One of the most popular early modems was made by Hayes Microcomputer Products. They became the IBM of the modem world, establishing a de facto standard. There are hundreds of modem manufacturers. Except for some of the very inexpensive ones, almost all of them emulate the Hayes standard.

Installing a modem

If you're adding a modem on a board to a system that's already assembled, the first thing to do is to check your documentation and set any jumpers or switches necessary to configure the board. You must usually set jumpers or small switches to enable COM1 or COM2. Once you've set the switches and jumpers, remove the computer cover, find an empty slot, and plug the board in.

If you have an I/O board in your system with external COM ports or if you have built-in COM ports on your motherboard, you must configure them for whichever port will be used for the modem. For instance, you might have COM ports built into the motherboard, a mouse connected to COM1 on the motherboard port, or an I/O board in your system that has COM1 and COM2 serial ports. If you use COM1 on the motherboard, then you must set the jumpers to disable COM1 on the I/O board.

If you're installing an external modem, you must go through the same procedure to make sure the COM port is accessible and doesn't conflict. You have a mouse, serial printer, or some other serial device, you'll have to determine which port it's set to. You can't have two serial devices set to the same COM port.

A simple modem test

It's often difficult to determine which COM port is being used by a device. You can use the AT command to determine if your modem is working, with the following simple test.

Switch to your communications software directory. At the DOS C: prompt, type the following (in uppercase): ECHO AT DT12345>COM1:. The AT stands for attention and the DT for dial tone. If you have pulse dial system, the command would be AT DP12345. If the modem is set properly, you'll hear a dial tone and the modem will dial 12345. The modem will then emit a continuous busy signal. You can stop the busy signal by invoking the command ECHO ATHO. The HO tells it to hang up.

If two devices are both set for COM1 or COM2, there will be a conflict. The computer will try for a while, then give an error message and the familiar "Abort, Retry, Ignore, Fail?" message. If the modem is connected to COM1 and you invoke the command ECHO AT DT12345>COM2, you'll get the message "Write fault error writing device COM2. Abort, Retry, Ignore, Fail?" You might not get a message nor hear the dial tone if the COM ports on both the I/O board and motherboard are enabled.

A diagnostic program, such as Check-It Pro from TouchStone at 714-969-7746, can determine which ports are being used. It also runs several very helpful diagnostic tests. Another essential program for finding port conflicts is Port Finder from mc-Tronic Systems at 713-462-7687.

It's very important to keep any documentation you get with your various plug-in boards. Many I/O boards have dozens of pins and jumpers. If you don't have the documentation, you might never be able to determine how it should be configured. It's also necessary to write down and keep a log of which ports and addresses are enabled. It can save a lot of time.

Connecting the modem

Plug in the modem board and hook it up to the telephone line. Unless you expect to do a lot of communicating, you might not need a separate dedicated line. The modem might have an automatic answer mode, where it always answers the telephone. Unless you have a dedicated line, this should be disabled. Check your documentation. There should be a switch or some means to disable it.

There should be two connectors at the back end of the board. One might be labeled for line in and the other for telephone. Unless you have a dedicated telephone line, unplug your telephone, plug in the extension to the modem and line, then plug the telephone into the modem. If your computer isn't near your telephone line, you might have to go to a hardware store and buy a long telephone extension line.

After you've connected all the lines, turn on your computer and try the modem before you put the cover back on. Use the simple test outlined in the previous section.

Enable your communications software and call a local bulletin board. Even if you can't get through or have a wrong number, you should hear the dial tone and then hear the modem dial the number.

Fax/modem/phone switch

Having a modem and telephone on the same line should cause no problems unless someone tries to use the telephone while the modem is using it. Life will be a lot simpler, though, if you have a switch that can detect whether the incoming signal is for fax, modem, or voice. Fax and modem signals transmit a high-pitched tone, called the CNG (calling) signal. A fax/modem switch can route the incoming call to the proper device. Note that some older systems don't use the CNG signals, and therefore let you manually transfer the call.

Command Communications, at 303-750-6434, has a model, ASAP TF 555, that I've used for some time. It has connections for a telephone answering device (TAD), telephone extensions, a fax machine or fax board, and an auxiliary device or modem. The alternative is to install a dedicated line for the fax machine and another one for the modem. This machine has given me all the utility of two extra telephone lines, and has paid for itself many times over. Figure 13-1 shows my ASAP TF 555. It's about three years old, but it still works perfectly. Command Communications has developed several newer and more sophisticated products in the last few years. Call them for a brochure.

There are several other fax and modem switchers available from different companies. One company that sells a fax/phone switch is Computer Friends, at 800-547-3303. Harmony Computers, at 800-441-1144, has a fax switch, and Business Computer Systems, at 800-333-2955, has several different models.

13-1
My command communications
phone/fax/modem/answering-machine
switch. If you don't have many fax or
modem calls, it can save you having to
install a dedicated phone line.

Telephone outlets for extensions

You need a telephone line or extension to hook up a computer modem or a fax-modem. You might also want telephone outlets in several rooms, at one or more desks, or at another computer. You can set up a fairly good, inexpensive network between two or more computers over a simple telephone line.

You can go to almost any hardware store, even a grocery or drugstore, to buy the telephone wire and accessories you'll need, but you might have trouble running telephone wires to the computer, desks, and other rooms. Cutting holes in the walls and running wires up in the attic or under the floor can be a lot of work.

There's a much simpler way. Just use 110-volt wiring. There are special adapters that plug into any wall outlet. It takes two or more adapters, one for the input telephone line and one or more to be plugged into any other outlet to provide a telephone extension. If you need an extension in another location, just unplug the adapter and plug it into another nearby wall outlet. The electronic circuitry in the adapters blocks the ac voltage from getting into the telephone lines, but allows voice and data to go through. Adapters such as these are carried by many discount stores. Call Phonex Corp. at 801-566-0100.

Bulletin boards

If you have a modem, you have access to several thousand computer bulletin boards. There are over 100 in the San Francisco Bay area and about twice that many in the Los Angeles area.

At one time, most bulletin boards were free of charge. You had to pay only the phone bill if they were out of your calling area. But there has been a lot of disreputable people who have uploaded software with viruses, downloaded commercial software, stolen credit card numbers, and performed many other loathsome and illegal activities. Because of this, BBS sysops (systems operators) have had to spend a lot of time monitoring their BBSs. Many bulletin boards now charge a nominal fee to join and some just ask for a tax-deductible donation.

Some bulletin boards are set up by private individuals and some are run by companies and vendors as a service to their customers. Some are set up by user groups and other special-interest organizations. Some people become addicted to bulletin boards and spend hours and hours hooked up to them. John Dvorak reported in one of his columns that a man in Israel sued his wife for divorce because she was carrying on a liaison with a man by way of a bulletin board. Her husband charged her with adultery, although it seems that all she ever did was to chat with the man over the modem. The husband was awarded a divorce.

Most bulletin boards are set up to help individuals. They usually have a lot of public-domain software and a space where you can leave messages for help, an advertisement, or just plain old chit-chat.

If you're just getting started, you probably need some software. There are all kinds of public-domain and shareware programs that are equivalent to many of the major commercial programs. And the best part is that public-domain software is free and shareware is practically free.

Where to find bulletin boards

Several local computer magazines devote a lot of space to bulletin boards and user groups. In California, *MicroTimes* and *Computer Currents* list several pages of bulletin boards and user groups each month. *Computer Shopper* has the most comprehensive listing of bulletin boards and user groups of any national magazine. It lists user groups one month and bulletin boards the next.

If you don't have a copy of *Computer Shopper*, you can call Allen Bechtold of the BBS Press Service, 913-478-3157. He can arrange to have a copy of the bulletin boards and user groups sent to you. If you have a bulletin board or belong to a user group and want them listed in the magazine, use your modem and submit your entry to 913-478-3088, 8NI, at 2,400 bps.

Viruses

A computer virus can be likened to the AIDS virus in some respects. A few years ago many people were a bit promiscuous, but AIDS put an end to that type of lifestyle. Now most people use safeguards and are quite selective about their partners.

A few years ago, you could access a bulletin board and download all kinds of good public-domain or shareware software. Or you could buy software and never have to worry about having it destroy your data. Because of computer viruses, however, you now have to protect yourself and be very careful about where you get your software and who you get it from.

I don't mean to diminish or lessen the terrible life-threatening danger of AIDS by comparing it to a computer virus. A computer virus isn't a live thing; it can't harm you, only the data in a computer or disk. A computer virus is usually a bit of program code, hidden in a piece of legitimate software. The virus is usually designed to redirect, corrupt, or destroy data and resembles an organic virus in that it can cause a wide variety of virus-type symptoms in the computer host.

The virus code might be written so it replicates or makes copies of itself. When it becomes embedded on a disk, it can attach itself to other programs that it comes in contact with. Whenever a floppy disk is inserted into the drive, it will come away with a hidden copy of the virus.

A few individuals have hidden "viruses" in public-domain, shareware, and even some commercial programs. The viruses can be spread and passed on through downloads from bulletin boards or on floppy disks. The affected software might appear to work as it should for some time, but eventually it will contaminate and possibly destroy many of your files. If a virus gets on a workstation or network, it can infect all the computers in the network.

McAfee Associates, at 408-988-3832, has one of the best antivirus programs available. It's shareware, so they encourage you to make copies and pass them out to friends. (Just make sure to register it if you use it!) McAfee has a bulletin board (408-988-4004) where you can download the latest version of their program. They constantly revise it to keep up with the latest viruses.

PC Tools at 503-690-8090, Disk Technician Gold from Prime Solutions at 619-274-5000, and Microsoft DOS 6.0 and later versions all have antivirus utilities. PC Tools, now a part of Symantec Corp., constantly upgrades their antivirus utilities. The antivirus utility in DOS is under the command MSAV, or MWAV for Windows.

Not all computer viruses cause damage other than growing and taking up more space on your hard disk. Some might just issue random sounds or present off-color messages on the screen. Well over 2,000 viruses have been created. The following are just a few of the different types:

Executable

This category actually contains several types of viruses, but they all work by attaching themselves to executable .EXE and .COM files. The virus can corrupt the file, prevent it from running, or redirect it to run another command. Here are the names of just a few executable viruses: AIDS II, Black Monday, Spyder, Leprosy Viper, and Yankee Doodle.

Boot sector viruses

These viruses attack the boot sector of hard and floppy drives. The boot sector is crucial to the data on a disk. If this sector is damaged or corrupted, you won't be able to boot from the disk. Some boot sector viruses will copy your boot sector information to another part of the disk, then write itself into the boot sector area. When you boot up, it reads the boot sector data from the other area, then reads its own bad data. You might not even notice there's anything wrong for some time. The boot sector is particularly vulnerable to viruses. A few of these viruses are: Spanish Trojan, 12 Trick Trojans, Liberty, Trackswap, and Anthrax.

Partition table viruses

Every hard disk has a partition table, even if it's only a single partition, and some viruses attach themselves to the partition table. They act somewhat like the boot sector viruses in that they make a copy of the partition table and store it somewhere else on the drive, then replace the table with their own bad data. If the partition table is damaged, DOS will display the message "Invalid drive specification" and you won't be able to access your hard disk. Here are a few of these viruses: Hong Kong, Michelangelo, Azusa, and Stoned III.

Memory-resident viruses

Some viruses load themselves into areas of memory, often in the memory allocated for COMMAND.COM. Some of them are written to prevent other programs from overwriting them. Some place themselves into memory above 640K.

Stealth viruses

A stealth virus can infect a file by adding a few bytes to it, then subtracting an equal number of bytes from the file. If you look only at the number of bytes in the file it will look fine, but of course it might not run properly.

Trojan horse viruses

This virus comes disguised as a legitimate program. It might lie dormant for a while, but then it can severely damage disks or destroy files. Files infected with a Trojan horse virus might not be recoverable.

Precautions and prevention

Most bulletin board sysops now scan all software offered on their systems. Many BBSs depend on software uploaded from their many users, which means that the sysops must spend an inordinate amount of time checking all the software.

Microsoft (MS-DOS 6.2), Symantec (PC Tools), and several other commercial software companies have excellent virus-detection programs. Symantec claims that their Anti-Virus can protect against 2,000 different viruses. It can also alert you to any suspicious activity that indicates infection by an unidentified virus. Anti-Virus can automatically scan and detect viruses and then clean and "immunize" your files against further infection.

One of the many features of Disk Technician Gold (619-274-5000) is that it can be loaded into memory with your AUTOEXEC.BAT file, where it will keep watch over any attempt to write to or change any .EXE or .COM file.

Most bulletin boards also have public-domain software or shareware to check for viruses. One of the better virus detectors is the McAfee Scan program. It's available for downloading from several bulletin boards or from the McAfee BBS, at 408-988- 4004.

If you download bulletin board software, check it with virus software. It's best not to install unknown software on your hard disk. Run it from a floppy disk until you're sure it's okay. Of course, the possibility of a virus infection is just one more reason to make sure you have a current backup of your hard disks.

PC Tools estimates that at least 100 new virus programs are created each month, and their antivirus program is frequently updated to combat these new viruses.

I've been very fortunate. I've never had a virus infect any of my computers. But a close friend of mine recently had a near disaster caused by a virus. His two children like to play computer games, and his son brought home a game someone had given him at school. My friend watched as the kids played the game. When they were finished he tried to boot up his computer to do some work. It wouldn't boot up, so he got out his DOS boot disk. He was able to boot up, but couldn't access his 540MB hard drive. He invoked the MSAV command and scanned his drive. Sure enough, it found the Michelangelo virus. He used the clean utility to remove the command and then tried to boot up. He was able to boot up, but he found that he now had a single 540MB drive C:. It appeared that all his data and the three partitions were gone. He got out his Norton Utilities rescue disk that was generated when he installed Norton. The Norton Rescue reinstalled his partitions and he was able to access all of his data. He now thinks Norton is one of the greatest programs of all time. He also has a very strict rule that his kids don't ever put any questionable software in his computer.

Online services

One of the most popular large, national online service companies is CompuServe, at 800-848-8199. They provide forums for help and discussion, mailboxes, and a large variety of information and reference services. You can search the databases and download information as easily as pulling data off your own hard disk. The company charges a fee for the connect time.

One of the forums on CompuServe is ZiffNet. Ziff-Davis publishes magazines such as *PC Magazine*, *Computer Shopper*, and *PC Computing*. The editors and staff members of these magazines will answer your questions on the ZiffNet forum.

Prodigy (800-284-5933) was unlike the other online services at first because they didn't charge for connect time. They charged only a very nominal monthly rate. They've recently revised their fee structures so that you're charged over and above the monthly rate for certain types of service. They have phone service to most larger cities, so there's no long-distance charge. They have an impressive list of services, including home shopping, home banking, airline schedules and reservations, and stock-market quotations. It's a real bargain. One of its faults is that it's relatively slow. But since it's so inexpensive, I can live with that.

America Online, at 800-827-6364, is one of the fastest-growing online services. It offers all the services provided by CompuServe and Prodigy and will give you 10 free hours just to try the service. All you need is a modem and Windows. They'll send you a sign-on disk with the connect software. They have a lot of local access numbers, so in most cases it shouldn't be a toll call. After the first 10 free hours, it costs $9.95 per month. For the $9.95, you get five hours each month. If you go beyond that, there's a nominal extra charge.

Delphi, at 800-695-4005, is another popular online service. Like the other systems, you can get stock quotes, access encyclopedias, newswires, and hundreds of other services. Also, it's currently the only service to offer full access to the Internet.

One very good reason to join online services is to save money. The cost of an automobile is second only to the cost of buying a house. You must be able to haggle and negotiate when buying a car. Many online reports give you the dealer cost, option price, and suggested retail price (SRP). Autovantage provides a very comprehensive report and is available from Ameria Online, Delphi, and Prodigy. To access it from America Online, log on and type AUTOVANTAGE. From Delphi, log on and type

SHOPPING, then type AUTO. From Prodigy, log on and then type JUMP AUTOMO-BILE. For more information about Autovantage, call 800-843-7777.

Prodigy also offers another report called AutoNet. To access that report, log on and type JUMP AUTONET. CompuServe has AutoQuot-R. To access it, log on and type GO AUTOQUOT. For more information, call AutoQuot-R at 800-992-7404.

About four million people subscribe to online services such as CompuServe, Prodigy, America Online, and GEnie. France has Minitel, which provides its users with a small computer screen along with a telephone. Minitel Corporation places the devices in homes for free, but then charges a monthly fee. They don't have phone vision, but they do provide several communications features. Subscriber can use the monitor to shop right from home.

The Clinton administration wants to implement a national network. It would be a broadband system that could transmit text, numbers, and voice, as well as quality sound, video, and graphics. The system should be available not only to businesses, but to homes and individuals. It would be great for everyone, but don't hold your breath waiting for it.

E-mail

Many national bulletin boards offer electronic mail, or e-mail, along with their other services. These services can be of great value to some individuals and businesses.

E-mail subscribers are usually given a "post office box," which is usually a file on a hard disk. When a message is received, it's recorded in this file. The next time the subscriber logs on to the service, he is alerted that there's "mail" in the in-box.

E-mail is becoming more popular every day and there are now several hundred thousand subscribers. The cost for an average message is about one dollar. The cost for overnight mail from the U.S. post office, Federal Express, and UPS ranges from $10 to $13.

It can be rather confusing trying to send or receive e-mail. E-mail Connection Software, at 800-234-9497, can make it fairly simple. With E-mail Connection, you can route messages through MCI, CompuServe, Prodigy, America Online, Delphi, and Internet services. It also handles fax and postal messaging. If you receive a lot of e-mail, E-mail Connection can help you organize and sort it. Some of the companies who provide e-mail at the present time are:

America Online	800-827-6364
AT&T Mail	800-624-5672
CompuServe	800-848-8990
DASnet	408-559-7434
MCI Mail	800-444-6245
Western Union	800-527-5184

Access to e-mail is another good reason to subscribe to one of the online services.

Banking by modem

Many banks offer systems to let you do all your banking with your computer and a modem from the comfort of home. You'll never again have to drive downtown, hunt for a parking space, then stand in line for a half an hour to do your banking.

Intuit, at 415-322-0573, offers Quicken, an excellent financial program, and CheckFree, a service that allows you to pay all your bills electronically. CheckFree also allows you to print your checks from your computer on a laser printer, which requires special checks with your account number imprinted in magnetic ink.

CheckFree costs about $10 a month, but if you spend at least four hours a month paying bills that's only $2.50 an hour. Another advantage to CheckFree is that it will automatically pay your bills when they're due. If you ordinarily write a lot of checks, CheckFree and Quicken can quickly pay for themselves.

Intuit is now merged with ChipSoft (602-295-3070), the developer of TurboTax, one of the best software packages for doing your taxes. The marriage of these two companies means that they can offer the most complete financial software available for your computer system. With a good financial program, you can get rid of the shoeboxes full of canceled checks. Then you can put the data in your computer onto TurboTax forms, making the onerous April 15 task a bit easier to accomplish.

Computer Associates, at 800-737-3382, also has an excellent financial program, called Kiplinger's CA-Simply Money. Microsoft Corporation is another big player who has seen the value of banking by computer and has developed a program appropriately called Money.

ISDN

ISDN is an acronym for Integrated Services Digital Network. Eventually the whole world will have telephone systems that can transmit voice, data, video, and graphics in digital form rather than the present analog. When this happens, we can scrap our modems. We'll need only a simple interface to communicate.

ISDN is already installed in several cities, but don't throw your modem away just yet. The new service might not be available in all locations for some time, and it will be rather expensive.

Fax machines

Facsimile (fax) machines have been around for quite a while. Newspapers and businesses have used them for years. Early machines were similar to early acoustic modems. Both used foam rubber cups that fit over the telephone receiver mouthpiece for coupling, and they were very slow and subject to noise and interference. Fax machines and modems have come a long way since those early days.

A page of text or a photo is fed into the fax machine and scanned. As the scanning beam moves across the page, white and dark areas are digitized as 1s and 0s, then transmitted over the telephone line. On the receiving end of the line, the digitized information is transformed back into images and text. Thus the original is reproduced.

When a text file is sent by modem, the digitized bits that make up each character are converted from digital voltage to analog voltage. A modem sends and receives the bits that make up each character. A fax machine or board, on the other hand, sends and receives scanned whole-page letters, graphics, images, signatures, etc. Since a modem recognizes individual characters, a computer program can be sent over a modem, but not over a fax. A fax sends and receives the information as digitized graphic data. A modem converts the digital information that represents individual characters into analog voltages, sends it over the line, then converts it back to individual digital characters.

There are millions of fax machines in use today. There are very few businesses that couldn't benefit from using one. You can use it to send documents, including handwriting, signatures, seals, letterheads, graphs, blueprints, photos, and other types of data, around the world, across the country, or across the room to another fax machine.

Express mail can cost more than $10. A fax machine can deliver the same letter for about 40 cents and do it in less than three minutes. Many programs will let you delay sending a fax until late at night to get the best rates. Depending on the type of business and the amount of crucial mail that must be sent out, a fax system can pay for itself in a very short time.

Computer fax and fax/modem boards

Several companies have developed fax systems on circuit boards that can be plugged into computers. Most fax boards are now integrated with a modem on the same board. These fax/modems cost little more than either board separately, and the combination saves having to use an extra plug-in slot. Most newer fax/modems are integrated onto a half board.

For some time the standard transmission rate for faxes was 9,600 bps, but many newer fax-modem boards are now capable of a 14,400-bps speed for both modem and fax. However, just like modem connections, both the sender and receiver must be operating at the same speed. Also like the modem, a fax can shift down to match the sending or receiving machine if it's operating at a slower rate.

Special software allows the computer to control the fax board. Using the computer's word processor, you can write letters and memos and send them out over the phone line. You can also store a letter or other piece of information, then retrieve it at a later date from the computer's hard disk and transmit it. Like some fax machines, you can also program some fax/modem boards to send transmissions at night when rates are lower.

But computer fax boards have one disadvantage. They can't scan information that isn't in the computer. Without a scanner, the information you can send is usually limited to that which you can enter from a keyboard or disk. As I pointed out earlier, stand-alone units scan pages of information, including handwriting, signatures, images, blueprints, and photos.

However, when your computer receives a fax, you can store it on a hard disk or print it out on a printer. Just remember that fax/modems send and receive digitized graphical images, not text you can change (unless you have special OCR software— see the section *Fax software* later in this chapter).

Installing a fax/modem

Most fax/modem boards are very easy to install and operate. Use the same basic instructions outlined earlier for installing a modem board. Check your documentation and set any switches that are necessary. Then plug the board into an empty slot and try the modem dial test. If it works properly, replace the computer cover and connect the telephone line.

You should have some software to control the fax installed on your hard disk. You should be up and ready to send and receive faxes.

If you use a word-processing program such as WordStar or WordPerfect to create letters or text for a fax transmission, you must save the text as an ASCII file before sending it. Word processors add control characters to the text that the fax won't recognize.

Fax on demand

Several companies have fax machines that can supply information to you 24 hours a day. Simply call them with your voice phone, tell them what documents you want, give them your fax number, and the documents will be sent immediately. Most of these companies also have a catalog that lists all their documents and document numbers. If you ask to have the catalog faxed to you, you can then determine which documents to order. FaxFacts, at 708-682-8898, publishes a small booklet that lists several companies who have fax-on-demand or fax-back capability.

Microsoft Corporation, at 800-936-4200, has an extensive library of fast tips for MS-DOS, Windows, and Windows for work groups. They also have fast tips for desktop applications (800-936-4100), for development tools (800-936-4300), and for advanced systems (800-936-4400). You can request a fast tips map from each of these numbers, which contain brief menus of what's available. Each menu offers several options, such as technical information, Microsoft support for network and customer service, and information about Microsoft's download service. You can access the download service by modem to download drivers, sample programs, and technical articles. It's best to order the fast tips map and fast tips catalog, then determine what other information you want.

Most fax-back information is free, but some companies, such as Consumer Reports, at 800-766-9988, ask for a credit card number and charges a fee for articles you request.

Here are just a few of the other companies who offer fax-back or fax-on-demand services (when you call, ask for new user instructions and navigation map):

Adaptec	408-957-7150
Borland TechFax	800-822-4269
Central Point Anti-Virus	503-690-2660
IBM	800-426-4329

Novell Support Line   800-638-9273
Symantec Corp.   800-554-4403
WordStar Fax Support   404-514-6333

If you prefer, most will send the information to you by mail rather than by fax.

Scanners

Scanners aren't absolutely essential to the operation of a PC-based fax, but there might be times when you need to transmit photographs, blueprints, documents, or handwritten signatures on contracts. So a scanner will let you get the most utility from a fax. Scanners were discussed in more detail in chapter 12.

Combination devices and voice mail

Compex International, at 800-626-8112, has an all-in-one fax, scanner, printer, and copier.

Speaking Devices Corporation, at 408-727-2132, has a unit with a fax, fax/phone switch, scanner, voice mail, and caller ID.

Boca Research, at 407-997-6227, has a 14.4-Kbps multimedia voice modem that has up to 1,000 password-protected voice and fax mailboxes, private and public fax on demand, remote message and fax retrieval, professionally recorded greetings, and voice prompts and personalized greetings for individual mailboxes. It can be used in small offices and home offices (SOHO) for voice mail, faxes, and as a modem. Call them for more details.

Tiger Software, at 800-888-4437, publishes a catalog that contains hundreds of software and hardware items. They advertise the Vomax 2000, which is a fax, voice, and modem system. It has one megabyte of digital storage that can store up to 20 minutes of voice-mail messages or up to 50 sheets of faxes. It has message forwarding so it can call another number and play your messages. It can also call your pager and relay messages. Call Tiger Software for a catalog and more information.

With a telephone line and any of these systems, you can make your office as difficult to reach as any of the big companies.

I sometimes wonder how any work is accomplished in this country. It seems that 90 percent of the times when I call people, they're away from their desk. I then have the opportunity to leave a message on their voice mail. It's frustrating not to be able to talk to a live person, but it's better than nothing. I can understand how voice mail can save money for a company, but I still don't like it.

Fax software

If you have a fax/modem you'll need fax software. There are several companies who provide it. Ordinarily, when you receive a fax it's in graphics form, so all you need to do is view it. Some newer fax/OCR software packages, such as UltraFAX from WordStar International, has optical character recognition (OCR) capabilities. This software can automatically scan the incoming fax and convert it to individual characters. You can then edit the fax, combine it with another file, or just save parts of it. You can also print it out on a laser printer for much better resolution than you'd normally get from a fax. Also, a fax that has been converted to digital characters takes up much less disk space than it does in graphical form.

WordStar's UltraFAX is about the least expensive fax/OCR software package, at $119. Intel's Faxability Plus/OCR has a list price of $249. They both have about the same features. Here are some of the other companies who offer fax/OCR software:

Program	Company	Phone
BitFax/OCR	Bit Software	510-490-2928
FaxMaster	Caere Corp.	408-395-7000
WinFax Pro	Delrina Corp.	800-268-6082
Eclipse Fax	Phoenix Tech.	617-551-4000
DataFax	Trio Information	800-880-4400
Faxability+OCR	Intel Corp.	800-538-3373
UltraFAX	WordStar	415-382-4859

Stand-alone fax units vs. fax boards

Fax machines have some advantages and some disadvantages compared to computer fax boards. The machines can send or receive at any time, and you don't need a computer that might have to be interrupted to receive or send a fax. They also have their own paper printout. And most are as easy to use as a copy machine. In fact, most of them can be used as a copy machine.

Some fax machines are fairly inexpensive, selling for as little as $300, but you might not be too happy with a low-cost machine. You'd be better off spending a bit more and getting one with a paper cutter, anticurl paper system, high resolution, voice/data switch on the system, document feeder for up to 20 sheets, automatic dialer with up to 50 speed-dial numbers, automatic retry, delayed transmission, transmission confirmation, polling, 16- to 24-character LCD readout, up to 16 shades of gray for printing photos and graphics, built-in answering machine with speaker phone, copy function, and large memory. You might not need, or be able to afford, all these features, but try to get a machine with as many as possible. Of course, the more features, the higher the cost.

The voice/data switch is important if you don't have a dedicated line for the fax machine. This built-in switch can recognize an incoming call as a fax or voice message. If it's a fax, it will automatically receive it. I mentioned the fax/phone switch earlier when discussing modems for use on a single line. You might need a fax/phone switch if the fax machine you buy doesn't have the automatic switch.

Telecommuting

Millions of people risk their lives in automobiles and fight frustrating traffic every day, and many of them have jobs that could allow them to stay home, work on a computer, then send the data to the office over a modem or a fax. Even if they had to buy their own computer, modem, and fax, it still might be worth it. You could save the cost of gasoline, auto maintenance, and lower insurance. Thousands are killed on the highways. Telecommuting can be a life saver.

Being able to work at home would be ideal for those who have young children, for handicapped people, or for anyone who hates being stuck in traffic jams. Over 6 million PCs were purchased for the home in 1993, which is about 30% of all units sold. It's expected that 42% of all PCs sold in 1996 will be for home use. A large percentage of those computers will be used for telecommuting.

Remote-control software

If you're on the road or working from home and have a computer at the office, it's often necessary to access the data on that computer. There are several software packages that allow you to connect from remote locations. You can be sitting with a notebook computer in a distant hotel room or at a PC at home and dial up the computer at your office. You can take control across a phone line or across a network and work just as if you were sitting in front of the office computer. You can review documents, update files, edit reports, and print out or download files. Here are a few software packages for remote control:

- Reachout, from Ocean Isle, at 800-677-6232
- Norton pcAnywhere from Symantec
- Carbon Copy from Microcom
- Close-Up from Norton Lambert
- CO/Session from Triton

You should be able to find these packages at most software stores, or listed in software catalogs such as MicroWarehouse, at 800-367-7080, or DellWare, at 800-847-4051.

All of these packages will work only if the remotely accessed computer is turned on and booted up. Server Technology has a device called Remote Power On/Off. This device plugs into the power line between the computer and the wall plug. The telephone line plugs into this device. When the device detects an incoming call, it automatically turns on and boots up the PC. When the call is ended, it turns off the PC. It even lets you reboot if the computer hangs up for some reason. Some companies bundle Remote Power On/Off with pcAnywhere and other remote-control software. A current DellWare catalog lists the price for Remote Power On/Off as $119.95 and the price for pcAnywhere also as $119.95. The price listed for both units together is $179.95.

Types of telecommuting

Most types of telecommuting involve the use of the telephone line. There have been some important advances in computers and telephone technology in the last few years, and even greater changes can be expected soon. All the items listed in the following sections can be used in a large business or in a small office/home office (SOHO). SOHO has become a very important element of business today.

Telephone conferences

It's very simple to have a telephone conference with as few as two persons or as many as several hundred. In conference calls, everyone is on the line and a person can talk to anyone else on the line. You can do teleconferences from home, a small office, or a large office. One of the disadvantages is that you can only talk.

Fax conferences

If you have a fax machine, you can send out a graphics design or any number of business papers, have other persons review it, make changes, sign it, and return it. You can have an interactive meeting with others in the same building or almost anywhere in the world over a simple telephone line. One disadvantage is that it's not in real time. You have to send the fax and then wait for a reply.

Modem teleconferences

With a computer modem, you can have a desktop conference. You can send data, graphics, and other materials over the telephone line to other computers in the same building or almost anywhere in the world over a local-area network (LAN). Other people sitting at these computers can view whatever you send, change the material, and send material to you. And you can interact with these other people in real time.

One of the better products for desktop conferencing is called TALKShow, from Future Labs at 415-254-9000, fax 408-736-8030. This small, simple program works under Windows. All the people in the conference must have a copy of TALKShow installed on their computer. TALKShow connects everyone together and automatically handles all the computer communications.

The same data appears on all the computer screens that are on the line. Many live conferences use a large white board in front of the conference room. The leader writes on the board, while the attendees watch and perhaps make comments for changes. With TALKShow, each computer screen becomes a white board and each individual can suggest changes or additions to the material on the screen. Of course, if the president of the company is leading a desktop conference, you might have to be careful of what you suggest. With TALKShow, you can save or print out anything that appears on the screen.

Systems like this weren't readily available when I worked at Lockheed years ago. It seemed that I spent half of my time sitting in meetings. Lockheed has a very large complex in Sunnyvale, California and some of the buildings are a mile or more apart. It would often take me 30 minutes to get to a meeting, then the same time to get back to my desk. The company could have saved thousands of dollars with a desktop conference system.

Integrated voice and data modems

AT&T, Multi-Tech, and several other companies are developing modem systems that integrate voice and data transmission. With such a system, remote users can talk to one another while they edit or share a document. It can be used for interactive presentations as well as conferencing, training, and entertainment.

AT&T's Paradyne unit at Largo, Florida has developed the DataPort 2001 modem. Multi-Tech, at 612-785-3599, has developed MultiModemPCS, a proprietary, stand-alone V.32terbo modem.

One of the problems with these units is that the voice slows down the transmission speed, from 14.4 Kbps to about 4.8 Kbps. The other very big problem is that there are no standards. Both parties must have the same equipment. AT&T has offered to license its technology, which should help toward setting some kind of standard.

Computer telephone integration

Computer telephone integration (CTI) is one of the hottest markets around today. CTI uses a computer and special software for various applications. Some CTI applications can convert voice to digital data and vice versa. In addition to fax-back services, discussed earlier in the book, here are just a few of the applications for CTI:

Financial reports

Investors can enter an automatic identification number (ANI) and check on their portfolios, bank balances, and transfer money. They can also access other banking services.

Real estate listings

Callers can enter information about what type of house they're looking for, including the location and price. A database reports what's available and what broker to contact.

Repair reports

The service manager of a large auto repair shop might spend half his time on the telephone with car owners. A CTI system would let customers enter the repair number, and a recording could inform customers of the repair status and how much more than the original estimate the repair will cost.

Shipping status

Customers can call in, enter their sales order number, and find out why the shipment is still sitting on the shipping dock.

Ticket sales

People could call up a ticket agency and order tickets for the next big Woodstock concert or opera season. They could request seat locations, dates, and other factors, enter a charge card number, and the tickets would be mailed to their home.

Here are a few CTI terms and acronyms:

Integrated messaging An application that handles voice mail, faxes, and e-mail.

IVR (interactive voice response) Uses touch tones or voice and a computer database.

Predictive dialer An application that has a computer dial numbers from a database. If a call is answered, a human operator takes over.

TAPI (telephone application programming interface) A part of Microsoft Windows that allows developers to write telephone-type Windows applications.

TSAPI (telephone services application programming interface) An interface for creating telephone applications for netware. It was created by Novell and AT&T.

Here are a few of the companies involved in the CTI revolution:

ACTAS/North American Telecom. Assoc.	202-296-9800
AnswerSoft, Inc.	214-612-5101
AT&T	800-FOR-PHON
	(800-367-7466)
Aurora Systems	508-263-4141
Dialogic Corp.	201-993-9000
Mitel Corp.	613-592-2122
Natural MicroSystems Corp.	508-650-1300
Northern Telecom	800-NORTHERN
	(800-667-8437)
NPRI Inc.	703-683-9090
Octus Inc.	619-452-9400
Pacific Bell	800-303-3000
Pronexus	613-839-0033
Rhetorex Inc.	408-370-0881

National telephone directories

I live in the Los Angeles area. In Los Angeles and Orange counties, there are over 100 suburban cities with over 12 million people. Can you imagine a single telephone directory that would list all these people? Or how about a telephone directory that would list all the millions of people in New York? Or Boston or San Francisco? Believe it or not, there are such directories. And they're smaller than ones you'd find in a small town—because they're on CD-ROMs.

ProPhone, from New Media Publishing at 617-631-9200, publishes a national directory on seven CD-ROMs, six discs for the white pages and one disc for businesses. There's over 600MB of data on each disc. They list telephone numbers, addresses, and zip codes, but they aren't very up-to-date. I'm listed, but at the address where I lived over two years ago. The separate disc for businesses makes it very easy to look up a company anywhere in the country.

PhoneDisc, from Digital Directory Assistance at 301-657-8548, has only five CD-ROMs. It lists over 90 million nation-wide residences and businesses. It doesn't have a separate business disc, but lists businesses along with the general population in the white pages. Figure 13-2 shows the ProPhone and PhoneDisc CD-ROMs.

These directories are ideal for business use. I hate to mention this because I hate telephone solicitations, but these systems would be great for those businesses because each listing provides the telephone number and complete address.

Neither PhoneDisc nor ProPhone lists all current phone numbers and addresses in the U.S., but there are some listings in ProPhone that aren't in the PhoneDisc and vice versa. Since PhoneDisc has only five discs, it doesn't have as many listings as

13-2 National telephone directories on CD-ROM from ProPhone and PhoneDisc.

ProPhone. I also like having a separate disc for businesses. With PhoneDisc, you might have to search all five discs, but only the one business disc in ProPhone.

If you're in a business where you have to contact a lot of people, then you need these two directories.

Sources

I haven't listed the names and manufacturers of modems and faxes because there are so many. Look in any computer magazine and you'll see dozens of ads. A recent copy of *Computer Shopper* had ads for about 200 modem/fax boards from several different companies.

One modem company I do want to mention is USRobotics. They manufacture a large variety of modems, especially high-end, high-speed ones. They'll send you a free 110-page booklet that explains about all you need to know about modems. For the free booklet, call 800-342-5877.

John Dvorak and Nick Anis have put together a very good book they call *Dvorak's Guide to PC Telecommunications*, published by Osborne McGraw-Hill. It was published in 1990, so it's a bit dated, but some of the information is timeless, so it's just as good today as it was in 1990. Another good book to have is *The Complete Guide to*

CompuServe, by Brad and Debra Schepp. It was published in 1990 by Osborne Mc-Graw-Hill, but it also has information that's as essential today as it was a short time ago.

Jerry Pournelle writes a very interesting column for *Byte* magazine, also published by McGraw-Hill. He teamed up with Michael Banks to put together *Pournelle's Complete PC Communications Bible*, published by Microsoft Press. It can tell you just about all you'd ever need to know about modems, fax machines, e-mail, online services, and most other aspects of electronic communications.

14
CHAPTER

Printers

For the vast majority of applications, a computer system isn't complete without a printer. This chapter discusses some of the features and functions of different types of printers.

Upgrading printers usually means buying a new one, but there are a few things you can do to upgrade an older printer. You can add plug-in font cartridges to some dot-matrix printers. If you own a laser printer, most of them will accept more memory. Most laser printers will also let you add larger paper bins. Depending on the type of printer you have, there are several other upgrades you can make and accessories you can add.

Printers usually last a fairly long time, so I've bought only a few different printers in the last ten years. When I need an excuse to buy a new printer, I just pass my old ones on to my children. Most of them are all still going strong.

Although printers usually last, printer manufacturers are constantly introducing new and improved models. Most of the time, however, the improvements aren't enough to make me want to abandon my older printers and buy a new one.

There are several types of printers, some of which are more suitable for certain applications than others. Right up front I want to admit that I haven't personally used some of the printers I'll be discussing, but I subscribe to over 50 computer magazines and most of them have reviews of printers every so often. *PC Magazine* devotes one issue each year to printers, usually in November. In that issue they usually have reviews of over 100 different kinds of printers, including dot-matrix, ink-jet, and laser printers.

If you don't subscribe to *PC Magazine*, you can order the November back issue by writing to the following address:

Back Issues Department
Ziff-Davis Publishing
P.O. Box 53131
Boulder CO 80322-3131

Enclose a check for $8 for each issue ordered.

Dot-matrix printers

Dot-matrix printers are available for a large range of prices. The print quality of low-priced 9-pin systems is fairly poor. Low-priced dot-matrix printers are also limited in the number of fonts and graphics capability. Some higher-priced dot-matrix printers can print in near-letter quality (NLQ) at a speed equivalent to some of the laser printers. Laser printer speed is measured by the average number of pages per minute it can print. Dot-matrix printer speed is measured by the characters per second (CPS) they can print. Most dot-matrix printers can print much faster in draft mode than in NLQ mode. There are some high-end dot-matrix line printers that can print a whole line at a time, and some of them can print up to 1,000 lines per minute. In order to get the high speed, some of them have four or more heads, each one of them printing a different line.

Many dot-matrix printers can also print different fonts, but the number of fonts are usually limited to less than ten. Only a few higher-priced units can print scalable fonts. Some can print limited graphics, but they're usually very slow. Some of them can even print fairly good color by using low-cost multicolor ribbons.

Advantages of dot-matrix printers

One of the distinct advantages of dot-matrix printers over laser printers is their low cost. You can buy some dot-matrix printers for less than $150. Of course, there are also some high-end dot-matrix printers, such as fast line printers, that can cost close to $10,000.

Dot-matrix printers aren't only lower in initial cost, they're usually lower in the cost of printing per page. *PC Magazine* estimated that it costs less than one cent per page for dot-matrix printing. It costs two to three cents per page for laser printers, and about six cents a page for ink-jet printers. It will cost from 50 cents to over a dollar per page to print high-resolution color graphics.

There are many applications where a dot-matrix printer is necessary. Wide continuous sheets are necessary for some spreadsheet printouts. My HP LaserJet can't handle anything wider than 8½ inches. With the wide carriage on my Star dot-matrix printer, however, wide sheets are no problem.

Another advantage is the number of sheets you can print without attending to the printer. Most laser printers have from 100- to 250-sheet bins. Dot-matrix printers can print up to a whole 5,000-sheet box of fanfold continuous sheets.

Many offices and businesses still use multiple-sheet forms. A laser printer can't handle these forms, but a dot-matrix can easily print them. Personally, I hate multisheet forms. In many cases, you can use a scanner to input the form into a computer, then print out as many copies as needed on a laser printer. But most companies have been doing things the same way for years and it's difficult to get them to change. I'm sure that 20 years from now companies that make multiple forms will still be doing a lot of business. Some things never change.

Dot-matrix printers can also print on odd sizes, shapes, and thicknesses of paper. I often use mine to address large manila envelopes.

The U.S. post office has adopted a postnet bar code that helps sort and speed-up mail. If you look at some of the envelopes you receive in the mail, you might see the postnet barcode below the address. Many companies that send out bulk mail use this code. Several dot-matrix printers have the postnet barcode built in and others offer it as an option. The post office will give you a discount when your envelope already has the postnet code on it. If you do a lot of mailing, a printer with this option could save you some money.

Dot-matrix color

Most major dot-matrix printer manufacturers offer printers that can produce color. These dot-matrix printers use a multicolored ribbon that are wider than standard ribbons, so one part is red, one part green, one part blue, and one part black. The ribbons are fairly inexpensive and the extra cost for the color option is quite reasonable.

You need special software, however, to print color on a dot-matrix printer. Under the control of the software, the printer heads move up and down and strike whatever colors on the ribbon that are needed. By striking the red, green and blue colors on the ribbon and overprinting them when necessary, all the colors of the rainbow can be printed. The result is definitely not of photographic quality and is a bit slow, but if you need color to jazz up a presentation or for accent now and then, they're great.

Maintenance cost

The maintenance cost of dot-matrix printers are usually less than that for laser and ink-jet printers. The main cost is to replace the ribbon about every 3,000 sheets. A dot-matrix ribbon costs from $3.00 to $10.00, and a color ribbon will cost from $20 to $35. A laser toner cartridge also lasts for about 3,000 sheets, but costs from $30.00 to $100.00 to replace.

Number of pins

There are still a few 9-pin dot-matrix printers being sold today, but most people buy those with a 24-pin print head. The 24-pin head has much better resolution and usually costs only a few dollars more. Twenty-four-pin printers form characters from two vertical rows, with 12 pins in each row.

There are small electric solenoids around each of the wire pins in the head. An electric signal causes the solenoid to push the pins forward. Dot-matrix printers are also called impact printers because the pins impact against the ribbon and paper. The solenoids press one or more of the various pins as the head moves across the paper, so they can usually form any character. It's also possible to print some graphics, although it's very slow.

Here's a representation of the pins for a 7-pin print head and how it would form the letter A:

```
1            o
2          o o
3        o     o
4      o         o
5    o   o   o   o
6  o               o
7  o               o
```

The numbers on the left represent the individual pins in the head before it starts moving across the paper. The first pin to be struck would be number 7, then number 6, then 5, 4, 3, 5 and 2, 1, 2 and 5, 3, 4, 5, 6, then 7.

A 24-pin head would be similar to the 7-pin representation, except it would have two vertical rows of 12 pins, side by side, in each row. The pins in one row are slightly offset and lower than the pins in the other row. Since the pins are offset, they overlap slightly and fill in the open gaps normally found in a 9-pin system.

There's a lot of competition between dot-matrix and laser printer companies for your dollar. Some vendors now sell laser printers for about the same price as some dot-matrix printers, which has forced the dot-matrix printer companies to lower their prices. In addition to lower prices, many dot-matrix printers have more features, such as more memory and more fonts, in order to attract buyers.

Some disadvantages

The biggest disadvantages is that dot-matrix quality can't come close to that of a laser printer. In draft mode with a 24-pin print head, only half the pins are hit and there's noticeable spacing between the dots. For NLQ on a 24-pin printer, all the pins are hit. In draft mode with a 9-pin head, all the pins are hit, but there are spaces between the dots. For NLQ on a 9-pin system, the printer makes a second run with the head slightly displaced so the pins hit different spots and fill in the open spaces. In draft mode, therefore, the printing is fairly fast but of poor quality. In NLQ mode, it slows down considerably but is of much better quality.

Most 24-pin dot-matrix printers have a resolution of 360×360 dots per inch (dpi). Until recently, the standard laser printer was rated at 300×300 dpi. If you compare the dot-matrix output to the laser output, however, you'll see that the laser printer has much higher resolution. This is because the laser printer produces a much smaller dot than the dot-matrix printer. So if an A is printed out on a dot-matrix printer, the jagged edges from the large dots is very apparent. Most laser printers can print scalable fonts, but only a very few high-end dot-matrix printers can. Most dot-matrix printers are limited to less than ten different fonts.

Most dot-matrix printers have only 8K or less of memory, although a few high-end ones have as much as 64K, or even 128K. The memory on a dot-matrix printer can be used as a print buffer. The computer can download a file to the printer and then go about its business doing other things. Laser printers use memory a bit differently. They take the file and format the whole page in memory before they start printing. Most laser printers come with a minimum of 512K, but you can add more. For higher speed and graphics, a laser printer should have a minimum of 2MB of memory.

Dot-matrix printers can print some graphics, but it's usually of very poor quality. They're also very slow when printing graphics.

Another problem that dot-matrix printers have is that they're noisy. If you're working in an office where there are several printers going, you might want to buy some earplugs. There are special enclosures that can be used to make them a bit quieter. Some companies have also developed dot-matrix printers that are a bit less noisy, but they still can't match the laser printer for quiet operation.

If you can get by with a dot-matrix printer, you should be able to find one at a very good price. Look for ads in computer magazines. Depending on what you want to use it for, I suggest you get a 24-pin unit with as many fonts as possible. A few offer scalable fonts, such as Panasonic, Epson, Tandy, and Digital Equipment Corp.

PC Magazine published a table listing about 40 different characteristics and features of the various printers they tested. They had sample printouts of each printer, the memory, the fonts, the prices, and many other features.

Ink-jet printers

Hewlett-Packard developed the first ink-jet printer, and now companies such as Brother, Canon, Epson, Texas Instrument, and Lexmark are manufacturing them. Some of the companies call them by a different name, such as Canon's BubbleJet printer, but they're all basically ink-jet printers. Ink-jet printers have a print output that approaches that of laser printers, but at a lower cost. One very big advantage of ink-jet printers over laser printers is that they can print color. Most ink-jet manufacturers have one or more color models. The models that can print in color usually have a C in the model number, such as the HP DeskJet 550C or the Canon BubbleJet BJC-600.

Ink-jet printers use a system that's similar to dot-matrix printers, but instead of pins that press a ribbon onto the paper they use a matrix of small ink jets that sprays dots of ink on the paper. They also have a much larger number of ink jets; dot-matrix printers have from 9 to 24 pins and ink-jet printers have from 48 to 128 small jets. The head also moves across the paper much like the dot-matrix system.

Most ink-jet printers come with one or more internal fonts, but they might be able to use several more, available on plug-in font cartridges. Some ink-jet printers can use scalable fonts.

Like dot-matrix printers, the speed of ink-jet printers is measured in characters per second. Depending on the type of print, the average speed is about two pages per minute.

Some high-end fax machines use ink-jet technology. FAX800, from Ricoh Corporation (408-432-8800), can be attached to a computer and used as a printer, it can print incoming faxes, or it can be used as a copy machine.

It's possible to buy different color ink cartridges and use them once in a while instead of the standard black. You could use red, for instance, to make a letterhead, or use the color for accent. The following are a few low-cost ink-jet printers:

Company	Model	Phone
Brother	HJ-400	800-284-4357
Canon	BJ-200	800-848-4123
C. Itoh	CJ-300	714-833-1165
Epson	Stylus 800	800-289-3776
HP	DeskJet 500	800-752-0900
Lexmark	ExecJet	800-358-5835
NEC	Jetmate 1000	800-632-4636
TI	microMarc	800-257-3500

If you're interested in buying an ink-jet printer, call one of these companies and ask them to send you a brochure and specification sheets.

Ink-jet color

It's now possible to buy color ink-jet printers for $500 to $600. Most are less expensive than quality laser printers. Most people would like to be able to print in both color and black for text, but color machines can be very slow. Ink-jet printers take about two pages per minute just for black text (as opposed to four to over ten pages per minute for a laser printer), and a color graphics printout could take several minutes for a single page.

Color ink-jet printers use a system of three different colored ink cartridges—cyan, magenta, and yellow—to print color. Some systems have a black cartridge for standard text, and some use the mixture of the three colors to make black. As the head moves across the paper, the software can spray any of the various colors onto the paper. It can blend the colors together much better than is possible on a dot-matrix printer. If you do any presentations using an overhead projector, ink-jet printers can handle transparencies very well. Color ink-jet printers are ideal for creating low-cost colored transparencies for presentations, graphs, and schematic plotting and drawings.

Most ink-jet cartridges are good for about 300 pages of text. They must then be replaced or refilled. The cartridges cost from $5 to $10 each. Table 14-1 lists a few of the color ink-jet printers and a current price comparison. Prices are for comparison only and will probably be different when you read this.

**Table 14-1. Color ink-jet printers
and current prices**

	Memory	Cost
HP DeskJet 560C	64K	$600
DeskJet 1200C	4MB–20MB	$1500–$2500
Canon BJC-600	60K	$600
IBM Jet 4079	4MB–16MB	$2500

The HP DeskJet 560C and Canon BJC-600 are about equivalent in speed, graphics capabilities, and cost. The HP DeskJet 1200C is a more sophisticated machine, has more memory, and can print faster. Hewlett-Packard also has a 1200C-PS, which has PostScript. The IBM Jetprinter PS 4079 is also a PostScript printer and is about equivalent to the HP 1200C-PS. Many companies have several different models of each product. Check through the ads in computer magazines. Here are some of the color ink-jet companies and their numbers:

Canon Corp.	800-848-4123
Hewlett-Packard	800-752-0900
IBM Jetprinter PS 4079	800-358-5835

Call the companies for brochures and specifications. The CJ10 from Canon Corporation is an all-around do-everything color ink-jet printer/copier/scanner. This is an amazing machine that not only copies in color, but is also a color printer and scanner. With available options, it can scan almost any kind of color graphic or text into a computer and print out almost any color graphic or text from a computer, a still video camera, video camera, video player, or 35-mm film projector. It also has an intelligent editor and other devices. It has a flat-bed scanner, 400-dpi resolution, printing and scanning, RGB 8-bit color, a 4-color process, halftones up to 256 gradations, and magnification 50% to 200%.

This machine would satisfy just about all the needs of an office. It could be used as a high-speed plotter or for presentations and color brochures.

Someone was bound to develop a machine like this sooner or later. The laser printer, copy machine, and scanner all have too much in common not to be integrated into a single machine. At this time, the CJ10 costs from $6,000 to $10,000, depending on the options.

I didn't mention several ink-jet and color ink-jet printers. There are many different models from different companies with different features, functions, and prices. Look for ads in the major computer magazines.

Ink-jet supplies

The original cost of a printer isn't the end. If you do much printing, the cost of supplies might end up being more than the cost of the printer. Ink-jet cartridges cost from $30 to $35, and some cartridges last for only about 300 pages. It's possible to refill some of them.

Laser printers

Hewlett-Packard developed the first laser printer, and they've remained in the forefront. They're the IBM of the laser printer world, and like IBM their products have always cost a bit more than other models. Because of the quality and the extras that Hewlett-Packard laser printers offer, they're worth the extra cost.

How laser printers operate

Laser printers are a combination of the copy machine and computer and laser technology. They have excellent print quality but a lot of moving mechanical parts, and they're rather expensive.

Laser printers use synchronized, multifaceted mirrors and sophisticated optics that write characters or images on a photosensitive rotating drum. A laser beam is then swept across the spinning drum and is turned on and off to represent white and dark areas. As the drum spins, it writes one line across the drum, then rapidly returns and writes another, similar to the electron beam that sweeps across the face of a TV screen or computer monitor one line at a time. The spinning drum is sensitized by each point of light that hits it. The sensitized areas act like an electromagnet. The drum rotates through the carbon toner and the sensitized areas are covered with the powder. The paper is then pressed against the drum. The toner that was picked up by the sensitized areas of the drum is left on the paper. The paper is then sent through a heating element where the toner is heated and fused to the paper. This is similar to what happens in a copy machine, except a copy machine takes a photo of the image to be copied and projects the image onto the rotating drum, which becomes sensitized to the light and dark areas.

The engine

The drum and its associated mechanical attachments is called an *engine*. Canon is one of the foremost makers of these type of engines. They manufacture them for their own laser printers and copy machines, and for dozens of other companies, such as Hewlett-Packard and Apple. There are several other Japanese companies who manufacture laser engines.

The Hewlett-Packard LaserJet was one of the first laser printers. It was a fantastic success and became the de facto standard. There are now hundreds of laser printers on the market, most of which emulate the LaserJet standard. Even IBM's laser printer emulates the Hewlett-Packard standard.

Low-cost laser printers

Because of the large number of companies manufacturing laser printers, there's a lot of competition, which is a great benefit to the consumer. The competition has driven prices of both laser printers and dot-matrix printers down. It has also forced many new improvements.

If you've used one of the high-end laser printers, such as the HP LaserJet III, you might be disappointed in the limited fonts provided with many low-cost lasers, but you can easily add font cartridges to them or use font software. Most of them will let you use Adobe Type Manager (ATM), which comes bundled with OS/2 2.1, or True-Type, which comes with Windows 3.1. Most of them will also operate with Bitstream facelift fonts. With these fonts, you can scale the type on most low-cost lasers. This will give you almost all the benefits of an HP LaserJet III at about one third the cost.

Until recently, most laser printers had a resolution of only 300 × 300 dpi. The Hewlett-Packard LaserJet IV has a resolution of 600 × 600 dpi, and some vendors are selling them for less than $1,000.

Laser printer memory

If you plan to do any graphics or desktop publishing (DTP), you'll need to have at least one megabyte of memory in your machine. Before it prints the first sheet, a laser printer loads the data into memory and determines where each dot will be placed on the sheet. Of course, the more memory, the better.

Not all laser printers use the same memory configuration. For some machines, you must buy a special plug-in board for the memory. Check the type of memory you need before you buy it. Several companies, including ASP (800-445-6190) and Elite (800-942-0018), offer laser printer memory.

Page-description languages

If you plan to do any complex desktop publishing you might need a page-description language (PDL) of some kind. Text characters and graphic images are two different species of animals. Laser printer controllers are somewhat similar to monitor controllers. Monitor controllers usually have all the alphabetical and numerical characters stored in ROM. When you press the letter A from the keyboard, it dives into the ROM chip, drags out the A, and displays it in a precise block of pixels wherever the cursor happens to be. These are called *bit-mapped characters*. If you wanted to display an A that's twice as large, you would have to have a complete font set of that type in the computer.

Printers are very much like monitors, and have the same limitations. They have a library of stored discrete characters for each font they can print. My Star dot-matrix printer has a single internal font and two cartridge slots. I can plug several different font cartridges into these slots, but the printer is limited to the fonts that happen to be plugged in. With a PDL, a laser printer can take one of the stored fonts and change it, or scale it, to any size you want. These are called *scalable fonts*. With a bit-mapped font, you have one typeface in one size. With a scalable font, you have one typeface in an infinite number of sizes. Most laser printers will accept ROM cartridges that have as many as 35 fonts. You can print almost anything you want with these fonts if your system can scale them.

Speed

Most laser printers can print from four to over ten pages per minute, depending on the model and what they're printing. Some very expensive high-end printers can print over 30 pages a minute. A dot-matrix printer is concerned with a single character at a time. Laser printers compose and then print a whole page at a time. With a PDL, you can print many different fonts and sizes of type, as well as graphics.

Because a laser printer must determine where every dot that makes up a character or image is placed on the paper before it's printed, the more complex the page the more memory it requires and the more time is needed to compose the page. It might take several minutes to compose a complex graphic. Once composed, however, it prints out very quickly. A PDL controls and tells the laser printer where to place the dots on the sheet. Adobe's PostScript is the best known PDL.

Resolution

Most low-cost laser printers still have a 300 × 300-dpi resolution, which is good, but not nearly as good as the 1,200 × 1,200 dots per inch that typesetters use for standard publications. Several companies have developed systems to increase the resolution to 600 dpi or higher. Table 14-2 lists just a few.

Table 14-2. Low-cost laser printers

Company	Model	DPI	Telephone
Hewlett-Packard	LaserJet 4M	600	800-752-0900
LaserMaster	1200XL	1200	800-950-6868
LaserMaster	WinPrinter	1000	800-327-8946
Lexmark (IBM)	4029-10P	600	606-232-6000
QMS	860	1200	800-631-2692
Xante	Accel-A-Writer 800	600	800-926-8839

PrintSprint, from Myriad Enterprise at 714-494-8165, allows low-cost laser printers to print at 600 × 600 dpi. It can also make the printer print from two to ten times faster. PrintSprint uses a printer controller board that plugs into one of the slots on the motherboard, and a small board that's installed in the laser printer options socket. LaserMaster (800-327-8946) has upgrade kits for the HP LaserJet III and LaserJet IV that can increase the resolution to 1,200 dpi. They also have several other upgrade kits. Call the company for details and brochures.

300 × 300 dpi means there are 90,000 dots in one square inch. On an 8½ × 11-inch page of paper, if you deduct a one inch margin from all four sides of the paper, you'd have 58.5 square inches × 90,000 dots = 5,265,000 possible dots.

600 × 600 dpi increases the number of dots per square inch to 360,000. For a full page, the number of possible dots is 21,060,000. You won't notice too much difference between 300 and 600 dpi for most applications; the difference is most noticeable when printing graphics.

Most laser printers print in the 8½ × 11-inch A format. CalComp, a division of Lockheed at 714-821-2000, has developed a 600 × 600 high-resolution laser printer that can print in the 8½ × 17-inch B format. CalComp has also developed several color laser printers. Call them for brochures.

Maintenance

Most laser printers use a toner cartridge that's good for 3,000 to 5,000 pages. The cost of an original cartridge is about $75. Several small companies now refill spent cartridges for about $30 each. It's probably a good idea to keep an extra cartridge on hand. Toner cartridges are sealed, so they'll last for some time on the shelf. I had a cartridge go out on a weekend when I was working on a tight deadline, and most stores that sell cartridges were closed. Since then I keep a spare on hand.

Most laser printers keep track of the number of sheets that have been printed. If you have a LaserJet, you can use the front-panel buttons to run a self test. This tells you the configuration, how much RAM is installed, any font cartridges that are installed, the type of paper tray, and how many pages have been printed.

When the toner gets low, the HP LaserJet III displays a warning message in the digital readout window. If you remove the toner cartridge and turn it upside down and shake it vigorously, sometimes you can get a few more copies out of it. This might help until you can get a replacement. Of course, there are other maintenance costs. These machines have a lot of moving parts that can wear out and jam up. Most larger companies give a mean time between failures (MTBF) rate of 30,000 up to 100,000 pages, but remember these are only average figures and not a guarantee. Most laser printers are expected to have an overall lifetime of about 300,000 pages.

Paper

There are many different types and weights of paper. Almost any paper will work in your laser printer, but if you use cheap paper it could leave lint inside the machine and cause problems in print quality. Generally speaking, any bond paper or a good paper made for copiers will work fine. Colored paper made for copiers will also work fine. Some companies mark copier paper with the word *laser* and charge more for it.

Laser printers will easily accept 18-pound up to 24-pound paper. I've even used 67-pound stock for making my own business cards. It's a bit heavy for wrapping around the drums and it jams once in a while. Some laser printers use a straight-through path, so heavier paper shouldn't cause any problems in these machines.

Many laser printers come equipped with trays to print envelopes. Hewlett-Packard recommends envelopes with diagonal seams and gummed flaps. Make sure that the leading edge of the envelope has a sharp crease.

Avery, at 818-858-8245, and a few other companies make address labels that can withstand the heat of the laser printer's fusing mechanism. There are other specialty supplies you can use with your laser printer. Integraphix, 800-421-2515, carries several different items you might find useful. Call them for a catalog.

Color printers

I worked in a small print shop while I was in high school. In those days we used engraved metal plates for printing, and it took four different engraved plates to print color. We would have to set the printer up and print one color, then change the engraving and ink color and print the next one. It was crucial that each printing was lined up exactly right or the colors wouldn't blend properly. It was very time-consuming and expensive to print color. Printing presses that could print color cost quite a bit of money and filled a large room. The technology has changed quite a bit in the last 40 years. Today, it isn't nearly as expensive or time-consuming to print color, and it can be done on a desktop printer.

Several color printers are available that cost from less than $1,000 up to $15,000. These printers are often referred to as color laser printers, but at this time only QMS and Xerox actually uses laser technology. The other companies use a variety of thermal transfer technologies using wax or rolls of plastic polymer. The wax or plastic is brought into contact with the paper, then heat is applied. The melted wax or plastic material then adheres to the paper. Very precise points, up to 300 dots per inch, can be heated. By overlaying three or four colors, all the colors of the rainbow can be created. Fargo Electronics offers a color printer that uses thermal wax for less than $1,000. Of course, it doesn't have all the goodies you'll find on the Tektronix Phaser or CalComp ColorMaster.

Another type of color printer uses dye sublimation, also called *thermal dye transfer* or *dye diffusion*. These systems use a ribbon with continuous series of four different color ink stripes across the ribbon. The paper is forced against the ink ribbon and dots of heat are applied to the various colors, which causes the color to diffuse onto the paper. The higher the temperature, the more color can be diffused. The dots of heat can be accurately controlled for up to 256 different colors. This process provides the best resolution and can produce prints that are near photographic quality. But as you might suppose, these printers are also the most expensive. Again, the least expensive dye-sublimation printer is manufactured by Fargo Electronics. You can buy the Fargo Primera thermal wax printer for $995, then upgrade to the dye-sublimation printer for another $249.95. The street price for these machines should be even less.

The QMS ColorScript Laser 1000 is a true laser color printer. It blends four different color toners—black, cyan, magenta, and yellow—to print color. The drum is sensitized for each color and that color toner is transferred to it. Once all the colors are applied to the drum, it prints out on ordinary paper or on transparencies. The QMS ColorScript is still rather expensive, at about $10,000, but it's still less than some high-end color laser printers, which can cost as much as $40,000. Xerox Corporation, at 716-264-5482, has also introduced a new color laser printer. Call them for a brochure and pricing information.

Most color printers either have PostScript or emulate PostScript. The Tektronix Phaser CP can also use the Hewlett-Packard graphics language (HPGL) to emulate a plotter, but can print out a page much faster than a plotter.

One disadvantage of color printers is the cost. Thermal wax costs up to 45 cents per page and dye sublimation up to $2.75 per page. Most of this cost is for the ribbons and wax rolls that are used by the color machines.

Color printers are rather slow but the technology is improving. There will be several other color printers on the market soon. There's also a lot of competition, so the prices are coming down. Table 14-3 lists just a few of the companies who manufacture color printers.

Table 14-3. Companies who produce color printers

Company/product	Telephone	Technology
CalComp, Lockheed	800-932-1212	Thermal transfer
Fargo Electronics	800-258-2974	Thermal transfer & dye sub.
General Parametrics	800-223-0999	Thermal transfer
QMS (ColorScript)	800-631-2692	Thermal transfer
QMS (Laser 1000)	800-631-2692	Laser technology
Tektronix (200i)	800-835-6100	Thermal transfer
Tektronix (Phaser III PXi)	800-835-6100	Solid ink
Tektronix (Phaser II SDX)	800-835-6100	Dye sublimation
GCC Technologies	800-422-7777	Dye sublimation
Kodak (ColorEase)	800-344-0006	Dye sublimation
Xerox (4900)	716-264-5482	Laser technology

One of the better color printers is from CalComp, and I'm not just saying that because I worked for Lockheed at one time. They build very high-quality equipment. On the downside, they're a bit expensive. General Parametrics has a desktop film recorder attachment for their printer, which allows you to make 35-mm color slides for presentations.

Plotters

Plotters can draw almost any two-dimensional shape or design under the control of a computer. They're a bit like a robot—an arm selects a pen and the pen can be moved from side to side while the sheet of paper is moved from top to bottom. The computer can direct the pen to any point across the paper and can move the paper up or down for any point on an X-Y axis. The motors are controlled by predefined X,Y coordinates. They can move the pen and paper in very small increments in order to trace almost any design. Values of perhaps 1 to 1,000 for both the X and Y elements can be assigned. The computer can then direct the plotter to move the pen to any point or coordinate on the sheet.

Some newer plotters use ink-jet technology instead of pens, which makes them faster. The different colored ink cartridges can be activated much more quickly than moving an arm to a rack, selecting a pen, replacing it, and selecting another.

Some less expensive plotters use a thermal paper such as that used by fax machines. This can be much faster than pen plotters, but you can't generate color and the resolution might not be very good. The thermal paper also fades when exposed to light.

Plotters are ideal for printing out circuit board designs and architectural drawings, making transparencies for overhead presentations, generating graphs, charts, and CAD drawings, and many other applications. And you can do it all in many different colors, which can be very helpful if you have a complex drawing, such as a multilayered motherboard. A different color could be used for each layer.

A plotter can have from one up to eight or more different colored pens. There are several different types of pens for various surfaces, such as different types of paper, film, or transparencies. Some pens are quite similar to ballpoint pens and others have a fibrous point. The points are usually made to a very close tolerance and can be very small, so you can control the thickness of the lines. The line thickness can be crucial in some precise drawings. You can also direct the plotter arm to choose any one of the various pens.

There are several different sized plotters. Some desktop units are limited to only A and B plots. There are other large floor models that can accept paper as wide as four feet and several feet long. A desk model might cost as little as $200 and as much as $2,000. A large floor model might cost as much as $10,000. If you're doing very precise work, for instance designing a transparency that will be photographed and used to make a circuit board, you'll want one of the more accurate and more expensive machines.

There are many very good graphics programs available for use with plotters, but there are several manufacturers of plotters and little or no standards. And just like the printers, each company has developed its own drivers. This can be very frustrating for software developers who must try to include drivers in their programs for all the various brands. Hewlett-Packard has been one of the major plotter manufacturers, so many other manufacturers now emulate their drivers. Almost all software that requires plotters include a Hewlett-Packard driver. If you're in the market for a plotter, try to make sure that it can emulate the Hewlett-Packard. Houston Instruments is also a major manufacturer of plotters. Their plotters are somewhat less expensive than the Hewlett-Packard.

One of the disadvantages of plotters is that they're rather slow. There are now some programs that allow laser printers to act as plotters. They're much faster than a plotter, but many are limited to black and white.

Plotter sources

Here are a few of the plotter manufacturers. Call them for a product list and latest prices.

Alpha Merics	818-999-5580
Bruning Computer	415-372-7568
CalComp	800-225-2667
Hewlett-Packard	800-367-4772
Houston Instrument	512-835-0900
Ioline Corp.	206-775-7861
Roland DG	213-685-5141

Plotter supplies

It's important to a good supply of plotter pens, special paper, film, and other plotter supplies because they're not as widely available as printer supplies. A very high-priced plotter will have to sit idle for some time if the proper supplies aren't on hand. Most plotter vendors provide supplies for their equipment. One company that specializes in plotter pens, media, accessories, and supplies is Plotpro, at 800-223-7568.

Installing a printer or plotter

Most IBM-compatible computers allow for four ports, two serial and two parallel. No matter if it's a plotter, dot-matrix printer, or laser printer, it will require one of these ports. Most printers use the parallel port LPT1 and most plotters use a serial port. Some printers have both serial and parallel connections.

If you're using the serial port, the printer can be up to 50 feet from the computer. If the parallel is used, it can only be about 10 feet. Serial printers use an RS232C connector, and parallel printers use a Centronics connector. When you buy your printer, buy a cable configured for your printer and your computer from the vendor.

Drivers

There are hundreds of printer manufacturers, and each manufacturer produces several different models. Every manufacturer and almost every model that's manufactured must have a unique software driver that tells the computer how to make it operate. The software drivers are special instructions for using the various and unique capabilities of each printer. There should be some sort of standard, but there isn't. Almost half the disks that are sent with some word-processing programs are filled with different drivers for various printers. Plotters must also have special software drivers.

If you don't have the proper driver for your printer or plotter, you might not be able to use it. Some printers and plotters can emulate some of the better-known brands. Many laser printers emulate the HP LaserJet, and many dot-matrix printers emulate the Epson.

Windows has helped somewhat because it comes with the drivers for most printers. When you install a program in Windows, just point to your printer name and model and the driver will automatically be installed.

Printer sharing

Printers normally sit idle most of the time. There are some days when I don't even turn my printer on. There are usually several computers in most large offices and businesses and almost all of them are connected to a printer in some fashion. It would be a terrible waste of money if each computer had a separate printer that was used only occasionally. It's fairly simple arrange so a printer or plotter can be used by several computers.

Sneaker net

One of the least expensive methods of sharing a printer is to generate the text on one computer, record it on a floppy disk, then walk over to a computer connected to a printer and print it out. In a large office, a single low-cost XT clone could be dedicated to running a high-priced laser printer.

I didn't originate the term *sneaker net*. You can tell it's dated; at one time, sneakers were about the cheapest footwear you could buy, but now they're about the most expensive.

Switch box

If there are only two or three computers and they're fairly close together, printer sharing isn't much of a problem. Manual switch boxes, which cost from $25 to $150, can allow any one of two or three computers to be switched on line to a printer.

With a simple switch box, if the computers use the standard parallel ports, the cables from the computers to the printer should be no more than 10 feet long. Parallel signals begin to degrade if the cable is longer than 10 feet, and could cause data loss. A serial cable can be as long as 50 feet.

If an office or business is fairly complex, then there are several electronic switching devices available. Some are very sophisticated and can allow a large number of different types of computers to be attached to a single printer or plotter. Many have built-in buffers and amplifiers that can allow cable lengths more than 250 feet. The costs range from $160 up to $1,400.

Networks

Of course, you can connect computers and printers together via a network. A large network can be very expensive and complicated to install. Moses Computers (408-358-1550) has some of the simplest and least expensive network systems. Microsoft's Windows for Workgroups is actually Windows 3.1 with peer-to-peer network software included. Windows NT is a complete operating system that replaces both DOS and Windows and is full-fledged network operating system (NOS) software.

Printer-sharing device sources

Here are a few of the companies who provide switching systems. Call them for their product specs and current price list.

Altek Corp.	301-572-2555
Arnet Corp.	615-834-8000
Belkin Components	310-515-7585
Black Box Corp.	412-746-5530
Buffalo Products (Buffalo XL-256)	800-345-2356
Crosspoint Systems	800-232-7729
Digital Products (PrintDirector)	800-243-2333
Extended Systems (ShareSpool)	208-322-7163
Fifth Generation (Logical Connection)	800-225-2775
Server Technology (Easy Print)	800-835-1515
Quadram (Microfazer VI)	404-564-5566
Rose Electronics	713-933-7673
Western Telematic	800-854-7226

Green printers

The entire computer industry is under pressure to produce energy-conserving products. The federal government will no longer buy computer products that don't meet Energy Star standards. Printers, especially laser printers, are notorious for being energy hogs. Hewlett-Packard and most other manufacturers are designing newer models that go into a "sleep mode" after a period of inactivity. Ordinarily, it takes from 20 to 30 seconds for a printer to warm up. Some of these models maintain a low-voltage input so they can warm up almost instantly.

If you have an older printer, you can purchase a PC ener-g saver from NEI, at 800-832-4007. The printer, monitor, and keyboard can be plugged into this unit. After a period of inactivity, the printer and monitor shut down. You can set the period for any amount of time. Of course, with this system, you do have to wait for the printer to warm up before it can be used. But if you know you'll be needing it, you can hit the print button a few seconds before you need it. NEI is also working on a model that will supply the printer with a small current while asleep so it can come online sooner. Call them for brochures and details. The PC ener-g saver can pay for itself many times over in saved electricity bills. Besides, you'll be doing your part for energy conservation.

Progress

If Gutenberg were around today you can bet he'd be using a laser printer, and I'm sure he'd be quite pleased with the progress that has been made in the printing business. We've come a long way since 1436.

15
CHAPTER

CD-ROMs

CD-ROMs and CD-ROM drives comprise one of the fastest growing segments of the computer industry. A CD-ROM (compact disc, read-only memory) can offer some very important benefits to individual end users—for entertainment, education, and business. Figure 13-2 shows a couple of the thousands of CD-ROM packages that are available. ProPhone contains seven discs, each of which holds over 600MB of information. PhoneDisc lists over 90 million names and addresses on only five CD-ROMs.

A CD-ROM drive can be a very important adjunct to your computer. Many of the computers sold within the next year will have a CD-ROM as standard equipment. It has become almost as essential as a hard disk drive.

Business

Many large businesses maintain huge databases of customers, invoices, prices, and other information. Businesses can use a single disc to replace these databases. A CD-ROM can store millions of part numbers, descriptions, drawings, costs, locations, names, addresses, and any other kind of information.

Businesses also use the telephone and telephone directories. Most larger businesses have dozens of phone directories for different cities. ProPhone, at 617-631-9200, publishes CD-ROMs with the phone numbers of every listed telephone in the U.S., on six separate discs. There's a separate disc for the Northeast, the Midatlantic, the South, the Midwest, the West, and the Pacific. They also include another disc of all the businesses in the U.S.

The discs include addresses and zip codes in addition to telephone numbers. You can download any of the information onto a hard disk, incorporating it with a database for business contacts or direct mailing.

In addition to stored paperwork records, some businesses keep important records on backup tape and floppy disks. Tape and floppy disks are good for only about 10 years before they start to deteriorate. A CD-ROM can store an enormous amount of data, and will last for 25 years or longer. And it's much, much easier to search and find an item on a CD-ROM than on a backup tape or stack of papers.

If businesses replaced the millions of file folders and cabinets with CD-ROMs, they could regain millions of square feet of office space. We could save thousands of trees if businesses saved documents electronically or on CD-ROMs instead of putting everything on paper, but many people still don't trust electronic documents. Quite often, even with an electronic file in the computer on their desk, many people still print out a paper copy. These people seem to have a need for something concrete to hold. We're cutting down more trees than are being planted. We need to join the green revolution by resisting the urge to have a paper printout unless it's absolutely necessary. We need to make the paperless office a reality.

Home entertainment

A large number of the CD-ROM titles are designed for entertainment, for both young and old. There are arcade-type games, chess and other board-type games, and role-playing games. Some CD-ROMs contain music, opera, art, and a large variety of other subjects to entertain you. Many of the titles are both educational as well as entertaining. Creative Labs, the company who's responsible for Sound Blaster audio boards, has an upgrade bundle that they call Edutainment.

Home library

Only one side of CD-ROMs are recorded on, but this single side can hold about 600MB of data. You can have a multitude of different programs on a single CD-ROM and a world of information at your fingertips. More books and information can be stored on just a few CD-ROMs than you'd find in an entire library. A 21-volume encyclopedia could be stored in just a fraction of one side of a single CD-ROM. When data compression is used, you can store the text of several hundred books on a single disc. And it takes only seconds to search through an entire encyclopedia or several hundred books to find any subject, sentence, or single word.

An easier way to learn

Text, graphics, sound, animation, and movies can be stored on CD-ROMs. There are several avenues to the brain. The more avenues used to input information, the easier it is to learn and to remember that information. You can learn by reading, most people will learn much better if sound is added to the text—and even better if graphics and motion is added. Schools can use CD-ROMs for teaching and businesses can use CD-ROMs to train their personnel.

Law

Lawyers have to spend hours and hours going through law books to find precedents, finer points of the law, and loopholes. If these books were recorded on CD-ROMs, they could find any subject immediately.

Health and medicine

The human body is a fantastic machine, and there are a tremendous amount of books written about medicine. Several medical CD-ROMs have been published for home users, such as Family Doctor, by Creative Multimedia Corporation at 503-241-4351, and the Mayo Clinic Family Health Book, published by Interactive Ventures at 507-282-2076.

Doctors must keep abreast of all scientific advances, new drugs, and treatments. A busy doctor can't possibly read all published medical papers so a CD-ROM can help. *American Family Physician* is the official journal of the American Academy of Family Physicians. It's available from the Bureau of Electronic Publishing, at 800-828-4766.

ADAM (for animated dissection of anatomy for medicine) Software, at 800-755-2326 has developed a disc that can take the place of dissection classes. The disc currently sells for about $3,000. The company is developing a female counterpart of ADAM called, appropriately, EVE.

Different formats

In spite of efforts to standardize CD-ROM technology, there are several companies who have developed competing technologies. This isn't necessarily bad, because it allows for new ideas and new methods, and keeps the technology from becoming stagnant and inactive.

There are several different CD-ROM formats. Philips and Sony developed the audio CD in 1982. It wasn't long before the importance of the technology was recognized and adopted for CD-ROMs. It was a fast growing technology, but there were no standards. The competing companies wanted to make their products a bit different, so there were several different formats.

In 1985 a group of industry leaders, including Microsoft, met at a hotel in Lake Tahoe to hammer out a set of standards. The standard they devised defined the table of contents and directory structure, as well as the logical, file, and record structures. Microsoft provided their Microsoft compact-disc extension (MSCDEX) software, a driver that allows DOS to access CD-ROMs using conventional DOS commands. All CD-ROM drives used in PCs use the MSCDEX driver. MSCDEX.EXE is now a part of MS-DOS 6.0 and higher. Every time a CD-ROM drive is installed in a PC using the MSCDEX.EXE, it makes Bill Gates richer by a few pennies.

There were several other specifications adopted at this Lake Tahoe meeting. Since they were meeting at Lake Tahoe, which is in the Sierra mountain range, they called the new standard the High Sierra specification. It was later adopted, with minor modifications, by the International Organization for Standards, as ISO 9660. Unless otherwise stated, most CD-ROM drives and discs conform to ISO 9660.

Besides the standards set forth in ISO 9660, several other standard specifications have been developed, most of which are recorded in four books: the red, yellow, green, and orange books (named as such because the specifications were originally issued in books bound in different colored covers). There are thousands of pages of specifications in each of these books. Sometimes a disc will have specifications from two or more books. For instance, if the disc contains text, audio, and graphics, it might conform to specifications in the red, yellow, and green books.

The red book sets forth the standards for audio or compact-disc digital audio (CD-DA). The yellow book sets forth the ISO 9660 standards for storing files that can be translated to DOS, Apple, or Amiga files. Microsoft MSCDEX drivers are used to accomplish the translation. The green book covers CD-interactive (CD-I) and CD-ROM extended architecture (CD-ROM/XA). The orange book covers write once, read many (WORM) and magneto-optic (MO) drives. It also covers multisession Photo CD drives.

How a laser works

The word *laser* is an acronym for light amplification by stimulated emission of radiation. As you probably know, white light encompasses all the colors of the rainbow. Each color has its own frequency of vibration, and the slower frequencies are at the red end. The frequencies increase as the colors move toward the violet end.

The particles that make up ordinary light are incoherent, that is they're scattered in all directions. Lasers are possible because a single color of light can be sharply focused and amplified. All the particles of one color are lined up in an orderly, coherent fashion.

The laser effect can be obtained from several different gases and materials. Most current CD-ROM lasers use light at the lower-frequency end of the spectrum, such as the red or yellow. Samsung has developed a green laser. They claim that by using this laser and their proprietary compression techniques, they can store up to 110 minutes of MPEG 2 video on a disc, five times more than standard. (MPEG is an acronym for Moving Pictures Experts Group, who developed a set of video compression methods). Scientist are working to develop a blue laser, which will have an even higher frequency. If they're successful, a CD-ROM drive with a blue laser will be able to store even more data on a disc than the green laser.

How discs are made

Data to be stored on a CD-ROM is usually assembled and organized, then copied on a large-capacity hard disk. A table of contents, index, and error-detection, error-correction, and data-retrieval software are usually added to the data.

A test disc can then be made from the organized data. A CD-ROM recorder similar to the Philips CCD 521 can be used to make this first disc. The disc is tested and, if it meets the proper specifications, then the data will be laser-etched onto a glass master disc. All of the duplicates are made from this disc.

All CD-ROMs are pressed, much like vinyl phonograph records, but a disc that's pressed from the original master is a mirror image of it. The pits and the lands on the copy are the reverse of those on the master. To make it identical to the master, a copy of a copy is made.

The first copy of the master is called the mother. Then a working copy of the mother is made, which is called the father. Virgin blank discs are pressed against the father to make all the commercial discs. Blank discs are 120 millimeters, about 4¾ inches, in diameter and are made from a polycarbonate plastic. After being pressed, the discs are coated with reflective aluminum. This coating is 1 micron thick. The discs are then coated with a thin layer of lacquer to prevent oxidation and contamination. The same process is used for both audio compact discs and CD-ROMs. Blank discs costs less than one dollar apiece.

How a CD-ROM operates

A CD-ROM is somewhat similar to a hard disk drive. Here is a brief explanation of how a CD-ROM works:

Density

There are several differences in laser recording and magnetic recording. In magnetic recording, a certain amount of space must be left between each track so the magnetism on one track doesn't affect that of another. The gap width and sensitivity of the heads used to read and write to disks can also be a problem if the tracks are very narrow. These types of problems don't occur with laser or optical technology. The laser beam is very small, so the track density can be much greater than on magnetic systems. The small pits in the laser tracks are also much smaller than the dots of magnetism in a hard disk track, so laser tracks can be much closer together and much more data can be stored on each track.

Tracks

Magnetic floppy and hard disks contain concentric individual tracks. CD-ROMs have a single track that begins at the center and winds toward the outer edge, similar to old phonograph records (which begin at the outer edge and wind to the center). The spirals are very close, about 1.6 microns from each other. This means that if you measured across the tracks, 16,000 spirals would fit in one inch. If the track was stretched out, it would be about three miles long.

Sectors

On magnetic disks, areas of the tracks are magnetized to represent 1s or left unmagnetized to represent 0s. To record on a CD-ROM, a laser burns spots on the disk, creating pits that represent 1s and leaving blank areas, or lands, that represent 0s.

When the disk is played back, a laser beam is focused on the track and its light is reflected. The amount of light reflected from a land is much greater than that from a pit, so it's easy to distinguish between the 1s and the 0s.

A sector on a floppy or hard disk is usually 512 bytes, but since there's so much more density on a CD-ROM, its track is divided into 2,048-byte sectors for user data. Just like floppy and hard disk systems, however, when CD-ROMs are formatted, a certain amount of data is written on the track to identify the track and sector numbers. The beginning of each sector on a CD-ROM contains a 12-byte sync field and a four-byte header field. Since the CD-ROM has a single spiral track, the header information contains the sector address in the form minutes:seconds:sector. The first sector is numbered 00:00:00 and the second one is 00:00:01. The first three seconds of each sector is therefore reserved and not available for user data.

There are two different modes for encoding data. Mode 1 adds 288 bytes to the sector for error-detection codes (EDC) and error-correction codes (ECC). So the 12-byte sync field plus the 4-byte header field plus the 288 bytes for ECD/ECC plus the 2,048 available bytes is actually 2,352 bytes per sector. Mode 1 is used in CD-ROMs that contain crucial data. There are about 270,000 sectors on a spiral track, so 270,000 × 2,048 bytes per sector is 552,960,000 bytes, or 552MB. Mode 2 doesn't use the 288 bytes for ECD/ECC, and it's usually fine for music where a lost byte now and then doesn't make much of a difference. So mode 2 offers 2,336 bytes per sector. Using mode 2, you get 270,000 sectors × 2336 bytes, which equals 630,720,000 bytes or 630MB.

Rotation speed

Although it takes both the inner and outer sections of a spinning disk or object the same amount of time to make a revolution, the amount of distance traveled in each revolution is greater on the outer edge than it is at the center (so the outer edge, in essence, moves faster). If you took a track at the two-inch diameter of a disk and stretched it out, it would measure a little over six inches long. On the same disk, if a track at the four-inch diameter was stretched out it would measure over 12 inches long. At a constant speed, it's easy to see that an inner track passes beneath the head in about half the time that it takes for an outer track to pass beneath the head.

On floppy disks and most hard disk systems, each track is divided into a fixed number of sectors. For instance, a 3½-inch 1.44MB floppy has 18 sectors on each of the longer outer tracks and 18 sectors on the much shorter inner tracks. Some of the sectors on the outer tracks are physically twice as long as those on the inner tracks, so there's a lot of wasted space on the outer tracks of a disk. Some hard disks have systems that allow more sectors to be recorded on the outer tracks, called zone-bit recording (ZBR). Using this technology, the disk capacity can be increased considerably. The physical length of the sectors on CD-ROMs are all the same.

Floppy and hard disks spin at a constant speed, or constant angular velocity (CAV). Floppy disk drives rotate at 300 RPM and hard disks rotate from 3,600 up to 6,600 RPM. The faster a hard disk rotates, the higher the density can be.

The CD-ROM uses a system that constantly changes the speed of the drive, depending on what area of the disk is being read. When reading the outer portion, the drive spins at about 200 RPM. When reading the inner portion, it spins at about 530 RPM. This is called constant linear velocity (CLV).

Double-speed CD-ROMs, with a 300K transfer rate, rotate at 400 RPM for the center tracks and at 1,060 RPM for tracks at the outer edge. Several companies have developed triple-speed drives, and there are also several drives on the market that are quadruple speed, that spin at about 800 RPMs for the center and over 2,000 RPMs for the outer edge. These drives will transfer data at 600K per second.

Transfer speed

From very early on until just recently, the transfer speed, or the amount of time it takes to read a track, was 75 sectors per second. A sector is 2,048 bytes (2K), and 2,048 times 75 equals 150K bytes per second.

NEC devised a multispin system, which doubled the speed of the drive for reading motion and certain applications. It also doubled the transfer rate to 300K bytes per second. This faster transfer times allows video and motion to be displayed in a smooth fashion. Faster drives can read all the CD-ROMs that slower drives can read, but they can do it twice as fast.

Text, graphics, and video is transferred at double the speed, but audio files must still be played back at the 150K rate. Audio must be placed at a speed of 200 to 530 RPM, according to the red book specifications. Digital audio is usually read from a disc, routed to a built-in digital-to-analog converter (DAC), and then sent to a headphone jack or sound card. (DACs are discussed in the next chapter). Most CD-ROM drives have a volume control and a headphone jack on the front bezel.

As you can see, it takes more than just doubling the speed of the drive to double the transfer rate. The electronics must also be able to detect when audio is present and drop back to the slower speed. Several other companies have since developed drives that have a similar performance to the NEC drives.

Data buffers

Data is read from the disc and stored in a buffer, or cache, then downloaded to the PC at a very fast rate. MPC specs call for a 64K buffer, but many newer systems have up to 256K buffers. Some older CD-ROM drives had as little as 16K or 32K buffers.

A 16K or 32K buffer would probably be okay for reading just text. But if you try to play back animation and full-motion video with a small buffer, it will quickly fill up and the output might be jerky and have interruptions. A large buffer can provide a smooth, continuous flow for animation and full-motion video.

Access or seek time

The access or seek time is the time necessary to find a certain block or sector on the track and begin reading it. The original MPC specification said that the drive should be able to find any block in 1,000 milliseconds (ms), or 1 second. Most older drives had access times of 300 to 400 ms. Most newer machines have about a 200-ms or less access time.

Disc caddy

On many older drives, you pressed a button and the disc holder was pushed out to receive the disc, similar to audio CD players with a hinged lid that receives the discs.

Newer drives use a caddy, which is quite similar to the jewel boxes that CD-ROMs are shipped in. The disc is placed in the caddy with the label facing up, then inserted into the drive. There's a metal cover on the bottom of the caddy that's similar to the metal cover on a 3½-inch floppy drive. The metal cover is pushed aside when the caddy is inserted.

If you're going to change discs frequently, you can buy extra caddies (for from $4.00 to $9.00 each) and have them loaded and ready to be inserted.

You must use both hands to open a caddy, which open somewhat differently than a jewel box. To open a jewel box, you use the thumb and middle finger of the left hand and press on both sides of the hinged top at the front. Then you hold on to the bottom part of the box with your right hand and open the top cover. For a caddy, use the thumb and middle finger of the right hand and press on the bottom part of the caddy at the front. Then with the thumb of your left hand, you can lift the top hinged cover of the caddy. It might not seem important that caddies and jewel boxes open differently, but if you're trying to switch discs in a hurry, it can slow you up.

CD-ROMs are an ideal learning tool for youngsters, but many won't be able to remove the discs from the jewel boxes and load them in a caddy because their hands aren't big enough. Someone could make a lot of money if they redesigned the jewel boxes and caddies so that they could be easily operated with one hand.

Internal and external drives

Not all CD-ROM drives are the same. Some mount internally, some are external, some use a SCSI interface, and some use a proprietary interface.

Internal drives are the same size and form as a standard 5¼-inch floppy drive, so they can be mounted in a standard bay. For power, they use the standard four-wire cable from the power supply.

If at all possible, I suggest that you buy an internal drive. An external drive will cost up to $100 or more than the same model internal drive and you still need a proprietary or SCSI interface board to drive it, so you'll have to plug a large ribbon cable into the back of the interface board. External drives also need more power, and will probably come with a small transformer to plug into a wall socket or into your power strip.

One reason to buy an external CD-ROM drive with a SCSI interface would be if you have both an IBM-compatible PC and a Macintosh. You could then use the CD-ROM drive on both machines. Of course, if you have no empty bays in which to install an internal drive, then by all means buy an external one.

Proprietary interface

A CD-ROM drive must have an interface or plug-in board to drive it, much like a hard disk needs a controller or interface. Most manufacturers, such as Sony, Philips, and Hitachi, have developed drives that have to use that company's interface. So much for standardization!

If the CD-ROM drive uses a proprietary interface, it will have a special card and ribbon cable, which might not be included in the price of the system. Read the ads carefully if you're buying by mail order.

The interface card will be plugged into one of the bus slots. Before plugging the card in, make sure any jumpers or switches on the board are set properly. The board must be configured so it doesn't conflict with the address or interrupt request (IRQ) of any of your other devices. Check your documentation. Always turn your computer off before unplugging or changing the settings of any card. Never plug in or unplug a card, cable, or device while the power is on.

Several sound cards, such as SoundBlaster, Pro Audio Spectrum, and Sound Galaxy have built-in interfaces for certain CD-ROM drives. The 16-bit Sound Galaxy card can control Panasonic, Sony, or Mitsumi drives. These proprietary interfaces mean you don't have to use one of your motherboard slots.

A CD-ROM can be difficult to set up and configure to work with your system IRQs and memory address locations. If the board conflicts with any other device in your system, it won't work. Sound board systems will usually check your system and tell you if there are any conflicts.

SCSI interfaces

More and more companies are now manufacturing CD-ROM drives for use with a SCSI interface. I strongly recommend that you look for a SCSI interface. If you have other SCSI products, such as a SCSI hard drive or tape backup, you already have an interface card. SCSI interface cards can drive up to seven different devices. It's amazing how quickly the slots get used up. With a SCSI, you don't have to install a separate interface for up to seven different devices. Connecting several devices to a single SCSI interface is called *daisy-chaining*. Most SCSI devices have two connectors, one for the input cable and an identical connector for the next item. If you don't already have a SCSI interface, you might have to pay $100 to $200 for one.

I have an older Sony CD-ROM drive on my 486DX2-66 computer. This drive has a proprietary interface. Windows NT comes on either 2 floppy disks or one CD-ROM. I tried to install Windows NT using the CD-ROM drive, but the installation software that comes with the disc checks for the type of CD-ROM drive and it would accept only drives that use the SCSI interface.

Kodak Photo CD

Eastman Kodak, at 716-742-4000, has developed a system that displays photos on a television set or computer monitor. You can take a roll of film to a photo developer and have the photos copied onto a CD-ROM. The Photo CD recorder is much too expensive for most small photo-finishing labs and they have to send them out to be done, so it usually takes about a week to get the disc back. It costs about $20 for the disk itself and roughly $20 to put 24 photos on it. If you later decide to add more photos to the disc, just take it back to the lab and they'll load them on.

Some of the advantages of the Photo CD system is that the photos can be recorded at a resolution of from 128×192 to $4,000 \times 6,000$ pixels. There are no televisions or even computers that will allow you to view photos at a $4,000 \times 6000$ resolution and, at this resolution, less than 100 photos in a 4×5-inch format can be recorded on a disc. The lower the resolution and the smaller the photo, the more photos can be stored on a disc. Most photos will be stored at 480×640 pixels. At a resolution of 128 × 192, as many as 6,000 small, thumbnail-sized photos can be stored on a disc. The 128 × 192 format is often used to make a small copy of each photo on the disc. These small copies are then used as an index or catalog for all photos on the disc. If you're using a computer, you can use a mouse to point and click on any of the small images to bring up the large photo.

A Kodak Photo CD player can be connected directly to a television or computer. You can display and enlarge the photos on a TV screen; rotate, mirror, flip, and crop them; copy them to a computer file; and then either print them out or export them. Kodak Photo CD players are also high-fidelity audio-CD players. The Kodak Photo CD player can be a great tool for business presentations. It's much more versatile than a slide projector.

You might ask why anyone would want to buy a Photo CD player when they could buy a camcorder for about the same price. But each system has advantages the other doesn't have.

Kodak has recently introduced a portable Photo CD player, the PCD 970. It's about the size of a VHS videocassette and operates off four AA batteries.

Philips CD-I

Philips CD-I, which stands for compact disc interactive, is a proprietary format. As the name implies, it offers a considerable amount of user interaction. The machine attaches directly to a television or stereo system. It can play CD audio in hi-fi stereo, Kodak Photo CDs and CD+Gs (compact audio discs with graphics), and standard ISO 9660 CDs.

The machine has a remote control for clicking on various functions and a joystick for playing games. It also has an optional trackball. The CD-I is ideal for home use, but it's also a great tool for business presentations, personnel training, and education.

The interactivity, of course, depends on the program. Basically, programs offer a menu of choices and each choice leads to more choices and different outcomes. CD-I is still fairly new and not too many titles are available, but you can be sure there will be before too long.

CD-ROM/XA

CD-ROM/XA, for CD-ROM extended architecture, is a format jointly developed by Philips, Sony, and Microsoft. The format allows the simultaneous display of video motion, graphics, and audio for extended play times. The discs can be played on the portable Sony multimedia player and also on standard CD-ROM and CD-I players with a special controller card. At the present time, there aren't very many titles available for this format.

Sony multimedia player

The Sony multimedia player is a small, two-pound, portable CD-ROM drive that can play most ISO 9660 titles, CD-ROM/XAs, and audio CDs. It's the CD-ROM equivalent of the Sony Walkman. It has jacks for stereo headphones or speakers and its own small, built-in display screen. It can be connected directly to a television set and has a serial port that can be connected to a computer, printer, or modem.

SyDOS personal CD

SyDOS, at 800-437-9367, has also introduced a small, portable CD-ROM drive. Most CD-ROM drives must have an interface card in the computer. SyDOS has a built-in SCSI interface and can be plugged into the printer port of a desktop or laptop PC. It's one of the few CD-ROM drives that can be used with a laptop computer.

CD-ROM recorders

One of the drawbacks of customized CD-ROMs is that you have to send data to a special factory to have recorded on a CD-ROM. It usually takes a tremendous amount of preparation and work to assemble and create a disc. If only a few specialized discs are to be recorded, it can be very expensive.

There's an alternative, however, to sending data out to have CD-ROMs made. Philips Consumer Electronics (800-835-3506) was one of the early pioneers in the development of CD-ROM technology and they've remained in the forefront. They have developed the Philips CCD 521 desktop CD recorder, which is about the same size as a desktop computer without a monitor. The CCD 521 can record ISO 9660 CD-ROM, CD-ROM/XA, CD-I, and CD compact audio data. When most commercial CD-ROMs are made, a single directory is recorded. Ordinarily, if the disc isn't completely filled, you can't add more data to it. These are called *single-session recordings*.

The CCD 521 is capable of multiple sessions. They're similar to the system used for hard disks. You can record some data today, then add more to it later if necessary. Most newer CD-ROM drives are now capable of reading multiple-session discs.

Eastman Kodak, at 800-242-2424, has a desktop CD-ROM recorder that's very similar to the Philips CCD 521 recorder. The discs can be recorded in the same formats as those used with the Philips recorder, and the Kodak system will also accept data in multiple sessions.

Both the Kodak and Philips recorder systems are a bit expensive, at about $6,000, but a large company could recover this cost in savings in a very short time. JVC and Pinnacle, however, offer recordable drives similar to the Philips CCD 521 whose starting price is $3,995, much less than the Philips. Pinnacle drives are manufactured by Victor of Japan, the parent company of JVC. You can be sure the competition is going to force Philips to reduce their prices. Many large businesses will find that CD-ROM recorders offer more benefits than WORM drives or almost any other type of storage.

Choosing a CD-ROM drive

Less expensive CD-ROM drives are usually the ones with a proprietary interface, which could be only 8 bits. Usually, the less expensive ones also have a smaller cache or data buffer, a transfer rate of only 150K, and an access time of 300 to 700 ms. Depending on what you intend to use your CD-ROM for and how much you want to spend, one of these low-cost drives could be all you need. You should be able to buy one of these drives for less than $200.

I recommend, however, that you buy a 16-bit SCSI unit with multispeed capability (NEC's QuadSpin, for instance). Try to find one with a large cache, at least 64K and up to 256K if possible. Make sure it's multisession Photo CD capable. It should have an access time no greater than 280 ms, and 200 ms is better. A drive such as this will cost from $400 to $750. The SCSI interface might be priced separately.

CD caching

Even the fastest CD-ROM drive is slower than most floppy drives. Sometimes it seems to take forever and a day to find a file and display it. Several companies have designed cache systems, similar to disk caching, when blocks of data are used over and over again. Data that's likely to be reused is stored on a fast hard disk, or better yet in a very fast RAM disk cache, so it's almost immediately available.

Bloc Publishing, at 305-445-0903, has developed CD Speedway, a software cache program they claim can speed up a CD-ROM by as much as 8,000 percent (80 times faster). Of course, this is the ideal, and you probably won't be able to achieve this speed very often. But if your time is worth anything at all, CD Speedway could pay for itself.

Power Pak from PC-Kwik, at 503-644-5644, is a caching system that not only speeds up CD-ROMs but also gives you hard disk caching, screen acceleration, keyboard acceleration, print spooling, and much more. It's also unlike most software in that it comes with a 90-day money-back guarantee.

Multimedia upgrade kits

Many companies are offering multimedia upgrade kits or bundles. Many of them sport the MPC logo, which means they conform to MPC specifications for all the products in the kit. Be aware that some of the kits have older CD-ROM drives and components. The kit should have a late model CD-ROM drive, an audio card (8 bits minimum, 16 bits is better), 22-KHz mono playback and 11-KHz recording (although 44-KHz stereo playback and recording is better), a multivoice MIDI synthesizer, an internal audio mixer for CD audio, MIDI and digitized sound, and MIDI and joystick ports. In addition, some vendors include several multimedia titles. In some cases, the list price of the titles alone exceeds the cost of the entire bundle. Some of these kits sell for as little as $350.

A few companies offer new hardware components and current software titles. Some even include speakers and a microphone. At this time, some of the better upgrade kits cost from $500 to $1,500.

Some audiophiles wouldn't dream of buying a bundled stereo sound system. They want to be able to pick and choose each individual component. One of the great things about PCs is that you can choose either individual components or bundled units. It's your choice. One of the better speaker systems is the Altec Lansing AC300.

Multiple-disc jukebox systems

Even though there's over 600MB on a disc, there will be times when it doesn't have the programs or information you need at the moment. You'll have to eject the disc, unload the caddy, and put the new disc in. Some systems, however, similar to audio CD players, have a carousel that can hold five or six discs.

Pioneer, at 800-444-6784, has a jukebox that can handle up to 18 discs. The CD-ROM changer operates much like the old jukeboxes. The system has three magazines that hold up to six discs. It takes about six seconds to switch a disc. The Pioneer jukebox is a SCSI device, and Pioneer supplies a Future Domain interface card and software drivers for it. The current list price is $2,495. For high-end applications, Pioneer offers a system that can hold five trays, with 100 discs in each tray. To reduce access time, you can install up to four drives. Cost for this system ranges from $20,000 up to $25,000.

NSM (516-261-7700) has a system, Model CDR-100SC, that holds two racks of magazines with 50 discs in each magazine. You can also have extra loaded magazines so either of the magazines can be quickly pulled out and replaced. You probably wouldn't need a system like this at home, but many large businesses could tie one of these to a network in order to provide gigabytes of information to users.

Multiple-drive systems

Tiger Software, at 800-888-4437, has a tower system that can hold up to seven different CD-ROM drives. The tower case has a lock for security. It was primarily designed for use on networks, but it could be used anywhere. The cost depends on the number of drives you want installed. It's $1,251 for the unit with two installed drives, and $480 for each additional drive. You can also add network printer ports and Ethernet connections.

Build your own and save a bundle

You can put together your own multiple-drive system that would be much less expensive than jukebox system and much faster. Just buy your own CD-ROM drives and daisy-chain them on a SCSI interface. I've seen good CD-ROM drives advertised for less than $200. Tiger Software advertises a double-speed CD-ROM drive for $199.90 on the page opposite their ad for their tower system. (On another page, Tiger advertises a CD-ROM drive with a proprietary interface card and a free CD-ROM with the 1994 Grolier's Encyclopedia, all for $99.90.)

You can attach up to seven drives to one interface, so for about $1,400, plus $150 for a SCSI interface, you could set up a very fast seven-drive system. The Adaptec AMM 1570 sound card includes an excellent SCSI-II interface. The tower system from Tiger Software, with seven CD-ROM drives, would cost over $3,600. If you had CD-ROM loaded in all the drives, it would take very little time to electronically switch from one drive to another. DOS simply assigns each drive a letter of the alphabet, and you can access them like you would another hard drive. It's definitely easier and faster than having the jukebox system use a robotic arm to unload and load a different disc.

Sources

There are several companies and vendors for CD-ROMs. Just look in any computer magazine and you'll see dozens of ads. If you're going to use a CD-ROM drive to read and import data, I recommend that you buy a drive capable of at least double spin.

16
CHAPTER

Computer sound and MIDI

Sound can be an important part of your computer system. Some Windows applications can make great use of sound, but you need a sound board to take full advantage of them. The Windows 3.1 Sound Recorder is an included utility that lets you record, edit, insert, mix, and play sound files that are in the .WAV format. You can add sound annotations to documents such as spreadsheets, or to programs that support object linking and embedding (OLE).

Not only can you play music through your computer, but even if you know nothing at all about music you can use your computer to compose and create music. A computer is very good at converting text and graphics into digital data. Music can also be represented as digital data just as easily. Once music is digitized, you can edit it, rearrange it, add new sounds to it, remove certain sounds, or change it in hundreds of different ways.

Sound boards

There are some very inexpensive 8-bit monaural sound boards. These might be okay for just adding a bit of narration to a file, but you can get a fantastic amount of sound capabilities if you spend just a bit more and get a good stereo sound board.

A good audio board should be able to digitally record narration, sound, or music and store them as *.WAV files. You should be able to record in mono or stereo and control the sampling rate. The board should have chips to convert the stored digital signals for analog conversion (DACs), and also chips to convert analog sound to digital signals (ADCs).

A good board will have a musical instrument digital interface (MIDI). With MIDI capabilities, you can use the board with MIDI instruments, such as piano keyboards, synthesizers, and sound modules.

The board should have an FM synthesis chipset that duplicates the 128 different MIDI voices and 46 percussion instruments. Instead of synthesized sound, some of the more expensive cards have samples of actual instruments and use a wave table for synthesis. The board should also have an audio mixer function that allows you to control the source and level of audio signals. Better boards will have tone controls for the bass and treble ranges. The board should also have a joystick port connector, a microphone input, and a speaker output jack.

Many boards have a proprietary interface for controlling CD-ROM drives. The interface might work with drives from three or four different manufacturers. A few companies manufacture sound boards with a SCSI interface, which allows you to control any SCSI CD-ROM drive. A SCSI interface will also control up to six other devices.

Sound, microphones, and speakers

Sound is made when an object vibrates and creates sound waves, which move through the air to your eardrums, which themselves vibrate, creating sound. If a microphone is placed in the vicinity of a sound, it can turn it into electrical impulses. There are several different types of microphones. One basic type has a diaphragm that vibrates in response to the pressure of the sound waves. The diaphragm is attached to a coil of wire that moves in and out of the field of a permanent magnet. The movement of the coil of wire in the magnetic field produces an analog voltage that varies according to the vibration of the sound. We can record the electrical pulses and, amplifying the small signals, cause a loudspeaker to reproduce the original sound.

Basically, a loudspeaker is quite similar to a microphone. The speaker has a coil of wire that's attached to the speaker cone. The coil of wire is surrounded by a strong permanent magnet. Moving the coil of wire through a magnetic field produces a voltage; passing voltage through the coil of wire produces a magnetic field. The polarity of the magnetic field created varies depending on the polarity of the voltage. As positive and negative pulses of voltage are passed through the coil of wire, it alternately attracts the coil into the magnet or repels the coil and cone outward. The movement of the speaker cone thus produces a replica of the original sound.

Recording on magnetic tape

The basic principles of magnetic recording were first discovered in the 1890s, but lacking the necessary electronics not much was done with the discovery.

The record or write head on a tape recorder looks somewhat like a C with a coil of wire wrapped around it (see Fig. 8-1). If voltage is passed through the coil, it causes a magnetic field to be formed between the ends of the C. The space between the ends of the C is called the *gap*. Depending on the type of head, the gap might be only a few thousandths of an inch wide.

The magnetic field varies, depending on the polarity and strength of the voltage. If the C is placed over a magnetic material such as tape or a disk, the area closest to the gap will be magnetized according to the strength of the voltage through the head. The magnetic image placed on the moving tape will then be a replica of the sound that caused the analog voltage.

Remember that a coil of wire that's passed through a magnetic field, or a magnetic field that passes a coil of wire, produces voltage. To play the tape back, the magnetic fields on the tape cause voltage to be produced as it moves past the wire coil in the head. The same basic principle is used to record or play back data on a hard or floppy disk.

Some of the original magnetic tapes were ¼ inch wide for monaural recording. Depending on the strength of the recording voltage, the recorded magnetic field on the tape would vary all the way across the tape. As the technology improved, you could record two sets of stereo, or four tracks, on a ¼-inch tape, which is ¹⁄₁₆ inch for each track. This is a huge amount of space when you consider that a hard disk can have up to 1,000 tracks per inch.

Digital recording

Digital recording is basically the same as analog recording, but digital voltages don't continuously vary. Digital signals are derived from chopping up of a steady direct current, or dc voltage. The dc voltage is turned on for a certain amount of time to represent a 1, then off for a certain amount of time to represent a 0. This chopped-up voltage passes through the head and magnetizes the area beneath the head each time it becomes positive to represent a 1.

Digital recording doesn't deal with the side-to-side variations of magnetic fields. In analog recording, the output voltage varies according to the strength of the magnetic field on the tape; the stronger the field, the greater the voltage output. Digital recording cares only if there's a signal that can represent a 1 or the absence of a signal to represent a 0.

Digital sampling

Some large network systems operate by giving each person a small slice of time, also called *time sharing*. If the time was divided into millionths of a second, one person might receive a couple of slices, then the next person would get a few slices, then a few millionths of a second later the first person would get a few more slices of data. It would be done so fast that the person wouldn't realize the data was being received only part of the time. Hundreds or even thousands of people could be on a single line, all receiving data at the same time.

Digitizing an analog voltage is somewhat similar to time sharing. Digital samples, or slices, are taken of the analog waves. If the number of digital samples per second is rather low, then there can be a lot of unrecorded space between each slice. When played back, the unrecorded space can usually be electronically reconstructed, but if the sample rate is too low and there are very wide spaces between each sample, the output sound will be somewhat less than high fidelity. The higher the frequency of the sample rate, the more closely the output sound matches the original. So why not take higher-frequency samples? Because the higher the frequency of the digital sample rate, the more storage space it requires. High-fidelity digital sound requires a tremendous amount of disk space.

Sampling rates and bits

Sound can be digitized using 8-bit (one-byte) or 16-bit samples. An 8-bit system can chop a wave form into a maximum of 256 steps, or 2^8. A 16-bit system (2^{16}) can save up to 65,000 pieces of information about the same wave form. As you can imagine, the 16-bit system offers much greater fidelity, but at a greater need for storage space.

Using an 8-bit mode with a sample rate of 11 KHz, you'd be recording 11,000 bytes of data each second × 60 seconds, or 661 kilobytes per minute. If you were recording in 8-bit stereo at the same rate, the storage requirement would double, to 1.3MB for one minute.

Speech has a frequency range from about 300 Hz up to about 6 KHz. Sampling at 11 KHz and 8 bits is good enough for speech, but it wouldn't be very good for high-fidelity music. Most systems are capable of sampling at 22 KHz and 44.1 KHz in both monaural and stereo modes. A sample rate for 44.1 KHz in monaural would be 82.2K per second × 60 seconds = 5.292MB. In stereo, it would be doubled to 10.5MB per minute. One hour of recording at this sample rate would require over 630MB of space. Most audio CDs have about 630MB of storage space and can play for about one hour. Standard digital sampling rates in the audio industry are 5.0125, 11.025, 22.05, and 44.1 KHz.

Why a 44.1-KHz sample rate?

If we had perfect hearing, we could hear sounds from 20 Hz, or 20 cycles per second, up to 20 KHz (20,000 Hz). Most of us, especially older people, have a much narrower hearing range. So why should we worry about a 44.1-KHz sample rate, which is more than twice the frequency we could hear even if we had perfect hearing?

Many instruments and other sounds have unique resonances and harmonics that go beyond the basic sounds they produce. These resonances and harmonics are what makes a middle C note on a piano sound different than the same note on a violin or trumpet. Many of the harmonics and overtones of sound is in the higher frequencies. In digital recording, the upper frequency must be at least twice what you'd expect when converted to analog. So a 44.1-KHz digital signal will produce a 22-KHz analog signal.

Resolution

We often speak of the resolution of our monitors. The more pixels displayed, the sharper the image and the higher the resolution. We also use the word *resolution* to describe digitized sound. The higher the sampling rate and the more bits of information about each sound wave, the higher the resolution and the better the fidelity. There is a limit to the resolution of an 8-bit system, no matter how fast the sample rate. The maximum number of samples of a wave form that can be captured by an 8-bit system is 2^8, or 256. You might think that 16-bit system could provide twice the resolution of an 8-bit system, but it can actually provide 256 times more resolution—2^{16}, or 65,536. A 16-bit system can obviously provide much better resolution and fidelity than an 8-bit system.

Signal-to-noise ratio (SNR)

Analog audio is made up of voltage sine waves that vary up and down continuously. Noise and static is also made up of similar sine waves. Noise and static is everywhere, especially so during electrical storms. It's in electrical lines and in almost all electronic equipment. It's very difficult to avoid.

The signal-to-noise ratio is the ratio between the amplitude of the audio or video signal and the noise component. The SNR is measured in dB (decibels), usually minus dB. The larger the negative number, the better.

Most sound boards, CD-ROM drives, and other sound systems list the SNR on their specifications. Most of the better systems have at least a –90 dB SNR. Since noise is analog voltage, a good digital system usually has less noise than an analog system.

Digital signal processors (DSP)

One thing that makes it possible to get so much music from a sound board is a digital signal processor (DSP). It can be very difficult just to assemble and determine which notes to output from a single instrument, but it can be mind-boggling to try to do it for several instruments.

The central processor unit (CPU) is the brains of your computer. Ordinarily, almost everything that transpires in your computer has to go through the CPU, but there are certain things, such as intensive number crunching, that can be speeded up with a coprocessor. All motherboards, from the lowly XT up through the 386DX, usually have a socket near the CPU for a coprocessor. The 486DX and Pentium CPUs have built-in coprocessors. When doing complex math and number crunching, the coprocessor can assist the CPU and speed up its operation by as much as 300 percent or more.

Digital signal processor (DSP) chips are quite similar in function to math coprocessors. A DSP can take over and relieve the CPU of much of its burden. DSP chips can be configured and programmed for several specific tasks, such as high-quality audio, complex graphics, or video. The DSP can be used for musical synthesis and many special digital effects.

At one time the DSP chips were rather expensive, but now the chips are quite reasonable. Since they add very little to the cost, more and more manufacturers are adding DSP chips to their sound boards. Before you buy a sound board, check the specifications.

Turtle Beach Systems was one of the first to design and implement the DSP technology on their MultiSound boards. Creative Labs followed soon after with their Sound Blaster 16 ASP. Several other companies are now manufacturing boards with the superior DSP technology. These chips add so much more function and utility to the sound board that eventually every manufacturer will be using them.

What sound board should you buy?

It all depends on what you want to do and how much you want to spend. If you can afford it, I would suggest that you look for a 16-bit card with a DSP chip. The

MultiSound card from Turtle Beach (717-843-6916) is without a doubt one of the best you can buy at this time. It's also the most expensive. There are many less expensive 16-bit cards that don't have a DSP or as many of the goodies as MultiSound. If you don't expect to use your computer for any type of high-fidelity music, then there are even less expensive, 8-bit cards. I've seen some no-name 8-bit sound cards advertised for as little as $25. There's a tremendous amount of competition in the whole multimedia business, so prices are coming down. Several sound cards have a built-in SCSI interface, but there are several levels of SCSI—so you might not be able to run anything other than a CD-ROM drive off these SCSI sound cards. Adaptec's AMM 1570/1572 Audio Machine sound card can run any SCSI device; it's one of the better sound cards you can buy.

If you're interested only in adding annotations to files and playing back incidental sound from files, then an inexpensive 8-bit system should be fine. Covox, at 503-342-1271, has the Sound Master II, an 8-bit system that comes with a headset microphone and two speakers. It also comes with Covox Voice Master Key voice-recognition software, which lets you train the computer to recognize and respond to as many as 1,023 voice commands or macros. Table 16-1 lists a few popular name-brand audio boards.

Table 16-1. Popular, name-brand audio boards

Board	Type
Sound Blaster Pro Deluxe	8-bit stereo
Sound Blaster 16 ASP	16-bit stereo
Pro Audio Spectrum	16-bit stereo
MultiSound	16-bit stereo
Sound Galaxy 16	16-bit stereo
Diamond Corp. Sonic	16-bit stereo
Adaptec Audio Machine	16-bit stereo

For sources, look in any computer magazine such as *Computer Shopper*, *New Media*, *PC World*, *PC Computing*, and *PC Magazine*.

Installing a sound board

Your computer's CPU is always busy and can be interrupted only by certain devices that need its attention. The obvious reason for this is to keep order. If all the devices tried to act at the same time, there would be total confusion. So computers have 16 interrupts, or IRQ, lines and each device is assigned a unique number. They're given a priority according to their ranking number. For instance, if the CPU received an interrupt request from the keyboard, which is IRQ 1, and a request from a mouse on IRQ 4, the keyboard request would be answered first.

If two devices are set for the same IRQ, it will cause a conflict. You might have to set one or more jumpers or switches on your board before you install it.

Just as your house has a unique address, areas of RAM have distinct addresses. Certain devices use portions of RAM to perform some of their processing, so you might have to set jumpers or switches for the input/output (I/O) address of the sound card. The default address, the one set by the factory, will probably be 220. This is the Sound Blaster standard and is used by many others.

You might also have to set jumpers for the Direct Memory Access (DMA) channel. Most PCs have three or more DMAs, but they don't usually cause a conflict if two or more devices are set to the same channel.

Many audio boards have built-in diagnostics that can detect a conflict with the IRQ or I/O settings, but you might have trouble determining which other device is causing the conflict. If you have DOS 6.0 or later, you can use the Microsoft Diagnostics (MSD) command. It will show all the IRQs and which components are using them.

Incidentally, the MSD command will give you a wealth of information about your computer. Besides the IRQs, it will show the memory usage, your AUTOEXEC.BAT and CONFIG.SYS files, and many other useful bits of information. You can view the information or print it out. Depending on what you have in your computer, it might take up to 20 pages.

An even better program for installing sound boards, or any board that uses IRQs and unique memory addresses, is CheckIt Setup Advisor from TouchStone, at 800-531-0450. This small, inexpensive program can save you hours of frustration. It can even help you before you install a board. It has a "what if" utility that tells you whether or not you'll be able to use a board before you install it. It has a large on-disk library of most popular boards. If you ask what would happen if you installed a Turtle Beach sound board, it would search your system and compare it to the Turtle Beach normal settings.

Connecting a CD-ROM to a sound board

One of the benefits of CD-ROM drives is that they can play sound and music along with the text, graphics, and motion. You can even play audio CDs on most CD-ROM drives. So it's necessary to be able to connect a CD-ROM drive to your sound board. Most CD-ROM drives have a small audio connector on its back panel. You must then use a special cable to connect the drive to the sound board. Unfortunately, there's no standardization, so the audio connector on the CD-ROM drive and on sound boards from different companies might be different. Because there are so many variations, the audio cable isn't often included with sound boards or CD-ROM drives. You might have to special-order it. They cost about $5. The audio cable plugs into a miniature connector, usually on the rear of the CD-ROM drive. The other end plugs into a small connector on the sound board.

Speakers

Most sound cards have an output of about 4 watts, which isn't very much, but you don't need much for your computer. You can attach any small speaker, but there are several companies who manufacture small speakers with a built-in amplifier. The speakers are powered by batteries or by a power supply, and cost from $20 to $100.

There are also high-end, high-fidelity systems available. Of course, high fidelity usually means high cost.

Some companies have developed computer cases with built-in speakers. At least one company, Proton Corporation (310-404-2222), has added speakers to their 15-inch monitors. The built-in systems help eliminate desktop clutter. You should be aware, though, that these speakers are definitely not high fidelity.

Just a few of the many companies who offer computer speakers are Labtec, Altec Lansing, Media Vision, Koss, and Roland. Look through computer magazines for others.

Some sound boards and speakers cost well over $500. If you need only Windows to add voice to programs and applications such as annotations for spreadsheets or financial reports, you might be interested in a system from Logitech, at 510-795-8500. The Logitech Audioman can be connected to the computer's parallel printer port, LPT1. Unlike most speakers, however, the Logitech Audioman doesn't need a sound board to drive it. Another plus is that you can connect it to the parallel port without opening your computer. It has a pass-through parallel connector so the printer can still be connected to LPT1. Audioman is supplied with a microphone that plugs into the base of the speaker for adding sound to files. It's strictly a monaural system.

Microphones

My Sound Blaster 16 ASP came with a microphone. A microphone for just voice annotations can be very inexpensive, such as those available from Radio Shack for about $5. If you expect to do any kind of high-fidelity recording, however, then you definitely need a good microphone. A sound system is only as good as its weakest link. A good microphone will cost from $35 to over $500.

There are two basic types of microphones: dynamic, which uses a diaphragm and a coil of wire that moves back and forth in a magnetic field, and condenser, or capacitor. A capacitor microphone is made up of two flat plates. When voltage is applied to the plates, a charged field, or capacitance, exists between the plates. The amount of capacitance depends on the voltage, the size of the plates, and the distance between the plates. If the plates are moved toward or away from each other, the capacity will change. In a capacitor microphone, one plate is fixed and the other is a flat diaphragm. Sound pressure on the flexible diaphragm moves the charged plate in and out, which changes the capacitance. Capacitor microphones can be very small, such as those made for lapels.

Most professional microphones sold today are wireless. They have a small, built-in transmitter that feeds the sound to a small receiver, which is connected to an amplifier or recorder.

Microphones can also be classified by their pickup directionality. Omnidirectional microphones pick up sound from all directions and bidirectional microphones pick up sound from opposite sides of the microphone. A cardiod microphone picks up sound in a heart-shaped, unidirectional pattern (*cardi* is a prefix meaning *heart*), and a unidirectional supercardiod picks up sound in a very narrow, straight path.

Musical instrument digital interface (MIDI)

Electronic circuits can be designed to oscillate at almost any frequency. The output of the oscillating circuit is a voltage that can be amplified and routed through a loudspeaker to reproduce various sounds.

In the early 1970s, Robert Moog used voltage-controlled oscillators (VCOs) to develop the Moog synthesizer. With a synthesizer, you can create sounds that imitate different instruments. The sounds from early systems, however, didn't sound much like real musical instruments.

Also in the early 1970s, John Chowning of Stanford University developed digital FM synthesis. Yamaha Corporation licensed the technology from Stanford and introduced the first FM digital synthesizer in 1982. Since that time there have been some tremendous technological advances. Today a person might not be able to tell whether a sound is synthesized or comes from a real instrument.

In some instances, the music from a sound board comes from real instruments. Sample notes from instruments are recorded and stored and, under computer control, they can be manipulated and played back. Notes can be lengthened or shortened, and samples from several instruments can all be playing at the same time. You can even make music sound as if it was being produced by a live, hundred-piece orchestra. All from a chip that's about one inch square. It's absolutely amazing.

Early voltage-controlled oscillators (VCOs) were rather crude since the electronics industry was still in its infancy and there were no integrated circuits. As technology evolved, newer and better VCOs were developed and incorporated into musical instruments.

The MIDI standard

There were no standards for the VCOs and new musical instruments. As usual, each vendor's product was a bit different than all others. In 1983 a group of companies got together and adopted a set of standards which they called the Musical Instrument Digital Interface. This was truly an historic agreement for the music industry. MIDI and the advances in electronic technology has made it possible to generate more new music in the last ten years than was generated in the last 100 years. Synthesized music is not only used for rock and roll, but for television commercials, for movies and for all types of music.

How MIDI operates

MIDI itself doesn't produce music; it's only an interface, or controller, that tells other devices such as a synthesizer or a sampler which particular sound to produce. In some respects, MIDI is similar to old-style player pianos that used a punched roll of paper.

Briefly, the MIDI specification says that a MIDI device must have at least two MIDI connectors, input and output. (These are DIN connectors, the same as those used for the computer keyboard connector on the motherboard.) A MIDI device includes adapter cards, synthesizers, piano-type keyboards, various types of instrument pickups, digital signal processors, and MIDI-controlled audio mixers. One of the great advantages of MIDI is that it allows many different electronic instruments to communicate with each other.

When two MIDI instruments are connected, the devices exchange information about the elements of a performance, such as the notes and how loud they're played. A master keyboard can be connected to two or more MIDI electronic keyboards or other MIDI devices. Any note played on the master can also be played on the connected MIDI "slaves." Electronic keyboards can emulate several different instruments. One person playing the master can use the slaves to make it sound as though a very large orchestra was playing. There are many options available, such as recording the notes played, changing them, then playing them back.

General MIDI signals

There are 128 common instrument sound signals for MIDI control, numbered 1 to 128. (You might also see them numbered 0 to 127). The standard was originated by the Roland Corporation and is now coordinated by the MIDI Manufacturers Association (MMA).

If MIDI receives a signal, and it's connected to a synthesizer, keyboard, or any MIDI instrument, it will trigger the device to play a note corresponding to the signal number. For instance, signal 3 would produce a honky-tonk piano sound and number 40 would be a violin. There are 16 different instrument classifications. Every eight numbers represent sounds from a basic class of instrument. For instance, the first eight sounds are made by piano-type instruments, the next eight are made by percussion instruments, etc.

There are an additional 46 MIDI note numbers for nonmelodic percussion instruments. These numbers include such things as drums, cow bells, wooden blocks, triangles, and cymbals.

Synthesizers

The MIDI specification was designed primarily as a standard for controlling synthesizers. It didn't specify how a synthesizer should create a sound or what sounds should be created.

The word *synthesize* means to combine or put together. Synthesizers can combine two or more wave forms to form new sounds. There are several types of sound waves or oscillations. Each musical note has a basic oscillation frequency. For instance, A2 has a frequency of 220 oscillations per second, or 220 Hz. Note E3 vibrates at 330 Hz, A4 at 440 Hz, and E6 at 660 Hz. You could generate pure, single-frequency sine waves for each of these notes, but they'd be rather dull and uninteresting. The actual notes are a combination of oscillation frequencies.

Even though it has the same basic frequency, if a note is played on different instruments, there are distinct difference in the sounds. The note A4 played on a trombone sounds quite different than A4 played on a guitar. They all sound different because they aren't pure sine-wave frequencies. The vibrations of a basic note causes other vibrations in the metal of a trombone or the strings and wood of a guitar. These extra vibrations are the timbre that adds tone and color to a sound and distinguishes it from a note played on another instrument.

Harmonics

An important difference in sounds are the harmonics that are created. A guitar string that's plucked to play A4 will vibrate at 440 Hz. If you photographed the vibrating string with a high-speed movie camera and then slowed it down, you'd see a primary node of vibrations, but there would also be several smaller nodes. These smaller nodes would be vibrating at twice the frequency of the primary node and some would even be vibrating at four times the primary frequency. The sounds made at the higher frequencies blend with the primary sound to give it tone and color. These higher frequencies are called *harmonics*. Harmonics are even multiples of the fundamental oscillation of a note, or its basic pitch.

Envelope generator

Bob Moog determined that there were four main criteria for each sound. He identified them as attack, decay, sustain, and release (ADSR). The attack determines how fast the initial sound rises. It might hold at the initial height for a while, then start to decay. Sustain determines how long the sound is audible while a key is held down. Release is the rate at which the sound intensity decreases to zero after the key is released. The ADSR electronic envelope is used in synthesizers to describe almost any sound.

Wave tables

FM-synthesized sounds aren't usually as good as the sound generated from an actual instrument. More expensive sound cards and many of the better MIDI instruments use digital samples of real sounds. This requires some memory to store the samples, but not as much as you might think. For instance, a piano has 88 notes, or keys, but it's necessary to sample only a few notes. Since they're all piano notes, the main difference is the pitch. Middle A, or A4, has a frequency of 440 Hz and A2 has a frequency of 220 Hz. A sample of a single A can be electronically altered to make it sound like any A on the piano keyboard, so you need samples of only an A, B, C, D, E, F, and G. With a small sample of each of these notes, you can create any note of the 88 on the piano.

The same type of system is used to sample notes from other instruments. It's a little simpler to store notes from other instruments because most of them don't have as large a range as a piano. And a piano is one of the few instruments that allows more than one note to be played at the same time.

The samples are stored in ROM. When a note is called for, the sample is read from ROM, placed in RAM, electronically adjusted for whatever note is needed, then sent to an amplifier and loudspeaker. Of course, the more instruments sampled and the more samples stored, the more memory is required, both ROM and RAM. Some high-end keyboards have 10MB or more of ROM and about 4MB of RAM.

Sequencers

Sequencers are a type of recorder that uses computer memory to store information about a performance. Like MIDI, it doesn't record the sound itself, just information about the sound.

Even if you know nothing at all about music, you can write and compose music with a sequencer connected to a synthesizer or other electronic instrument. If you know a little bit about music, you can become an expert composer with a sequencer. Most sequencers are software programs that allow you to create, edit, record, and play back musical compositions in the MIDI message format.

A sequencer memorizes anything you play and can play it back at any time. They're similar to multitrack recorders, except they're much faster since the tracks are on a computer. The computer also lets you do hundreds of things better, more quickly, and more easily than a tape recorder. You can edit music in thousands of ways not possible with a tape machine. You could record an entire album with a single MIDI instrument.

A sequence can be part of a song, a single track of a song, or the whole song. The sequences are laid down in tracks. Several tracks of different instruments can be laid down separately, then all played back together. A single track can be edited or changed. Tracks can be recorded at different times, then blended together. A song or an album could be created by a group even if one is in New York, one is in Los Angeles, and the others scattered all over the country. All the members of the group could record their individual parts on a disk, then ship it to a studio where all of the tracks could be edited and blended together.

Some sequencers allow you to record channels while playing back existing channels. Tracks can be laid down over an existing track or tracks without erasing what's already there. Portions of a track can be erased and new material inserted. The editing capabilities are almost unlimited.

Some synthesizers and keyboards have a built-in hardware sequencer, which lets you do many of the same things you can do with sequencer software. But a hardware sequencer doesn't have the added capabilities of a computer.

Sequencer software, such as Cakewalk, will let you record in real time as an instrument is being played, or you can use the step entry mode and enter one note at a time. The notes can be entered from a computer keyboard or a piano-type MIDI keyboard connected to the computer.

The software is intelligent enough to take step entry notes and combine them with the proper staff notation and timing. Some software will even add the proper chords to the step entry. Several Windows sequencer software programs are Cakewalk Professional, Cadenza, Master Tracks Pro, and Midisoft for Windows. Many music software programs will also print out music scores.

When you consider that modern technology allows songs to be edited and re-edited until they're perfect, you just have to admire the works of some of the early recording artists. They usually didn't get the opportunity to go back and change a mistake or to improve a lick here and there.

Keyboards

It's possible to use a computer keyboard to edit or create music, but it's a lot easier to work with an electronic piano keyboard. Many of electronic keyboards have built-in synthesizers and MIDI connections.

If you're interested in computerized music, you should definitely subscribe to *Electronic Musician* (800-888-5139). They have excellent articles about music and new devices. They also publish an annual *Digital Piano Buyer's Guide*, available from Mix Bookshelf, at 800-233-9604. Mix Bookshelf specializes in books for musicians, and one of the books they carry is the *The Musical PC*. It's an excellent book for anyone who wants to learn more about music and computers. Another book they carry is *Making Music with Your Computer*, which could be helpful to anyone just getting into electronic music.

If you're thinking about buying a keyboard, there are a lot of choices available. You won't find an electronic keyboard that sounds exactly like an acoustic piano, but some come pretty close. Keyboards can produce sounds and tones that acoustic pianos can't, as well as providing an easier way to learn, private practice with earphones, and the ability to record and compose—all in a small size that can be easily transported, and often at a very affordable price.

Some electronic keyboards and instruments have more keys, switches, and buttons than you'd find in a 747 cockpit. It can be a bit daunting if you're just getting into the music scene.

There are two basic types of digital keyboards: the portable digital keyboard and the larger digital piano. More expensive units have a velocity sensor that can detect how hard a key is hit and how long it's depressed. A standard acoustic piano has 88 keys, but many smaller portable keyboards have 49 or less. The better ones have 61 keys.

Portable keyboards cost from $100 up to $3,000, depending on the options and features.

Digital pianos

Digital pianos are usually fairly expensive. Many of them are fine pieces of furniture; some upright and others shaped like a grand piano. They usually have a lot of built-in features: MIDI, synthesizers, sequencers, powerful amplifiers, and speakers. They might also have a floppy disk drive and a built-in CD-ROM drive.

There are several other goodies on some of the higher priced keyboards, such as a DSP, bass reflex audio system, one-finger ad-lib (one-finger chords), pitch bend /mod wheels, reverb, chorus sound effects, expert logic accompaniment, auto harmony, and programmable drum pads.

A few machines have only 76 keys, but the majority of them have a full 88. Most have a weighted hammer effect, so they play very much like an acoustic piano. Most digital pianos have three foot pedals, just like an acoustic piano. The right pedal is the damper pedal. When depressed it actually undampens the keys so notes sound until they decay naturally. The middle pedal is the sostenuto or sustain pedal, and the left pedal is the una corde, which shifts the keys so that only one string of the normal trio of strings are struck. Some digital models have only two pedals by leaving out the rarely used sostenuto pedal, but digital pianos offer a whole lot more than just foot pedals.

Just like acoustic pianos, there are two types of digital pianos: uprights and grands. The uprights are generally a bit less expensive and have less features compared to the grands. Many digital pianos have fewer sounds than portables, but the sounds are usually cleaner and have better fidelity. There might be several on-board effects, such as tremolo, reverb, chorus, and vibrato. They might also have features such as transposition, touch sensitivity, performance memory, headphone jacks, programmable layers and splits, automatic accompaniment, automatic rhythms, on-board sequencers, floppy disk drives, and RAM and ROM. In addition, the piano cabinets are usually made from fine wood and have superb finishes.

Some of the less expensive uprights cost as little as $1,200, with a median price of about $3,000. Some high-end digital grand pianos will cost as much as $40,000.

In the early 1920s, broadcast radio was still unknown to most of the public, and the majority of pianos sold were player pianos. Today, many high-end digital pianos are purchased by people who don't play. Many digital pianos have floppy disk drives that can do much the same thing that the player piano did. Slip a floppy disk in the drive and hear someone like George Gershwin tinkle the ivories in your own living room.

Acoustic MIDI pianos

There are still a lot of people who don't like digital pianos, no matter how much they cost. They much prefer the old-fashioned acoustic sound. But many people would like to be able to take advantage of the many features offered by MIDI and digitization. Yamaha and several other manufacturers have added digital and MIDI features to some of their finest acoustic pianos, which can give you the best of both worlds.

If you already own an acoustic piano, you can also upgrade it to take advantage of the modern digital technology. Gulbransen, at 619-296-5760, has several kits you can attach to an acoustic piano to give it a full range of MIDI capabilities. They offer several kits with different features, ranging from $1,190 up to $2,800 depending on the features included.

The following programs will teach you how to play your portable keyboard or digital piano:

The Miracle Piano Teaching System

Many people would like very much to be able to play the piano, but don't want to spend the long hours practicing. The Miracle is a 49-key keyboard from Software Toolworks (415-883-3000) that's designed to make it easier for anyone to learn to play the piano. It comes with the Miracle Piano Teaching System, which can be used with ISA machines, the Macintosh, the Amiga, Nintendo, or Super NES systems.

The system is designed for young people up to adults. Some of the exercises make use of juvenile arcade and musical games that might not suit some adults, but it can make learning interesting and entertaining.

Floppy disk learning software

Ibis Software, at 415-546-1917, has developed several good software programs to help you learn music.

Play it by ear

This contains a variety of self-paced exercises in a realistic learning environment, and features an on-screen piano keyboard and guitar fretboard. You control the content and difficulty of each exercise.

Soloist

This disk can be used by anyone from beginner to advanced musician. In the game mode you progress through 36 levels of instruction, or you can use Soloist to practice or explore. The 32-page manual includes a tutorial.

Rhythm Ace

This program helps you to learn, practice, and play rhythm. A variety of interactive exercises will sharpen your ability.

Note Play

This is a game to help you learn to read and play music. Designed primarily for keyboard players, NotePlay displays musical phrases on a grand staff, where you make points by playing notes quickly and accurately.

Super Jam

Super Jam, from Blue Ribbon Soundworks, Ltd. (P.O. Box 8689, Atlanta, GA, 30306), lets you write and compose your own music whether you can read music or not. Comes with everything you need, including an interactive on-screen keyboard and the new Eas-o-matic Music Maker. It works with Windows 3.1 and either a compatible sound card or MIDI instrument.

Keyboard and digital piano sources

If you're planning to buy a portable keyboard or a digital piano, learn all you can about the instrument. If you live in or near a large city, several stores will probably carry portable keyboards, but there probably won't be many who carry expensive high-end digital pianos. If it isn't convenient to visit a store, here's a brief list of vendors and manufacturers of portable keyboards and digital pianos. This is not a complete listing. Call the manufacturers and ask for catalogs and specification sheets.

Akai Professional	817-336-5114
Bachman General Electro Music	708-766-8230
Baldwin Piano & Organ Co.	513-576-4500
Casio, Inc.	201-361-5400
Daewoo International	213-774-1746
Kawai America Corp.	310-631-1771
Korg Corp.	516-333-9100

Kurzweil Corp.	310-926-3200
Peavey Electronics	601-483-5365
Roland Corp.	213-685-5141
Samick Music Corp.	818-964-4700
Suzuki Corp.	619-566-9710
Technics Musical Instruments	201-392-6140
Yamaha Corp.	714- 522-9011

Catalogs

Soundware, at 800-333-4554, publishes a catalog listing hundreds of music software programs, including a comprehensive and detailed description of each program. Even if you don't intend to order the program, the descriptions in the catalog can give you a good idea of what's available.

Musician's Friend, at 800-776-5173, American Musical Supply, at 800-458-4076, and Manny's Mailbox Music, at 800-448-8478, all produce catalogs listing hundreds of musical instruments, supplies, videotapes for training, and books. Another catalog for all sorts of musical instruments and software is Rock 'n Rhythm, at 800-348-5003.

Roland magazine

Roland publishes a magazine that contains articles, tips, and suggestions for using Roland products as well as news about the music business. It's sent free to anyone who purchases any Roland product and sends in the warranty card. Even if you aren't a Roland customer, if you call 213-685-5141 they'll send you a copy of the magazine.

Musician trade shows

Partly due to the success of the COMDEX show, there are now a lot of trade shows. The National Association of Music Merchants (NAMM) has two large shows each year, usually one near Los Angeles in the winter and one in Nashville during the summer. There are usually hundreds of exhibitors at these shows. You can find just about every imaginable musical product at these shows. There are dozens of rooms where they demonstrate amplifiers and loudspeakers, and hundreds of electronic keyboards, everything from the small toys up to very expensive grand pianos. To find out when and where the next NAMM show will be held, call 619-438-8001.

The Consumer Electronics Show (CES) also presents two large shows each year, one held in Las Vegas during the first week in January and one in Chicago during the first week in June. To find out more about this show, call 202-457-8700.

Summary

Advancing computer and MIDI technologies have made it possible for most people to play music or even to compose their own music. Acoustic pianos are very expensive, but digital technology has made it possible for many more people to own inexpensive keyboards and be able to have hands-on musical experience.

Some people don't like synthesized music because they say it's artificial, but music, like all technologies, is constantly evolving, changing, and improving. If no changes were allowed, we might still be beating on hollow logs for drums, blowing on reed flutes, or plucking a single-stringed harp.

17
CHAPTER

Essential software

You cannot operate a computer without software. It's equally as necessary as hardware. Software tells the hardware what to do. Computers are dumb. They do only what the software tells them to do.

I can't possibly list all the thousands of software packages available. The computer magazines listed in chapter 19 often have detailed reviews of software, and they usually have many advertisements for software in every issue.

Off-the-shelf and ready-to-use software

A software upgrade might be one of the better ways you can enhance your computer's operation. There's more software, already written and immediately available, than you could use in a lifetime and software companies are constantly revising and updating their software.

Except for very unusual applications, ordinary users should never have to do any programming. There are off-the-shelf programs that can do anything you'd ever want to do with a computer. It's somewhat like the clothing business. Most people can buy what they need off the rack, but it's still nice to have a sewing machine at home.

To begin with, BASIC is something most people should have, and GW-BASIC from Microsoft is more or less the standard. Before MS-DOS 5.0, GW-BASIC was included with all versions of DOS. It has since been changed and is now called QBASIC. If you want to run any old BASIC program, you have to convert it to QBASIC, but many applications still use BASIC. Even if you aren't a programmer, it's simple enough to use to design a few special applications.

There are several categories of programs, such as a disk-operating systems, word processors, databases, spreadsheets, utilities, shells, communications, graphics, and computer-aided design (CAD). Depending on what you intend to use your computer for, there are hundreds of others for special needs.

Cost

Software is priced much like the products at foreign bazaars and flea markets. There are several tiers of pricing and, if you aren't savvy, you might end up paying three or four times more than what you should. Few other products can match software for its pricing structure.

In the first place, software is primarily an intellectual product. Sure, it takes some effort and time to type in the program code, but much of the programming is done with computer-aided software engineering (CASE). So how is the ultimate price determined? It seems likely that a group of upper-management VIPs get together and determined how much the market will bear.

Software can be more expensive than the hardware, but the prices vary from vendor to vendor. Quite often software will have an inflated list price that's about twice the discount price. For instance, one of the catalogs listed later in this chapter gives the price for Lotus SmartSuite 2.1 as $795, which they've discounted to $449.95. WordPerfect 6.0 has a list price of $495, but the discount price from this company is $289.95. The software vendor can say "Look at how much you're saving. We cut the price almost in half just for you." Most people are a bit wiser now, though, so many companies have stopped listing unreasonable prices and just list the "discount" price. If you look through the catalogs, you'll find that the discount price is the same, or within just a few dollars, in most of the catalogs. However, there are a few that have prices considerably lower. Order all the catalogs and do your own comparisons.

Software upgrades and surplus software

Quite often a new version of a program is released when there's still quite a lot of the older version that haven't been sold. The software business is somewhat like the soap business. Companies have to come out with a new and improved version every year. Quite often, however, the new and improved soap doesn't clean much better than the old does.

Most people never use all the capabilities of software, so in most cases the older version does all you need it to do. So if you don't mind having your friends point and laugh at you for using older software, then go ahead and order it. Surplus Software International (800-753-7877) publishes a catalog that sells hundreds of older software packages still in their original shrinkwrap.

Live upgrade discounts

There's another very important reason to buy older software. If you really must have the latest, Microsoft Word 6.0 is advertised in a discount software magazine for $299.95, but you can get it for about one third of this price by buying a live upgrade. A live upgrade is a program that updates your previous version of the same product. MicroWarehouse advertises that if you have any previous version of Word for Windows, you can trade it in for 6.0 and pay only $95.95 instead of $299.95. Well, you can buy Microsoft Word 2.0 for $49.95 from Surplus Software and then buy the upgrade for $95.95 for a total cost of $145.90, a savings of $154.05.

Competitive upgrade discounts

You can get an even better deal if you trade in an older copy of one of Microsoft Word's competitors, such as WordPerfect, Ami Pro, or WordStar. The cost of a competitive upgrade is $119.95, but you get a $30 rebate from Microsoft, which brings the price down to $89.95. The Surplus Software catalog offers earlier versions of all of these packages.

Microsoft isn't the only one who plays this game. WordPerfect 6.0 is listed for $289.95, but you can trade in any previous version of WordPerfect or any of the competition's older version and get WordPerfect for only $69.95.

You might call the software company and ask what qualifies as a competitive package to trade in for what you want to buy. There's usually quite a bit of latitude.

Proof of purchase

You need to have a proof of purchase for the previous or competitive version in order to get an upgrade, and it varies among the different software publishers. You might need to provide one or more of the following:
- The title page of the user manual.
- A copy of a sales receipt or invoice.
- The serial number of the software program.
- A photocopy of the original program disk.

If you're buying through mail order, you can mail or fax a copy of the required items. To verify the proof of purchase requirements, call several of the catalog companies listed later in this chapter and they'll send you their catalogs.

Shareware and public-domain software

Also, remember that there are excellent, free, public-domain programs that can do almost everything that high-cost commercial programs can do. Check your local bulletin board, user group, or the ads for public-domain software in most computer magazines. There are also some excellent shareware programs you can register for a nominal sum.

CD-ROMs

Here's another excellent reason to install a CD-ROM drive. DellWare, at 800-551-3355, offers CorelDraw 5.0 on three CD-ROMs for $475. If you want it on 3½-inch disks, it will cost you $609. For the $134 difference, you could buy a low-cost CD-ROM drive. Of course, you'd be better off spending a bit more for a better quality drive. CorelDraw 5.0 is discussed in more detail later. It's an excellent program that now includes the Ventura desktop publishing program.

Incidentally, you can buy CorelDraw 3.0 from DellWare for $136, then turn around and upgrade to CorelDraw 5.0 for $179.95 (the upgrade price listed in the current MicroWarehouse catalog, 800-367-7080). This means that instead of paying

$475, you could pay just $315.95 for CorelDraw 5.0, a savings of $159.05, or $293.05 when compared to the cost of the 3½-inch disks.

Again, please note that these prices are for comparison only. They'll be different, probably lower, by the time you read this.

Software Dispatch, at 800-289-8383, can send you a CD-ROM that has several software programs on it. Look at them and try them. If you find one that you want to buy, just give them a call and have your credit card ready. They'll give you a password you can use to unlock that particular program and copy it to your hard disk.

The software on the CD-ROM range from first-class programs, such as Claris-Works, to kids' games. ClarisWorks is an integrated word processor, database, spreadsheet, communications, graphics, and charting program. It's listed for $99.

Software catalogs

There are several direct-mail discount software companies. If you're undecided about what you need, call the companies for their catalogs. By all means check out the Surplus Software catalog. It could save you hundreds of dollars.

Many of the companies who send out catalogs sell both software and hardware, and the catalogs usually contain very good descriptions of what they sell, along with the current prices. Some of the companies, however, aren't exactly discount houses. You might find better prices at your local store or in some of the computer magazines.

Note that some of the catalogs don't have a date on them. Prices of software and hardware changes almost overnight. So if you don't have the latest catalog and you place an order, you might not be paying the latest price. Here are just a few of the available software catalogs:

MicroWarehouse	800-367-7080
Tiger Software	800-888-4437
PC Connections	800-800-5555
The PC Zone	800-258-2088
Global Software & Hardware	800-845-6225
JDR Microdevices	800-538-5000
DellWare	800-847-4051
PowerUp! Direct	800-851-2917
Computer Discount Warehouse (CDW)	800-330-4239
Desktop Publishing (DTP Direct)	800-325-5811
Elek-Tek	800-395-1000
J&R Computer World (mostly Mac)	800-221-8180
Insight CD-ROM	800-488-0002
Shareware Express	800-346-2842

Profit margins and markups

After considering the list, discount, and upgrade prices for the same product, you'll probably agree that there must be a very good profit margin on software.

There are currently over 150 million PCs in existence, about 90% of them using Microsoft's MS-DOS operating system. But Bill Gates isn't content with ruling the operating system world; he'd also like to be your single source for software. Microsoft has developed hundreds of other kinds of software, including Windows, Windows for Workgroups, Windows NT, Word for Windows, Excel, Microsoft Works, and Access. Microsoft has also taken over other companies, such as FoxPro, and bought into others, such as Stac Electronics. Very few of those 150 million computers aren't using one or more Microsoft programs. Until recently, all PCs sold by major vendors had to pay Microsoft a license fee, whether they had MS-DOS installed or not. This means that you could ask for a PC with Novell DR DOS, but the vendor still had to pay Microsoft a fee.

Many companies, such as Lotus, Borland, and Novell, think that perhaps Microsoft has become too big and too aggressive, and that they're stifling competition and innovation. The Justice department recently slapped Microsoft on the wrist and told them not to impose license fees on PCs that don't use MS-DOS.

Operating system software

DOS to a computer is like gasoline is to an automobile. Without it, the computer won't operate. DOS is an acronym for disk-operating system, but it does much more than just operate the disks. In recognition of this, IBM dropped the D when naming their operating system (OS/2).

If you're new to computers, DOS should be the first thing you learn. DOS has over 50 commands, but you'll probably never need to know more than 15 or 20 of them. DOS 6.2 has a very poor manual, but if you have trouble trying to remember a command, DOS 6.0 and higher come with very good on-disk help. At the prompt, just type HELP and the command name or HELP ?.

You can use any version of DOS on your computer. I don't know why anyone would want to, but you can even use MS-DOS version 1.0. Of course, you'd be severely limited in what you could do. I recommend that you buy the latest version of MS-DOS, DR DOS, or IBM DOS. If you're still using an older version, then you should upgrade to the latest version. It's not that expensive.

When you run a program, it's copied from the hard disk, or wherever it's stored, into your 640K of conventional RAM. Older versions of operating systems loaded the entire system, COMMAND.COM, CONFIG.SYS, buffers, drivers, and TSRs into conventional memory, often leaving less than 400K of free memory to load and run programs. Sometimes there wasn't enough memory left to load other programs. Later versions, however, load the operating system, TSRs, buffers, drivers, and others files in memory above 640K.

At one time, some operating system commands, such as FORMAT, DEL, ERASE, COPY, and RECOVER, could be disastrous when invoked. Later versions have now rectified most of those problems. In versions of MS-DOS before 5.0, for instance, if you used the RECOVER command, it would rename all the files on your disk into FILE0001.REC, FILE0002.REC, etc. The disk would no longer be bootable and crucial files might be garbled. The RECOVER command has been removed from newer versions of MS-DOS.

MS-DOS 6.0 and later also let you unformat a disk and easily undelete a file with the UNDELETE command. Before MS-DOS 6.0, the COPY command could cause problems. If you copied a file onto a disk that had another file with the same name, the original file would be replaced and gone forever. If you erase or delete a file, you can possibly recover it, but if it has been copied or written over, it's history. MS-DOS 6.0 and later versions ask if you want to replace the file before copying over it.

MS-DOS

Microsoft has come a long way since they developed MS-DOS 1.0 for IBM. MS-DOS has gone through a lot of changes and has consistently been improved, but it has always remained backward compatible. You can still read any software that was created for the earlier versions of DOS with the latest DOS version. Each new version has advantages over any previous version.

Gary Kildall and DR DOS

The DR stands for the Digital Research Corporation, founded by Gary Kildall. He developed the control program for microprocessors (CP/M) in 1973, which was the first operating system for personal computers. There's a story that IBM sent representatives to Gary's home in Monterey, California in 1980 to ask him to develop an operating system for their new PC. Gary wasn't home so the representatives got back on a plane and went to Redmond, Washington and talked to Bill Gates. The rest is history.

In my job at Lockheed, I learned and used CP/M. When we got our first IBM PCs with MS-DOS, I was amazed how easy it was to use. Most of the commands in MS-DOS were very similar to the CP/M commands I had already learned. MS-DOS was a direct descendent of CP/M. Later, IBM offered their PCs with the option of either MS-DOS or CP/M. It cost $40 extra for an MS-DOS machine and $240 extra for CP/M.

Gary set up Digital Research and developed several very good software products. A few years later, he developed DR DOS, which was completely compatible with MS-DOS. In addition, he included some functions and utilities that weren't in MS-DOS. Since MS-DOS had no competition, they hadn't done much to improve or upgrade MS-DOS, but when DR DOS was introduced, they immediately started releasing new and improved versions to match the improvements in DR DOS.

Unfortunately for DR DOS, there were already millions of MS-DOS users when DR DOS was introduced, and DR DOS didn't have the money or resources to be able to capture anymore than a small share of the market.

Digital Research has now merged with Novell, the network company, and is developing new and more powerful versions of DR DOS for both single users and high-end networks. Every time MS-DOS comes out with a new version, DR DOS comes out with an improved version. The competition between Novell, Microsoft, and IBM can only benefit users.

Besides the standard DOS commands in DR DOS, here are some of the other features you'll find:

Peer-to-peer networking Lets you share files, printers, and other resources with other computers.

Universal netware client Lets you easily access Netware networks.

Network management agents Supports the industry standard, simple network management protocol (SNMP) systems.

Multitasking Runs multiple DOS applications at the same time.

Stacker disk compression Both DR DOS and MS-DOS now includes Stacker data compression technology.

DR DOS has virus protection, a backup utility, password security, and a full on-screen manual for very easy help and information on any command or topic. It also includes a computer game, NetWars, which can be played on a stand-alone computer or a network.

There are several other excellent features in DR DOS, like fax, modem, and telephone support. Unlike some other companies who are now charging for support with a 900 number, Novell still offers a toll-free 800 number.

I met Gary at computer shows several times, and he impressed me as a real engineer's engineer. Gary Kildall died in July of 1994 at 52 years of age. He was an innovator and a true pioneer in the computer industry.

IBM PC DOS

IBM and Microsoft are no longer the good buddies they once were. The relationship started turning sour when Microsoft dragged their feet in developing OS/2 because they were so busy working on Windows. IBM finally had to take over and finish it.

IBM recently released PC-DOS 6.3, which they claim is not only smaller and faster than MS-DOS 6.2, but also has several features not found in MS-DOS 6.2. Like Microsoft, IBM went to outside companies and licensed some of the features. To match MS-DOS, they also used Central Point's (Symantec's) backup software and several other very useful utilities. One thing that seems strange is that many IBM computers sold through their companies are loaded with MS-DOS. I'm sure this was an oversight and will be corrected by the time you read this.

IBM has set up Ambra and several other companies that now compete with direct-mail companies like Dell and Gateway.

OS/2

OS/2 breaks the 640K barrier and can seamlessly address over 4 gigabytes of RAM. It can do true multitasking and run several programs at the same time. If one program crashes, it doesn't affect the other programs. It can run all DOS software and anything developed for Windows.

OS/2 also offers Adobe Type Manager (ATM), which allows scalable fonts for the screen and for printing. It has several other excellent utilities, and even a few games such as solitaire and chess if you have nothing else to do.

IBM claims that OS/2 runs Windows applications better than Windows under MS-DOS. For some time, IBM sold OS/2 with a copy of Windows, but they had to pay Microsoft a license fee for each copy. They now have OS/2 for Windows; It doesn't include Windows, but if you happen to have Windows it will work with it.

Many people have bought Macintosh computers because they're easy to use and learn. IBM's OS/2 is similar to the Macintosh in this respect. For some applications, it might even be easier to use than the Macintosh.

Windows

Windows isn't a true operating system because it runs "on top of" MS-DOS (or any DOS), but in most respects it acts like an operating system.

Windows 3.0 was one of the most phenomenal successes of all time, but it had some flaws. Microsoft revised 3.1 extensively and added several new features, including TrueType scalable fonts for the screen and for printing, which can give you a true what-you-see-is-what-you-get (WYSIWYG). One flaw in 3.0 was that it often caused the computer to hang up with unrecoverable application errors (UAEs). The whole system would then have to be rebooted. If you had work that wasn't saved to disk or you had two or more windows open, everything was lost.

The 3.1 version did away with the UAEs. If there's an error, the program will analyze it and give you several options. Dr. Watson, a diagnostic utility, might ask you to describe the details of what happened, then save these comments as a record, which can be useful to help Microsoft or other developers eliminate the problems. If the program does crash, only that operation goes down without affecting other open windows.

Windows was a giant step forward for the computer industry. Windows is a graphical user interface (GUI), and thousands of software programs have been developed to run under Windows. These programs all have to obey certain rules and specifications in order to run under Windows, which has made life a bit easier for software developers in some areas.

There are at least 500 different printers and printer models in existence, and every one must have its own software driver. At one time, word processor, databases, spreadsheets, and any other program that needed to be printed out had to provide separate printer drivers for every make and model. A software package might include three or four floppy disks for just the printer drivers. Windows now has all of the drivers, so software written for Windows doesn't have to include a lot of printer drivers. Windows also supplies the different drivers for mice.

Windows 3.1 has some built-in sound capabilities, but you'll need a sound board, such as Sound Blaster (408-986-1461), Pro AudioSpectrum (800-638-2807), Soundcard (213-685-5141), or MultiSound (717-843-6916) to use them. Windows also offers an object linking and embedding (OLE) utility, which allows data or graphics in one file to be imported and embedded in another.

There are too many other features in Windows to name. Besides, by the time you read this, Windows 95 (code name Chicago) should be out, and it will add even more features to make computing easier and more productive. These new features, functions, and utilities will make you wonder how you ever got along without them.

Windows for Workgroups

Microsoft Windows for Workgroups is an enhancement of Windows 3.1, with built-in networking capability that allows two or more computers to be tied together so they can share resources. If the computers are already on a network, it will actually enhance the network by adding the Windows graphical user interface.

Windows NT

Microsoft Windows 3.1 is a great system, but it's still 16 bits. All 386 and 486 computer systems have a 32-bit CPU architecture, which communicates with RAM over a 32-bit bus.

Microsoft began working on Windows NT (new technology) in 1988. It's a 32-bit operating system that has a lot of goodies. It's a scalable system, which means it's a multiprocessing operating system that allows a user to run the same applications on both single processor and multiprocessor computers. Windows NT conforms to the U.S. government's POSIX procurement standard. POSIX is an acronym for portable operating-system interface for UNIX. Windows NT is downward compatible and will operate on any ISA-type machine from a 386 up to a Pentium. When installed as server software on a network, it will operate the lowly XT and 286 as workstations. There are NT versions that will even work on the Macintosh, as well as reduced instruction-set (RISC), UNIX, and VMS computers.

Windows NT will run all previous applications written for DOS or Windows and, for new applications written to take advantage of the 32-bit system, there will be no 640K barrier. Windows NT can access up to 4GB of RAM, and a single application can address up to 2GB of memory. According to the Microsoft installation guide, Windows NT can access 17 billion gigabytes of disk storage. These kind of figures hurt my brain, and it's probably a bit more than I'll ever need in my small office. But as software keeps getting more user friendly, it also gets bigger. Windows NT software is compressed to fit on 21 1.44MB floppies. It's also distributed on a CD-ROM. A hard disk with 80MB of free disk space is necessary for installation, 20MB of which is set aside for virtual memory. A minimum of 8MB of RAM is required, but 12MB is recommended.

Windows 3.1 runs on top of a DOS, but Windows NT is an actual operating system, so you don't need MS-DOS, PC DOS, OS/2, or DR DOS in order to run it. It can run existing DOS and Windows applications all by itself.

Microsoft is currently doing an interim revision of Windows NT, the code name of which is Daytona. It was supposed to have been available in the first half of 1994, but it didn't make it. It should be available by the time you read this. The full revision is code-named Cairo and is scheduled to be finished sometime in 1995. For information on Windows and related products, call Microsoft at 206-882-8080.

DESQview

This is similar to Windows in that it runs on top of DOS. It allows multitasking and multiple users; you can have up to 50 programs running at the same time and have as many as 250 windows open. It runs all DOS software, and is simple to learn and use.

DESQview is one of the better programs for managing memory. It can load memory-resident software (TSRs) into memory above 640K, and seems to be able to find little niches and spaces above 640K that most other memory managers can't find or use. Now that MS-DOS has MemMaker, people don't need the Quarterdeck memory managers anymore, so they're trying to develop other products. For information on DESQview, call Quarterdeck Office Systems at 310-392-9851.

Cost of OS software

When you buy a new computer, the operating system software is usually included with the overall price. If you have an older version and you want to upgrade, it's currently $77 for IBM PC DOS 6.3, $77.95 for MS-DOS 6.22, and $69.95 for Novell DOS 7.0. These prices are listed for comparison only and will probably be different from different vendors. There will probably also be newer versions available soon.

Word processors

The most common of all software is word processing. There are literally dozens of word-processing packages, each one slightly different than the others. It amazes me that they can find so many different ways to do the same thing. All the major word-processing programs come with a spelling checker and a thesaurus, which can be very handy. They usually also include several other utilities, such as a calculator, communications programs for your modem, outline maker, and print merge.

WordStar

I use WordStar. I'm almost ashamed to admit it because I'm afraid people will laugh at me behind my back. At one time, WordStar was the premier word processor—number one in its field—but it has lost a lot of its luster and has been displaced by others, such as WordPerfect and Microsoft Word.

I started off with WordStar 3.0 on my little CP/M Morrow, with a hefty 64K of memory and two 140K single-sided disk drives. It took me some time to learn it, but I've been using it for so long now that it's like second nature. I've tried several other word processors and found that most of them would require almost as much time to learn as WordStar did originally. Learning to use a new word processor is almost like learning a new language, and it's a proven fact that the older you get the more difficult it is to learn a new language. I don't have a lot of free time and WordStar does all I need. In fact, WordStar, like most other programs, has a lot of utilities and functions that I've never used. I have several other word processors I use once in a while because I have to write about them, but when I write about them I usually use WordStar to do it. WordStar has both DOS and Windows versions.

Most word processors come with a dictionary and thesaurus, but they're often quite limited. WordStar publishes the up-to-date and very comprehensive *American Heritage Dictionary, 3rd edition* on ten high-density disks. The installation requires about 15MB of disk space and is designed to work under Windows. WordStar also has Roget's II thesaurus, which contains over 500,000 synonyms. You can use Word Hunter to find words you don't know how to spell or can't quite recall. WordStar also publishes Correct Quotes and several other writing aids.

For information on WordStar, call WordStar International at either 800-227-5609 or 800-843-2204. WordStar also has an educational division (800-543-8188) that offers an excellent discount to schools for both site licenses and student purchases.

WordPerfect

This is one of the hottest selling word processors, so it must be doing something right. One thing they were doing right was providing free, unlimited, toll-free support, but this has now ended.

WordPerfect has simplified printer installation and offers many desktop-publishing functions. With WordPerfect, you can make columns, import graphics, and select fonts by their proper names. WordPerfect 6.0 is probably their last upgrade for DOS. They'll be concentrating on WordPerfect for Windows for future upgrades and improvements.

WordPerfect also has several other software products, such as WordPerfect Presentation, WordPerfect Office (for e-mail and scheduling), DataPerfect (a database), and WordPerfect Works (an integrated software package).

WordPerfect has now merged with Novell, which will make it a bit easier for them to compete with Microsoft Word. For information on WordPerfect, call WordPerfect Corporation at 800-451-5151.

Microsoft Word for Windows

Microsoft Word for Windows lets you take full advantage of all the features and utilities of Windows. It's one of the best-selling programs in the country. If you've previously learned a different word processor, such as WordPerfect, Word for Windows can let you use WordPerfect commands.

Besides an excellent word processor, Word for Windows does just about everything necessary for desktop publishing, reports, charts, drawings, and presentations. It does columns, imports graphics, and imports data from databases, spreadsheets, and other files. It even has an automatic corrector, for people like me who constantly type *teh* instead of *the*. It has many more features than I would ever use, even if I could learn them all.

For information on Word for Windows, call Microsoft Corporation at 206-882-8080.

PC-Write

PC-Write 4.0 is the least expensive of all the word processors. It's shareware, so if you get a copy from another user, they ask for a $16 donation. Full registration with manual and technical support is $89. It's easy to learn and is an excellent personal word processor. PC-Write is available from Quicksoft Inc., at 206-282-0452.

There are many other good word processors. Look for ads and reviews in computer magazines.

Grammar checkers

Even if you're the most intelligent person alive, you might not be able to write a simple intelligible sentence. There are several grammar-checking programs that can work with most of the word processors. They can analyze your writing and suggest ways to improve it. A couple of these programs are Right Writer from Que Corporation, at 800-992-0244, and Grammatik from Reference Software, at 800-872-9933.

Database programs

Database packages are very useful for business purposes. They allow you to manage a large amount of information: storing it, searching it, sorting it, doing calculations, and making up reports.

There are currently almost as many database programs as there are word processors. Some of them allow the interchange of data from one program to another. There's a strong effort in the industry to establish some standards under the structured query language (SQL) standard. Several of the larger companies have announced their support for this standard.

The average price for better-known database packages is almost twice that for word processors.

dBASE 5.0

dBASE II was one of the first database programs for the personal computer, and it has since gone through several revisions and improvements. It's now up to dBASE 5.0 for both DOS and Windows. It's a very powerful program, with hundreds of features. Previous versions were highly structured and could be a bit difficult to learn, but the new Windows version is very easy to use; in many cases, all you have to do is just point and click. You can create forms and design reports quickly and easily. It also has excellent built-in help and tutorials.

dBASE 5.0 is downward compatible, so the 7 million users who have databases generated by the older versions can still use their old data. The MicroWarehouse catalog offers dBASE 5.0 at a list price of $339.95, or $189.95 with an upgrade trade-in.

dBASE is available from Borland International, at 408-438-8400. Philippe Kahn is the founder and president of Borland. He's young, about the same age as Bill Gates, Steve Jobs, and several of the other young computer pioneers. He was penniless when he came to this country from Belgium. His first product was Sidekick, then Turbo Pascal, then pretty soon dozens of products.

askSam

This funny-looking name is an acronym for access knowledge via stored-access method. It's a free-form, text-oriented, database-management system, and works very much like a word processor. In fact, if you can use a word processor you'll have no trouble using askSam. Data can be typed in randomly, then sorted and accessed. Data can also be entered in a structured format for greater organization. It's not quite as powerful as dBASE 5 or Paradox, but it's much easier to learn and use. It's also much less expensive. It's ideal for personal use and for many business needs.

The Windows version even has a spell checker and hyperlink ability. Hyperlinks connect related parts of a document or database, or even different documents or reports.

There's an askSam discount program for students. Students can buy the $395 program for only $99 when the order is placed by an instructor. Any instructor who places an order for 10 or more copies will get a free copy. Upgrades from a previous version are available for $79.95. For information on this unusual database program, contact Seaside Software at 800-327-5726.

FoxPro

FoxPro is very easy to use. It can be controlled by a mouse or the keyboard, and has several different windows. The View Window is the master control panel you use to create databases, open files, browse, set options, and other functions. You don't have to be a programmer to type commands and operate FoxPro. The Browse Window lets you view, edit, append, or delete files. It also has memo fields, a built-in editor, a macro utility, extensive context-sensitive help, and much more. FoxPro is now a part of Microsoft Corporation, at 206-882-8080.

Paradox 4.5

Paradox is fairly easy to learn and use, and is fast and powerful. It's designed for both beginners and expert users. It's a full-featured relational database that can be used on a single PC or network. The main menu has functions like View, Ask, Report, Create, Modify, Image, Forms, Tools, Scripts, and Help. Choosing one of these items brings up options associated with that item. Extensive use is made of the function keys. There are Paradox versions for both DOS and Windows. Paradox also has a very powerful programming language, PAL. Experienced programmers can easily design special applications. Paradox is available from Borland International, at 408-438-5300.

Spreadsheet programs

Spreadsheets are primarily number crunchers. They have a matrix of cells where you can enter data. Data in a particular cell can be acted on by formulas and mathematical equations. If the data in a cell that's acted on affects other cells, recalculations are performed. Several tax-preparation programs use a simple spreadsheet. The income and all the deductions are entered in cells and, if you discover an additional deduction, you can easily enter it and the program will automatically recalculate the rest of the equations.

In business, spreadsheets are essential for inventory, expenses, accounting, forecasting, and dozens of other important areas. There are a large number of spreadsheet programs. Here are just a few:

Lotus 1-2-3

Lotus was one of the first spreadsheets. The current version is 4.01 for Windows, which is a spreadsheet, database, and graphics package all in one. It's still one of the most powerful and popular spreadsheets.

The discount price listed in several catalogs is $309.95, and the upgrade price is $95.95. Any previous version of 1-2-3 can be used for a live upgrade. Competitive spreadsheets such as Excel, Quattro, Quattro Pro, and SuperCalc qualify for a competitive upgrade. Check through any of the software catalogs or call Lotus Development at 617-577-8500.

Microsoft Excel

Microsoft Excel 5.0 is a very powerful spreadsheet program, with pull-down menus, windows, and dozens of features. You can even use it as a database. It has a long list of other features. Excel is one of the products that makes up Microsoft Office.

Several catalogs have a discount price for Excel of $299.95. A live upgrade is only $89.95 and a competitive upgrade is $119.95. Check the catalogs or call Microsoft at 206-882-8080.

Quattro Pro

The Quattro Pro spreadsheet looks very much like Lotus 1-2-3, but it has better graphics capabilities for charts, calculates faster, has pull-down menus, can print sideways, and has several other features not found in Lotus 1-2-3. It's fully compatible with Lotus 1-2-3 spreadsheet files. It's very easy to learn and offers an interactive tutorial.

Quattro Pro is one of the least expensive of the major spreadsheets. The list price of the package is $49.95. A live upgrade is listed in the Global catalog (800-845-6225) for $39.95, plus you'll get a $10 rebate from Borland. Or you can get a $20 rebate from Borland for any competitive upgrade. It's amazing. You can buy a major spreadsheet that's equivalent or better than Lotus or Excel for as little as $29.95. You probably couldn't register a shareware spreadsheet for that price. Check the catalogs or call Borland International at 408-438-8400.

There are many other spreadsheet programs. Check the ads and reviews in computer magazines.

Suites

Several companies bundle several software packages together as a suite. Suites usually have a word processor, database, spreadsheet, and perhaps one or two other packages. The software in the suite is integrated so it works together, and there are import/export capabilities for the packages. A suite usually costs much less than buying each package separately. Here are just a few of the more popular suites:

Microsoft Office

Microsoft Office has several different versions. One version includes Microsoft Word 6.0 for word processing, Excel 5.0 for spreadsheets, PowerPoint for presentations, and Mail for e-mail and fax systems. Another version includes all of these plus Access 2.0 for databases.

Office for Windows

Borland and WordPerfect teamed up to put together a suite of applications. Office for Windows has WordPerfect 6.0 for Windows for word processing, Quattro Pro for spreadsheets, and Paradox as a database application.

Lotus SmartSuite

Lotus SmartSuite includes AMI Pro for word processing, Lotus 1-2-3 for Windows for spreadsheets, Lotus Approach for databases, Lotus Organizer (a personal information manager), and Freelance Graphics for creating presentations.

CorelDraw 5

Corel Corporation has now acquired Ventura Publisher from Xerox Corporation, one of the premier desktop-publishing packages. Ventura will be sold separately, or you can purchase a version that contains several of Corel's graphics and other features as CorelDraw 5. This package includes over 22,000 clip-art images, 825 fonts, and 100 royalty-free photos on CD-ROM. Graphics, text, and other materials can be imported under the Windows OLE and placed in Ventura files.

Microsoft Works

Microsoft Works could be called a poor man's suite. It has word processing, spreadsheet, and database features, plus communications, charting, and drawing, all in one package. A discount house is offering this software package for $79.95. The same discount house offers the previously discussed suites from $279 to $559, so you know the Microsoft Works package can't be nearly as powerful or have as many features as the full-featured suites.

Depending on what you want to do, however, Microsoft Works might be all you need. Many people never come close to using all the features and functions of high-powered software packages.

Phoenix Ultimate Utilities Suite

Phoenix, at 800-452-0120, was one of the first companies to make a legitimate clone of the IBM BIOS, which allowed the clone makers to manufacture IBM-compatible PCs. Phoenix still designs BIOS chips, but they've also diversified into the software business. They don't have that many software packages, but they wanted to market a suite. So they went to four other companies and purchased the rights to their software to make up a suite of five "ultimate utilities" for Windows. Here are the excellent and useful utilities:

Eclipse Find from Phoenix

Eclipse Find is a text-retrieval program that lets you find and view files in less than three seconds. You can view, archive, copy text to the clipboard, or print.

Dashboard from Hewlett-Packard

Dashboard is similar to the dashboard of an automobile. You can set up favorite icons, just like presetting the stations in your car radio. You can work with several screens or switch or launch any one of them. It has several other very useful and time-saving features.

Folderbolt from Kent Marsh

Folderbolt is a security utility that offers several options. You can set full password protection or mark files as read-only. You can also prevent access, copying, alteration, and deletion of files.

Uninstaller from MicroHelp

Every time you install a Windows program, it loads bits and pieces of the files in many nooks and crannies. If you decide to delete the file, you might leave several of the bits and pieces behind. Every time you run Windows from then on, you could get error messages. Uninstaller will search your system, find all the bits and pieces that were left behind, and delete them. This program alone is worth the price of the package.

Uninstaller can also be purchased as a stand-alone package. It's discussed in more detail later in the chapter.

SuperQueue from Zenographics

When printing a long document, SuperQueue takes over and feeds the document to a special file on disk. It then returns control to you and feeds the file to the printer in the background. It allows you to batch-print several documents, handling them while you go about your business.

Utilities

Utilities are essential tools that you can use to unerase a file, detect bad sectors on and unfragment a hard disk, diagnose problems, sort files, and many other things. Norton Utilities was the first, and is still foremost, in the utility department.

SpinRite and Disk Technician are excellent hard disk tools for defragmenting and detecting potential bad sectors on a hard disk. They're essential tools for hard disk preventive maintenance.

Norton Utilities

This is a program that everyone should have. It has several excellent utilities that can save you time and money. Norton Disk Doctor (NDD) can automatically repair disk problems, both hard and floppy. Norton Disk Editor lets you explore and repair sectors of a hard disk. File Fix lets you repair data files. The Unerase command is great for recovering accidentally erased files (it's so useful that Microsoft now includes a similar utility in MS-DOS 6.0 and later versions). Norton also has Norton Commander, a shell program, and Norton Backup, a very good hard disk backup program. Norton Backup is available for both DOS and Windows.

The latest version of Norton Utilities is 8.0. It improves many of the old standard features and adds several new ones, including several Windows utilities that can help in diagnosing, troubleshooting, and repairing Windows problems.

When you install it, you're given the option to have your AUTOEXEC.BAT file changed. If you agree, Norton will automatically check all your hard drives for cross-linked files, fix any corrupted files, and ask if you want to make out a report. It will then make a mirror image of the FAT and store it in a second location. If the primary

FAT is damaged, you'll still be able to access your data from the second FAT. For information on Norton Utilities, contact Symantec at 408-253-9600 or 800-441-7234.

PC Tools Pro

This is an excellent program that just about does it all. It has data recovery, hard disk backup, and antivirus utilities, a DOS shell, a disk manager, and lots more. This program is available from Central Point Software, at 503-690-8090.

SpinRite 3.1

SpinRite 3.1 has several new features that weren't in the original versions. It performs the most rigorous hard disk tests of any software. It can detect any marginal areas and move the data to a safe area. SpinRite can maximize hard disk performance and prevent hard disk problems before they happen.

Steve Gibson, the developer of SpinRite, writes a very interesting weekly column for *InfoWorld*. Contact Gibson Research, at 714-362-8800.

Disk Technician Gold

Disk Technician, at 619-274-5000, does essentially the same type of tests that SpinRite does, but not quite as thoroughly. Disk Technician also has several automatic features and can now detect most viruses. It will work in the background to detect any errors as they happen when writing to a hard disk.

CheckIt PRO: Analyst

CheckIt PRO: Analyst for Windows, from TouchStone Software Corporation (714-969-7746), quickly checks and reports on the configuration of a computer, the type of CPU, the amount of memory, number of installed drives, and types of peripherals. It runs diagnostic tests of the installed items and can do performance benchmark tests.

Directory and disk management programs

There are dozens of disk management programs that help you keep track of files and data on the hard disk. With these programs, you can find, rename, view, sort, copy, and delete files. They can save an enormous amount of time and make life a lot simpler.

XTreePro Gold and XTree for Windows

XTree, from XTree at 805-541-0604, was one of the first and is still one of the best disk management programs available. I use it to view my files and delete unnecessary ones. I also use it to copy and back up files from one disk or directory to another. With XTree, you can order your files either chronologically or alphabetically. I often look at the date stamp so I know which files are the latest. It also has many other features. I don't know how anyone can get along without XTree.

Norton Commander

Norton Commander, from Symantec Corporation at 800-441-7234, is a shell program that offers speed and convenience for file management, file viewing, PC-to-PC file transfer, and even electronic mail. It lets you view many different database, spreadsheet, and word-processing programs, as well as graphics and compressed files. It lets you edit, copy, rename, move, and delete files. It's very easy to learn and use.

Computer-aided design (CAD) programs

Most high-end CAD programs require very good, high-resolution monitors and powerful computers. The Pentium is an ideal computer for computer-aided design.

AutoCAD

AutoCAD, from Autodesk, is a complex, high-end design program with an abundance of capabilities and functions, and it's also rather expensive, at about $3,000. Autodesk (415-332-2344) is the IBM of the CAD world and has more or less established the standard for the many clones that have followed.

Generic CADD

Autodesk has several modules and other programs that cost less than the full-blown AutoCAD. One of them is Generic CADD 6.0. Call 800-228-601, extension 803.

Home Series

Autodesk offers a set of five low-cost programs they call the Home Series. They are Home, Kitchen, Bathroom, Deck, and Landscape. You don't have to be an architect to design an up-to-date kitchen, bathroom, or deck, or plan your landscape. Each of the five programs are listed at $59.95. The programs come with a library of professional symbols for doors, outlets, furniture, fixtures, and appliances that you can import and place in your drawing. The program tracks the materials specified in your drawing and automatically creates a shopping list.

3D PLAN

Autodesk has recently added 3D Plan, a program that lets you work with any of the plans created in Home, Kitchen, Bathroom, Deck, or Landscape in three dimensions. Surfaces are shaded to add a realistic appearance.

I recommend these programs if you're planning to design your own home or do any remodeling on an older home. They can save you hours of time and a lot of money.

DesignCAD 2D and DesignCAD 3D

These CAD programs will do just about everything AutoCAD will, at a lesser cost. DesignCAD 3D allows you to make three-dimensional drawings. These programs are available from American Small Business Computers, at 918-825-4844. Several other companies offer CAD software. Check the computer magazines.

Miscellaneous software

There are many programs for things such as accounting, statistics, finance, graphics, and many other applications. Some are very expensive and some are very reasonable.

CorelDraw

CorelDraw can be used for drawing, illustration, page layout, charting, animation, desktop publishing, and presentations. It has word processing, OCR, over 5,000 drag-and-drop symbols and shapes, over 18,000 clip-art images, over 750 fonts, and many other features and utilities. This is all in CorelDraw version 3. It comes on a 600MB CD-ROM. They've also added more fonts, features, and functions to Corel-Draw and released it as CorelDraw 4. It comes on two CD-ROMs. Corel has several other excellent software packages. Call them for a brochure at 613-728-3733.

CorelSCSI

CorelSCSI has software and several SCSI drivers that work with most major SCSI host adapters, such as Future Domain, Ultrastor, and Adaptec. It also has SitBack, a software program for unattended backup, Corel tape-backup software, and several other programs and utilities.

Stacker

Stacker, from Stac Electronics at 619-431-7474, is an excellent software compression program. Software programs keep getting bigger and bigger. No matter how big your hard drive is, it never seems to have enough empty space. Most software has a lot of empty space in between the 0s and 1s. Some time ago engineers figured out how to compress the software. Software compression is somewhat like taking all the text on this line and pushing it together so there's no space between the words. There are also special symbols for more frequently used letters, such as *e* and *s*. The software can have a 2:1 or even higher compression ratio.

Software compression has been around for some time. BBSs have been using it for several years, but it was quite a bit of trouble to compress and decompress the data. A few years ago, Stac Electronics came up with a system that compressed and decompressed seamlessly and automatically. It's great. It can double your disk storage. It is just like adding another hard disk, except that it is considerably less expensive and less trouble to install.

When Stacker was first introduced, many people were afraid that it might destroy their precious data. I was a bit leery myself when I first started using it. I used it for files that weren't very important, or for data that I had backed up on floppy disks. I've now been using Stacker compression software for almost five years. I've installed it on several hard disks, and I haven't had any problems whatsoever.

You can also use Stacker data compression on floppy disks. You can use it to store 2.88MB on a 1.44MB floppy, and even configure it so it can be used on any other system, even one that doesn't have Stacker.

MS-DOS 6.2 DoubleSpace

With the release of MS-DOS 6.0 Microsoft finally acknowledged the value of data compression. MS-DOS 6.0 has compression utility, DoubleSpace, that let you store up to twice as much data on your hard disk. I was one of the beta testers for MS-DOS 6.0, so I was duty bound to try it. Unfortunately, a lot of people (including myself) lost data. Microsoft wouldn't admit there were any problems with the DoubleSpace utility, but they quickly released MS-DOS 6.2 which fixed the bugs. I am using it on a couple of my hard drives and haven't had any problems.

You probably heard that Stac Electronics sued Microsoft and won for patent infringement because of DoubleSpace. Microsoft bought a large percentage of Stac, so they can now legally use Stacker code as part of the new compression utility in MS-DOS 6.22.

Screen Craze

Screen Craze is three packages in one. It contains a screen saver, an animated wallpaper, and an editor that allows you to create your own animated movies to use with the screen saver and animated wallpaper.

Screen savers help you avoid burning images into your monitor. You can use one of the included movies or create your own using the editor. It also prevents information from being accessed from your screen when you aren't at your computer.

The animated wallpaper option lets you liven up your Windows desktop by running a movie in the background. The option is disengaged when you use a full-screen (maximized) application.

The Screen Craze editor lets you create your own animated movies, incorporating the supplied backgrounds, actors, and sounds to customize your screen saver and animated wallpaper. You can also create messages to leave on your screen, or bring in your own graphic files to give a personal feel to your movie. Importing a graphic of your company logo for use as a screen saver or animated wallpaper can give your office a professional corporate look. Screen Craze is available from Gold Disk, at 408-982-0200.

Uninstaller for Windows

When a program for Windows is installed on your computer, it copies files into several different areas. If you decide later that you don't want that application, you can use DOS to delete the program, but you won't delete all references to the program. Every time you load Windows, it might hunt for that program and tell you it can't find it. Even some demo programs load themselves into several areas that are difficult to clean out. Use the DOS editor and look at the WIN.INI. You might find references there to programs that you erased months ago. These leftover bits and pieces can clutter up your disk considerably.

Uninstaller from MicroHelp can track down all the different parts of a Windows program and delete them. Even if you're a Windows pro, Uninstaller can save you time. For information on this program, call MicroHelp, Inc. at 404-516-0899.

Quest multimedia authoring system

The Quest multimedia authoring system, from Allen Communication at 801-537-7800, is a software tool for developing professional-quality multimedia courseware. It allows training professionals at every level of computer skill and knowledge to create effective computer-based training.

Quest is a two-level authoring system that includes both interactive authoring capability and an authoring language. The interactive authoring program (called AUTHOR) uses dialogue boxes or prompt windows to interface with the user. It requires no programing experience.

Computer-managed instruction (CMI) functions are available in Quest. These functions allow you to control access to the Quest software with a log-on process that restricts access to registered users. You can further control access to courseware by assigning courses to students. You can record student performance and course data, and generate reports to help evaluate students and courses.

Utility programs provide a variety of functions to enhance courseware and aid courseware maintenance. They include editors to create and maintain character fonts, shape libraries, group libraries, etc., and other programs to print lessons, generate flow diagrams, globally replace objects in lessons, and capture screen images. In addition, the Inspect Spelling program helps you find and correct spelling problems in a frame or a complete lesson.

LIPS for Windows

LIPS for Windows lets you add verbal reminders to your documents, spreadsheets, and graphics. It can even be used to teach a foreign language. It works with standard WAV files and version 3.1 Windows-compatible sound cards. No programming skills are required. LIPS is available from LIPS Software Inc., at 516-271-6500.

WinMaster

WinMaster for Windows is a launch program that gives you one-click access to your programs and files. It also gives you dynamic, graphic information on system performance and the state of your disk drives. It features drive optimization, archiving, and management. Contact PC-Kwik Corporation at 503-644-5644 for more information.

Power Pak

Power Pak is a caching program that can accelerate your computer's effective speed by three to nine times. Disks can run up to 20 times faster, screens three times faster, keyboards up to 14 times faster, and printing up to 20 times faster. It also speeds up CD-ROM transfer. Power Pak is available from PC-Kwik Corporation, at 503-644-5644.

StreetSmart

StreetSmart, from Charles Schwab at 800-334-4455, lets you use your computer and modem to trade stocks, options, mutual funds, and bonds; research Dow Jones

News and Dow Jones databases, use MarketScope for S&P databases and news, stock ratings, and buy/sell recommendations; and use company reports to do comprehensive research on earnings and financials. You can create your own performance graphs, import and export crucial financial data, and customize your portfolio reports. If you have any interest in the stock market, then you should have a copy of StreetSmart.

Money Counts

This is a very inexpensive program that can be used at home or in a small business. With it you can set up a budget, keep track of all your expenses, balance your checkbook, and several other functions. The cost is $40. This program is published by Parsons Technology, at 800-223-6925.

It's Legal

This program helps you create wills, leases, promissory notes, and other legal documents. It's also published by Parsons Technology.

The Random House Encyclopedia

This is an entire encyclopedia on disk. You can use it to find any subject very quickly. This one is available from Microlytics, at 716-248-9150.

ACT!

This program lets you keep track of business contacts, schedules, business expenses, reports, and about 30 other features. Contact Software was one of the first companies to develop this type of software and they're still in the forefront of contact programs. For more information on ACT!, call Contact Software at 800-228-9228.

Maximizer for Windows

This is another contact program that lets you keep track of people and organizations. It's a powerful database you can use for fax support and to automatically dial a client in the database, search, keep histories, create letters, and provide direct mailing. It has several other very good features that should appeal to most businesses. Call 604-229-2121.

Form Express

Most businesses have dozens of forms that must be filled out. Quite often, the information must then be transferred to a computer. Forms Express lets you easily design and fill in almost any kind of form on a computer and print it out. This program is available from Forms Express, at 415-382-6600.

Que's Computer User's Dictionary

There are thousands of computer terms. One of the better ways to find out what most of them mean is to get an electronic edition of Que's Computer User's Dictionary, which runs under Windows. You can enter a partial word and it will search for it. It provides links for related topics. For more information on this electronic computer dictionary, contact Que Software at 800-992-0244.

Stedman's Medical Dictionary for WordPerfect

This medical dictionary is ideal for anyone who writes about medical or health-related fields. It's a good tool for doctors and nurses, medical transcriptionists, medical records personnel, hospital administrators, attorneys specializing in medical cases, and health-care insurance professionals. It has over 40,000 medical definitions and allows you to scroll through, browse, and compare words to choose the best one. It checks for correct usage and is a spell checker. It also has a listing of 20,000 drugs. This dictionary would be good for anyone who wanted to check the meaning of a health term or look up the symptoms of a disease. The program is available from Stedman's Software, at 800-527-5597.

PharmAssist

PharmAssist, The Family Guide to Health and Medicine, from Software Marketing at 602-893-3377, gives details on drugs, corresponding brand names and generic names of drugs, drug interactions, drug application, first-aid information, signs of drug abuse, and abuse hotlines. It contains hundreds of full-color illustrations of different pills, capsules, tablets, and much more. It's a great reference for the world of health care and drugs.

WillMaker

WillMaker, from Nolo Press at 415-549-1976, is a low-cost program that can help you create a will. Everyone should have a will, no matter what age. Many people put it off because they don't want to take the time nor pay a lawyer a large fee. This inexpensive software can help you create a legal will.

Software training

Most software manuals are very poorly written. You can usually tell how bad the manuals are by the number of books written telling you how to use the software. Microsoft is the largest software publisher in the world. They also have a very large book-publishing company, Microsoft Press, which publishes hundreds of books each year to help people learn to use their software. A cynical person might suspect that Microsoft publishes poor manuals so they can sell more books.

Several companies conduct training classes and seminars where you can learn some of the more popular software. If you pay $500 or $600 for a software package, you shouldn't have to spend an additional $500 or $600 to learn how to use it. Plus, many of the seminars are single-day cram courses. I can't learn enough in one day to justify the cost of some of them.

One of the better ways to learn software is by using videotapes. ViaGrafix, at 800-842-4723, has about 200 different videotape courses. They have tapes on all the most popular software and even some that's not so popular—they even have interactive videotapes. You should be able to find a tape for almost any program imaginable. They even have instructional tapes on networking, telecommunications, programming, and much more. You can view the tapes at your leisure and learn at your own pace. Call them for a catalog.

Software for kids

One of the big reasons to have a home computer is for the kids. In today's society, children need all the help they can get in order to make it as an adult. There are thousands of software programs—commercial, shareware, and public domain—that have been developed for children. Most software catalogs listed in this chapter and in chapter 19 have children's software listings.

A good example of a children's educational program is the Smithsonian Institution Dinosaur Museum from the Software Marketing Corporation, at 602-893-2042. Many of the programs like this come on CD-ROM. This one also comes on five 1.44MB floppies. The program is in 3-D, so a pair of plastic 3-D video glasses come with it.

Summary

I can't possibly mention all the fantastic software that's available. There are thousands and thousands of ready-made software programs that allow you to do almost anything with your computer. Look through any computer magazine for the reviews and ads. You should be able to find programs for almost any application.

18
CHAPTER

Some applications

Now that you've upgraded your computer, there are many, many ways to make it more useful and get more out of it. I can't possibly list them all, but here are just a few ways to do so.

Home office

SOHO, a new acronym meaning small office, home office, has recently been created. Many businesses can be operated from home. Several advantages in having a home office are no commuting, no high office rent, being able to take care of young children at the same time, and setting your own hours. More and more businesses are allowing their employees to work from home and telecommute. There are some jobs that can be done from home as easily as at a big office.

Several computer programs let you connect your home computer to an office computer. Almost any communications software, such as CrossTalk, ProComm, or QModem, will let you access another computer.

I commuted back and forth to work for many years, and I hated fighting traffic and sitting in traffic jams. I also worried that I might become one of the 55,000 annual traffic fatalities. I would have taken a large pay cut if I could have stayed home and worked.

Deductions

If you have a home office for a business, you might be able to deduct part of the cost of your computer from your income taxes. You might even be able to deduct a portion of your rent, telephone bills, and other home expenses that are also legitimate business expenses.

I can't give you all of the IRS rules for a home office, but there are several deductions available if you use a portion of your home exclusively and regularly to operate your business. These deductions might include portions of your computer, rent, telephone bills, real estate taxes, mortgage interest, operating expenses (such as home insurance premiums and utility costs), and depreciation allocated to the area used for business. You might even be able to deduct a portion of home-repair expenses.

Before you make any deductions, however, I recommend that you buy the latest tax books and consult with the IRS or a tax expert. There are many, many rules and regulations, and they change frequently. For more information, call the IRS and ask for publication #587, "Business Use of Your Home." Look in your telephone directory for the local or 800 number for the IRS.

Preparing your own taxes

Congress and the IRS change the tax rules every year, and every year they become more complicated. It's almost impossible for the ordinary person to be aware of and understand all the rules and regulations. Some of the rules are even difficult for the IRS.

If a person works at a single job and has a single source of income, the forms are fairly simple, but if you have several sources of income or a small business, preparing your taxes can be a nightmare. It's an impossible task for many people, so they hire a tax preparer. Many tax preparers charge from $50 to over $100 dollars an hour.

If you have any inclination for accounting and tax preparation, then you might consider taking a course. Many community colleges offer courses in accounting, but H & R Block is probably the best place to learn tax preparation. They conduct several classes throughout the year in various locations.

It's not absolutely necessary to be an accountant in order to prepare your taxes, but it helps. Another reason to learn accounting is that many small businesses can't afford to hire full-time accountants. Many of them hire accountants on a part-time basis to keep their books and accounts in order.

There are several good software programs to use for accounting. The ACCPAC accounting package from Computer Associates Company, at 516-324-5224, is a very good accounting program for both small and larger businesses. Call them for brochures. Another low-cost accounting package is Peachtree Accounting for Windows. This program is available from most software companies or from PC Zone mail-order, at 800-258-2088. Other accounting packages available from PC Zone are StageSoft Accounting for Small Business and One-Write Plus Accounting. Call PC Zone for a current catalog. There are several other software catalogs listed in chapter 19.

Tax programs

If you have a computer, it might not be necessary to pay a tax preparer to do your taxes. There are several tax programs that can do the job for you. Unless you have a very complicated income, it should be fairly quick and easy. In many cases, the cost of the program will be less than the cost of having a tax preparer do your taxes.

Besides doing your own taxes, most of these programs let you set up files and do other people's taxes. Many software companies offer tax-preparation programs for professional tax businesses, but usually at a much higher price.

All the programs operate much like a spreadsheet in that the forms, schedules, and worksheets are linked together. When you enter data at one place, other affected data is automatically updated. Most of the programs have a built-in calculator so you can do calculations before entering figures. Many of them allow "what if" calculations to show what your return would look like with various inputs. Most of the companies also have software for state income taxes, and allow you to print out acceptable IRS forms. Here are brief reviews of some of the better-known programs:

Andrew Tobias's TaxCut

This program will handle most of the average returns. It can be interfaced with Andrew Tobias's Managing Your Money, which is an excellent personal financial program. The program is available from Meca Ventures (203-222-9150) at the following address:

Meca Ventures
325 Riverside Ave.
Westport, CT 06880

TurboTax

TurboTax is unique because it offers modules for 41 states. It's an excellent program that's fairly easy to install and learn. It starts out with a personal interview about your financial situation for the past year, then lists forms you might need. Based on the present years taxes, it can estimate what your taxes will be for next year. The program is available from ChipSoft, Inc. (619-453-8722) at the following address:

ChipSoft Inc.
5045 Shoreham Pl., #100
San Diego, CA 92122-3954

ChipSoft and Intuit, at 415-322-0573, have now merged. Quicken, from Intuit, is a financial software program that's an ideal adjunct to TurboTax. You can use Quicken to keep track of all your financial records, then at the end of the year import the records into TurboTax.

Your Income Tax

This program is available from J. K. Lasser (800-624-0023 or 800-624-0024) at the following address:

J. K. Lasser
1 Gulf, Western Plaza
New York, NY 10023

The program has several state modules. It has a scratch pad, calculator, and next-year tax planner. The popular *J. K. Lasser's Tax Guide* is included with the package.

Electronic filing

The IRS is now accepting electronic filing from certain tax preparers and companies. Eventually, you should be able to complete your taxes with one of these programs, then use your modem to send it directly to the IRS. This, of course, would save both you and the IRS a lot of time. Ordinarily, the IRS has to input the data from your return into their computers by hand. Can you imagine the amount of time saved if they received it directly into their computers? The IRS, therefore, encourages electronic filing. Electronic filing also offers advantages to you. Here are just a few:

- Faster refund (up to three weeks faster)
- Direct deposit of the refund
- More accurate return, resulting in fewer errors
- IRS-acknowledged receipt of the return
- Reduced paperwork
- Less filer and IRS labor

There are still some limitations. For more information, call 800-829-1040 and ask for an electronic filing coordinator, or check with your local IRS office to see if electronic filing is possible in your area.

Other tools of the trade

The following are some other tools that can go very well with your computer in business uses:

Point-of-sale terminals

A point-of-sale terminal (POS) is usually a combination of a cash drawer, computer, and special software. It provides fast customer checkout, credit-card handling, audit, and security; reduces paperwork; and provides efficient accounting. By keying in codes for various items, the computer can keep a running inventory of everything that's sold. Store owners can immediately know when to reorder certain goods. A POS system can provide instant sales analysis data of which items sell best, buying trends, and of course profit and loss.

There are several POS systems. A simple cash drawer with a built-in 40-column receipt printer might cost as little as $500. More complex systems will cost $1,500 and more. Software will cost from $175 up to $1,000. The entire system, however, can replace a bookkeeper and an accountant. In successful businesses that sell goods, a POS system can easily pay for itself. Here are a few POS hardware and software companies:

Alpha Data Systems	404-499-9247
CA Retail	800-668-3767
Computer Time	800-456-1159
CompuRegister	314-365-2050
Datacap Systems	215-699-7051
Indiana Cash Drawer	317-398-6643
Merit Dig. Systems	604-985-1391
NCR Corp.	800-544-3333
Printer Products	617-254-1200
Synchronics	901-761-1166

Bar-code scanners

Bar codes are a system of black-and-white lines arranged in a system much like the Morse code of dots and dashes. By using combinations of wide and narrow bars and wide and narrow spaces, any numeral or letter of the alphabet can be represented.

Bar codes were first adopted by the grocery industry. They set up a central office that assigned a unique number, a universal product code (UPC), for just about every manufactured and prepackaged product sold in grocery stores. Different sizes of the same product have a different and unique number assigned to them. The same type of product from different manufacturers were also given unique numbers.

When the clerk runs an item across the scanner, the dark bars absorb light and the white bars reflect light. The scanner decodes the resulting number and sends it to the main computer. The computer then matches the input number to the number stored on its hard disk. Linked to the number on the hard disk is the price of the item, the description, the amount in inventory, and several other pieces of information about the item. The computer sends back the price and the description of the part to the cash register, where it's printed out on the receipt. The computer then deducts that item from the overall inventory and adds the price to the overall cash received for the day.

A store might have several thousand items in different sizes and prices. Without a bar-code system, either the clerk must know most of the prices or the prices must be laboriously attached to each item, then the prices must be entered in the cash register by hand. There's a much higher margin for error with this kind of system. With bar codes, the human factor is eliminated. The transactions are performed much faster and with almost total accuracy.

At the end of the day managers can look at the computer output and immediately know how much business was done, what inventories need to be replenished, and what items were the biggest sellers. With the push of a button on the computer, they can change any or all of the prices of the items in the store.

Bar codes can be used in many other ways—to keep track of time charged to a particular job or track inventory, just to name two. There are very few businesses, large or small, that can't benefit from the use of bar codes.

There are several different types of bar-code readers or scanners. Some are actually small, portable computers that can store data, then be downloaded into a larger computer. Some systems require their own interface card, which must be plugged into one of the slots on the computer motherboard. Key Tronic has a keyboard with a built-in bar-code reader.

If you're interested in bar-code and automatic identification technology, there are two magazines that are sent free to qualified subscribers:

ID Systems
174 Concord St.
Peterborough, NH 03458
603-924-9631

Automatic I.D. News
P.O. Box 6158
Duluth, MN 55806-9858

Call or write for subscription qualification forms. Almost everyone who has any business connections can qualify.

Bar-code printers

Special printers have been designed for printing bar-code labels. Labels can also be printed on better dot-matrix and laser printers. Several companies specialize in printing labels to your specifications.

Radio frequency IDs

Another system of identification is the use of small tags on materials that can be read by an RFID system. These systems can be used on production lines and many places that are difficult to access.

One RFID system is being used in California for toll-bridge collection. A person buys a small tag that's good for a month of tolls. The tag is placed in the window of the auto and is automatically read as the driver passes through the toll gate. He doesn't even have to slow down for the tag to be read and fed to the computer.

RFID systems can also be used in stores, libraries, and other places. Many clothing stores use a system that has detectors at the exits. If someone tries to walk through with an item that hasn't had the tag removed, it will set off an alarm.

Networks

The term *network* covers a lot of territory. Some networks are worldwide. The telephone system is a good example of a worldwide network. Some computer networks, on the other hand, connect only two or three computers.

Networks are made up of two major components, hardware and software. The hardware might consist of boards, cables, hubs, routers, and bridges. There are several different companies who supply network operating software (NOS). The main ones are Novell, Microsoft, and IBM.

There are network standards, so most hardware and software from the major companies is compatible. For instance, software from either Novell or Microsoft will work on boards and systems from several different vendors and manufacturers.

There are several different types of networks, such as zero-slot, proprietary, and peer-to-peer systems, as well as local-area networks (LANs) and wide-area networks (WANs). A LAN is usually a system within a single building, plant, or campus, and a WAN might include several different types of systems.

A zero-slot network is usually two computers tied together with a cable through their serial or parallel ports. Special software can allow each unit to access the hard disk of any of the other units. Files can be viewed, copied, and transferred between computers. It's a very inexpensive way to share resources. A disadvantage is that it's limited to a maximum of 115,000 bits per second, which is relatively slow. Another disadvantage is that the distance between the two computers is limited to about 50 feet.

Some companies have proprietary systems for small networks and peer-to-peer systems. Moses Computer, at 408-358-1550, has several systems that are ideal for

18-1 An inexpensive network system from Moses Computer.

small networks. I have a MosesALL! IV computer network system in my office. Figure 18-1 shows two MosesALL! boards.

Some large network systems can be very complicated and difficult to set up, but Moses systems are very easy to set up and use. MosesALL! IV has a small card that plugs into each computer, and a cable similar to telephone extension cables is used to connect the computers. Software allows each computer to share printers, disk drives, and other resources. Up to 53 computers can be connected with this system. Moses Computers has several other systems for small networks, and they're about the least expensive system you can buy. Call them for brochures on their various systems.

For small businesses or small groups, a proprietary system might be all you need. They're usually inexpensive, yet can have many of the utilities and functions of the large systems.

I also have two other types of network interface cards (NICs) in my office. They're both Ethernet boards. I have several software programs that these boards will work under, such as Microsoft's LAN Manager, Windows for Workgroups, Windows NT, and Novell's NetWare Lite. Figure 18-2 shows an Ethernet network interface card.

A disadvantage to using proprietary systems is that they have their own non-standard software and hardware. Thus they might not work with standard network operating software and hardware.

A peer-to-peer network is rather sophisticated. It requires a network card and special software in each computer. Depending on the type of system, it might operate from 1 MHz to more than 10 MHz.

A peer-to-peer network is different from a file-server network in that the computers on a peer-to-peer network communicate with each other rather than with a large file server. They can share and transfer files and use the resources of all the computers on the network.

In a file-server network, one computer is usually dedicated as the server. It usually has a very large hard disk that contains all the company's files and records. The individual computers attached to the server are called workstations, and can access the files and records and change or alter them as necessary.

18-2 An Ethernet network interface card.

The Pentium is an ideal machine to be a file server on a network. It can support a very large hard disk and has a very fast processing speed. You could have several low-cost computers tied to such a file server, and the resources stored on the Pentium hard disk would be available to each of the low-cost computers. To all the people on the network, the large hard disk with all of its resources would appear to be on their machine. This network system distributes the resources to each person on the network.

A file-server network also offers several advantages to the company. They have to buy software for only one machine. They do have to pay for a license for each of the networked computers, but it costs much less than having to buy software for each machine.

With a network, you can keep all records and data in one place, which can allow for close control of updating and revising the data. A network allows for communication between each of the networked computers. It also allows the users to share a single printer, fax, modem, or other peripheral.

One disadvantage is that if the main server goes down, the whole system is down. The data and records must also be routinely backed up. For crucial data, it might be necessary to have a redundant array of inexpensive disks (RAID) in order to have two or more copies of all data. A less expensive system would be to use a couple of large IDE hard disks and a couple of SCSI hard disks. Since they use different interface controllers, there's less chance that both of them would fail.

For crucial data, it's also necessary that the server be supplied with an uninterruptible power supply (UPS). A UPS is essential in areas where there's frequent lightning and electrical storms. It's also necessary in areas where there are wide variations in the electrical supply and occasional brown-outs.

Of course, you'll need network operating software (NOS). Novell is the leader in both software and network interface cards (NICs). Windows NT can also be used as a NOS. It might cost less for a Windows NT license than a Novell license.

Several companies provide NOS and NICs for small networks. Lantastic, from Artisoft (602-670-7326), is one of the better-known suppliers. Novell also has Novell

Lite for small networks. Microsoft Windows for Workgroups can also be used for small networks.

A good example of a large file-server network is the airline ticket system. A ticket agent in any part of the country can access the main server, see what seats are available on any flight, sell tickets, and assign seats.

There are three main methods, or topologies, of tying computers together: Ethernet, token ring, and star. Each system has some advantages and disadvantages. The Ethernet system is the most popular.

If you'd like to learn more about networks, you might want to order my *Build Your Own LAN and Save a Bundle*, available from Windcrest/McGraw-Hill.

Desktop publishing

If you use outside printing for brochures, manuals, and documents, desktop publishing (DTP) could save you a lot of money. The Pentium or comparable computer, and a good laser printer are about all you need. There are some high-end DTP programs, such as PageMaker and Ventura Publisher, that are necessary if you expect to do a lot of DTP, but for many projects Word for Windows 6.0, WordPerfect for Windows, or WordStar for Windows would be all you need.

One of the better high-end packages is CorelDraw 5.0, which contains Ventura. Corel, of course, has several graphic and drawing packages. They have clip art and just about everything else necessary for desktop publishing.

You'll probably also need a good laser printer and scanner for DTP. If you plan to do any color work, you'll need a color printer and scanner. Scanners were discussed in chapter 12 and printers were discussed in chapter 14.

DTP Direct, at 800-395-7778 or 800-325-5811, is a desktop publishing catalog. They list several DTP software packages and also several DTP hardware products. The ads in many of the computer magazines don't have much information about products because the space is expensive, but many of the catalogs have a fairly good summary of the various features of the products. Call them for a copy of their catalog.

Several magazines specialize in DTP, and almost every computer magazine carries DTP articles. Check the list of magazines in chapter 19.

Presentations

The word *presentation* as used in this chapter has several meanings. A presentation can be used for sales and promotions, training employees, informing employees and other people of policies, benefits, events, changes, updates, news, and many other things.

A presentation can be a directory in a large mall. It might even be interactive, offering a menu with buttons or a touch screen that presents several different options. Several large department stores have directories where brides-to-be can enter their choices for their bridal registry. These type of systems are connected to a computer where the registry is recorded and a list of already purchased items is kept track of.

A presentation can display and print forms, charts, maps, directions, and almost any type of information needed. A museum in Boston uses this kind of presentation to demonstrate how things work. One shows a complete medical procedure for an artificial hip-joint replacement.

Presentations are not only for businesses. Almost any communication is a presentation. Even a discussion with your spouse about upgrading your computer is a presentation. Every time you have a conversation with a person, you're usually presenting ideas that you want the other person to "buy." There might be no monetary reward if the person buys your ideas, but there might be a substantial reward in some other sense. Whether we realize it or not, most of us are nearly always presenting and selling our ideas.

For this type of casual, one-on-one presentation, you don't usually need a lot of software and hardware, but for an old-fashioned presentation where you stand up before a group with a projector and pointer, you'll probably need software and hardware for text, graphics, sound, and video. A few years ago you would have needed large studios full of equipment costing many thousands of dollars to accomplish all of this. Today it can be done relatively inexpensively with a desktop multimedia PC.

The cost of a bad presentation

Good presentations are essential to most all businesses. I've sat through a few presentations that were very important, but it was all I could do to keep from falling asleep (especially so if the presentation was held in the afternoon just after I had eaten a big lunch). Quite often most of the other people in the darkened room were also struggling to keep awake. For many of us, the very important message never got through. In order to keep awake, I would look around the room and count the number of people there, estimate how much each person was making per hour, and then estimate the amount of money the presentation cost. If there were 50 people in the room and each person was making $30 an hour, the presentation cost $1,500. Then you have to add another $1,500 for the time lost while these people weren't doing their regular jobs. A poor presentation can be a terrible waste of a company's valuable resources.

Presentations are very important business tools, but just like any tool if they aren't used properly they can do more damage than good. Quite often, it isn't the message that's at fault, but the messenger. In some cases it would even seem justifiable to shoot the messenger—or at the very least take away his projector and pointer for the rest of his life.

Designing a good presentation

It isn't always the presenter's fault for giving a bad presentation. He might not have the proper tools to make a good presentation. There are several new electronic tools, but one of the most important tools is proper training. A few people are born with a certain charisma that makes them perfect silver-tongued orators. They don't need to be trained. But if you're like most of us, you need to learn a few basic rules to become a better presenter. They're summarized in the following list:

- Know the basics of public speaking. You might be very talented and intelligent, but if you don't know the basics of public speaking, you could end up sounding like an idiot. The main lesson to be learned in public speaking is to communicate better. One way to learn public speaking is to join a Toastmasters club.

- Consider your appearance. You could have the greatest message in the world, but the way you look might end up getting more attention than the message.
- Know your audience. If you know the general likes and dislikes of your audience, you can tailor your presentation. You probably wouldn't give the same presentation to a group of liberal Democrats that you would give to a group of conservative Republicans.
- Know your subject. It can be very embarrassing if members of your audience know more about your subject than you do. Study and learn all you can about your subject. If someone asks a question you can't answer, admit it and promise to try to find the answer.
- KISS (Keep it simple, stupid). If you try to prove to your audience how superior you are, you can quickly lose them. The message should be simple and easy to understand. Use the classic rule of composition: Tell them what you're going to tell them, tell them, then tell them what you've told them.
- Be dynamic. If you just stand at a podium with your head down and read your presentation, very few people will get the message. Use your voice to add inflection and variation. You can't expect your audience to be excited about your subject if you aren't.

The AskMe Multimedia Center, at 612-531-0603, has an excellent software package, Super Show & Tell, for developing presentations. Michael O'Donnel, the company president, has written a booklet called *Making Great Presentations Using Your PC*. AskMe also produced *A Guide to Multimedia on the PC*, a 52-page spiral-bound book that has a wealth of information. Call them for copies of these very helpful resources.

Electronic notes

If you're giving a talk and need notes, put them on a laptop computer. Use a large type, and arrange the notes so each time you press PgDn, new notes roll up. Pressing PgUp will let you easily go back and review. Set the computer on the podium, then glance down now and then at your notes.

Laptops are now very inexpensive, unless you're looking for one with color and an active-matrix display. If you do much public speaking, notes on a laptop are much better than handwritten notes.

New presentation tools

Just a few years ago, about all the presenter had was an overhead projector or slide projector and a pointer. For the vast majority of presentations, these simple tools are still used most often, but there are now an abundant number of electronic hardware and software presentation tools.

Windows 3.1 has made it a lot easier to develop presentations on the PC. It lets you exchange elements and import text, graphics, and charts. You can edit files, export them, or embed them with Windows' object linking and embedding (OLE), but you'll need more than Windows to create and produce a first-class presentation.

Presentation programs

I subscribe to a lot of magazines in order to try to keep up with the computer industry. *Windows Sources* is one of the many computer magazines published by Ziff-Davis. It's an excellent magazine. It has great articles, advice, tips, and product reviews. Ziff-Davis has set up several testing labs to help them evaluate products reviewed in their various magazines. Since I don't quite have the resources that Ziff-Davis has, I often rely on their reviews and evaluations.

The May 1993 issue of *Windows Sources* had extensive reviews of several presentation products, written by Susan Glinert. She tested and evaluated seven different major presentation programs: Freelance Graphics from Lotus at 617-577-8500, Harvard Graphics from Software Publishing at 408-986-8000, Hollywood from Claris Corporation at 408-727-8227, Persuasion from Aldus Corporation at 206-622-5500, PowerPoint from Microsoft at 206-882-8080, SoftCraft Presenter from SoftCraft at 608-257-3300, and Stanford Graphics from 3-D Visions at 310-325-1339. She also looked at CA-Cricket Presents from Computer Associates at 800-342-5224, and WordPerfect Presentations from WordPerfect at 801-225-5000.

Tempra Media Author

A good program the review didn't cover is Tempra Media Author, from Mathematica at 813-682-1128. This program is an excellent presentation and authoring package. It has all the features necessary to create a presentation, a commercial design, training programs, and multimedia productions. It allows you to integrate audio, video, animation, graphics, and text, and it's very easy to learn and to use.

Necessary components

Ziff-Davis felt that all presentation programs should include the following:

An outliner   An integrated outliner is essential to help you organize your ideas. The outliner should flow into any slides, and any changes made in a slide should be reflected in the outline. They considered evaluating CorelDraw, which is probably the most comprehensive and best of any current graphics program, but decided against it because the program doesn't have a built-in outliner. It does have excellent text handling, a spell checker, a thesaurus, and a lot of fonts. CorelDraw also has the remaining necessary components for a presentation program, and more.

Spreadsheet import   The program should be able to import charts and data from major spreadsheet programs, such as Lotus, Excel, and Quattro Pro.

Thumbnail slide preview   After creating several slides, the program should let you preview all of the slides at once, then allow you to rearrange them if necessary.

Speaker's notes and handouts   The program should let you generate speaker's notes and handouts directly from the slides.

Runtime screen show   Some programs require as much as 18MB or more of hard disk space. The program should also offer a small stand-alone runtime version so you can use it on a laptop or other PC to make the presentation.

The programs were checked and evaluated for several other features, such as types of charts and chart features, types of files that could be imported, drawing features and tools, editing tools, fonts, slide show features, and multimedia features.

One other feature checked for was dynamic data exchange (DDE). This is a feature of Microsoft Windows 3.1 that allows information to be transferred automatically between certain Windows applications. Six of the seven programs tested supported DDE. The only program that didn't support DDE was PowerPoint 3.0, the program from Microsoft.

The multimedia features included in most of the programs were sound, animation, and full-motion video. Two of the programs, Persausion and Stanford Graphics, don't support any of these multimedia features. Hollywood supports sound but doesn't support animation or full-motion video.

All of the programs tested were rated very good, but it was decided that Lotus Freelance Graphics was a bit easier to run and had a few more features than the others. One criticism of Freelance was that it was the biggest program of those tested. It requires 18MB of hard disk space.

I have a copy of the Lotus Freelance Graphicsm, and I have to agree that it's an excellent program for designing presentations. The program is also good for many other uses and applications, such as creating graphics, drawings, charts, and outlines.

Compel

Another very good presentation program the review didn't look at is Compel, from Asymetrix at 800-448-6543. This program does everything in the required list and more. MediaBlitz, which comes with several sound and graphics clips, is bundled with Compel. The program comes on several 3½-inch floppy disks, but also comes on a CD-ROM. It's a mainstream, quality presentation program and sells for only $99.

Q/Media

Q/Media for Windows, from Q/Media Software at 604-879-1190, is another low-cost presentation program with a list price of $99. It has all the requirements and also comes with unlimited free support and a 60-day money-back guarantee. Q/Media, version 2.0 works with OLE 2.0, has an integrated outliner and automated bulleting of text, and comes with a 500MB CD-ROM graphic clip library.

Bravo

Bravo, from Alpha Software at 800-852-5750, is the least expensive presentation program available. Some of the previous programs have a list price for as much as $795. Bravo has all the required features, such as an outliner, powerful drawing tools, spelling checker, animation, movies and sound via OLE, slide sorter, speaker notes, handouts, and runtime player. It even has Windows OLE and DDE support. It has a list price of only $79.

Astound

Astound, from Gold Disk at 800-982-9888, does everything the previous programs do, and it also comes with a CD-ROM filled with clip art that can be used in your presentations. Astound can interface with all the major presentation packages and import data from them. It's very easy to learn and use.

Design tips for better presentations

In the *Windows Sources* article, Susan Glinert offers some tips to help you create a better presentation. Briefly, here are some of her suggestions:

Choose the proper chart There are several different types of charts. Use a line chart to represent data that changes over time, such as sales. Bar charts should be used to compare individual data points. Pie charts are good to show proportions. Organizational charts should be used to show relationships and processes.

Format the charts Bars should be differentiated with solid shades or simple cross-hatch patterns. Limit pie charts to no more than 10 parts. Use grid lines and reference points to make the graph readable.

Tables Use tables for detailed data.

Text Use text lists for simple information. Follow each point or bullet with no more than six words and no more than six lines per slide. Don't use several types of fonts.

Color Emphasize strong points by setting them in a contrasting color. Don't use more than seven colors. Use most vivid colors for emphasis. Foreground and background colors should have a high contrast. Avoid color combinations, such as red and green, that might be difficult for color-blind people to see. Avoid large areas of a single color, such as red, that might tire the eyes. Blue is the most restful color.

Fit the presentation to the type of room For slides shown in a dark room, use light objects on a dark background. For overhead projectors that will be used in a lighted room, use dark objects on a light background.

Adding clip art

There are several programs that have thousands of clip-art images you can import into your presentation. You can use the images to illustrate a point or just give the presentation a bit of life. CorelDraw 4.0 has two CD-ROMs that contain several thousand clip-art images, symbols, and shapes that can be imported. It also has several animations and cartoons.

Task Force, from New Vision Technology at 613-727-8184, has over 3,500 images that can be imported. The images are both black-and-white and color, and can be used with all the major word processors and presentation packages.

Adding sound

A little sound can be an excellent addition to a presentation. Not only will it help to keep your audience from going to sleep, you can use it to enhance the presentation. Sound can help illustrate or emphasize a point or make a presentation enjoyable and unforgettable. You'll need a sound card (see chapter 13).

Just as you can add graphics clips to a presentation, you can also add music clips. Magiclips Music, from Wolfetone Publishing at 800-949-8663, has a large number of music clips on a CD-ROM. There are various styles and types of music to fit almost any type of presentation. You can also play the music on the CD-ROM on a standard home CD player. The clips can be embedded into your presentations and are royalty-free. If there's nothing on the CD-ROM that satisfies you, they can provide custom music. The list price is $89.95.

Adding photos and video

To add photos, animation, and motion pictures, you'll need a video capture card. Some of the less expensive video boards can capture only a single frame. The more expensive cards can capture full motion.

Digitizing a frame from a motion picture or color photograph is somewhat similar to a paint-by-numbers painting. The electronics break the image down into small dots as it scans across the image. The color, hue, and brightness of each dot is assigned a digital number. These digital numbers are then stored on the hard disk. When the image is played back, the assigned number of each dot causes the original color to be reproduced.

If the image is a monochrome line drawing, the dot numbers will be either 1 or 0. It doesn't require much disk memory for this type of storage. For color, the resolution is a factor. A 16-bit 640 × 480 resolution will require over 600K for a single photo or frame from a movie. If a movie is shown at 30 frames per second, it would be 600,000 × 30 = 18MB for one second. At this rate it wouldn't take long to fill up a hard disk. Higher resolutions require even more storage space.

Fortunately, three compression methods have been developed that can help considerably. Intel's digital video interactive (DVI) standard takes the digital information from the first frame and stores it. Ordinarily, the next frame is quite similar to the first, so only the changes in the second frame and each successive frame are saved. The Motion Picture Expert Group (MPEG) adopted a compression standard similar to the Intel DVI, and the Joint Photographers Expert Group (JPEG) adopted a compression standard that was originally designed for single frame-photos but is now used in some video systems. JPEG looks at blocks of pixels and stores an averaged generalization of the color of the block. Compression ratios of up to 25:1 don't cause too much degradation, but higher ratios would cause a noticeable change. MPEG can have a compression ratio as high as 50:1 or more without too much degradation.

Even with a compression ratio of 50:1, however, you'd still need about 21MB to store one minute of a motion picture.

Table 18-1 lists some of the boards used to display and capture photos and video. Most boards come with software, and some require that Microsoft Video for Windows be used. The street prices are considerably less than the quoted list prices.

Table 18-1. Boards to display and capture photos or video

Program	Company	Phone	Price
Video Clipper	Advanced Dig. Sys.	800-888-5244	$465
ProColor	Aitech	408-946-3291	$795
PIB/NTSC	ATronics	510-656-8400	$970
Video Blaster	Creative Tech.	800-647-9933	$500
Watchit-TV	New Media	508-663-0666	$350
Super Motion	New Media	508-663-0666	$1995
Sweet 16	Omnicomp	713-464-2990	$775
FrameBuffer	Videolinx	408-395-9593	$695

Scanners

If you create a lot of presentations, a good color scanner is almost essential. You can use a color scanner to scan in color brochures and photographs. Several color scanners are listed in chapter 7. There's a wide range in the cost, from about $1,000 to over $20,000. The output of some of the less expensive scanners, such as the Hewlett-Packard ScanJet IIC, at $1,500, appears to be as good as that of some of the $20,000 machines.

Printing overhead transparencies

Once a presentation is completed, you can print it out. If your presentation doesn't include color, you can use the printout to make overhead transparencies. Avery (800-472-8379) has transparencies that print directly from a laser or ink-jet printer. The transparencies are placed in the paper tray and feed automatically just like paper. If you call them, they'll send you a sample.

Printing color presentations

A presentation can also be a printed brochure or prospectus. Adding color to a presentation is like adding frosting to a cake. There are several color printers available. The least expensive are dot-matrix printers that use a multicolored ribbon. They're slow because they usually require multiple passes of the print head. The colors don't blend very well, so this kind of printer isn't suitable for most professional presentations.

The Hewlett-Packard DeskJet 550C (800-752-0900) is a fairly inexpensive color printer, at a list price of about $1,000. The Canon BJC 800 bubble-jet printer (800-848-4123) is a bit more expensive, at a list price of about $2,700. The Jetprinter PS 4079, from Lexmark at 800-358-5835, and the HP PaintJet XL300 are both high-end ink-jet color printers with a list price of about $3,400. All ink-jet printers can use plain paper, coated paper, or transparencies.

There are several thermal color printers. They provide excellent color by melting wax and then spraying it onto special paper. They can also make color transparencies. The Primera color printer, from Fargo Electronics at 800-327-4622, is one of the least expensive thermal printers with a list price of about $950. One reason it's inexpensive is because it doesn't have PostScript. The QMS ColorScript 230, from QMS at 800-523-2696, has a list price of about $7,900. The Phaser IIIPXi, from Tektronix (800-835- 6100) and the HS-1PS, from Brother International (908-356-8880) each have a list price of about $9,900.

Another type of color printer uses dye sublimation. These printers produce photographic-quality output that's top of the line. The Tektronix Phaser IISD is a dye-sublimation printer, as is the Shinko ColorStream/DS from Mitsubishi International at 914-997-4960. Both printers have a list price of about $9,900.

Making slides

There are several software and hardware tools that will let you import and store photos and high-quality color in your presentations, but the ordinary desktop computer system can't print out a slide. Not to worry. There are several service bureaus who will gladly take your presentation and create the slides for you.

You can copy your presentation onto a floppy disk and send it to such a company by courier or by an overnight service, and they'll create the slides and ship them back to you. Some of them offer overnight service. For even faster service, you can simply use a modem to send the presentation.

Besides making slides, most service bureaus also offer other services, such as making color overhead transparencies, color posters, and color prints. Prices range from $3 to $5 per slide, more if it's a rush overnight job.

If you use a lot of slides and overhead transparencies, then you might want to have your own desktop system. 2Film Technology, at 416-633-5523, has a file-to-film recorder for $2,995. It includes a 35-mm camera back, a digital interface board, film, and cables. If you need slides and colored transparencies only once in a while, then it's a lot cheaper to use a service bureau. Here's a list of some of the service bureaus:

Artform Communications	800-279-7298
Autographix	800-548-8558
Better Image Production	408-441-0955
DigiColor	800-967-3714
Elegant Graphics	303-879-4334
Genigraphics	800-638-7348
Graphicsland	800-347-2744
Lazertouch,Inc	415-348-7010
LightCraft Graphics	708-394-8380
Magicorp	800-367-6244
Slide Imagers	800-232-5411
Slidemasters,Inc.	800-969-8228

Do-it-yourself slides

You can also take your own 35-mm slides and have them developed at any film-developing center. If your subject is something you can photograph, then do it yourself. If you're like me, take some extra shots. I've contributed greatly to Kodak's success because I waste so much film.

Displaying the presentation

Slides and an overhead projector are still the most popular medium used for presentations, but there's no sound or motion on these systems. There are more sophisticated ways to display your presentation, as follows:

Computer screen

Any image that appears on a computer screen can be projected onto a wall or a large theater screen. The output of a computer is plugged into an LCD panel, which is then placed on the bed of an overhead projector. Whatever appears on the computer screen appears on the LCD panel, which is then projected onto the screen. If the computer also has a sound board and speakers, a complete presentation with color, sound, and motion is possible.

Some LCD panel systems are rather expensive. They have an active-matrix screen, the same type of screen used in the more expensive notebook computers. The term *active-matrix* means that separate transistors are required for every pixel in the panel, which could be several hundred thousand. One reason the active-matrix panels are so expensive is that a single defective transistor makes the whole panel defective.

There are some less expensive LCD panels that are monochrome, but can display several shades of gray. The list prices for the monochrome panels start at $1,595; color active-matrix panels start at $4,295 and go as high as $9,995. Table 18-2 lists a few companies who manufacture LCD panels, and each company produces several models. List prices are for comparison only.

Table 18-2. A few companies who manufacture LCD panels

Company	Telephone	Prices
In Focus Systems	800-327-7231	$3,995 and up
nViwew Corp.	800-736-6439	$2,495 and up
Proxima Corp.	800-447-7694	$5,000 and up
Sayett Technology	800-678-7469	$1,895 and up
Sharp Electronics	201-529-9636	$1,595 and up
3M Corp.	800-328-1371	$6,795 and up

Projection monitor

NEC, at 800-632-4636, has a couple of Multisync projection monitors. This system takes the output from a computer, VCR, or other video source and projects it onto a large screen. The system uses red, green, and blue projection lamps such as those used on projection television sets. There are several other companies who make similar projection monitors.

Large-screen TV

Several companies have developed small devices that allow the output of a computer to be plugged into a large-screen TV. Advanced Digital Systems (310-865-1432) has the VGA-to-TV Elite. The price is $399.

Consumer Technology (800-356-3983) has Presenter and Presenter Plus, small pocket-sized devices that can connect a computer output to a TV. You can use them with either a desktop PC or a small laptop. You can carry your presentation with you on a laptop and display it on a large television. These devices work with standard TVs and S-Video TVs.

Comedge (818-855-2784) has Audio/Video Key, similar to the previous devices. You can use it to connect a computer to a TV, VCR, or camcorder. It has both standard video and S-VHS outputs.

Ordinarily, there's a lot of degradation when a video signal is copied. If you've ever seen a videotape copy of a copy, you can see just how much is lost. Many newer VCRs and television sets are now equipped with the S-VHS or S-Video option, which separates the chrominance signals from the luminance signals of composite video.

The resulting image is much cleaner, with a lot less signal loss. If you're thinking of buying a new TV or VCR, look for S-Video input and output types.

Camcorder

All three of the devices in the previous section can be used to record a presentation on a camcorder. If you record your presentation on an 8-mm tape recorder, you can easily take it with you. Palm-sized camcorders are small, relatively inexpensive, and can be connected to any TV. The 8-mm tape cartridges can hold up to two hours of text, graphics, speech, and music. The cartridges are small enough to fit several in a coat pocket. Camcorders can run off a small battery so they don't have to have an external power source. I recommend HI-8 camcorders.

Gold Disk, at 800-465-3375, produces a program called VideoDirector, which comes with cables that plug into your computer and camcorder video recorder. You can use the software and cables to edit and record clips of your tapes. It works under Windows, so it's very easy to use. VideoDirector is ideal for editing both home videotapes and professional presentations. There are both PC and Macintosh versions.

Summary

There are many other ways you can benefit from and use the power of your computer. One way to learn more about your computer and what it's capable of doing is to subscribe to some of the magazines listed in chapter 19.

19
CHAPTER

Component sources

How much you save by doing it yourself depends on what components you buy and where you buy them. You'll have to shop wisely and be fairly knowledgeable about the components in order to take advantage of bargains.

Computer shows and swap meets

I've done almost all of my buying at computer shows and swap meets. There's at least one computer show or swap almost every weekend in larger cities. If you live in or near a large city, check your newspaper for ads. In California, several computer magazines, such as *MicroTimes* and *Computer Currents*, list the coming events.

To set up a computer swap, an organizer usually rents a large building, such as a convention center or a hall. Booth spaces are then rented out to the various local vendors. Most booths are run by reputable local businesspeople.

One of the best features of swap meets is that almost all the components you need are on display in one place. Several booths will have similar or the same components. I usually take a pencil and pad with me, walk around, write down the prices of the items I want to buy, and then compare the prices at the various booths. There can be quite a lot of variation in the pricing. I bought a good printer at one show for $695 and, about 50 feet away, another dealer was offering the same printer for $995.

You can also haggle with most of the dealers, especially near closing time. Rather than pack up the material and lug it back to their stores, many will sell it for a lower price.

Interface, at 617-449-6600, puts on the biggest computer shows in the country. They have the spring Computer Dealers Exposition (COMDEX) in Atlanta or Chicago, and a fall COMDEX in Las Vegas. The attendance goes up every year. When I first started attending in 1984, they had only about 60,000 people at Las Vegas. The 1994 show attracted close to 200,000. Every hotel room in Las Vegas is usually sold out six months before the show. They've now started a New Media Expo, which will be held in Los Angeles in the spring. Interface also puts on international shows in several countries.

Since the COMDEX shows have been such a huge success, many other companies are now putting on shows. *New Media* magazine publishes a calendar each month that lists shows for the current month. *New Media* is sent without charge to qualified new media professionals; for others, the subscription rate is $48 a year. Call 415-573-5170 and ask them to send you a qualification form.

Your local store

Most of the vendors at swap meets are local businesspeople who want your continued business, but there might be a few vendors from other parts of the country. If you buy something from a vendor who doesn't have a local store, be sure to get a name and address. Most components are reliable, but there's always a chance something might not work. You might need to exchange it or get it repaired, or you might need to ask some questions to get it working.

Again, computers are very easy to assemble. Once you've bought all the components, it usually takes less than an hour to assemble a computer. But it's possible to make a mistake. Although most components are now fairly reliable, a new part you buy and install could possibly be defective. Most dealers will give you a warranty of some kind and will replace defective parts. If there's something in the system that prevents it from operating, you might not be able to determine just which component is defective.

It can take a considerable amount of time to remove a component, like a motherboard, and return it to someone across the country, so if at all possible try to deal with a knowledgeable vendor who will support you and help you if you have any problems.

Magazines and mail order

Every computer magazine has pages and pages of advertisements for components and systems that can be sent to you through the mail. If you live in an area where there are no computer stores or shows, you can buy by mail.

One of the biggest magazines in size and circulation is *Computer Shopper*, which is usually over 1,000 tabloid-sized pages. A large percentage of the magazine is made up of full-page ads for computer components and systems. They do manage to get a few articles in among the ads. For subscription information, call 800-274-6384. Another good magazine you can have sent to you free is *Processor* (800-334-7443). It's a tabloid-sized magazine with over 100 pages of advertisements. It's a good source for all kinds of components.

Another reason to use mail order is because it's usually less expensive than local vendors. Local vendors have to pay overhead for their stores, which are usually in fairly high-rent districts; mail-order houses can be run out of a back bedroom. Most local vendors have to buy their stock from a distributor, who usually buys it from the manufacturer or a wholesaler. By the time you get the product, it has passed through several companies, each of whom has made a profit. One reason an IBM or Apple computer is more expensive is because they have several middlemen. Most direct marketers who advertise by mail have cut out most of the middlemen and passed their profit on to you.

IBM has recently fallen on hard times and has lost a lot of money. They finally realized they can't compete with the direct marketers, so they've also entered the direct market. They offer not only their own products, but products of other companies. Call 800-426-2968 for their latest IBM direct catalog.

Without computer magazines there would be no mail order, and without mail order there would be no computer magazines. Advertisements are the life-blood of magazines. The subscription price of a magazine doesn't even come close to paying for the mailing costs, so they must have ads to exist.

Most mail-order vendors are honest, but a few bad advertisers could ruin a magazine. *PC World* has a regular Consumer Watch column. If you have a problem with a mail-order vendor you can't resolve, write to them. They can usually get it resolved. For *PC World* subscription information, call 800-234-3498. Several other magazines publish letters to the editor, which can also help you if you have a problem. Most of the computer magazines have formed the Microcomputer Marketing Council (MMC) of the Direct Marketing Association (212-297-1393), at the following address:

Direct Marketing Association
6 East 43rd St.
New York, NY 10017

If you have a problem with a vendor you can't resolve, they may be able to help. They police the advertisers fairly closely.

Make sure of what you need and what you're ordering. Some advertisements aren't written very well and might not tell the whole story. They're also expensive, so a lot of information must be abbreviated or even left out. If possible, call the company to make sure. Ask what their return policy is for defective merchandise. Also ask how long before the item will be shipped. And ask for the current price. The ads are usually placed about two months before the magazines are delivered or hit the stands. The way prices are coming down, there could be quite a change in cost at the time you place your order. Of course, if you send them the advertised price, I'm sure they won't refuse it. A two- or three-dollar phone call could save you a lot of time, trouble, grief, and maybe even some money.

Ten rules for ordering by mail

Here are some brief rules you should follow when ordering by mail:

Rule 1: Look for a street address.
Make sure the advertiser has a street address. Some ads give only a phone number. If you decide to buy from this vendor, call and verify that there's a live person on the other end with a street number. But before you send any money, do a bit more investigation. If possible, look through past issues of the same magazine. If the company has been advertising for several months, it's probably okay.

Rule 2: Compare other vendor prices.

Check through the magazines for other vendors prices for this product. The prices should be fairly close. If it appears to be a bargain that's too good to be true, then . . . well, you know the rest.

Rule 3: Buy from MMC members.

Buy from a vendor who's a member of MMC or other recognized association. There are now about 10,000 members who belong to marketing associations, and they've agreed to abide by the ethical guidelines and rules of the associations. Except for friendly persuasion and the threat of expulsion, the associations have little power over the members, but most realize what's at stake and put a great value on their membership. Most who advertise in the major computer magazines are members.

Rule 4: Do your homework.

Read the advertisements carefully. Advertising space is very expensive. Many ads use abbreviations, and many aren't entirely clear. If in doubt, call and ask. Know exactly what you want, state precisely the model, make, size, component, and any other pertinent information. Tell them which ad you're referring to, ask them if the price is the same, if the item is in stock, and when you can expect delivery. If the item isn't in stock, indicate whether you'll accept a substitute or not. Ask for an invoice or order number. Ask for the person's name. Write down all the information, the time, date, company's address and phone number, description of the item, and promised delivery date. Save or make a record of any correspondence.

Rule 5: Ask questions.

Ask if the advertised item comes with all the necessary cables, parts, accessories, software, etc. Ask what the warranties and the return and refund policies are, and ask for the name of someone to contact if there's a problem.

Rule 6: Don't send cash.

You can't keep a record of cash, and many people request that you don't send it by mail. If possible, use a credit card. A personal check could cause a delay of three to four weeks while the vendor waits for it to clear. A money-order or credit-card order should be filled and shipped immediately. Keep a copy of the money order.

Rule 7: Ask for a delivery date.

If you haven't received your order by the promised delivery date, notify the seller.

Rule 8: Try the item out as soon as you receive it.

If you have a problem, notify the seller immediately by phone, then in writing. Give all the details. Don't return the merchandise unless the dealer gives you a return material authorization (RMA). Make sure to keep a copy of the shipper's receipt, packing slip, or some evidence that the material was returned.

Rule 9: Take steps if the product is defective.

If you believe the product is defective or if you have a problem, reread your warranties and guarantees. Reread the manual and any documentation. It's very easy to make an error or misunderstand how an item operates if you're unfamiliar with it. Before you go to a lot of trouble, try to get some help from someone else. At least verify that you do indeed have a problem. Many times a problem will disappear and the vendor won't be able to duplicate it. When you call, try to have the item in your computer and be at the computer so you can describe the problem as it happens.

Rule 10: Try to work out your problem with the vendor.

If you can't resolve your problem with the vendor, then write to the consumer complaint agency in the seller's state. Also, write to the magazine and to the DMA (the address is listed in the previous section).

Federal Trade Commission rules

Here is a brief summary of FTC rules:

Rule 1: Seller must ship within 30 days.

The seller must ship your order within 30 days unless the ad clearly states that it will take longer.

Rule 2: Seller has the right to cancel.

If it appears that the seller can't ship when promised, he must notify you and give a new date. He must give you the opportunity to cancel the order and refund your money if you desire.

Rule 3: Seller must notify buyer if an order can't be filled.

If the seller notifies you that he can't fill your order on time, he must include a stamped, self-addressed envelope or card so you can respond to his notice. If you don't respond, he can assume that you agree to the delay. Then he must ship within 30 days of the end of the original 30 days or cancel your order and refund your money.

Rule 4: Buyer has the right to cancel if product is delayed.

Even if you consent to a delay, you still have the right to cancel at any time.

Rule 5: Seller must refund money if buyer cancels the order.

If you cancel an order that you've paid for by check or money order, the seller must refund the money. If you paid by credit card, your account must be credited within one billing cycle. Store credits or vouchers in place of a refund are not acceptable.

Rule 6: No substitutions are allowed.

If the item you ordered isn't available, the seller may not send you a substitute without your express consent.

Online services

If you have a modem, there are several BBSs and online companies who offer all kinds of shopping services. You can call up from your computer and buy airline tickets, furniture, clothing, toys, electronics, computers, and just about anything else you can imagine.

Online services offer some advantages over mail order. The prices quoted in some magazines might be two or three months old by the time the magazine is published. As you know, computer prices come down almost daily. The prices quoted by online services are up-to-the-minute prices. Here are just a few of the BBSs who offer online buying:

First Capitol Computer
16 Algana
St. Peters, MO 63376
314-928-9889
BBS: 314-928-9228

Leo Electronics
Box 11307
Torrance, CA 95124
213-212-6133
BBS: 213-212-7179

JDR Microdevices
2233 Branham Lane
San Jose, CA 95124
408-559-0253
BBS: 408-559-1200

Swan Technologies
3075 Research Dr.
State College, PA 16801
814-234-2236
BBS: 814-237-6145

Here are some online companies:

America Online	800-827-6364
CompuServe	800-848-8990
Delphi	800-544-4005
Prodigy	800-776-3449
GEnie	800-638-9636

Magazines

There are several good magazines that can help you gain the knowledge necessary to make sensible purchases and learn more about computers. These magazines usually carry very interesting and informative articles and reviews of software and hardware. They also contain many advertisements for computers, components, and software.

I suggest you subscribe to the following magazines: *Computer Shopper*, *PC Sources*, *Byte*, *Computer Buying World*, *Computer Monthly*, *PC World*, and *PC Magazine*. Most of these magazines are available on local magazine racks, but you'll save money with a yearly subscription and you can have them delivered to your door. If you need a source for components, you only have to look in any of these magazines to find hundreds of them. If you live near a large city, several vendors will probably advertise in your local paper.

Many of the magazines, such as *Computer Shopper*, *PC Computing*, and *Computer Monthly*, have a section that lists all the products advertised in that particular issue. The components and products are categorized and listed by page number. It makes it very easy to find what you're looking for.

There are hundreds of computer and computer-related magazines. Even if you read everyone of them, you still won't be able to keep up with the flood of computer information. Here are just a few of the magazines that will help you keep abreast to some degree:

Audio-Forum
96 Broad Street
Guilford, Connecticut 06437

Black Box Corporation
P.O. Box 12800
Pittsburgh, PA 15241

Byte
P.O. Box 558
Hightstown, N.J. 08520

CD-I World
P.O. Box 1358
Camden, ME 04843-1358

CD-ROM Multimedia
720 Sycamore St.
Columbus, IN 47201
800-565-4623

CD-ROM Professional
462 Danbury Rd.
Wilton, CT 06897-2126

CD-ROM Today
Subscription Department
P.O. Box 51478
Boulder, CO 8032-1478

Compute!
P.O. Box 3245
Harlan, IA 51593-2424

ComputerCraft
76 North Broadway
Hicksville, NY 11801-9962

Computer Currents
5720 Hollis St.
Emeryville, CA 94608

Computer Graphics World
P.O. Box 122
Tulsa, OK 74101-9966

Computer Pictures
Knowledge Industry Publications, Inc.
Montage Publishing, Inc.
701 Westchester Ave.
White Plains, NY 10604

Computer Shopper
P.O. Box 51020
Boulder, CO 80321-1020

Computer World
P.O. Box 2044
Marion, OH 43306-2144

Desktop Video World
P.O. Box 594
Mt. Morris, IL 61054-7902

Digital Video Magazine
P.O. Box 594
Mt. Morris, IL 61054-7902

Electronic Musician
P.O. Box 41525
Nashville, TN 37204-9829

High Color
P.O. Box 1347
Camden, ME 04843-9956

Home & Studio Recording
Music Maker Publications Inc.
7318 Topanga Canyon Blvd., Suite 200
Canoga Park, CA 91303

Home Office Computing
P.O. Box 51344
Boulder, CO 80321-1344

Imaging Magazine
1265 Industrial Highway
Southampton, PA 18966
(800) 677-3435

Insight Direct Inc.
1912 West Fourth Street
Tempe, Arizona 85281

International Spectrum
10675 Treena Street, Suite 103
San Diego, CA 92131

LAN Magazine
P.O. Box 50047
Boulder, CO 80321-0047

MicroComputer Journal
Classified Dept. 76
N. Broadway
Hicksville, NY 11801

MicroTimes
5951 Canning St.
Oakland, CA 94609

Musician's Friend
P.O. Box 4520
Medford, OR 97501

Nuts & Volts
430 Princeland Ct.
Corona, CA 91719-1343

PC Computing
P.O. Box 50253
Boulder, CO 80321-0253

PC Magazine
P.O. Box 51524
Boulder, CO 80321-1524

PC Novice
P.O. Box 85380
Lincoln, NE 68501-9807

PC Today
P.O. Box 85380
Lincoln, NE 68501-5380

PC World
P.O. Box 51833
Boulder, CO 80321-1833

PRE-
8340 Mission Rd., #106
Prairie Village, KS 66206

Publish!
P.O. Box 51966
Boulder, CO 80321-1966

Video Magazine
Box 56293
Boulder, CO 80322-6293
800-365-1008

Videomaker
P.O. 469026
Escondido, CA 92046
800-334-8152

Voice Processing Magazine
P.O. Box 6016
Duluth, MN 55806-9797

Open Computing
P.O. Box 570
Hightstown, NJ 08520-9328

Windows Magazine
P.O. Box 58649
Boulder, CO 80322-8649

In addition to magazines like these, some are sent free to qualified subscribers, like *PC Week* and *InfoWorld*. These excellent magazines are so popular that the publishers had to limit the number of subscribers. They can't possibly accommodate all the people who request subscriptions, so they set standards you have to meet in order to qualify.

To get a free subscription, write to the magazine for a qualifying application form. The form will ask several questions, such as how you're involved with computers, the company you work for, and whether you have any influence in purchasing the computer products listed in the magazines.

There are hundreds of trade magazines that are sent free to qualified subscribers. Cahners alone publishes 32 different trade magazines, many of which are highly technical and narrowly specialized. Here's a list of some of the more general of these kinds of magazines:

Advanced Imaging
445 Broad Hollow Rd.
Melville, NY 11747-4722

Automatic I.D. News
P.O. Box 6158
Duluth, MN 55806-9870

*AV Video Production &
Presentation Tech.*

701 Westchester Ave.
White Plains, NY 10604
914-328-9157

Beyond Computing (IBM)
1133 Westchester Ave.
White Plains, NY 10604

California Business
P.O. Box 70735
Pasadena, CA 91117-9947

CD-ROM News Extra
462 Danbury Road
Wilton, CT 06897-2126

Client/Server Computing
Sentry Publishing
1900 West Park Dr.
Westborough, MA 01581-3907

Computer Design
Box 3466
Tulsa, OK 74101-3466

Computer Systems News
600 Community Dr.
Manhasset, NY 11030

Communications Week
P.O. Box 2070
Manhasset, NY 11030

Computer Reseller News
P.O. Box 2040
Manhasset, NY 11030

Computer Products
P.O. Box 14000
Dover, NJ 07801-9990

Computer Tech. Review
924 Westwood Blvd.
Los Angeles, CA 90024

Communications News
2504 Tamiami Trail North
Nokomis, FL 34275
813-966-9521

Data Communications
P.O. Box 477
Hightstown, NJ 08520-9362

Designfax
P.O. Box 1151
Skokie, IL 60076-9917

*Document Management & Windows
Imaging*
8711 E. Pinnacle Peak Road, #249
Scottsdale, Arizona 85255

EE Product News
P.O. Box 12982
Overland Park, KS 66212

Electronic Design
P.O. Box 985007
Cleveland, OH 44198-5007

Electronics
P.O. Box 985061
Cleveland, OH

Electronic Manufacturing
P.O. Box 159
Libertyville, IL 60048

Electronic Publish & Print
650 S. Clark St.
Chicago, IL 60605-9960

Federal Computer Week
P.O. Box 602
Winchester, MA 01890

Identification Journal
2640 N. Halsted St.
Chicago, IL 60614-9962

ID Systems
P.O. Box 874
Peterborough, NH 03458

InfoWorld
P.O. Box 1172
Skokie, IL 60076

LAN Times
122 East, 1700 South
Provo, UT 84606

Lasers & Optronics
301 Gibraltar Dr.
Morris Plains, NJ 07950

Machine Design
P.O. Box 985015
Cleveland, OH 44198-5015

Managing Office Technology
1100 Superior Ave.
Cleveland, OH 44197-8092

Manufacturing Systems
P.O. Box 3008
Wheaton, IL 60189-9972

Medical Equipment Designer
29100 Aurora Rd., #200
Cleveland, OH 44139

Micro Publishing News
21150 Hawthorne Blvd., #104
Torrance, CA 90503

Mini-Micro Systems
P.O. Box 5051
Denver, CO 80217-9872

Mobile Office
Subscription Department
P.O. Box 57268
Boulder, CO 80323-7268

Modern Office Technology
1100 Superior Ave.
Cleveland, OH 44197-8032

New Media Magazine
P.O. Box 1771
Riverton, NJ 08077-7331
415-573-5170

Network Computing
P.O. Box 1095
Skokie, IL 60076-9662

Network Journal
600 Harrison St.
San Francisco, CA 94107
800-950-0523

Network World
161 Worcester Rd.
Framingham, MA 01701
508-875-6400

Office Systems
P.O. Box 3116
Woburn, MA 01888-9878

Office Systems Dealer
P.O. Box 2281
Woburn, MA 01888-9873

PC Week
P.O. Box 1770
Riverton, NJ 08077-7370

Photo Business
1515 Broadway
New York, NY 10036

Programmer's Shop (The)
5 Pond Park Rd.
Hingham, MA 02043-9845

Quality
P.O. Box 3002
Wheaton, IL 60189-9929

Reseller Management
Box 601
Morris Plains, NJ 07950

Robotics World
6255 Barfield Rd.
Atlanta, GA 30328-9988

Scientific Computing
301 Gibraltar Dr.
Morris Plains, NJ 07950

Software Magazine
Westborough Office Park
1900 West Park Dr.
Westborough, MA 01581-3907

Stacks
P.O. Box 5031
Brentwood, TN 37024-5031

Sun Expert
P.O. Box 5274
Pittsfield, MA 01203-9479

Surface Mount Technology
P.O. Box 159
Libertyville, IL 600048

Component and software catalogs

Several companies publish special catalogs for components and software through direct mail. Even IBM has gotten into the act. Most of these companies, however, charge a bit more than those who advertise in the major magazines, but ads cost a lot of money so there usually isn't too much information given about a product. Direct mail-order companies usually give fairly good descriptions of products. The catalogs are free. Here are just a few:

CompuClassics
P.O. Box 10598
Canoga Park, CA 91309

Compute Ability
P.O. Box 17882
Milwaukee, WI 53217

Computers & Music
647 Mission St.
San Francisco, CA 94105

Damark
7101 Winnetka Ave N.
P.O. Box 29900
Minneapolis, MN 55429-0900

Data-Cal Corporation
531 East Elliot Rd.
Chandler, AZ 85225-1152

Dell Direct Sales L.P.
11209 Metric Blvd.
Austin, TX 78758-4093

Digi-key Corporation
701 Brooks Ave. South
P.O. Box 677
Thief River Falls, MN 56701-0677

DTP Direct
5198 West 76 Street
Edina, MN 55439

Edmund Scientific Company
101 E. Gloucester Pike
Barrington, NJ 08007-1380

Global Computer Supplies
11 Harbor Park Dr., Dept. 48
Port Washington, NY 11050

Global Office Products
11 Harbor Park Dr., Dept. 30
Port Washington, NY 11050

Hello Direct
5884 Eden Park Place
San Jose, CA 95138-1859

IBM PC Direct
P.O. Box 12195
Bldg. 203, Dept. WN4
Research Triangle Park, NC 27709-9767
1-800-426-2968

JDR Microdevices
2233 Samaritan Drive
San Jose, CA 95124

Mailer's Software
970 Calle Negocio
San Clemente, CA 92673

MicroWarehouse
1720 Oak Street
P.O. Box 3014
Lakewood, N.J. 08701-3014

Momentum Graphics Inc.
16290 Shoemaker
Cerritos, CA 90701-2243

Mr. CD-ROM
P.O. Box 1087
Winter Garden, FL 34787
800-444-6723

Multimedia World
P.O. Box 58690
Boulder, CO 80323-8690

One Network Place
4711 Golf Road
Skokie, IL 60076

Paper Direct
205 Chubb Ave.
P.O. Box 680
Lyndhurst, NJ 07071

Pasternack Enterprises
P.O. 16759
Irvine, CA 92713

PC Connection
6 Mill Street
Marlow, NH 03456

Personal Computing Tools
90 Industrial Park Road
Hingham, MA 02043

Power Up!
P.O. Box 7600
San Mateo, CA 94403-7600

PrePress
11 Mt. Pleasant Ave.
East Hanover, NJ 07936-9925

Presentations
Lakewood Building
50 South Ninth Street
Minneapolis MN 55402-9973

Processor
P.O. Box 85518
Lincoln, NE 68501
800-334-7443

Projections
P.O. Business Park Drive
Branford, CT 06405

Queblo
1000 Florida Avenue
Hagerstown, MD 21741

Software Labs
100 Corporate Pointe, #195
Culver City, CA 90230-7616

Soundware
200 Menlo Oaks Drive
Menlo Park, CA 94025

South Hills Datacomm
760 Beechnut Drive
Pittsburgh, PA 15205

TENEX Computer Express
56800 Magnetic Drive
Mishawaka, IN 46545

TigerSoftware
800 Douglas Tower, 7th Floor
Coral Gables, FL 33134
800-888-4437

Tools for Exploration
4460 Redwood Hwy., Suite 2
San Rafael, CA 4903

United Video & Computer
724 Seventh Ave.
New York, NY 10019
800-448-3738

UnixReview
P.O. Box 420035
Palm Coast, FL 32142-0035

Public-domain software and shareware

Several companies provide public-domain software, shareware, and low-cost software. They also publish catalogs listing their software. Some charge a small fee for the catalog.

PC-Sig 1030D	800-245-6717
MicroCom Systems	408-737-9000
Public Brand Software	800-426-3475
Software Express/Direct	800-331-8192

Selective Software	800-423-3556
The Computer Room	703-832-3341
Softwarehouse	408-748-0461
PC Plus Consulting	818-891-7930
Micro Star	800-443-6103
International Software Library	800-992-1992
National PD Library	619-941-0925
Computers International	619-630-0055
Shareware Express	800-346-2842
PsL News ($24 year)	800-242-4775
MMI Corporation	800-221-4283
Computer Discount Warehouse	800-330-4CDW
The PC Zone	800-258-2088
PrePress Direct	800-443-6600
Numeridex	800-323-7737
Industrial Computer Source	800-523-2320
J&R Computer World	800-221-8180
Jameco Electronic Components	415-592-8097
Zenith Data Systems	800-952-3099

Computer books

There are several companies who publish computer books, two of which are Windcrest/McGraw-Hill (Blue Ridge Summit, PA 17294-0850, 800-822-8158) and Osborne/McGraw-Hill (800-227-0900). Call them for a current catalog, listing the many books they publish. I admit that I'm a bit prejudiced, but I recommend them highly.

20
CHAPTER

Troubleshooting and repairing your PC

I don't want to discourage you, but I have to tell you up front that you might not be able to find the answer to your problem in this chapter. There are thousands of little things that can go wrong in a computer, in both hardware and software. This chapter could be ten times as long and still not cover every possible problem. However, I will try to cover most of the major problems you could experience.

When you say "troubleshooting," most people think of hardware problems, but I've had far more trouble with software than with hardware. And software problems tend to be more difficult to solve.

Finding the cause of a problem is the first step in fixing it. There are several hardware and software diagnostic tools available that can help you find and fix the problems, a few of which will be discussed.

Computer basics

Troubleshooting is a little easier if you know the basics. Computers are possible because of electricity. Under the control of software and hardware, small electrical on/off voltages are formed when you type from the keyboard, when data is read from a disk, or when information is input in some other manner. This voltage turns transistors on and off to perform various tasks.

An electric charge is formed when there's an imbalance or an excess of electrons at one pole. The excess electrons flow through whatever path they can find to get to the other pole, much like water flowing downhill.

Most electrical paths have varying amounts of resistance, so work or heat is created when the electrons pass through them. For instance, if a flashlight is turned on, electrons pass through the bulb, which has a resistive filament. The heat generated by the electrons passing through the bulb causes the filament to glow and create light. If a light is left on for a period of time, the excess electrons from the negative pole of the battery will pass through the bulb to the positive pole of the battery. Electrons will continue to flow until the amount of electrons at the negative and positive poles are equal, at which time there is a perfect balance and the battery is dead.

A computer is made up of circuits and boards that have resistors, capacitors, inductors, transistors, motors, and many other components. These components perform certain functions when electricity passes through them. Circuits are designed so the paths of the electric currents are divided, controlled, and shunted to do the work that you want done. The transistors and other components can force the electrons to go to the memory, disk drive, printer, or wherever the software and hardware directs it to go.

If an electronic circuit is designed properly, it should last several lifetimes. Nothing in a semiconductor or transistor can wear out, but occasionally too many electrons find their way through a weakened component and cause it to heat up and burn out. Or for some reason electrons are shunted through a path or component where they shouldn't go. This might cause an intermittent, partial, or complete failure.

Electrostatic voltage

Before you touch any of the electronic components, ground yourself to discharge any electrostatic voltage that has built up on your body. It's possible for a person to build up a charge of 4,000 volts or more of electrostatic voltage. If you walk across a carpet and then touch a brass doorknob, you can get a shock. If you were to touch a fragile electronic component, this high voltage could be discharged through the component, weakening and possibly ruining it. Most electronic assembly lines have workers wear a ground strap whenever they're working with any electrostatic-sensitive components. You can discharge yourself by touching an unpainted metal part of the computer case or other device that's plugged into a wall socket. The computer or other grounding device doesn't have to be turned on.

Document the problem

The chances are if a computer is going to break down, it will do it at the most inopportune time. This is one of the basic tenets of Murphy's immutable and inflexible law.

If it breaks down, try not to panic. Ranting, cussing, and crying might make you feel better, but it won't solve the problem. Instead, get out a pad and pencil and write down everything as it happens. It's very easy to forget. Write down all the particulars, how the cables were plugged in, the software that was running, anything that might be pertinent. Make sure to record any error messages on your screen. Use the PrtSc (Print Screen) key to print them out if possible.

If you can't solve the problem, you may have to call technical support or your vendor for help. If you have all the written information in front of you, it will help. Try to call from your computer. If it's a software problem, have your serial number handy. Most technical support will ask for that before anything else.

Instruments and tools

For high levels of troubleshooting, you need sophisticated tools and expensive instruments to do a thorough system analysis. You'll also need a good high-frequency oscilloscope, a digital analyzer, a logic probe, and several other expensive pieces of equipment. And you'll need a test bench with a spare power supply, disk drives, and plug-in boards.

It's essential to have a diagnostic card, such as POST-PROBE or Ultra-X, and several diagnostic and utility programs. It's also very important to have a reliable computer with some empty slots so you can plug in suspect boards and test them.

You'll need a voltohmmeter, some clip leads, a pair of side-cutter dikes, a pair of long-nosed pliers, various screwdrivers, nut drivers, a soldering iron, solder, a good workbench with plenty of light over the bench, and a flashlight or small light to light up the dark places in the computer case.

And last but certainly not least, you need quite a lot of training and experience.

Fortunately, you don't need all the expensive and sophisticated tools and instruments for most computer problems. Just a few simple tools and a little common sense is all that's needed for the majority of problems. In addition to a pad and pen, so you can write down everything that happens if you have a problem, here are some tools you should have close to your computer:

Several sizes and types of screwdrivers A couple of these should be magnetic for picking up and starting small screws. You can buy magnetic screwdrivers, or you can make them yourself. Just take a strong magnet and rub it on the blade of the screwdriver a few times. The magnets on cabinet doors or the voice coil magnet of a loudspeaker will do. Be very careful with any magnet around your floppy disks; it can erase them.

A small screwdriver with a bent tip You can use this to pry up ICs. Some of the larger ICs are very difficult to remove. One of the blank fillers for the slots on the back panel of the computer can also make a good prying tool.

A couple pairs of pliers You should have at least one pair of long-nosed pliers.

A set of nutdrivers Many of the screws have slotted heads for screwdrivers as well as hexagonal heads for nutdrivers. Using a nutdriver is usually much easier to use than a screwdriver.

A pair of side-cutter dikes Use these for clipping leads of components and cutting wire. You can buy a pair of cutters that also have wire strippers.

A voltohmmeter There are dozens of uses for a voltohmmeter. You can use it to check for the wiring continuity in your cables, phone lines, and switches, and for the proper voltages in your computer. There are only two voltages to check for, 12 volts and 5 volts. The newer DX4 and Pentium 90 and 100 CPUs require 3.3 volts, but a voltage regulator on the motherboard or CPU socket usually reduces the 5-volt supply to the required 3.3 volts. You can buy a relatively inexpensive voltohmmeter at any electronics store.

A soldering iron and some solder You shouldn't have to do any soldering, but you never know when you might need to repair a cable or some other minor job. I recently set up some computer systems with CD-ROM drives and speaker systems for my grandchildren and one of the speakers didn't work. I could have sent it back to the vendor, but it would have cost me a lot of time and trouble. I used my voltohm-meter, comparing resistance measurements with a good unit, and found a bad solder joint. I resoldered the joint and saved a lot of time.

Several clip leads Clip leads are insulated wires with alligator clips on each end. You can use them to extend a cable, short out two pins, or hundreds of other uses. You can buy them at your local electronics store.

A flashlight This is for looking into the dark places inside the computer or at the cable connections behind the computer.

Chances are you'll never need most of these tools, but it's nice to have them available if you ever do need them.

Solving common problems

Many common problems don't require a lot of equipment. You can often solve a problem by using four of your five senses:, sight, hearing, smell, and touch.

Sight If you look closely, you might be able to see a cable that isn't plugged in properly, a board that isn't completely seated, or a switch or jumper that isn't set properly.

Hearing Listen for any unusual sounds. Ordinarily, electrons don't make any noise as they move through your computer at almost the speed of light. The only sound from your computer should be the noise of your drive motors and the fan in the power supply.

Smell If you've ever smelled a burned resistor or capacitor, you'll never forget it. If you smell something very unusual, try to locate where it's coming from.

Touch If a component seems to be unusually hot, it could be the cause of your problem. Except for the inside of your power supply, there should not be any voltage above 12 volts in your computer, so it should be safe to touch, even when the power is on. Before touching a component, be sure to discharge yourself of any electrosta-tic voltage.

The number-one cause of problems

If you've added something to your computer or done some sort of repair and the computer isn't up and running, there's always the possibility that something isn't plugged in correctly or some minor error was made in the installation.

By far the greatest problem in assembling a unit, adding something to a com-puter, or installing software is not following the instructions. Quite often it isn't nec-essarily the fault of the person trying to follow the instructions. I've worked in the electronics industry for over 30 years, but sometimes I have a hard time deciphering and following the instructions in some manuals. Sometimes a very crucial instruction or piece of information is inconspicuously buried in the middle of a 500-page manual.

If you've just added something to your computer and it doesn't work, read the in-structions again. Recheck all the cables and any boards. Make sure the boards are configured properly and that they are properly seated. If your computer doesn't work at all, remove the item and see if it works without it. Never install more than one item at a time. Install an item, check to see if it works, then install the next one.

Use the documentation

You should have some sort of documentation or manual for all your computer components and peripherals. You should also have a written record of the switch and jumper settings of each of your boards. It's very important that you have the drive type and CMOS information of your hard disk written down with your records or on a special floppy disk. If for some reason your system fails, you might not be able to access your hard drive and its data if you don't know the drive type listed in your CMOS configuration. You should know what components are inside your computer and how they're configured.

Norton Utilities lets you make a rescue disk that has a copy of your CMOS, boot record, partition tables, AUTOEXEC.BAT, and CONFIG.SYS. This disk is bootable so you can use it anytime you lose your CMOS or any other vital information. PC Tools will also let you make an emergency disk similar to the Norton rescue disk.

What to do if it's completely dead

There are several software diagnostic programs that are great in many cases, but if the computer is completely dead, the software won't do you any good. If it's completely dead, the first thing to do is check the power outlet. If you don't have a voltohmmeter, plug a lamp into the same socket and see if it lights. Check your power cord. Check the switch on the computer. Check the fan in the power supply. Is it turning? The power supply is one of the major components that frequently becomes defective. If the fan isn't turning, the power supply might be defective, but the fan might be operating even if the power supply is defective. Do any of the panel lights come on when you try to boot up? Does the hard disk motor spin?

If there's a short anywhere in the system, the power supply won't come on. The fan won't turn and none of the drives will come on. I once connected a miniature power plug to a combo drive and it shorted out the power supply. Only after I had removed the power supply and tested it did I find that I had improperly plugged the power cord into the drive connector.

You can check any of the cables from the power supply with a voltohmmeter. The power supply won't work unless it has a load, so have at least one disk drive plugged in. There should be +12 V between the yellow and black wires and +5 V between the red and black wires. If there's no voltage, then you probably have a defective power supply.

If you hear the fan motor and the panel lights come on, but the monitor is dark, check the monitor's power cord, the adapter cable, and the adapter. The monitor also has fuses, but they're usually inside the monitor case. Also, check the monitor's brightness and contrast controls. If you've just installed the monitor, check the motherboard or adapter for any switches or jumpers that should be set. Check your documentation and your CMOS setup to make sure that the BIOS knows what type of monitor you have.

If you've added a board or some accessory and your computer doesn't work, remove the item and try the computer again. If the computer works without the board, then you know that it must be the board. A short in a board or a peripheral may prevent the computer from working.

CONFIG.SYS and AUTOEXEC.BAT

If you've just added a new piece of software and your system doesn't work, or it doesn't work the way it should, check your AUTOEXEC.BAT and CONFIG.SYS files. Many programs change these files as they're being installed, and might introduce commands and statements that conflict with your system. I try out a lot of different software and systems and I've had problems when a statement or command was left in the AUTOEXEC.BAT or CONFIG.SYS file from a system no longer being used. The statement or command might ask the computer to perform a command or access a file that isn't there and the computer will go off into never-never land trying to find the command or file. You'll usually have to reboot to get out.

You might get the error message "Unrecognized command in CONFIG.SYS" and possibly "Bad or missing file, driver, or path." You could have a misspelled word in CONFIG.SYS or you might have left out a backslash or forward slash. It's quite easy to type in a / for a \, or vice versa. The structure of CONFIG.SYS is rather strict and doesn't provide much room for error.

Whenever you make a change to your AUTOEXEC.BAT or CONFIG.SYS file, always keep the old one as backup. Call the old files something like AUTOEXEC.OLD and CONFIG.OLD. If your new AUTOEXEC.BAT or CONFIG.SYS doesn't work, you can always go back and rename the old file back to its original name.

If you have a long AUTOEXEC.BAT file that doesn't work, you might try editing out parts of it, then rebooting and retrying it. (Use the DOS EDIT command, which uses ASCII text. Don't use a word processor because it will add symbols and characters that will confuse the system.) You can temporarily change lines in your AUTOEXEC.BAT or CONFIG.SYS by adding a REM (for remark) at the beginning of a line you don't want to be executed.

If you press F8 while booting up, DOS 6.2 will let you look at each line of the CONFIG.SYS file and give you the option of loading it or not.

You should always have a "clean" boot disk that has a very lean AUTOEXEC.BAt and CONFIG.SYS on it. There might be times when you don't want any TSRs or anything in your 640K in order to run a special program.

Beep error codes

Every time a computer is turned on or booted up, it does a power-on self test (POST). It checks the RAM, floppy drives, hard disk drives, monitor, printer, keyboard, and any other peripherals you've installed. If everything is okay, it will give a short beep and then boot up.

If it doesn't find a unit or if the unit isn't functioning correctly, it will beep and display an error code. It might beep two or more times depending on the error. If the power supply, motherboard, CPU, or possibly some other crucial IC is defective, it might not beep at all.

You can check the beep system by holding a key down while the system is booting up. You might hear a continuous beep and, after the boot is complete, the system will give two short beeps and display the message "Keyboard error. Press F1 to continue."

There are several other beep error codes that are in the system BIOS. Some BIOS manufacturers use slightly different codes for the errors. Some of the beep codes are for fatal errors, which will cause the system to hang up completely. The beeps are arranged so you might get a beep, a pause, another beep, then three beeps close together, or 1-1-3. This code might indicate that there was a failure in the CMOS setup system. One long and two short beeps, accompanied by a POST code of 400, 500, 2400, or 7400, might mean that there was an error in the CMOS RAM, a motherboard switch setting, or defective video card. A 1-1-4 code might indicate that there was an error in the BIOS itself. A continuous beep or repeating short beeps could indicate that the power supply or motherboard had a fault.

POST codes

The POST codes start at 100 and go up to 20000. The codes aren't normally displayed if there's no problem. If there is a problem, the last two digits of the code will be something other than 00. The BIOS manufacturers develop their own codes, so there are slight differences, but most of them are similar to the following:

101	Motherboard failure
109	Direct-memory access test error
121	Unexpected hardware interrupt occurred
163	Time and date not set
199	User indicated configuration not correct
201	Memory test failure
301	Keyboard test failure or a stuck key
401	Monochrome display and/or adapter test failure
432	Parallel printer not turned on
501	Color graphics display and/or adapter test failure
601	Diskette drives and/or adapter test failure
701	Math coprocessor test error
901	Parallel printer adapter test failure
1101	Asynchronous communications adapter test failure
1301	Game control adapter test failure
1302	Joystick test failure
1401	Printer test failure
1701	Fixed disk drive and/or adapter test failure
2401	Enhanced graphics display and/or adapter test failure
2501	Enhanced graphics display and/or adapter test failure

POST cards

Several companies have developed diagnostic cards or boards that can be plugged into a slot on the motherboard to display the POST codes. If there's a failure in the system, it can tell you immediately what's wrong.

If you've eliminated the possibility of a defective plug-in board or peripheral, then the problem is probably in your motherboard. If the power supply is okay, you could use a diagnostic card such as the POST-PROBE, from Micro 2000 at 818-547-0125, or R.A.C.E.R. II, from Ultra-X at 800-722-3789. These two cards are quite similar in the tests they perform. They can be plugged into a computer that's completely dead except for the power supply, and they'll check every chip and component on the motherboard. Each card has a small digital display that gives you a code for the condition of each component.

These cards will work on any ISA or EISA machine—XT, 286, 386, 486, or Pentium. POST-PROBE comes with a Micro Channel architecture (MCA) adapter so it can also be used on IBM PS/2 systems. R.A.C.E.R. II has a separate board designed for MCA PS/2 systems.

Ultra-X's R.A.C.E.R. II is shown in Fig. 20-1. R.A.C.E.R. is an acronym for real-time AT/XT computer equipment repair. This card can be used on any ISA machine—XT, 286, 386, or 486—to diagnose and find faults in the computer hardware. There are several POST cards on the market, but most of them aren't very sophisticated. R.A.C.E.R. II has several ROMs that run over 70 diagnostic tests. In addition to displaying the test codes on the plug-in board, the progress of the tests can be displayed on a monitor. If there's a failure in one of the tests, the program will display a fault tree, listing which chips might be at fault. In a computer where several chips interact, it's often difficult to determine exactly which chip is at fault. R.A.C.E.R. II can narrow it down to a very few. At the end of the test, you can print out a report.

20-1
The Ultra-X R.A.C.E.R. II diagnostic card. It can check all components, even if the computer is dead.

The POST-PROBE card is shown in Fig. 20-2. It's a good product, but I have to tell you that I am a bit biased toward R.A.C.E.R. II. I worked with the people who first originated the Ultra-X diagnostic cards, and I know how much hard work went into designing and developing this card. I recommend them highly.

20-2
The Micro 2000 POST-PROBE
diagnostic card.

The R.A.C.E.R. II and POST-PROBE diagnostic cards are tools that every professional repair shop should have. Most businesses have their own maintenance departments, and every computer maintenance department should also have R.A.C.E.R. II and POST-PROBE. If you have to take your computer to a repair shop, at $50 to $100 an hour, the repair could be rather expensive. You'll also have to take the time just to get the computer to the shop. If the shop is busy, it might be some time before you get your computer back. If your computer is crucial to you, then it might be a good idea to have R.A.C.E.R. II or POST-PROBE on hand in case of a failure.

QuickPost-PC

QuickPost-PC, also from Ultra-X, is low-cost card that can do many of the diagnostic tests done by the R.A.C.E.R. II, except that it isn't as sophisticated or expensive (see Fig. 20-3). It monitors the POST as the computer boots up. If there's a fault, the code will be displayed. The accompanying manual has a list of all major vendor POST codes. Ultra-X has several other diagnostic products, both hardware and software. Call them for a brochure.

Diagnostic and utility software

Several excellent diagnostic programs are available. Some of the programs contain similar utilities and tests, and most test and report on your system configuration and system memory. Many of them test your hard drives. Some, such as SpinRite and Disk Technician, are primarily designed for hard disk tests and preventive maintenance.

Most BIOS chips have built-in diagnostic routines and other utilities. These routines allow you to set the time and date, tell the computer what type of hard and floppy drives are installed, the amount of memory, the wait states, and several other functions. The AMI and DTK BIOS chips have a very comprehensive set of built-in

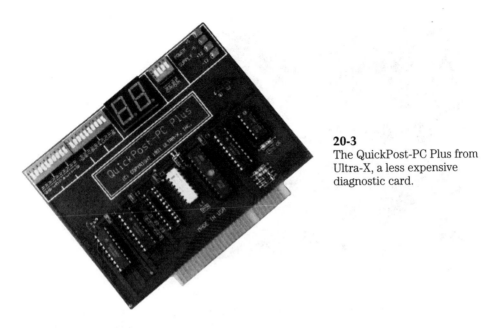

20-3
The QuickPost-PC Plus from
Ultra-X, a less expensive
diagnostic card.

diagnostics. They allow for hard and floppy disk formatting, checking the rotation
speed of the disk drives, performance testing of hard drives, and several other tests.

QuickTech PRO

QuickTech PRO is another diagnostic product from Ultra-X (see Fig. 20-4). This
software has a pull-down menu and is very easy to use. It can check and isolate RAM
and component failures, run floppy and hard disk tests, run parallel and serial port
tests, check the monitor and video, and run system performance tests and evaluations. It can save hours trying to find the cause of a problem.

MS-DOS MSD command

If you own a copy of MS-DOS 6.0 or later, you have the MSD (Microsoft diagnostics) command. This utility can search for files or subjects and can provide you with
a wealth of information about your computer. It can show you the IRQs, memory usage, AUTOEXEC.BAT and CONFIG.SYS files, and much more. You can view the information or print it out. Depending on what you have in your computer, it could
take up to 20 pages to print it all out.

Norton Utilities

Norton Utilities, from Symantec Corporation at 408-253-9600, includes several
diagnostic and test programs and essential utilities. One of the programs is Norton
Diagnostics (NDIAGS). This tests the memory, CPU, DMA controllers, real-time
clock, CMOS, and serial and parallel ports.

Software can't recognize and test the serial and parallel ports unless you have
a loopback plug installed. These are 9- and 25-pin connectors that plug into the se-

20-4 QuickTech PRO, diagnostic software from Ultra-X.

rial and parallel sockets. Some of the pins in these connectors are shorted out so the software can recognize them. There's a coupon in the back of the Norton Utilities manual for a loopback set. Symantec sells them for $19.95. Call them for more information.

Of course, Norton Utilities has all the standard utilities, most of which are periodically updated and improved with new releases. Some of the standard utilities are Unerase, Disk Doctor, Disk Test, Format Recover, Directory Sort, and System Information.

PC Tools

PC Tools, from Central Point Software (now part of Symantec) at 503-690-8090, has even more utilities than Norton Utilities. PC Tools can diagnose and repair disk partitions, boot records, FATs, lost clusters, and other disk problems. It also lets you create an emergency disk, similar to the Norton rescue disk. It has a utility that can recover data from a disk that has been erased or reformatted, and several other data recovery and DOS utilities. It can also be used for hard disk backup and can detect well over 1,000 different viruses.

MicroScope

MicroScope, from Micro 2000 at 818-547-0125, is an excellent diagnostic software tool (see Fig. 20-5). It can test the CPU, IRQs, DMAs, memory, hard disk drives, floppy drives, video adapters, and much more. It can search for a network card and display its I/O and node address. It shows IRQ and I/O address, tests memory and displays available memory space, displays CMOS contents and lets you run CMOS setup, run video tests for memory and character sets, do a read, write, and random seek test of the hard drives. It will even allow you to edit sectors of the hard drive. You can set it up to run any or all of the tests continuously, and either halt on an error or log the error and continue. MicroScope is a very good adjunct to POST-PROBE. Micro 2000 is a small company, and they provide excellent support.

20-5 Microscope, diagnostic software from Micro 2000.

QAPlus/FE

QAPlus/FE, from DiagSoft at 408-438-8247, is a very sophisticated program. Among its many functions is the ability to diagnose problems on the disk systems, memory, video, IDE and SCSI drives and interfaces, interrupts, BIOS, and serial and parallel ports. In order to test the serial and parallel ports you need loopback plugs, which come free with QAPlus/FE diagnostic software.

If a semiconductor or system is going to fail, it will usually do so within the first 72 hours of use. Many vendors test their products in order find any such systems before they're shipped, but many vendors don't have the time nor the software to properly exercise the units. QAPlus/FE can perform rigorous and continuous tests on systems.

If you buy an expensive system or component, it might be well worth the cost to buy a copy of QAPlus/FE just for this capability. If you find a defective component early, you can usually send it back to the dealer and have it replaced at no cost.

CheckIt PRO: Analyst for Windows

CheckIt PRO: Analyst for Windows, from TouchStone Software at 800-531-0450, is comprehensive analysis tool that can be used by beginning as well as advanced users. It can collect configuration and performance data, test hardware integrity, evaluate a system to compare performance with other systems, determine upgrade needs, and assess the compatibility of hardware and software.

CheckIt was developed several years ago, then they improved it and called it CheckIt PRO. CheckIt PRO: Analyst is yet another improvement, and contains several new features. It's a very good diagnostic tool.

The Troubleshooter

The Troubleshooter, from AllMicro at 800-653-4933, has its own self-booting operating system that bypasses DOS. It can test the motherboard, run memory tests, test the hard and floppy disk drives, check and test the serial and parallel ports, and test the video adapter, keyboard, and mouse. It can identify the system hardware and print out a report. It's a good, low-cost diagnostic tool.

WinSleuth Gold Plus

WinSleuth Gold Plus from, Dariana Software at 714-236-1380, is another good, low-cost diagnostic software tool. It even has an 800 technical support line, which is something unheard of today. They also have a BBS number for technical support. WinSleuth Gold Plus can check hardware configuration, give you BIOS information and CMOS settings, and perform CPU and keyboard tests.

WINProbe

WINProbe is available from Landmark, at 800-683-6696. The PC Certify program that comes with WINProbe can save you a lot of time and trouble. PC Certify can also be used to test all types of hard and floppy drives and controllers.

Besides the drives, PC Certify does complete diagnostic tests on the whole computer. It tests the memory, serial and parallel ports, BIOS, video adapter, monitor, keyboard, and printer. You can run the tests continuously as many times as you want. These tests are ideal for "burning in" a computer, that is, running them for about 72 hours to see if there are any defects. PC Certify will even print out a form for a technician to fill out. The form shows what tests were run and has a space for the technician to verify and sign.

The WINProbe portion of the program also has an audio sound test, communications serial-port test, floppy drive RPM test, floppy and hard drive surface analysis, keyboard test, math coprocessor test, motherboard CPU function test, mouse driver test, printer cable test, RAM chip test, and video mode test.

WINProbe also comes bundled with a DOS for Windows program. This is a very low-cost package that everyone should have.

SpinRite

SpinRite, from Gibson Research (714-362-8800), does the most thorough and complete testing of hard disks than any other software. If you decide to use it on a fairly large drive, it could take from 24 to 72 hours to complete its tests. Run the program at night or over a weekend when you won't need your computer.

The software scans and tests every bit of the hard disk. If it finds any defects or areas that are questionable, it will move the data to a safe area and lock the defects out of the usable space. SpinRite is an excellent preventive maintenance tool that everyone should have.

Disk Technician

Disk Technician, from Prime Solutions at 619-274-5000, has utilities that allow you to diagnose, analyze, and optimize your hard disk. Disk Technician can be loaded as a small terminate-and-stay-resident (TSR) program.

DOS has several terse error messages if it can't read a disk, such as "Data error," "General failure," "File allocation table bad," "Bad data," and "Bad sector." The Disk Technician manual refers to these as "terror messages" because that's what they do. Disk Technician can automatically prevent most of these terror messages.

Disk Technician claims that the U.S. Air Force did a study of 210 new computers and found that 63 percent of the computers had problems, 33 percent of which were hard disk problems. They installed Disk Technician and, after five months, they had no hard disk problems at all. Amazing!

If you choose to include Disk Technician in your AUTOEXEC.BAT and CONFIG.SYS files, a small TSR will be loaded into your computer's memory. Every time you boot up, it will do a thorough disk check of all of your drives and report any problems. If it finds any cross-linked files or other problems, you can use CHKDSK/F or SCANDISK to fix them.

Disk Technician also checks for viruses and will beep at you every time you try to copy or change any files with .EXE and .COM extensions, as well as your CONFIG.SYS and AUTOEXEC.BAT files. It will continue to beep until you press a key to turn it off. It's very alert and conscientious, almost like an overzealous chaperone at a high-school prom. It might be slightly annoying if you need to change these files on a regular basis.

Which one should you buy?

If I could afford only one program, I would be hard pressed to choose. All are good tools and many are very similar in their utilities and performance, but there are also different utilities in every one of them.

Spares

One of the easiest ways to check a part is to have a good spare handy. If you suspect a board, it's very easy to plug in one you know is good. It's a good idea to have a few spare boards and components on hand, especially if your computer is crucial and you can't afford any downtime. I suggest that you also have a spare floppy disk drive, floppy disk controller board, and keyboard. These items are all fairly inexpensive. Depending on how important your computer is, you might even want to have spares of all your components, such as a motherboard, power supply, and all your plug-in boards.

You might have very expensive video adapters, VL-bus IDE interfaces, or other boards that cost hundreds of dollars, but you can buy very inexpensive boards to keep as spares. For instance, you can buy a simple IDE interface for less than $10 and an adapter that doesn't have all the goodies for about $30. A low-cost board can help you pinpoint a problem. If your monitor doesn't light up but it works with a replacement adapter, then you can probably make a pretty good guess as to the problem.

DOS error messages

DOS will give you several error messages if you try to make the computer do something it can't do, but many of the messages aren't very clear. And don't bother looking in the DOS manual for an explanation of error messages. I have dozens of books on DOS. One of the better ones is *DOS, the New Complete Reference* by Kris Jamsa, published by Osborne/McGraw-Hill at 800-227-0900. His *DOS Secrets, Solutions, and Shortcuts* is another good book on DOS. He explains DOS error commands and tells you what to do about them. These reference books should be in your library. The following are some common DOS error messages:

Access denied
You might have tried to write on or erase a file that was protected. Files can be hidden or protected by the ATTRIBUTE command. Use ATTRIBUTE to change it.

Bad command or file name / File not found
You might have made a mistake in typing in the command, or the command or file doesn't reside in the current directory.

CHKDSK errors
Run CHKDSK often. Some people put CHKDSK/F in their AUTOEXEC.BAT file so it runs every time the system is booted. (Disk Technician can do it for you.) CHKDSK might give you the error message "n lost clusters found in n chains. Convert lost chains to files? Y/N." Reinvoke CHKDSK with the /F switch (for fix) and the lost clusters will be converted to FILE000n.CHK. When you delete a file, portions of it are sometimes left in a sector, or something might have caused an error in the FAT, writing portions of two different files to a single sector or cluster. The files created by CHKDSK/F are usually incomplete. In most cases they can be deleted.

General failure reading or writing drive n:. Abort, Retry, Fail?
The disk might not be formatted. It's also possible that track 0 on the disk, which stores the FAT, has become defective. You might be able to restore the disk by using Norton's Disk Doctor (NDD) on it.

Invalid Directory

You'll get this message if you're currently in one directory off the root directory, say C:\WORDSTAR, and you try to access another directory off the root directory, say C:\NORTON, without using the backslash. If you were to issue the command CD NORTON in such a situation, you'd get this error message. You must use CD \NORTON. You'll also get this message if you use the forward slash, /, rather than the backslash, \.

Non-system disk or disk error. Replace and strike any key when ready.

You have a nonbootable disk in drive A:.

Not ready error reading drive A. Abort, Retry, Fail?

You might have asked the computer to access drive A: and there was no disk in the drive.

Glitches

Sometimes when the computer is booting up, something will go wrong that causes all kinds of weird problems. I recently booted up, went to my WordStar program, and started working. I have several WordStar macros that save me a lot of keystrokes. This particular day, some of the macros worked, but others caused all kinds of unexpected events. I finally gave up, turned off the computer and rebooted. This time everything worked fine.

Glitches can happen when running almost any kind of program. Sometimes you can get out of them with a warm boot (pressing Ctrl–Alt–Del) and other times you have to turn off the computer, wait a few seconds, then turn it back on.

Remember that anything you've created or changed since last saving your file is in memory only, so when you turn off the computer or reboot, this information will be gone forever. By all means try to save your work before rebooting.

Power supply

The power supply is one of the most frequent causes of problems. Most of the components in your computer are fairly low power and low voltage. The only high-voltage component in your system is enclosed in the power supply. There's no danger of shock if you open your computer and put your hand inside it, but you should *never* connect or disconnect a board or cable while the power is on. Fragile semiconductors could be destroyed if you do.

Most power supplies have short-circuit protection. If too much of a load is placed on them, they'll drop out and shut down, similar to what happens when a circuit breaker is overloaded. Most power supplies are designed to operate with a load and if you take one out of the system and turn it on without a load, it won't work. You can plug in a floppy drive to act as a load if you want to check the power-supply voltage when not plugged into the motherboard.

Semiconductors have no moving parts. If the circuits are designed properly, a semiconductor should last indefinitely. Heat is an enemy, however, and can cause semiconductor failure. The fan in the power supply should provide adequate cooling. Make sure that all the openings on the back panel that correspond to the slots on the motherboard have blank fillers. Even the holes on the bottom of the chassis should be covered with tape. This forces the fan to draw air in from the front of the computer, pull it over the boards, and exhaust it through the opening in the power-supply case. Nothing should be placed in front of or behind the computer that would restrict airflow.

If you don't hear the fan when you turn on your computer, then the power supply could be defective.

Table 20-1 lists the disk drive and motherboard power connections. The 8-bit slotted connectors on the motherboard have 62 contacts, 31 on the A side and 31 on the B side. The black ground wires connect to B1 of each of the eight slots. B3 and B29 have +5 VDC, B5 –5 VDC, B7 –12 VDC, and B9 +12 VDC. These voltages go to the listed pins on each of the eight plug-in slots.

**Table 20-1.
Power-supply connections to the
disk drives and motherboard**

Pin	Color	Function
1	Yellow	+12 VDC
2	Black	Ground
3	Black	Ground
4	Red	+5 VDC

P8 Pin	Color	Function
1	White	Power good
2	(No connection)	
3	Yellow	+12 VDC
4	Brown	–12 VDC
5	Black	Ground
6	Black	Ground

P9 Pin	Color	Function
1	Black	Ground
2	Black	Ground
3	Blue	–5 VDC
4	Red	+5 VDC
5	Red	+5 VDC
6	Red	+5 VDC

I'm not going to list the functions of the other contacts on the slots. Most of them are for address lines and data input/output lines. They're not often involved in problems.

Intermittent problems

Intermittent problems can be the most frustrating and maddening, and they can be very difficult to find.

If you suspect a cable or a connector, try wiggling it to see if it goes away or gets worse. I once spent several hours trying to find the cause of a floppy disk problem. It turned out to be a loose wire in the connector. It was just barely touching the contact. A slight vibration would cause the disk drive to become erratic. A wire or cable can be broken and still make contact until it's moved.

You might also try unplugging a cable or a board and then plugging it back in. Sometimes the pins are slightly corroded or not seated properly. I recently turned on one of my computers that hadn't been used for about a month, and got a message that the FDC (floppy disk controller) had an error. This board also controls my hard disks, so I was a bit concerned. I unplugged the controller board, cleaned the contacts, and plugged it back in. (The copper contacts on a plug-in board can become corroded. You can clean them with an ordinary pencil eraser.) But I still got the FDC error message. I got out another FDC and prepared to plug it in, but I had to change the setting of a shorting bar on the controller board. On a hunch, I slipped the shorting bar on and off my original controller a few times, then tried the board again. The floppy drives worked perfectly. The shorting bar and the pins had become corroded during the time it wasn't used.

The contacts of the edge connectors on floppy drives and hard drives can also become corroded. Sometimes just unplugging then plugging them back in several times can wipe away the corrosion. Before unplugging a cable, you might want to put a stripe on the connector and cable with a marking pen or nail polish so you can easily see how they should be plugged back in.

The problem could also be in a DIP switch. Try turning it on and off a few times. Caution! Always write down switch positions before touching them. Make a diagram of the wires, cables, and switch settings before you disturb them. It's easy to forget how they were plugged in or set before you moved them. You could end up making things worse. Make a pencil mark before turning a knob or variable coil or capacitor so it can be returned to the same setting when you find out what you did didn't help. Better yet, resist the temptation to reset these types of components. Most were set with highly sophisticated instruments and don't usually change enough to cause a problem.

If too much current flows through a chip, it can get hot and fail. It might fail only at certain times, like when you're running a particular program. If you suspect a chip and it seems to be warmer that it should be, you might try using a hair dryer to heat it up. If it fails due to the extra heat, then you've found the problem. Be careful that you don't heat up a good chip and cause it to fail.

If a component seems to be too hot, you can spray a coolant on it such as freon. Because of environmental concerns, however, you might not be able to buy freon. You might try using ice water in a plastic bag. If the component works properly when cool, you've found your defect.

Some of the diagnostic software will run a system in an endless loop to try to force the system to fail.

Monitor problems

Monitors are usually rather long-lived and don't cause too many problems. If you're having monitor problems, check the switch settings on the motherboard. There are several different motherboards. Some have DIP switches or shorting bars that must be set to configure the system for the type of monitor you're using, such as monochrome, CGA, EGA, or VGA. Most monitors also have fuses. Check them and also check the cables for proper connections.

Serial ports

Conflicts in setting up serial-port devices can cause a lot of problems. Like parallel ports, pins for serial ports are available on any of the bus plug-in slots. Serial ports might be available as a group of ten pins on the motherboard, on a multifunction plug-in board, as a male DB25 connector with pins, or as a male DB9 connector. The original RS232 specification called for 25 lines, but most systems use only four or five lines, so the DB9 connector with 9 pins is more than sufficient. Many mice sold today have the DB9 connector, so if your system has the DB25 connector you'll need to order an adapter. The adapter costs about $3.

Serial ports are used most often for a mouse or other pointing device, modems, fax boards, plotters, scanners, and several other devices. DOS supports four serial ports—COM1, COM2, COM3, and COM4—but has only two interrupt request (IRQ) lines for the serial ports: IRQ4 for COM1 and IRQ3 for COM2. So COM3 and COM4 must share the IRQ lines with COM1 and COM2, and you need special software in order to permit sharing. They can share because it's not likely that all four IRQ lines would be used at the same time.

If two devices are set for the same COM port, it will cause a serious conflict. Neither device will operate properly. When installing a mouse, modem, or fax board, the interface plug-in boards must be configured so that none of the devices use the same port. If you have devices already installed on your system, you might not know which ports they're set for.

Several programs can help you determine which ports are being used. One of the better ones is a low-cost shareware program called Port Finder, available from James McDaniel of mcTRONic Systems, 713-462-7687.

Computer hanging up

Sometimes the computer will hang up. Either you or the software you're running might have told the computer to do something it couldn't do. Since it's very obedient, it will go off to never-never land and try to do the task. You can usually do a warm reboot of the computer by pressing Ctrl–Alt–Del. Of course, this will wipe out any file in memory.

I've had a couple of problems with Windows. I usually assemble a system on a bench and try it out there before installing it in a case. I tried for quite a while to install Windows on a system that I had set up on the bench but it would hang up about halfway through the installation. I was really concerned about what was wrong with the system I was putting together. It seemed to run everything else except Windows. I went ahead and put it in the case and hooked up all the front-panel wires. I tried Windows again. When I got to the point where it had stopped before, the program beeped, then completed loading. I found that if the speaker isn't hooked up, it will sit there forever trying to beep.

I had another computer that had an 80MB hard drive. I used the Microsoft DoubleSpace utility on it, then tried to load Windows. It seemed to load okay, but when I tried to run it I got a brief message telling me the swap disk file was corrupted. I hadn't read the manual so I wasn't aware that you must have an uncompressed disk in order to run Windows in the 386 enhanced mode. In this mode, windows sets aside a portion of your hard disk and uses it as virtual RAM for large programs. You can run Windows in the standard mode on a compressed disk if you use WIN/S to start it.

Occasionally the computer won't respond to a warm boot. You can pound on the keyboard all day long and it will ignore you. In that case, you have to switch off the main power, let it sit for a few seconds, then power up again. Always wait for the hard disk to wind down before turning the power on again.

Software problems

I've had far more trouble with software than I've had with hardware. Quite often it's my fault for not taking the time to completely read the manuals and instructions, but I don't usually have the time to read a manual every time I want to run a program. Many programs are getting easier to run, but there are still thousands and thousands of software problems you can run into. Many companies support their products. If something goes wrong, you can call them. Some companies charge for their support and some even use a 900 telephone number.

If you have a software problem, write down everything that happens. Before you call, try to duplicate the problem. Carefully read the manual. When you call, it's best to be sitting in front of your computer, with it turned on and with the problem on the screen if possible. Before you call, have the serial number of your program handy. One of the first things they'll probably ask for is your name and serial number. If you've bought and registered the program, it will be in their records.

Most software is reasonably bug-free, but there are millions of things that can go wrong if you don't follow certain procedures exactly. And in many cases, the instructions for these procedures aren't very explicit. It seems that most software manuals are written by people who know the software very well, but they forget that the person using it for the first time doesn't know it.

You know the manuals are bad when you see a lot of books written by third parties to supplement the original manuals. There are hundreds of books written to help you learn DOS, Lotus 1-2-3, Windows, WordPerfect, and most other popular programs. If the original manuals were done properly, there would be little need for these supplemental books.

User groups

There's no way to list all possible software or hardware problems. Computers are dumb and very unforgiving. It's very easy to plug a cable in backwards or forget to set a switch. There are thousands of things that can go wrong. Sometimes it can be a combination of both software and hardware and sometimes it's a hardware problem caused by software or vice versa. There's no way every problem can be addressed.

One of the best ways to find answers is to ask someone who has had the same problem. One of the best places to find those people is through a user group. If at all possible, join one and become friendly with all the members. They can be one of your best sources for troubleshooting. Most of them have had similar problems and will be glad to help. Many local computer magazines list user groups in their area. The nationally distributed *Computer Shopper* lists bulletin boards one month and user groups the next.

This chapter should help you cope with many of the problems you'll experience. Thank you for buying my book. I wish you all the best, and I hope all your problems are easy ones.

—Aubrey Pilgrim
73740,2561 (CompuServe)
TJJC38A (Prodigy)

Glossary

active-matrix LCD System used for high-resolution liquid-crystal diode (LCD) display panels used on color laptop and portable computers. This type of display is fairly expensive since it requires an individual transistor for each pixel. *See also* passive-matrix LCD.

adapter card A printed wiring board with digital circuitry that plugs into connectors on the motherboard of a personal computer, usually performing input/output functions.

ADC An abbreviation for analog-to-digital converter. The electronic device converting conventional analog audio and video signals to digital form, which can be processed by computer and stored as data.

address The numerical value, usually in hexadecimal format, of a particular location in a computer's random-access memory (RAM).

ADPCM An abbreviation for adaptive differential pulse-code modulation. A method of digital waveform sampling that encodes the difference between successive samples rather than their actual values (DPCM). The differences are assigned values based on the content of the sample. ADPCM is the storage format used by CD-ROM XA and CD-I discs.

algorithm A digital set of instructions for solving a problem, or the configuration of operators in an FM synthesizer.

amplitude The strength or intensity of sound or signal, or the measure of a current's deviation from its zero value.

amplitude modulation A term describing the interaction of two signals, a carrier and a modulator. The modulation signal varies the amplitude (intensity) of the carrier. In AM radio transmission, the carrier is a medium-frequency signal (550–1550 KHz) and the modulator is the sound signal. In sound synthesis, a low-frequency oscillator modulates a carrier that is the sound's fundamental frequency.

analog A term describing a circuit, device, or system that responds to continuously variable parameters generated by hardware rather than by software.

analog-to-digital converter A circuit that periodically samples a continuously variable voltage and generates a digital representation of its value, also called an ADC, A-to-D, or A/D converter.

ANSI An abbreviation for the American National Standards Institute. It also refers to the ANSI character set that Microsoft uses for Windows.

API An abbreviation for application programming interface. Generically, it's a method of accessing or modifying the operating system for a program. In Windows, API refers to the functions provided by Windows 3.*x* that allow applications to open and close windows, read the keyboard, interpret mouse movements, and so on. Programmers call these functions "hooks to the operating systems."

APM Abbreviation for advanced power management from Intel and Microsoft. It allows certain programs and operating systems to slow down various hardware components, thereby saving power. Also called SMM, which stands for system management mode, a group of instructions built into the CPU.

ASCII Pronounced *ask-ee*, it's an acronym for American standard code for information interchange, the digital code for display alphanumeric characters. It originally consisted of 128 codes, but was later extended to 254 characters. Some of the characters are smiley faces, playing cards, and musical notes. You can see what some of them look like by using the DOS TYPE command to view almost any .EXE, .COM, or word-processed file. Most word processors add control characters to display bold, underline, page formats, and other characteristics. Text generated on one word processor is usually quite different than that of another, almost like a foreign language. But most programs can handle pure ASCII characters, and allow you to strip the control characters out of files so only ASCII characters are left.

artifact An extraneous sound or effect on an image not present in the source signal, introduced by one of the components in the recording or reproduction chain.

aspect ratio An image's ratio of width to height, usually expressed as W:H. The aspect ratio of digital images is expressed as the ratio of the number of pixels in each dimension (640:480 for VGA images).

ASPI An acronym for advanced SCSI programming interface, it's the industry standard for SCSI interface cards. If the card conforms to this standard, then several different peripherals from different manufacturers can be used. Adaptec was the original creator of this standard. *See also* CAM.

ATM Either asynchronous transfer mode, a wide-band high-frequency protocol for data transmission, or Adobe Type Manager, Adobe's system for managing True-Type fonts.

AVI An abbreviation for audio video interleaved, the Microsoft application programming interface (API) designed to compete with Apple's QuickTime methodology. AVI techniques provide a software synchronization and compression standard for audio and video signals, competing with DVI.

BitBlt Abbreviation for bit block transfer, an assembly-level function for copying graphic images in Windows applications to a destination graphic context.

buffer A section of RAM where data is stored temporarily, usually containing data to be edited or inserted.

CAM Common access method, a standard developed for SCSI devices. It's similar to the ASPI standard except that the interface cards have their own on-board BIOS.

Camcorder A contraction of the words *camera* and *recorder*. The term describes a video camera and videocassette recorder combined into a single, hand-held unit.

carpal tunnel syndrome (CTS) Pain and numbness in the hand, wrist, and arm along the path of the medial nerve. It's often caused by the repetitive action of typing on a computer keyboard. *See also* repetitive strain injury (RSI).

CAV An abbreviation for constant angular velocity devices, such as computer hard disks and CAV video laserdiscs, depending on the distance of the read write head from the drive spindle.

CCD Abbreviation for charge-coupled devices, integrated circuits consisting of a linear array of semiconductor photoreceptor elements. CCDs are used to create bit-mapped images. Each photoreceptor creates an electrical signal representing the luminance of one pixel. CCDs are used primarily in scanners, color xerographic printers, and video cameras.

CCITT An abbreviation for the Consultative Committee International for Telephone and Telegraph. The CCITT establishes standards for telephone interchange and modems in Europe, several of which have been adopted in the United States. Recently renamed the International Telecommunications Union (ITU).

CD An abbreviation for compact disc. CDs are the original format for distributing compact optical discs for audio reproduction (CDAudio). This early format was jointly developed by Phillips N.V. and Sony Corporation, and is described in Phillips N.V.'s yellow book. Control of yellow-book CD-ROMs, such as starting and stopping the drive and file selection with your computer, requires Microsoft's MSCDEX.DRV driver.

CD-DA An abbreviation for compact-disc digital audio, also called "red-book audio." CD-DA requires compatibility with MPC specification 1.0. It enables interleaving of audio with other types of data, so recorded sound can accompany images. The CD-DA format is defined in the International Electrotechnical Commission's (IEC) standard BNNI-5-83-095.

CD+G A format in which the subchannel (s) of an audio CD contain graphic images that can be displayed on a computer or television set.

CD-I An abbreviation for compact disc interactive. CD-I refers to a class of CDs designed to be viewed on conventional television sets by means of a CD-I player. CD-I players incorporate at least 1MB of RAM, special pointing devices, and remote-control systems. CD-I players can also be used for training and other commercial and industrial applications. CD-I formats are covered by Phillips N.V.'s green-book specification.

CD+MIDI A format in which the subchannel (s) of an audio CD contain data in standard MIDI file format that can be routed to a MIDI out connector and played on external MIDI synthesizers or internally by audio adapter cards.

CD-MO An abbreviation for compact disc magneto-optical. Magneto-optical CDs and CD-ROMs can be erased and rerecorded. The standards for CD-MOs are incorporated in Phillips N.V.'s "orange book 1" specification. CD-MO technology is used for high-capacity, 3½-inch floptical disks.

CD-ROM An acronym for compact disk read-only memory. CD-ROMs can incorporate text, audio, and graphic images. Phillips N.V.'s documentation for this standard has a yellow binding, hence the term "yellow-book audio." MPC specification 1.0 requires multimedia PCs to include a CD-ROM.

CD-ROM XA An abbreviation for CD-ROM extended architecture, jointly developed by Phillips N.V., Sony Corporation, and Microsoft Corporation in 1989. CD-ROM XA provides storage for audio and other types of data interleaved on a CD-ROM, enabling simultaneous access.

channel message A MIDI command or data sent over a specific MIDI channel.

chrominance A term used in television broadcasting to describe the signal (a subcarrier of the basic black-and-white signal) containing the color information in a composite video signal. Chrominance has two components: hue (tint) and saturation (the degree to which the color is diluted by white light). Chrominance is also called chroma and abbreviated as C.

clipping Audible distortion of an audio signal, usually caused by overloading a circuit of transducer.

clock An electronic circuit that generates the pulses used to synchronize bits of information.

clock-doubling Refers to CPUs that operate internally at double the external frequency, such as the Intel 486DX2. Other CPUs triple or quadruple the external frequency, such as the IBM Blue Lightning and Intel's 486DX4.

CLV An abbreviation for constant linear velocity. The recording technique used with CD-ROMs and other CD devices specifying that the velocity of the media at the point of reading or writing remain constant, regardless of the distance from the spindle. CLV devices have a constant data transfer rate. To achieve this, the rotational speed of the spindle motor must be inversely proportional to the distance of the read or write point on the media from the spindle video. Laserdisc drives are produced in CLV and constant angular-velocity models.

codec Acronym for compression-decompression for video data.

coprocessor A processor support chip that can vastly improve intensive calculations and graphics. It can be used only if the software is written to take advantage of its capabilities. Coprocessors have the designation $x87$, for instance, the 386 CPU uses the 387 coprocessor. The 486DX CPU has a built-in coprocessor.

CP/M Stands for control program for microprocessors. CP/M was the first operating system for personal computers. It was written by Gary Kildall in 1973 and used by all the early PCs, such as Osborne, Kaypro, and Morrow. In 1980 IBM approached Gary to develop a system for the first IBM PC. IBM later went to Bill Gates and you know the rest of the story.

CPS for the frequency of electronic circuits, it's cycles per second; for printers, it means characters per second.

CTI Computer telephone integration, or connecting a computer to a telephone.

cycle A single, complete wave—the basic unit of oscillation.

DAC An abbreviation for digital-to-analog convertor. DAC is the electronic device used to convert digital audio and video signals stored on CD-ROM, DAT, or disk to analog signals that can be reproduced by conventional stereo and television components.

daisy chain Connecting several devices on a SCSI. Also, a network in which data flows from one receiving device's MIDI through port to another receiving device's MIDI in port.

DAT Acronym for digital audio tape. DAT is a process of recording sound in helical bands on a tape cartridge, similar to recording video signals.

default A parameter value that exists when hardware is turned on or an application is run.

Dhrystones A benchmark that measures millions of instructions per second (MIPS).

digital-to-analog converter A circuit that generates a digital representation of a continuously variable signal, also called a DAC (D/A converter).

DIN An acronym for Deutches Institute fur Normalization. DIN is an organization similar to ANSI that establishes and coordinates standards for Germany. It has become the de-facto standards bureau for Europe.

DLL An abbreviation for dynamic link library. DLL contains a collection of Windows functions that are called (invoked) as necessary by applications to perform certain operations.

drag and drop Using the mouse to move (drag) an icon representing an object, such as a file, to another location, such as a different directory, and placing (dropping) it in that location. Visual Basic provides drag-and-drop capabilities for control objects.

DSP An abbreviation for digital signal processing. Although all synthesized sound involves DSP, the term is usually applied to the creation of electronic, acoustic effects such as reverberation, chorusing, flanging, and panning.

DTV An abbreviation for desktop video, the production of videotape presentations using the multimedia capabilities of personal computers. DTV implies being able to edit videotapes by using the playback and record functions of VCRs, remotely controlled by a computer.

DVI An abbreviation for Intel's digital-video interactive standard. DVI simultaneously displays compressed video images and sound files. IBM has adopted the DVI standard for its Ultimedia product line. Microsoft adds DVI capability through its DVMCI extensions.

EISA An abbreviation for extended industry standard architecture. A bus specification used to interconnect adapter cards employing 32-bit memory addresses or providing multiprocessor capabilities. The EISA standard was declared by a group of PC-compatible hardware suppliers to compete with IBMs Micro Channel architecture.

Energy Star The EPA requirement that PCs implement automatic sleep modes when not being used to save energy. Many laptop computers have used similar systems for some time. Newer CPUs have a variety of power-saving options.

EPROM Acronym for erasable programmable read-only memory. The type of chips usually used for ROM BIOS.

Error correction code (ECC) A coding system that, in conjunction with an error detection coding scheme, can reconstruct erroneous data to its original value.

Error detection code (EDC) A coding system that detects errors in a single byte or in blocks of data. Single-byte errors are caught by parity checkers such as the ones employed in the PC's memory system. Errors in blocks of data are commonly determined by using techniques such as cyclic redundancy codes (CRC), which are used for data transfer by modem. More sophisticated EDC methods are employed when error correction is required, such as with CD-ROMs.

field In video terminology, one half of a television image. A field consists of either the even or odd lines of a frame. In relation to computer databases, a field is a single, distinct element of a complete database record.

filter A circuit or function that alters a signal's frequency spectrum by attenuating or accenting certain portions.

firmware Software that's embedded in the computer's ROM or elsewhere in the computer circuitry. You cannot ordinarily change or modify firmware.

FM synthesis Stands for frequency-modulation synthesis, a method of generating complex waveforms by modulating the frequency of the audio waveforms (carriers) with other waveforms (modulators).

frame rate In film or video, the frequency at which single frames are shown, usually equal to 24, 25, or 30 frames per second.

frequency The rate of oscillation, which determines pitch, measured in cycles per second, or Hertz.

fundamental frequency A sound's primary frequency, the first harmonic.

harmonic A simple component of a complex waveform that's a whole-number multiple of the fundamental frequency.

genlock A process for synchronizing the video display of a computer to the frame synchronization signal of NTSC, PAL, or SECAM video. This process allows a computer-generated graphics to be viewed on a television set or recorded with a VCR. Genlock capability is required to add computer-generated titling to video productions.

GIF Acronym for graphic interchange format. GIF is the file format (and extension) storing most graphic images in CompuServe forum libraries.

global Pertaining to a computer program as a whole. Global variables and constants are accessible to and can be modified by program code at the module and procedure level.

grayscale Monochrome (black-and-white) images displayed in various shades of gray. The most common format is an 8-bit grayscale, which provides 256 shades of gray. Four-bit grayscale images with 64 shades are also used.

HDTV Abbreviation for high-definition television, a form of television transmission that results in clearer images, especially on large-screen TV sets. The present standard is 525 lines, from top to bottom. HDTV would increase the number and give much better resolution.

Hi8 An abbreviation for high-band 8 mm, a format developed by Sony Corporation for camcorder videotapes. Hi8 provides the capability of recording PCM digital audio- and time-code tracks, as well as conventional analog audio and enhanced-quality video information.

High Sierra format A name assigned to the predecessor of ISO standard 9660, defining the table of contents and directory structure of CD-ROMs for computer applications. Microsoft's MSCDEX.DRV driver reads these structures and converts the directory to a structure used by DOS. This function enables you to treat CD-ROM files as if they were located on a conventional hard disk drive.

HMS time Time expressed in the format hours:minutes:seconds.

Hz An abbreviation for Hertz, the fundamental unit of frequency of audio and radio waves. Hertz was previously called cycles per second (CPS). Most people can discern sounds that range in frequency from about 20 to 20,000 Hz.

icon In Windows, a 32×32-pixel graphic image, usually in color. An icon identifies the application in the Program Manager window when the application is minimized and in another location.

interlaced A method of displaying television signals on conventional TV sets, and computer images on video display units. Alternative fields of images, consisting of even or odd horizontal lines comprising the image, are displayed in succession.

interleaved A method for containing sound and video information in a single file but in separate chunks, so digital images and audio signals can be transferred from a file to the computer's memory without the delays incurred by CD-ROM seek operations.

ITU International Telecommunications Union, formerly called the CCITT. A United Nations committee that tries to convince nations and companies to standardize telecommunications devices and protocols. *See also* CCITT.

ISA An abbreviation for industry standard architecture, the specification of the connections to plug-in adapter cards with 16-bit memory-addressing capability. ISA is the bus structure used in conventional IBM-compatible computers using 8088, 80286, 80386, and 80486 CPU chips.

ISO An abbreviation for International Standards Organization. The ISO is a branch of the United Nations, headquartered in Geneva. ISO coordinates international standards for a wide variety of products and equipment. The CD-ROM standard for table of contents and file-directory entries, originally called the High Sierra format, has been established as the ISO-9660 standard.

IVRU Interactive voice response unit, a system whereby the computer can play back digitized speech and accept requests from a touch-tone telephone. These systems are now used by many companies to replace human beings. It saves them a lot of money because these systems never take a coffee break, go on vacations, or ask for a raise.

JPEG An acronym for the Joint Photographic Experts Group that has established an industry standard for photographic image compression.

.JPG The file extension for graphics files stored with JPEG compression.

jumper A small, plastic-enclosed spring clip making an electrical connection between two adjacent square metal pins, usually in the form of a header. Jumpers are used to select device addresses, interrupt levels, and other optional features of adapter cards. They're also found on motherboards.

luminance One of the characteristics defining a color in the hue-saturation-luminance (HSL) system. Luminance is the collective intensity (lightness) of the color, defined by hue and saturation. In television broadcasting, the signal containing the black-and-white image is referred to as the luminance signal.

MIDI Musical instrument digital interface, a means of communicating musical information among computers and microprocessor-based devices.

MIPS An acronym for millions of instructions per second, a measure of how fast a CPU operates.

NAMM Abbreviation for the National Association of Music Merchants. NAMM is an industry association of music dealers and musical instrument manufacturers that holds a yearly exhibition where new MIDI devices and audio components are introduced.

nanosecond One billionth of a second, abbreviated ns. The speed of memory chips is measured in nanoseconds, usually ranging from about 30 to 100 ns. Faster computer clock speeds require memory chips with lower nanosecond response times. 33-MHz computers, for instance, use 70- to 80-ns memory chips.

NLQ Near letter quality. Many printers, especially dot-matrix printers, can print fairly fast in a draft mode. In draft mode, there are usually spaces and jagged edges in the characters. In NLQ printing, more pins in the head are struck so the characters are better defined.

noninterlaced The preferred method of displaying computer images, usually on a multisynchronous video display unit, in which the image is created by displaying consecutive rather than alternate scanning lines.

OCR Optical character recognition, the system used in scanners to recognize printed text and convert it into digital data.

OLE An acronym for object linking and embedding. OLE is a Windows protocol developed by Microsoft Corporation that provides for the creation of compound documents in which elements of a document in an OLE client application are created, edited by, or linked to a file in another application acting as an OLE server. Applications such as Word for Windows 2.0 and Excel 4.0 can act as either clients or servers. Applets such as Media Player and Microsoft Draw and Chart are OLE servers only. OLE is an extension of the Windows dynamic data exchange (DDE) protocol. Apple Macintosh System 7.*x* also supports the OLE protocol. OLE version 1 accommodates BMP, DIB, and WMF graphics file formats.

oscillator A circuit or software that generates voltage signals.

PAL An acronym for phase-alternative line system. PAL is the television transmission standard for Western Europe, excluding France. PAL displays 625 lines per frame at a rate of 25 frames per second.

palette A Windows data structure defining the colors of a bit-mapped image in RGB format.

parallel interface A connection between devices that transfers one or more bytes of information simultaneously.

parameter A variable characteristic or value.

passive-matrix LCD A system used on less expensive display panels for color laptops and portables. It uses single transistors to activate rows and columns of pixels. It's much less expensive than an active-matrix LCD, but the colors aren't as bright. *See also* active-matrix LCD.

PCM Pulse-code modulation, a means of digitally encoding and decoding audio signals.

PCI Peripheral component interconnect, a system that allows plug-in boards and devices to communicate with the CPU over a 32- or 64-bit high-speed bus.

PCX The file extension created by ZSoft Corporation for storing images created by its PC Paintbrush application. PCX bit-mapped files can be monochrome or color and are used by many other bit-mapped image-creation (paint) and display applications.

Photo CD A trademark of Eastman Kodak for its technology and CDs that provide copies of photographic color images in a format compatible with CD-I and CD-ROM XA drives. Photo CDs are produced from 35-mm film images produced by licensed photo-finishing facilities. These facilities have equipment that can write to the special Photo CD media.

pipeline An arrangement of registers within the CPU, also called execution units. Each register performs part of a task, then passes the results to the next register. PCs such as the 486 have a single pipeline and can process only one instruction per clock cycle. The Pentium has two pipelines and can process two instructions per cycle.

POSIX An acronym for a portable operating system interface based on UNIX. It refers to a collection of international standards for UNIX-style operating-system interfaces. U.S. government agencies specify POSIX as a procurement standard for government computing contracts.

presentation A multimedia production consisting mainly of still images or simple animation covering a single topic.

prosumer A contraction of *professional* and *consumer*. The word describes video components, such as camcorders and VCRs, bridging the gap between consumer-grade products and industrial-quality devices.

QIC Quarter-inch cartridge, magnetic tape used for tape backup.

RAM Random-access memory, a computer's main memory in which data is temporarily stored.

RAID An acronym for redundant array of inexpensive disks. When data is crucial, you can use a RAID system of two or more hard disks to mirror each other so the same data is recorded on each disk.

repetitive strain injury (RSI) Pain and numbness to areas of the hand, wrist and arm. RSI is similar to carpal tunnel syndrome, except that RSI can occur to any part of the body that's subject to frequent motion or trauma. The injury usually occurs in tendons and the synovial sheaths that surrounds nerves. This injury is sometimes called repetitive motion injury, which is probably a better term.

ribbon cable A flat multiconductor cable having parallel individual conductors that are molded together. One side of the ribbon cable is marked with a printed line, usually blue or red, that identifies the conductor corresponding to pin 1 of the attached connectors.

RIFF An acronym for the Windows resource interchange file format. RIFF is used in conjunction with multimedia extensions. Depending on their definition, these files might contain MIDI sequence, sample dump, or system-exclusive data; waveform audio files; or data to create graphic images. RIFF is the preferred file format for Windows multimedia files, but few third-party applications currently create RIFF files except in wave (.WAV) format.

sample To digitally encode an analog signal.

sawtooth wave A waveform that contains every component of the natural harmonic series, also called a ramp wave.

scalable Multiprocessing operating system that allows a user to run the same application on single-processor and multiprocessor computers.

SCSI Small computer system interface (pronounced "scuzzy"). An interface standard for connecting peripherals to a PC. The standard supports several different peripherals such as hard drives, CD-ROMs, and scanners. As many as seven different devices can be connected to one interface card.

SECAM The acronym for systeme couleur avec memoire. SECAM is the French standard for television transmission (819 horizontal lines per frame, displayed at 25 frames per second). SECAM is the standard for most of Eastern Europe, including the former USSR, as well as African countries where French is the secondary language.

seek To locate a specific byte, sector, cluster, record, or chunk within a disk file.

serial interface A connection between devices that transfers information one bit after another.

signal-to-noise ratio (SNR) The ratio between an audio or video signal of a specific amplitude (level) and the underlying noise contributed to the signal by a component. Signal-to-noise ratio is expressed in dB (decibels) or dBr (relative decibels). A large negative number is preferred.

sine wave A pure, simple waveform comprised of a single frequency with no overtones. It's a voltage signal that goes from zero to a certain positive number, then back to zero, then negative for a minus voltage, then back to zero. Alternating voltages are sine waves.

slave A device receiving signals from and controlled by a master device.

SOHO An acronym for small office, home office.

SMPTE A type of time code adopted by the Society of Motion Picture and Television Engineers used to indicate location in time and synchronize playback.

SPEC92 This stands for Systems Performance Evaluation Cooperative (SPEC), a group of organizations who got together in January of 1992 and developed a suite of benchmark programs that effectively measure the performance of computing systems in actual application environments.

SPECint92 An effective benchmark to measure integer application performance.

SPECfp92 A benchmark that measures floating-point performance.

square wave A pulse wave with a 50% duty cycle, consisting of odd harmonics only.

streaming Technique used to transfer information from a file structure, such as on a disk or CD-ROM drive, to the computer's memory. Streaming takes place in groups of bytes less than the entire file's length, usually processed in memory as a background activity.

stripe A synchronization signal recorded on one track of a multitrack tape recorder.

superscalar Refers to the fact that the Pentium architecture has two parallel pipelines and can process instructions in both pipelines simultaneously, or two instructions per clock cycle.

S-VHS A VHS-format videocassette recorder with S-video capability.

S-video Abbreviation for Super-video. S-video is a video signal with enhanced quality used for recording. S-video separates the chrominance signal from the luminance signals of composite video.

sync Abbreviation for synchronization.

.TGA A file extension for files created in the format used by Truevision's Targa series of graphics adapter cards.

.TIF An acronym for tagged image format. Black-and-white, grayscale, and color bit-mapped images developed by Aldus Corporation are stored in .TIF files.

time code A method of identifying the time an event (such as a single motion-picture or video frame) occurs in a format that can be understood by a computer.

time stamp The date and time data attributes applied to a disk file when created or edited. In MIDI files, a time stamp identifies the time MIDI events (such as Note On or Note Off) should occur, so the correct tempo is maintained.

triangle wave A waveform with a strong fundamental tone and weak overtones, comprised of odd-numbered harmonics only.

trigger A control signal that indicates the beginning of an event.

truncate In sampling, removing recorded data before or after a sample.

TrueType Apple Computer's outline-based typeface design and display system that creates display and printer fonts in a manner similar to Adobe's PostScript. Microsoft Corporation has incorporated an improved version of TrueType technology in Windows 3.1.

TSR Terminate-and-stay-resident program, software that loads itself into RAM and stays there. It's then available at any time, but it might use up a lot of the valuable 640K of conventional memory.

twip Window's smallest unit of graphic measurement. A twip is a twentieth of a point, or $\frac{1}{1,440}$ of an inch.

typeface Print or display type of a single design. Typeface is often confused with the term *font*, which means a particular size of a typeface. A typeface might be a member of a type family, including related designs.

UART Universal asynchronous receiver and transmitter, a chip that processes data through the serial port. For example, it takes eight bits to make a character, and a parallel port can send an entire 8-bit character eight lines at a time. To send data over a serial port, the chip takes the digital data and sends it through the port one bit at a time in a serial string. The early UARTs use an 8250 chip, which is rather slow. Newer devices use the 16550, which is much faster. Many of the less expensive multi-I/O boards still use the older 8250. To find out what you have, use the DOS MSD command.

VESA An acronym for the Video Electronic Standards Association. VESA is a group of manufacturers and software developers who create standards for graphic and video display adapter cards.

VLB VESA local bus, a system that allows plug-in boards or other devices to communicate with the CPU over a fast 32- or 64-bit bus.

WAVE file A RIFF (resource interchange file format) file containing PCM waveform audio data, usually with a .WAV extension. Microsoft and IBM have adopted .WAV files as their standard format for multimedia sound applications.

waveform audio A data standard of Windows multimedia extensions. Waveform audio defines how digitally sampled sounds are stored in files and processed by Windows API functions.

wave table A term describing the synthesis technique of simulating the sounds of musical instruments with short digitized recordings (PCM samples).

wildcard A character that substitutes for and allows a match by any character or set of characters in its place, such as the ? and *.

WinBench A benchmark for use with Windows.

WinMark A benchmark for use with Windows.

WORM An acronym for write-once read-many. WORM systems use a laser to write on special optical discs. CD-WO (the write-once CD standard) is a special type of WORM format.

Write-back cache A write-back system that writes only data that has been modified back to main memory.

Write-through cache A system where all data is immediately written back to memory.

YC An encoding method used in S-Video. In YC, the luminance (Y) and chrominance (C) signals are separated, and the chrominance signal incorporates both hue and saturation information.

ZIF An acronym for zero insertion force. A 238-pin chip like the Pentium requires a large amount of force to insert and remove. It's a fragile device and the pins can be easily damaged. A ZIF socket has a lever that opens the socket contacts so the device can be dropped in. When the lever is pressed down, the socket contacts close around the pins.

zoom To magnify an image on a video display.

Index

About the author

Aubrey Pilgrim was the originator of the "Save a Bundle" series of books for McGraw-Hill. Named one of the 100 most influential leaders in the computer industry by *MicroTimes* for two consecutive years, Pilgrim is the author of McGraw-Hill's *Build Your Own LAN and Save a Bundle*, *Build Your Own 386/386SX Compatible and Save a Bundle, 2nd edition*, *Upgrade Your IBM Compatible and Save a Bundle, 2nd edition*, *Build Your Own 486/486SX and Save a Bundle*, *Build Your Own Multimedia System and Save a Bundle*, and *Build Your Own Pentium Processor and Save a Bundle*. Over 250,000 copies of his books have been sold.

Other Bestsellers of Related Interest

Easy PC Maintenance and Repair, Second Edition
—Phillip Laplante
Even the average PC user can provide ongoing maintenance, or fix difficult problems using the most basic tools. Unlike other PC repair texts that assume the reader has electronics knowledge and software design capability, this guide provides simple, step-by-step instructions for troubleshooting PC's and their peripherals. The easy-to-read text is arranged in advancing degrees of difficulty so readers can focus on the sections appropriate to their level of expertise.
0-07-036432-X $27.95 Hard
0-07-036433-8 $17.95 Paper

Troubleshooting, Maintaining, & Repairing Personal Computers:
A Technician's Guide
—Stephen J. Bigelow
Focusing on hands-on repair procedures rather than complex theory, it is the only guide with all of the nuts-and-bolts information technicians must have. The largest set of computer diagnostic freeware and shareware ever made available is included on disk. Covering IBM PCs and compatibles, including the Pentium, this manual features extensive coverage of multimedia PCs and contains crucial information on how to use diagnostic software.
0-07-912099-7 $44.95 Paper/Disk

Troubleshooting and Repairing Computer Monitors
—Stephen J. Bigelow
Ranging across all types of conventional CRT-based monitors—as well as the newer, fast-growing LCD variety—this one-stop guidebook provides an overview of monitor concepts, components, technologies, and test equipment . . . and then describes a broad spectrum of potential malfunction symptoms, along with details on the appropriate remedy for each.
0-07-005408-8 $36.95 Hard

Easy Laser Printer Maintenance & Repair
—Stephen J. Bigelow
The author takes you step-by-step through the laser printer from operational concepts and the design and function of each component to using the tools and testing equipment needed to solve operational problems. Tips on comprehensive troubleshooting techniques and what to look for are included along with a quick reference appendix for cleaning and maintenance procedures and resources for parts, materials, and service vendors.
0-07-035976-8 $18.95 Paper

Build Your Own Pentium Processor PC, Second Edition
—Aubrey Pilgrim
Build-It-Yourself guru Aubrey Pilgrim delivers a top-to-bottom update of his best-selling guide to building a complete, custom-made Pentium-chip system—including peripherals—at a fraction of dealer prices. Pilgrim provides new, updated, or expanded coverage of all the latest Pentium chips, multispeed CD-ROM's and other new multimedia components, Windows '95 and OS/2 Warp, and the latest hard drive specs. Step-by-step assembly instructions and numerous clear photographs make it simple to build a Pentium system without advanced skills or special tools.
0-07-050183-1 $32.95 Hard
0-07-050184-X $19.95 Paper

The McGraw-Hill Illustrated Dictionary of PC's, Fourth Edition
—Michael Hordeski
More than 2,400 new entries covering the latest computer hardware and software, architectures, network terminology, and more add to what was already the most comprehensive computer-specific dictionary available. Detailed definitions for terms, buzzwords, jargon, and acronyms. Over 11,900 terms defined and more than 650 illustrations make this PC dictionary the best available anywhere.
0-07-030409-2 $32.95 Hard
0-07-030410-6 $21.95 Paper

Start Your Own Computer Repair Business
—Linda Rohrbough and Michael Hordeski
This hands-on guide shows you the specifics of how to capitalize on the lucrative field of PC repair and maintenance. You'll get valuable insights into: launching your business, tools to buy and how to use them, maximizing profitability by specializing, licensing, insurance, getting paid for what you do, and more. Whether you are looking for secure self-employment or a way to make extra money, this guide is for you.
0-07-911901-8 $32.95 Paper/Disk

IBM Dictionary of Computing
—IBM
This book defines 18,000 terms and abbreviations, it's a one-of-a-kind desk reference covering virtually all information processing, personal computing, telecommunications, office systems, and IBM specific terms. No other dictionary of computing terms even comes close to the breadth of this one, nor is there anything available from such an authoritative source.
0-07-031489-6 $24.95 Paper

How to Order

 Call 1-800-822-8158
24 hours a day,
7 days a week
in U.S. and Canada

 Mail this coupon to:
McGraw-Hill, Inc.
P.O. Box 182067
Columbus, OH 43218-2607

 Fax your order to:
614-759-3644

 EMAIL
70007.1531@COMPUSERVE.COM
COMPUSERVE: GO MH

Shipping and Handling Charges

Order Amount	Within U.S.	Outside U.S.
Less than $15	$3.50	$5.50
$15.00 - $24.99	$4.00	$6.00
$25.00 - $49.99	$5.00	$7.00
$50.00 - $74.49	$6.00	$8.00
$75.00 - and up	$7.00	$9.00

EASY ORDER FORM—
SATISFACTION GUARANTEED

Ship to:

Name ⎯⎯⎯⎯⎯⎯⎯⎯⎯⎯⎯⎯

Address ⎯⎯⎯⎯⎯⎯⎯⎯⎯⎯⎯

City/State/Zip ⎯⎯⎯⎯⎯⎯⎯⎯⎯

Daytime Telephone No. ⎯⎯⎯⎯⎯⎯⎯

Thank you for your order!

ITEM NO.	QUANTITY	AMT.

Method of Payment:	
☐ Check or money order enclosed (payable to McGraw-Hill)	Shipping & Handling charge from chart below
	Subtotal
☐ DISCOVER ☐ AMERICAN EXPRESS Cards	Please add applicable state & local sales tax
☐ VISA ☐ MasterCard	TOTAL

Account No. ☐☐☐☐☐☐☐☐☐☐☐☐☐☐☐☐

Signature ⎯⎯⎯⎯⎯⎯⎯⎯ Exp. Date ⎯⎯
Order invalid without signature

**In a hurry? Call 1-800-822-8158 anytime,
day or night, or visit your local bookstore.**

Key = BC95ZZA

CompuServe.

The difference between your PC collecting dust and burning rubber.

No matter what kind of PC you have, CompuServe will help you get the most out of it. As the world's most comprehensive network of people with personal computers, we're the place experts and novices alike go to find what's hot in hardware, discuss upcoming advances with other members, and download the latest software. Plus, for a low flat-rate, you'll have access to our basic services as often as you like: news, sports, weather, shopping, a complete encyclopedia, and up to 60 e-mail messages a month. And it's easy to begin. All you need is your home computer, your regular phone line, a modem, and a CompuServe membership.

To get your free introductory membership, just complete and mail the form on the back of this page. Or call 1-800-524-3388 and ask for Representative 449. Plus, if you act now, you'll receive one month free unlimited access to basic services and a $15 usage credit for our extended and premium services.

So put the power of CompuServe in your PC — and leave everyone else in the dust.

CompuServe
The information service you won't outgrow.™

Put the power
of CompuServe
at your fingertips.

Join the world's largest international network of people
with personal computers. Whether it's computer support,
communication, entertainment, or continually updated
information, you'll find services that meet your every need.

Your introductory membership will include one free month
of our basic services, plus a $15 usage credit for extended and
premium CompuServe services.

To get connected, complete and mail the card below. Or call
1-800-524-3388 and ask for Representative 449.

Yes! I want to get the most out of my PC. Send me my FREE
CompuServe Introductory Membership, including a $15 usage credit and
one free month of CompuServe basic services.

Name: _____

Address: _____

City: _____ State: _____ Zip: ____

Phone: _____

Clip and mail this form to: CompuServe
P.O. Box 20212
Dept. 449
Columbus, OH 43220

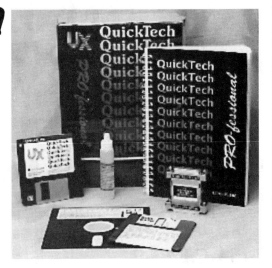